Writing by Numbers

Writing by Numbers
Legal Writing Made Easy

Melissa Shultz
ASSISTANT PROFESSOR &
DIRECTOR OF LEGAL WRITING
UNIVERSITY OF NORTH TEXAS AT DALLAS
COLLEGE OF LAW

Christine Tamer
ASSISTANT PROFESSOR &
ASSISTANT DIRECTOR OF LEGAL WRITING
UNIVERSITY OF NORTH TEXAS AT DALLAS
COLLEGE OF LAW

CAROLINA ACADEMIC PRESS
Durham, North Carolina

Library of Congress Cataloging-in-Publication Data

Names: Shultz, Melissa, author. | Tamer, Christine, author.
Title: Writing by numbers : legal writing made easy / Melissa Shultz, Christine Tamer.
Description: Durham : Carolina Academic Press, 2020.
Identifiers: LCCN 2019046142 | ISBN 9781531014438 (paperback) | ISBN 9781531014445 (ebook)
Subjects: LCSH: Legal composition.
Classification: LCC KF250.S37 2020 | DDC 808.06/634—dc23
LC record available at https://lccn.loc.gov/2019046142

Carolina Academic Press
700 Kent Street
Durham, North Carolina 27701
Telephone (919) 489-7486
Fax (919) 493-5668
www.cap-press.com

Printed in the United States of America
2021 Printing

Table of Contents

3 | Persuasive Legal Writing 135

Acknowledgments

As you can imagine, we have a handful of shout-outs we need to make to acknowledge the key people who made the drafting of this book possible. Very clearly, and always primarily, thanks go to our children—Reagan, Bennett, Tennyson, and Austen—who all deserve serious accolades for understanding weeks of abbreviated bedtime reading and longer than usual work hours. Related to that, we also want to deeply thank our husbands for taking care of the children while we were editing or writing and for (probably more importantly) tolerating our incessant moaning (and necessary procrastinating) while we finalized this book.

In addition, we owe a huge thank you to our three diligent and deadline-compliant research assistants who helped finalize this book: Tara Bush, Eric Knudsen, and Emily Worland. Their pages and pages of editorial marks are proof that one—no matter how great an editor—cannot catch her own errors.

We also want to thank our academic colleagues, especially those at UNT Dallas College of Law for their unending support, additions, and critiques. Particular thanks to Brian Owsley for his early review, Loren Jacobson for being our "phone a friend," and Stuart Caton, Shannon Conway, and Diana Howard for their guidance and input on particular sections of the book. We are privileged to call each of you colleagues. In addition, thanks to the editorial staff at Carolina Academic Press, who helped and shepherded us—brand-new professors to the world of book publication—through the process. Your input and edits made the book what it is today.

Finally, thank you to our students—past and present—who have, each year, made us better teachers. Your stories, your grit, and your perseverance amaze us. You are the inspiration for this book.

Introduction and How to Use This Book

Let's begin with an admission: despite the title of this book, legal writing is not easy. It is difficult. And, it is difficult for innumerable reasons, just a couple of which are worth mentioning here.

The first reason legal writing is difficult is because all law students have written in some form or another since they turned probably about five years old. Given this reality, all law students know how to write at least in the very basic sense of the word (and have known how to do so for quite some time). Moreover, many—top college graduates, English or journalism majors, prior novelists—excel in at least one form of writing. Yet, despite any past experience or success as a writer, no first-year law student comes into law school as a strong ***legal writer***. This is because legal writing requires not only good writing (good grammar, good sentence structure, good style, etc.), but it also requires good legal analysis. How to conduct legal analysis is a new skill. Good legal analysis requires an understanding of what the law is, how the law works, and how the law is communicated by lawyers. Learning the law and, specifically, learning how to write using it is a bit like learning a foreign language. Mastery—especially mastery of writing in a new language—takes time, patience, and practice. Law students—especially those who have excelled in other areas of writing—struggle to appreciate the reality that legal writing is much like writing in a new language. Learning to write like a lawyer requires time, patience, and—most importantly—lots of practice in order to master it.

The second reason legal writing is difficult (and confusing) for students is because legal writing is more like math with words than like quintessential excellent writing, such as poetry. Often students with backgrounds in science or engineering—which are not normally thought of as synonymous with strong writing—excel in legal writing. This is because scientists and engineers are familiar with carefully plotting out the steps they took to reach their result in a logical and methodical fashion. Scientists and engineers are used to formulas and formulaic writing. In legal writing, to conduct sound legal analysis, you also must "show your work"—that is, show the reader step by step how you derived your conclusion from applying the law to the facts of your case. The way you "show your work" in legal writing is formulaic like scientific writing. Courts reach and write decisions in a methodical way and pursuant to an accepted formula, and lawyers must do the same. This can be frustrating to students (especially to students who have their own "style" of writing that has suited them well in the past). As a beginning legal writer, you must set your style aside and first master the math-like content required for excellent legal analysis (and, thus, excellent legal writing).

Given the reality that legal writing is difficult for most new law students, this book aims to demystify the legal writing process by providing concrete formulas—both "macro" formulas and "micro" formulas—for mastering the content required for objective and persuasive legal analysis. The "macro" formula we start with in this book is CRAC, which stands for Conclusion ("C"), Rule ("R"), Analysis ("A"), and Conclusion ("C"). Within this macro formula, we use "micro" formulas to help you draft the different parts of CRAC. This book also breaks down different parts of legal work product, such as the introduction to a motion or the question presented of an objective memo, into smaller components so that you can see how they are constructed. Put simply, at each juncture of your legal writing journey, this book will give you a roadmap to follow (and a step-by-step list of directions). Our goal is that you will never find yourself lost—that is, facing an entirely blank page without directions as to how to start filling it.

Remember those paint-by-numbers kits you received as a gift for your eighth birthday? A bigger picture was broken up into numerous small parts, each with a number indicating which color you were to paint it. Going number by number, following the directions, even the most inexperienced artist could create a beautiful and complex picture. Those paint-by-numbers kits were the inspiration for our method of teaching first-year legal writing and for this book. After working with law students from unique backgrounds, of all different ages, with varied educational experiences, and with diverse core writing abilities, we have learned that the best way to teach beginning legal writing to a diverse set of students is to employ the "paint-by-number technique." First, break down the "picture" into small, bite-sized parts. Then, like assigning colors to the numbers in a paint-by-numbers kit, provide formulas and explicit instructions to law students to help them populate their legal product (the picture) with the necessary content (the color). The result is the same: just like the novice artist colored in the small parts in the painting-by-numbers kit to generate a beautiful and complex picture, beginning law students can put the small pieces of legal analysis (CRAC) together to create larger and excellent pieces of legal writing.

Also, just like those paint-by-number kits do not confuse the novice artist with a bunch of choices but instead tell the novice artist that "anything with a number 8 should be painted blue," this book aims to not confuse novice law students with a bunch of choices. We have found that, in teaching beginning legal writing, giving a lot of choices to novice legal writers can paralyze them from putting pen to paper (or fingers to keyboard) and writing. If we say, "Here are nine ways to write a case illustration," students think, "I literally just learned what a case illustration is. I have never written a case illustration before. How do I know which of the nine ways I should use to illustrate my case?"

So, in this book, instead of giving you multiple choices for how to—for example—write a rule statement, we show you one way to write a rule statement that works. We then give you an example of that same rule statement in the context of objective writing and persuasive writing (and, in persuasive writing, how the same rule could be written by both sides). In this way, you will not be paralyzed by choices, but, instead, you will be equipped, from the outset, to write your own rule statements by following the instructions, the formulas, and the examples provided.

That said, just like an experienced artist would scoff at a paint-by-numbers kit, an experienced legal writer may scoff at the lack of choices in this book and its strict formulaic approach. But you must learn to crawl before you can walk. You must learn to walk before you can run. Once you master the basics taught in this book, you will have the confidence and skills to take your legal writing to an advanced level and to stray from the strict formulaic approach in this book. That is, once you have learned to talk, you can then learn to make your legal writing sing.

This book is organized into seven parts that can be categorized into three groups. Part One is the longest part of the book. It provides you with an overview of foundational, basic skills that apply to both objective and persuasive writing. Part One discusses (i) the overview of the federal and state legal systems; (ii) the hierarchy of authority; (iii) introductory legal research; (iv) how to read the law; and (v) basic grammar rules. Part One also introduces you to formulaic writing (and its backbone, CRAC—Conclusion, Rule, Analysis, and Conclusion) and why it is important.

Parts Two and Three explicitly address how to draft key legal documents. Part Two dives into objective writing and discusses, in detail, two of the more popular vehicles for objective writing: the formal objective memorandum and the e-mail memorandum. Part and parcel to its discussion of how to draft a formal objective memo, Part Two explains how to use the CRAC formula in the context of objective writing. Part Three discusses persuasive writing and, specifically, persuasive writing to the audience of a trial court via a motion or opposition to a motion. Part Three teaches you to apply the drafting techniques you learned in objective writing and make those techniques persuasive. Part Three builds upon the CRAC formula used in objective writing and shows you how to use it in the context of persuasive writing.

Parts Four through Six expand on the core skills discussed in Parts Two and Three. Part Four, which applies equally to objective writing and persuasive writing, discusses how you edit and polish your written work product (the work product that you so tirelessly drafted according to Part Two or Part Three). Part Five discusses how to take your written work and convert it into an oral presentation, specifically how to convert a motion or opposition into an oral argument. Part Six discusses how the skills at the center of legal writing—Parts One through Four—translate to success on bar-style law-school essay exams, on actual bar essay questions, and on the bar's Multistate Performance Test ("MPT").

The last part—Part Seven—is the appendix, which consists of sample objective and persuasive written documents. What makes the appendix unique is that it includes, among other documents, an objective memo, a persuasive motion for summary judgment, and a persuasive opposition to the motion for summary judgment—all of which are written from the same problem and set of facts (although the facts are more developed for the motion and opposition than the memo because those would have been written well after the memo in the life cycle of the case). You will be able to use these documents as examples of not only objective legal writing and persuasive legal writing but also of how each compare to one another. For example, you will be able to see how an objective rule statement for an element compares side by side with a persuasive rule statement for the same element, In addition, you will be able to see how a persuasive rule statement for the same element compares when written by two different sides (the plaintiff and the defendant). The appendix also includes the underlying assigning memo for the objective memo and the factual record for the motion and opposition. From this, you will see how the facts were taken from the assigning memo versus the more complete factual record and then transformed into a statement of facts in the objective memo, the motion, and the opposition.

Learning how to write—specifically how to write like a lawyer—will be critical to your success both in law school and in your practice as a lawyer. Legal writing is a different kind of writing than any type of writing you have ever done. So buckle up, get comfortable, and get ready to take off into the strange and new world of legal writing!

Note on Permissions

The Westlaw Edge screenshots in Part One and the *Rothermel* case in Appendix H are taken from Westlaw and are used with permission of Thomson Reuters. The reprint of *In re Estate of Fiedler* in Part One is used by permission of LexisNexis.

Writing by Numbers

I | Basic Skills of Legal Writing

In this part of the book, you will learn the basic skills you need to become a proficient—if not an excellent—legal writer. Interestingly, many of these basic skills involve competency in areas different than what may first come to mind when you think of writing. These areas include understanding the state and federal judicial systems, grasping the different types of legal authority and which type of authority is the best to use, finding legal authority using Westlaw and LexisNexis, and reading and comprehending the legal texts you find. Skills in these areas, even though they do not involve putting pen to paper, are critical to your ability to formulate (and then ultimately write) legal analysis and, thus, are critical to your ability to master legal writing. For example, if you do not know how to read and comprehend a judicial opinion, how will you be able to find the legal rules housed in that judicial opinion that you will need to include in your memo, motion, or brief?

In addition to these "pre-writing skills," this part of the book will introduce you to a number of skills that are more obviously tied to writing, such as ordering your legal analysis the way lawyers expect analysis to be ordered (Conclusion, Rule, Analysis, Conclusion—CRAC), placing and formatting legal citations, and demonstrating competency in basic rules of grammar.

Part One of the book will serve as the backbone of your legal writing course. Although sections of it will be assigned as reading early in the year, you will often find yourself referring back to these lessons.

I. The U.S. and state legal systems

As they navigate reading, analyzing, and writing about the law, law students often struggle with the constant requirement to "zoom in" to grasp the specifics and then to "zoom out" to see where those specifics fit into a larger picture. In order to engage in thoughtful legal analysis, however, you, as a law student, must grapple with and understand both the details of the area being studied as well as how the particular area of study relates to the bigger picture. For example, when analyzing whether an act constitutes a battery, you should ("zooming in") also "zoom out" to understand the requirements for battery, how battery relates to other intentional torts, and how that analysis fits into the larger legal system. Given the importance of understanding the larger picture, even when studying a limited area of law, we will begin by reviewing the organization of the U.S. legal system so that you can grasp how the cases you read in law school relate to and affect the larger system of government.

The U.S. Constitution divides the U.S. government into three branches—the judicial branch, the legislative branch, and the executive branch.[1] At first blush, it might seem like only the judicial and legislative branches of government are relevant to the study of law, but, in fact, all three branches of government deeply affect the creation and enforcement of law in this country. In brief, the legislative branch makes the laws, the executive branch carries out and enforces the laws, and the judicial branch interprets the laws. As part of a carefully created system of checks and balances among the three branches of government, each branch can affect the acts of the other branches. For example, the president can veto legislation created and passed by Congress; Congress can remove the president from office under certain circumstances or override the president's vetoes; and the Supreme Court of the United States (also referred to as the U.S. Supreme Court) can overturn laws passed by Congress that it deems unconstitutional. Given that this is law school, the next section will provide more detail about the judicial branch of government, which includes the Supreme Court of the United States and any inferior courts that Congress or state constitutions establish.

II. Hierarchy of authority: hierarchy of courts

The judicial branch of government—in both the state and federal systems—interprets the meaning of laws, applies laws to individual cases, and decides the legality of laws (under the state and federal constitutions). There are three basic levels of court: trial, intermediate appellate, and appellate court of last resort. These courts are hierarchical in nature, meaning that cases proceed through the three levels of courts in a set order, from lowest to highest. The trial court is the lowest court and a court of original jurisdiction. As such, the trial court is the court where an action is first filed.

---

1. U.S. Const. art. I (legislative branch), art. II (executive branch), and art. III (judicial branch).

The intermediate appellate court ("appellate court") and appellate court of last resort are generally not courts of original jurisdiction. That means, as a general matter, cases are not filed originally in those courts. Instead, appellate courts and courts of last resort review cases from courts below them. The appellate court is the next level up from the trial court—it is the court where the party losing its case (or an aspect of its case) can seek review of ("appeal") the trial court's decision in hopes of achieving a different result. The losing party in the appellate court can then appeal the appellate court's decision to the appellate court of last resort, which is often called a supreme court.

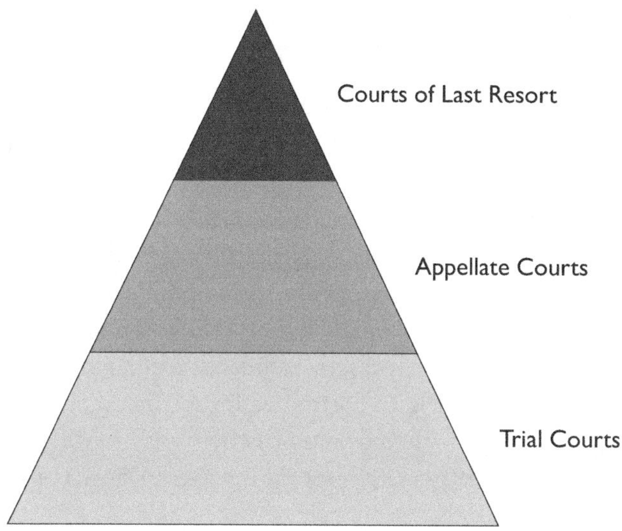

To make things more complicated, however, in each state there are two distinct court systems—the state judicial system and the federal judicial system. These two systems operate separately from one another, are organized differently, and name their courts differently. Although there is some overlap,[2] generally speaking, the hierarchical structures of the federal and state judicial systems remain distinct. More specifically, what separates the federal and state systems is the types of cases they hear, because each of the 50 states and the federal government retain their own sovereignty, set their own laws, and have their own constitutions.

2. In certain circumstances, state courts can hear cases brought under federal law and federal courts can hear cases brought under state law. For example, and as you will study in first-year Civil Procedure, federal courts can have jurisdiction over cases involving questions of state law when the parties on opposite sides are from different states and the amount in controversy exceeds $75,000.00. This exception to the separation of the state and federal systems is called "diversity jurisdiction."

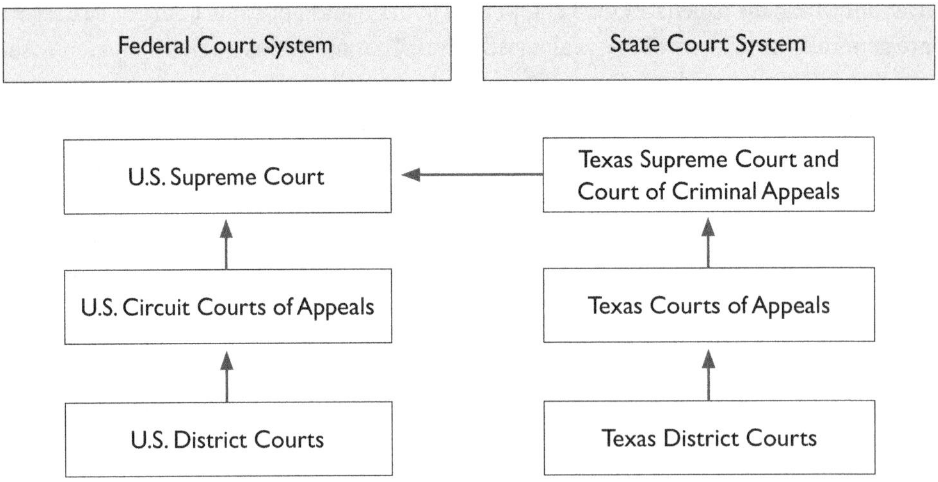

Courts in the federal system apply and interpret federal law.[3] In the federal system, the trial level courts are called district courts, the appellate level courts are called circuit courts of appeals, and the appellate court of last resort is called the Supreme Court of the United States. Federal district courts handle trials—both civil and criminal—within the federal system. There are 94 federal districts that house more than 670 district judges nationwide. For example, in Texas, there are four federal district courts: United States District Court for the Northern District of Texas, United States District Court for the Eastern District of Texas, United States District Court for the Western District of Texas, and United States District Court for the Southern District of Texas.

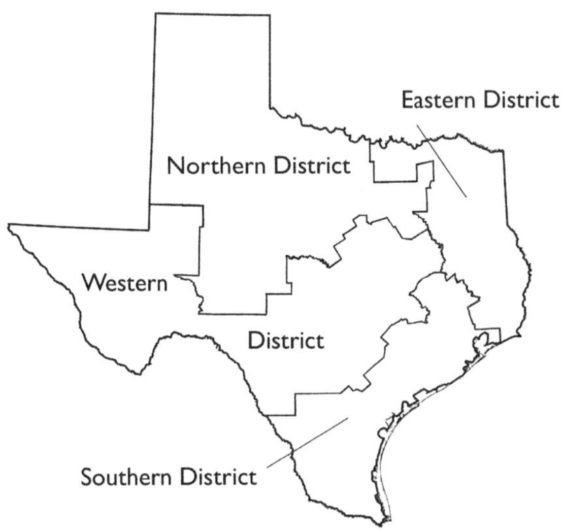

3. Federal courts have jurisdiction over most federal questions and review decisions of some administrative agencies such as the Food and Drug Administration (FDA), the Internal Revenue Service (IRS), or the Drug Enforcement Agency (DEA).

Some smaller states, e.g., Connecticut, only have one federal district court.

Once a federal district court has decided a case, the case can be appealed to the federal circuit court of appeals in which the district court sits. There are a total of thirteen federal circuit courts of appeals, as set forth in the picture below:[4]

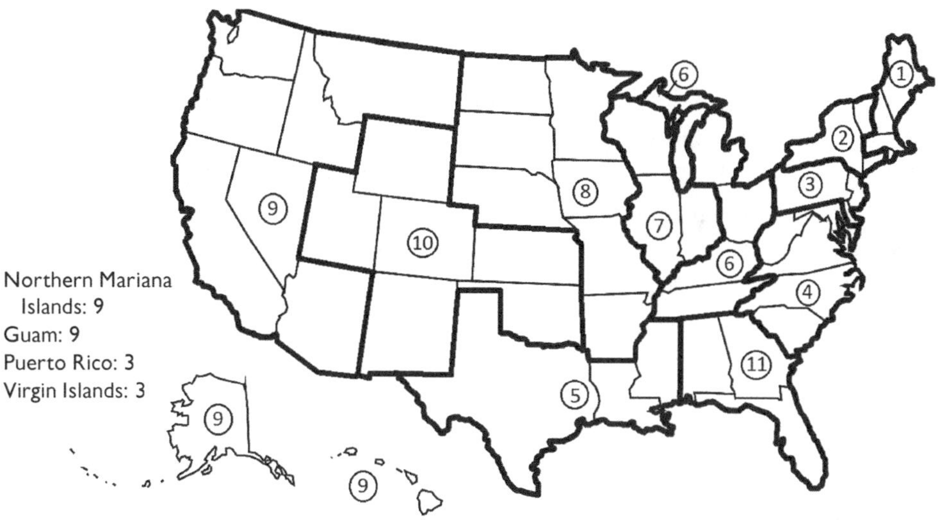

For example, all of the federal district courts located in Texas are in the Fifth Circuit. In addition to Texas, the Fifth Circuit also includes the federal courts in the states of Louisiana and Mississippi. Cases from the federal district courts in all three of those states are appealed to the United States Court of Appeals for the Fifth Circuit, which is headquartered in New Orleans, Louisiana.[5]

The U.S. Supreme Court is the highest court in the federal judicial system. In addition, the U.S. Supreme Court is the ultimate decision-maker when it comes to interpreting federal law as well as interpreting the U.S. Constitution and determining whether either the federal government or a state government has violated rights granted under the U.S. Constitution. The limit on the U.S. Supreme Court's jurisdiction can be confusing for law students—on one hand, the U.S. Supreme Court does **not** have the

---

4. In addition to the 12 location-based circuit courts, the Federal Circuit Court of Appeals, in Washington, D.C., is a nationwide circuit court that has appellate jurisdiction over very specific issues, such as patents.

5. This description of the federal system is a bit over-simplified. In reality, in addition to the federal districts there are also a few specialty "district" courts, including the United States Tax Court, the United States Court of International Trade, and the United States Court of Federal Claims. Similarly, in addition to the 11 numbered United States Courts of Appeals, there are two additional courts of appeals—the District of Columbia Circuit and the Federal Circuit. The hierarchical structure for these specialty courts is a bit different. Decisions from cases heard in the United States Tax Courts are appealed to one of the United States Court of Appeals. However, decisions from the United States Court of International Trade and the United States Court of Federal Appeals are appealed in the United States Court of Appeals for the Federal Circuit, which was created in 1982 to review decisions of these specialty courts as well as some administrative decisions.

power to hear cases involving only questions of state law (did the plaintiff commit a battery), but it **can** hear cases that involve whether a state law violates rights granted under the U.S. Constitution (does Texas's battery statute somehow violate the U.S. Constitution). Not all cases that are appealed to the U.S. Supreme Court are heard because it is a court of discretionary review. The U.S. Supreme Court hears only about one percent of the cases that it is asked to hear. On average, it hears about "70 cases out of the roughly 7,000 petitions for review it receives each term."[6]

In the state judicial system, the names for each type of court—whether trial, appellate, or last resort—vary from state to state. For example, in Texas, there are several different types of trial courts—state-level district courts, county-level courts (which include constitutional county courts, statutory county courts, and statutory probate courts), justice courts, and municipal courts. These trial-level Texas state courts are under the court of appeals in the area where the trial-level court is located. Texas has 14 districts, where 14 courts of appeals are located:

Amarillo	Tyler	Eastland
Beaumont	Houston (2)	Waco
Dallas	Corpus Christi—Edinburgh	Texarkana
El Paso	Austin	
San Antonio	Fort Worth	

In this way, a state district court located in Dallas falls hierarchically under the court of appeals in Dallas. The Texas state system has two appellate courts of last resort: the Court of Criminal Appeals and the Texas Supreme Court. The Court of Criminal Appeals has final appellate jurisdiction over Texas criminal cases. The Supreme Court has statewide, final appellate jurisdiction over most Texas state civil and juvenile cases. Like the U.S. Supreme Court, these two courts are courts of discretionary review.

Why does the judicial hierarchy matter? Understanding the hierarchical structure of the federal and state judicial systems is important because where a case is within that structure dictates whether a decision from a particular court is mandatory or persuasive on the court you are before. If a particular decision is mandatory or binding, it means that the lower court must follow that decision with respect to the issue that has been decided by the court or courts above it. On the other hand, decisions issued out of a lower court will not be mandatory on a court higher in the judicial hierarchy in the same system; instead, such decisions will merely be persuasive. Similarly, more often than not, decisions from federal courts are not binding on state courts and vice versa.[7]

6. Elizabeth Slattery, *Overview of the Supreme Court's 2017–2018 Term*, The Heritage Foundation (Sept. 5, 2017), https://www.heritage.org/courts/report/overview-the-supreme-courts-2017-2018-term.

7. Generally, the federal court system hears cases involving federal law and the state court systems hear cases involving state law. There are a few areas—such as criminal law—where state and federal jurisdiction overlaps. In such instances, federal law preempts (i.e. controls) state law when the two laws conflict, when

Determining whether a particular statute or case is mandatory or persuasive requires you to engage in a two-step process. First, you must determine which jurisdiction's law applies: is it federal or state law, and which state or federal circuit are you in? Second, you must determine which of that jurisdiction's cases or statutes will be binding on the court that will be deciding your case.

Let's look at an example. You are an attorney handling a case in Texas related to whether termination of your client's parental rights is in her child's best interest—purely a state law question. The statute implicated by your client's issue is in the Texas Family Code—a Texas law. Your case is being heard by Judge Moyé in the 14th District Court in Dallas County. In support of your motion for summary judgment, you need to cite a case for the standard for summary judgment in Texas. Which cases from the courts below would be mandatory authority for the 14th District Court?

Step one: Determine what jurisdiction's law applies.

Here, you are dealing with a Texas state statute and are in a Texas state court.

Step two: Determine which of that jurisdiction's cases or statutes will be mandatory or binding on the court you are in.

Here, you are in the 14th District Court in Dallas County. Federal courts (in Texas and elsewhere) and other state courts (e.g., Oklahoma or Arkansas) would—at most—be persuasive. Texas state courts "above" the court you are in (the 14th District Court in Dallas County)—the Court of Appeals for the Fifth District of Dallas (not to be confused the federal Fifth Circuit Court of Appeals) and the Texas Supreme Court—would be mandatory. All other Texas state courts (those courts at your same level and those courts above you but overseeing different districts) would be merely persuasive.

COURT	FEDERAL OR STATE COURT	MANDATORY OR PERSUASIVE
An opinion from the 44th District Court in Dallas County	State	Persuasive
Oklahoma Supreme Court	State	Persuasive
An opinion from the 14th District Court in Dallas County	State	Persuasive
Court of Appeals for the Fifth District of Texas at Dallas	State	Mandatory

continued on next page

Congress expressly or implicitly says so, or when federal laws are so pervasive that they occupy the entire field of law.

Texas Supreme Court	State	Mandatory
Court of Appeals for the 14th District of Texas at Houston	State	Persuasive
U.S. Supreme Court	Federal	Persuasive
An opinion from the United States Court of Appeals for the Fifth Circuit	Federal	Persuasive

Put in the simplest terms, cases which are both (1) in the same jurisdiction, and (2) from a higher court are considered mandatory authority.

On top of all of this, sometimes mandatory authority conflicts with other mandatory authority and you have to figure out which of the mandatory authority is likely to have more weight. We know that sounds daunting, but it is not that difficult to discern. The "weight" a court gives to the conflicting authority may turn on a number of factors, including prestige of the issuing court, the date of the opinion, the strength of the opinion's reasoning, the subsequent treatment of that authority by other authorities, whether the issue you are using the case for is dicta or part of the court's holding, the factual similarity to your case, whether the opinion is published, the number of judges subscribing to the opinion, or the reputation of the judge who drafted the case opinion. Similarly, some persuasive authority is more persuasive than other persuasive authority. Again, the weight given to a certain piece of persuasive authority will turn on the same factors.

III. Types of authority

In addition to assessing how a judicial opinion fits within the judicial hierarchy in order to determine whether it is mandatory or persuasive, you must also determine whether the source relied on is primary or secondary authority. Primary authority includes cases (judicial decisions) and enacted law, such as constitutions, statutes, and regulations. Depending on which jurisdiction the case you are handling is in, primary authority may be, as explained above, either mandatory or persuasive.

Secondary authority, on the other hand, takes a variety of forms. Secondary authority includes such sources as treatises, legal encyclopedias, law review articles, and summaries of the law. Typically, secondary sources seek to explain or comment on primary authority. Secondary authority is **always** persuasive. To the extent secondary authority conflicts with primary authority, the primary authority will control.

For law students and lawyers, secondary authority sources serve as helpful resources to understand the context and background of an area of the law. Secondary sources can also help you locate relevant primary authority. Secondary sources, however, are not themselves law and, as such, should be used only where primary authority is absent or as background for giving context to primary authority.

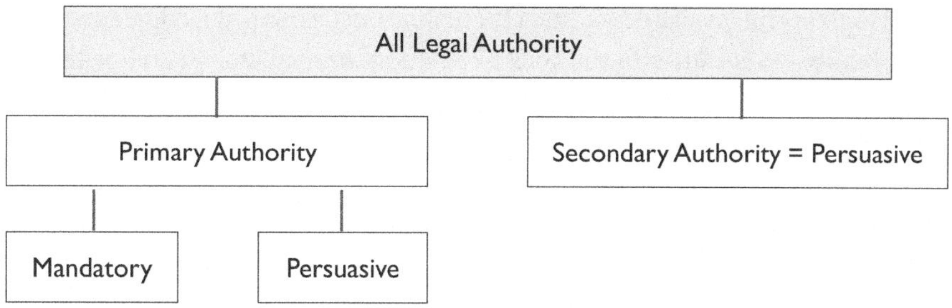

IV. How to find the law

Now that you have a general overview of how the legal system is organized, let's discuss how you, as a law student, will find the law. In most first-year legal writing programs, during the first semester, students' big writing assignment is a "closed-packet" objective memorandum. "Closed packet" means that students are not supposed to do legal research. Instead, all legal authority (statutes, cases, secondary sources, etc.) is provided to them. The reason for using a closed-packet problem to start is to allow students to focus on legal **writing** only, which is a new and difficult skill in and of itself. However, in real life as a lawyer, when given a legal "problem"—whether that be an issue from a client, a memorandum to write for a partner, a motion to draft, or a brief to which you must respond—you are not given an accompanying "closed packet" of legal authority upon which you may rely. Instead, after understanding the problem, in whatever form it takes, your first step is usually to find the legal authority or, in other words, to conduct legal research. Through your legal research you will find the legal authority upon which you will rely to write your analysis of the issue(s).

Because legal writing and legal research go hand in hand, during the second semester of first-year legal writing, most law schools switch to persuasive writing, and the problem used is "open." This means that students must do their own legal research to find the legal authority upon which they will rely for the arguments they will include in their persuasive motion, opposition, or brief.

A. *Introduction to research*

How to do legal research is well beyond the scope of this book. Indeed, there are numerous books devoted solely to teaching you how to conduct legal research. Additionally, in law school, you will likely take an entire class devoted to legal research. For purposes of this book, we will provide you with only a brief overview of how lawyers conduct legal research.

And, as the world is rapidly moving online, we will focus on online legal research. This is not to say that there is not value in conducting research in books, but truth be told, today most lawyers are doing their research online, especially when it comes to searching for primary authority like statutes and cases. Moreover, many secondary sources—treatises, periodicals, reports, restatements, and so forth—are now, in addition to being in print, available online. Often, it is much easier to navigate these sources online because you can, with the click of a button, immediately search within them, and, from the online secondary sources, you can click on internal links that will take you directly to the primary authority (cases, statutes, regulations, etc.) that the secondary sources summarize or discuss.

The most commonly used online legal research services are Westlaw® (Westlaw Edge®) and LexisNexis® (Lexis Advance®). For the sake of simplicity, the quick tips below use Westlaw Edge as an example. Note that, while Lexis Advance is similar, there are a few small differences, such that what is below will not perfectly translate to searching on Lexis Advance.

B. *Quick tips for researching online*

When you first begin researching online using either Westlaw or Lexis, you may feel overwhelmed. Unlike in your first-year, first semester, where you were given a closed packet of legal authorities, you now have a whole world of legal authority at your fingertips. You are no longer in a closed universe but are instead in what seems like an endless universe of information. How do you get started? There are lots of theories on how to conduct legal research and discussing each of them (or any of them) is beyond the scope of this book. However, we have set forth some general principles tailored to the problem accompanying this book to help give you an overview of one way to approach researching.

Step one: Make your universe smaller.

Although there are tens of thousands of databases on Lexis and Westlaw, most of them will be entirely irrelevant to the problem you are researching. Therefore, after you understand your problem, before researching, you must narrow your universe so that you will look only in databases that are relevant to your problem. For example, if you look at the problem accompanying this book, you will see that it involves a will being contested on the ground of undue influence in a state probate court (trial level court) in Dallas. Therefore, the problem (1) is set in a Texas state trial court; and (2) involves the legal issue of undue influence (a state common law claim). From this, you can narrow your universe of potentially relevant legal authority considerably. Because the problem is in Texas state trial court and involves an issue solely involving state law, you need to figure out what primary legal authority will be mandatory and persuasive to the Texas trial court you are before.

As noted, the issue (undue influence) involves a state common law claim. Common law claims mean claims that come from caselaw, as opposed to statutes. This means the primary authority upon which you will rely for your rules (law) that govern the issue will be caselaw, not statutes, such that your endgame is finding relevant cases (as opposed to constitutions, statutes, or regulations). This narrows your universe even more.

Now that you know you are ultimately looking for cases, next, ask, where should the cases be from? To answer this question, you need to look at where your problem is set;

that is, what court you are before. Here, you are in a Dallas County Probate Court. This is a state, trial-level court in Texas. The only mandatory authority to a state trial court on an issue of state law will be the state intermediate appellate court (court of appeal) above it and the state appellate court of last resort (supreme court). In Texas, the only cases that will potentially be mandatory (binding) authority on a Dallas County Probate Court case will be cases from the Court of Appeals for the Fifth District of Texas at Dallas and the Texas Supreme Court. Does this mean you are only looking for cases from these two courts? No! Other primary authority may be persuasive, especially cases from other courts of appeals in Texas. Additionally, if a federal district court in Texas or the federal Fifth Circuit Court of Appeals interpreted or applied a Texas common law undue influence claim, that would be persuasive—although maybe not as persuasive as a Texas state appellate court interpreting the issue. Therefore, your universe, in order of priority, should be:

MANDATORY:
Texas Supreme Court
Court of Appeals for the Fifth District of Texas at Dallas

PERSUASIVE:
Other Texas State Courts of Appeal
Fifth Circuit Court of Appeals (Federal)
Texas District Courts (Federal)

Do you need to be searching for legal authority from other countries? No, a Texas trial court does not care what Canada does. Do you need to be searching for legal authority from other states? No, a Texas trial court will not care what a Maryland court does because the issue is a Texas state common law issue.

As you can see, your universe continues to get smaller. To capture searching only Texas state cases and related federal cases (Texas federal district court and the Fifth Circuit Court of Appeals cases), you tailor your search. On Westlaw Edge, your beginning screen will look similar to the below image. If you simply type into the search bar, you will be searching **all content types** from **all state and federal jurisdictions** ("All State & Federal"). This is not only an expensive search from a cost standpoint (yes, in practice, searches cost money), but it is also way too broad.

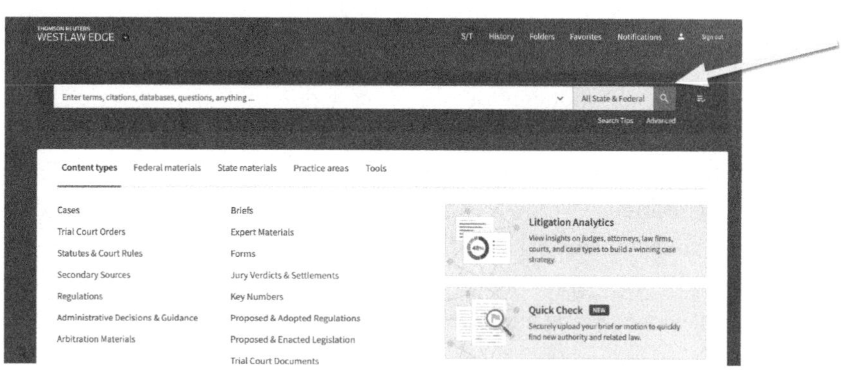

First, you do not want to search all content types; you need to narrow your search to caselaw (not trial court orders, statutes, rules, secondary sources, forms, briefs, etc.). Therefore, you should click on the "Cases" link under "Content types." This will limit your search to only cases, as you can see on the left side of the search bar.

Second, you do not want to search all cases, but only Texas state court cases and Texas-related federal court cases. To do this, you click on the right grey box in the tool bar and change it to "Texas" and click the box at the bottom that says "Include related federal."

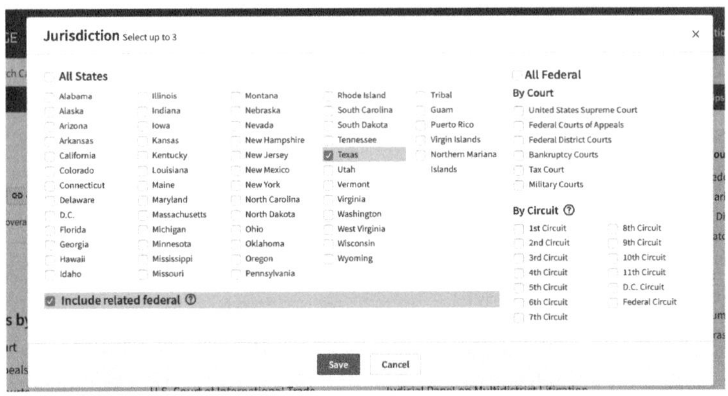

Now your search will be limited to only cases and only cases from Texas state courts or from federal courts as long as the cases are Texas-related.

Step two: Craft your search terms.

The universe in which you are searching is Texas state and Texas federal cases ("Texas cases"). What kinds of Texas cases do you want to find? Certainly, you are looking for cases that discuss undue influence. If a case does not discuss undue influence, it is probably not going to be very helpful to you.

Therefore, you need to conduct a search within your Texas cases universe for the term "**undue influence.**" One way to do this is by simply typing the words undue influence (without quotations) into the search bar like you would on Google. This is called a "natural language" search. While this natural language search feels comfortable and easy, it is less exacting and does not provide the same strong results as the other type of search—a "terms-and-connectors" search. As you can see, the natural language search of undue influence yielded almost 3,000 results.

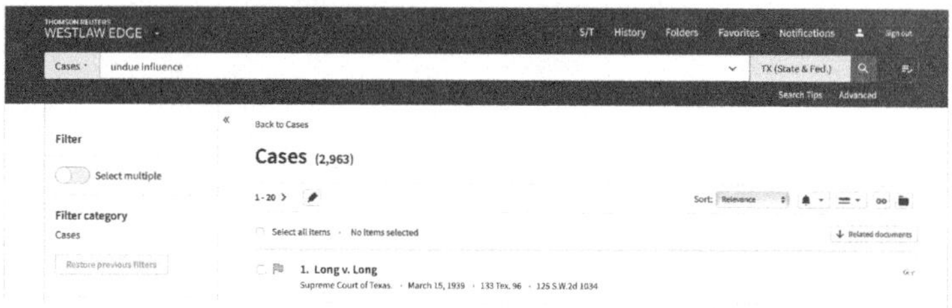

A terms-and-connectors search (also called a "Boolean" search) allows you to specify relationships between search terms and, therefore, allows your searches to be more precise. There are lots of terms and connectors you can use when crafting a search. We will discuss our favorite ones, but a complete list can be found in both the Westlaw and Lexis free, online quick guides for researching.[8] The favorite term-and-connector we use is /#, which specifies that terms must be within a certain number of words from each other. For example, you do not want cases that simply have the word "undue" and the word "influence" anywhere in them, rather you want the words to be either right next to each other or close to each other. To capture this, you could search "**undue influence**" in quotations, which would return only cases that have the term undue influence as reflected in the quotation marks. However, if that search turned out to be too narrow or was not capturing the results you needed, you could use the term and connector **/#** and search **undue /4 influence**, which would return cases with the word **undue** within four words of the word **influence**. Doing this search narrows the results some (to 2,622), but not nearly enough.

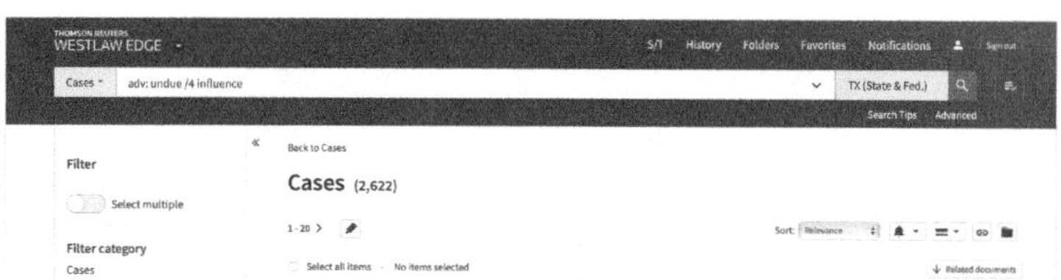

What you really need is undue influence not in any context, but rather in the context of contesting a will. You could search: **undue /4 influence /20 will /20 contest!** Note that by using an explanation mark [!], which is a root expander, you will capture not

8. *Searching with Boolean Terms and Connectors*, Westlaw Next, https://lscontent.westlaw.com/images/content/WLN_Boolean-Connectors-S023352_Final.pdf (last visited June 20, 2019); *Using Search Commands and Connectors at Lexis Advance*®, LexisNexis, https://www.lexisnexis.com/pdf/lexis-advance/terms-and-connectors.pdf (last visited June 20, 2019).

only the term "contest," but also all variations of the word (contests, contestant, contested, etc.). This search will capture cases where **undue** is within four words of **influence**, which is within 20 words of **will**, which is within 20 words of all variations of **contest**.

This narrows the results to 529 cases, which is still a lot, but it is much less than the original almost 3,000 case results.

Step three: Narrow and refine.

When searching, it is best to start broad and then refine or narrow the results. For example, let's say you ran the search **undue /4 influence**, which yielded about 2,600 results. You can narrow this search by searching within those results using the search box ("Search within results") in the left panel. Let's say you searched within the left search bar, **execut! /10 exert! /20 undue /4 influence**. This search translates to the following: all variations of the word **execute** within 10 words of all variations of the word **exert** within 20 words of **undue** within four words of **influence**. Now, the initial almost 2,600 results are limited to 149, which is a much more manageable number.

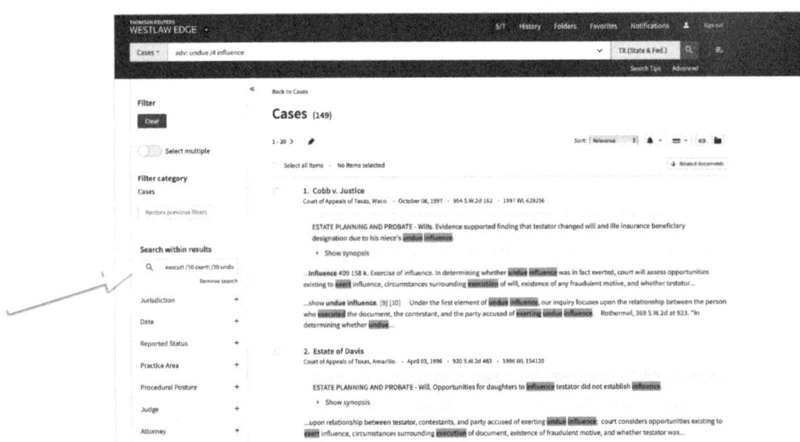

Note that you could make this number even smaller by filtering the results using the options on the left panel. You can see under the "Jurisdiction" heading to the left of the 147 case results that 7 cases are federal and 142 are state.

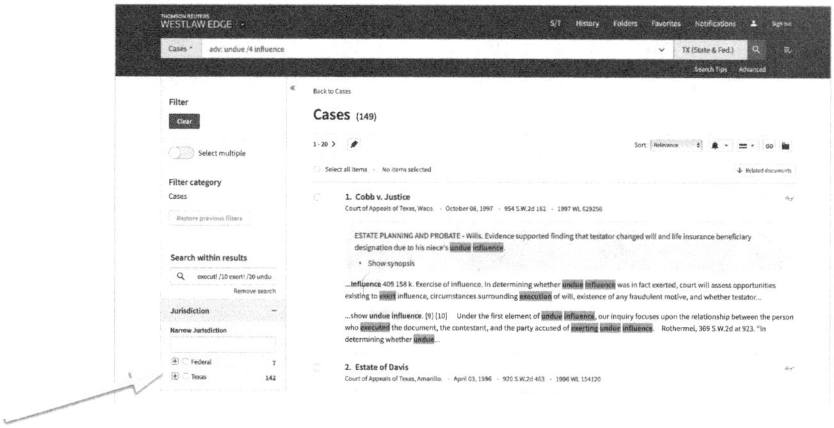

Step four: Use good cases to find other good cases.

From the above results, the first case listed is *Cobb v. Justice.* If you were to read this case, you would realize that this Texas court of appeals case is on point because it involves a will being contested on grounds of undue influence and the facts are at least somewhat analogous to the facts in the problem. Put another way, it is a "good" case. We can use this "good" case to find other "good" cases in a couple of ways. First, we can see which cases *Cobb v. Justice* cites and read those cases by clicking the link to them from within the *Cobb v. Justice* case. Second, we can click "Citing References" to see which cases cite *Cobb v. Justice.* Given that *Cobb v. Justice* is on point, it is likely that many of the cases it cites or many cases that cite to it will be on point and useful to you as well.

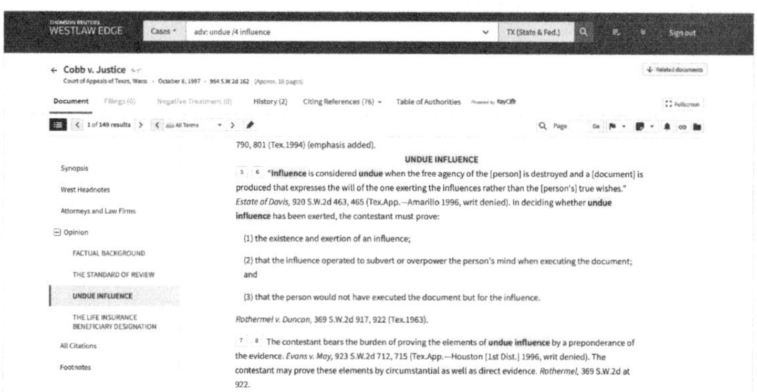

Step five: Secondary sources = your friend.

Refer to secondary sources to refine you understanding of the law. Secondary sources are very helpful in understanding the area of law and leading you to relevant primary authority. Oftentimes, it is wise to start looking in secondary sources before conducting a search of primary authority like caselaw. For the problem in the book, because it is a Texas common law claim, you would want to look at Texas-specific secondary sources. You can find state-specific secondary sources on Westlaw Edge by clicking "Secondary Sources" under "Content types." On the next screen, you will be able to narrow your secondary sources search by type and/or by state.

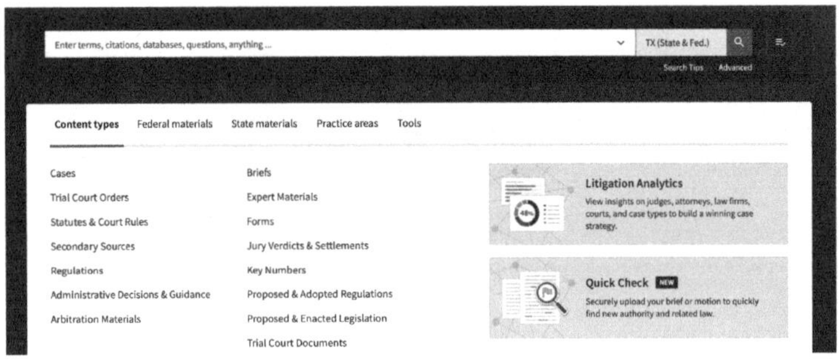

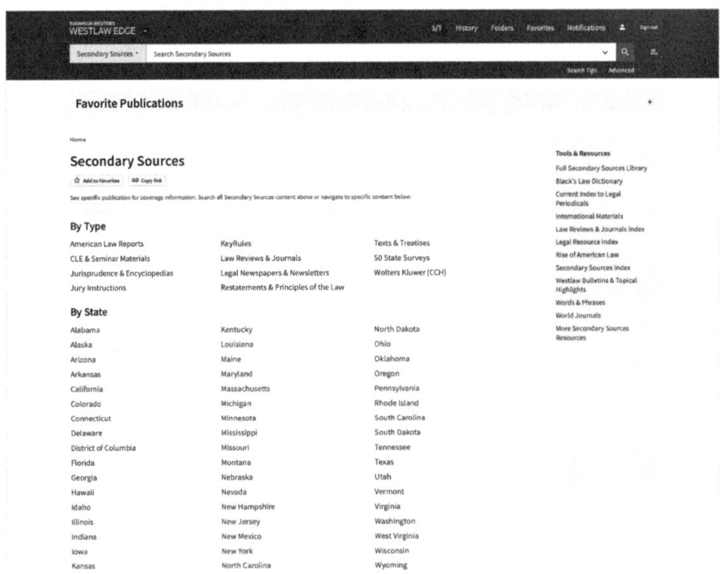

Another place to find secondary sources is in your law school's library. While we find it easier to search for cases online rather than in print, the same is not true of secondary sources, and it can be easier to navigate secondary sources in book form. For example, if you wanted to become familiar with will contests in Texas, the book *Texas Practice Guide: Wills, Trusts and Estate Planning* by Ronald R. Cresswell, Sarah Patel Pacheco, and Patrick Pacheco would be a smart place to start. Much like you probably enjoy having your textbooks in hard copy, flipping through a secondary source in hard copy is, simply put, easier than navigating its contents online, although you will not have the ease of following the linked references as discussed above.

V. How to read the law

Reading for law school and reading for the practice of law are different from other types of reading law students have been asked to complete in the past. Law school reading is different in terms of sheer quantity;[9] but, more importantly, it is different in terms of the skills required to parse the text and the depth and breadth of the take-aways that a legal reader is expected to glean from the readings. Instead of assigned readings that are descriptive and tell the reader what he or she needs to learn from the text, law school readings are nuanced, contextual, and evaluative. This difference means that the popular techniques—such as "speed reading" and "power-browsing"—that are taught and valued in other reading-heavy contexts can end up being a disservice, rather than a tool, for law students trying to understand the law through reading cases and statutes.

Instead of powering through a text with the purpose of capturing the highlights and key terms, students reading legal texts must take a slower, multi-staged approach to reading.

Step one: Identify the purpose for which you are reading the source. What part of the law are you trying to understand?

Step two: Skim the source, paying attention to any headings and any conclusions, to get the source's context. Do not use a highlighter or take notes during this step. Sit on your hands.

Step three: Slowly read the source. Look up terms you do not know, interact with the text, and note what is said, as well as what is not said, in the text. During this step, you may take notes and highlight key text.

Step four: Think about how this source relates to others you have read and/or how it helps you resolve client problems.

As you progress, legal reading will become—and must become—faster. This increased speed stems from familiarity with terms and with the structure of legal readings. It also comes from an appreciation for the fact that some parts of a case can be skimmed, while others must be more carefully parsed, depending on the issue with which you

9. Law students are assigned on average three to four hours of reading daily. Law School Numbers, *How to Determine if the Law Is for You*, available at http://lawschoolnumbers.com/application-prep/is-law-for-you (last visited June 28, 2019). Such extensive reading, however, does not end in law school because a central part of practicing lawyers' work involves reading. In fact, most lawyers read "at least ten hours per week," and younger lawyers read closer to "thirty hours" a week. *Id.*

are grappling. For example, you may be doing research for a case that involves a potential battery. The judicial opinion that you are reviewing may address the requisite elements of battery, but it may also resolve procedural issues or even the presence/absence of other related torts. When you first begin reading cases, you will need to deeply read the entire case in order to discern which parts of the opinion are relevant to your research issue. As you fine-tune your legal reading skills, however, you will be able to focus on the parts of the opinion relevant to your precise issue and skim (or skip) those parts that involve, for example, other torts irrelevant to your research. Again, when you first begin navigating legal texts, you need to read texts in their entirety to begin to build your legal vocabulary and to develop your ability to discern what is (or is not) relevant.

Given this reality, law students are best served by setting aside their preconceptions of how to successfully complete reading assignments from their prior educational or vocational experiences, and, instead, treat being a legal reader as a new skill they must grapple with and, ultimately, master. Moreover, different types of legal texts require unique skills in order to successfully parse them. This section aims to identify the key skills and processes lawyers need to read the two most common legal texts: statutes and caselaw.

A. *How to read a statute*

Statutes are formal written laws enacted by legislative bodies, such as the U.S. Congress, a state legislature, or a city council. Unfortunately, statutes are complex, and because they are often the result of "group thinking" and extensive compromise, they can be dense and difficult to parse (even when they are only a single paragraph long).

As a result, it is important for new law students to understand that reading a statute is an art as much as it is a science. As such, it is critical for new law students to approach statutory reading slowly and deliberately with a multi-step plan and a significant amount of time allotted for the task. When given an assignment to read a statute, one of the most common mistakes that new law students make is they do simply that: they take five minutes to read the words of the statute. Reading a statute like an article, a chapter from a book, or even a case, will not likely yield a meaningful understanding of the statute, much less how it may or may not apply in other contexts. Thus, you should read a statute like you would read Ikea assembly instructions for a bunkbed: slowly, closely, and with attention to detail.

A legal reader faced with the task of grappling with a new statute should, generally speaking, use the same basic steps set forth above. In an effort to provide you with a bit more guidance, the table below fine-tunes the four steps recommended for general legal reading to conform to the nuances of statutory reading, which requires extra care.

Step one: Identify the purpose for which you are reading the statute. What part of the law are you trying to understand and how does the specific statute you are reading fit into the larger context of the law?

Step two: Skim the statute, paying attention to any headings and any conclusions, to get the statute's context. Make an effort to decipher how the statute operates and to whom or to what it applies. Do not use a highlighter or take notes during this step. Sit on your hands.

Step three: Slowly read the statute with painful particularity. Look up terms you do not know, interact with the text, and note what is said, as well as what is not said, in the text. Pay close attention to "watchwords" and grammatical construction. During this step, you may take notes and highlight key text.

Step four: Think about how this particular statute relates to other statutes or other pieces of law (cases possibly) that you have read and/or how it helps you resolve client problems.

To better understand the process you should use when you read a statute, let's try reading a statute together.

Congratulations, after three years of law school and after successfully passing the Bar Exam, you are a family law attorney in the great state of Texas! One afternoon, a client calls your office and says she has been served with divorce papers by her long-time boyfriend. She explains that they were never formally married. Trying to figure out the basis for the divorce filing, she asks you what the requirements are for an informal marriage in Texas. You set up a meeting to review the law with her tomorrow. You pull up section 2.401 of the Texas Family Code and read it by engaging in each of the four steps above. Below is the text of the relevant statute as it appears in the Texas Family Code.

SUBCHAPTER E. MARRIAGE WITHOUT FORMALITIES

Sec. 2.401. PROOF OF INFORMAL MARRIAGE. (a) In a judicial, administrative, or other proceeding, the marriage of a man and woman may be proved by evidence that:

(1) a declaration of their marriage has been signed as provided by this subchapter; or

(2) the man and woman agreed to be married and after the agreement they lived together in this state as husband and wife and there represented to others that they were married.

(b) If a proceeding in which a marriage is to be proved as provided by Subsection (a)(2) is not commenced before the second anniversary of the date on which the parties separated and ceased living together, it is rebuttably presumed that the parties did not enter into an agreement to be married.

(c) A person under 18 years of age may not:

(1) be a party to an informal marriage; or

(2) execute a declaration of informal marriage under Section 2.402.

(d) A person may not be a party to an informal marriage or execute a declaration of an informal marriage if the person is presently married to a person who is not the other party to the informal marriage or declaration of an informal marriage, as applicable.

Added by Acts 1997, 75th Leg., ch. 7, Sec. 1, eff. April 17, 1997. Amended by Acts 1997, 75th Leg., ch. 1362, Sec. 1, eff. Sept. 1, 1997.

Amended by:

Acts 2005, 79th Leg., Ch. 268 (S.B. 6), Sec. 4.12, eff. September 1, 2005.

Step one: Identify the purpose for which you are reading the statute. What part of the law are you trying to understand and how does the specific statute you are reading fit into the larger context of the law?

The first step you should take when reading a statute is really a two-part step: first, identify the purpose for reading the statute; and, second, determine how the statute you are reading fits into the larger, statutory context.

In our hypothetical situation, your purpose for reading the statute is relatively straightforward: your client, who was not formally married but has a long-time boyfriend who served her with divorce papers, wants to know the requirements of an informal marriage to determine whether she and her boyfriend were, in fact, ever married. In other words, you are reading the statute to discern the requirements for an informal marriage.

Next, with this in mind, you must figure out how the statute you are reading fits into the overall statutory scheme to determine whether the section you are reading will give a complete answer to your client's question or whether you need to review additional statutory sections. To do this, you must "zoom out" a bit, so you can see beyond the particular statute in front of you. This requires that you understand how statutes are organized and where the statute you are reading fits into that larger organizational structure.

1. Organization and structure of Texas state statutes

Like other states, Texas statutes are—for the most part—organized by subject matter. Each "code" or book of Texas statutes includes the state laws—statutes—on a particular topic. For example, Texas has the Alcoholic Beverage Code, Election Code, Estates Code, Family Code, Penal Code, etc. Each subject matter code is then broken up into multiple titles, chapters, subchapters, and sections. In our hypothetical, you are tasked with finding out what is required to prove an informal marriage. In which subject matter code do you think you would find this information? Below is a list of all the current Texas codes.

Agriculture Code
Alcoholic Beverage Code
Business and Commerce Code
Business Organizations Code
Civil Practice and Remedies Code
Education Code
Civil Statutes (Education Auxiliary)
Election Code
Estates Code
Family Code
Finance Code
Government Code
Health and Safety Code
Human Resources Code
Insurance Code
Labor Code
Local Government Code
Natural Resources Code
Occupations Code
Parks and Wildlife Code
Penal Code
Property Code
Special District Local Laws Code
Tax Code
Transportation Code
Utilities Code
Water Code
Civil Statutes (Water Auxiliary)
Civil Statutes (Titles 1 to 32)
Civil Statutes (Titles 33 to 77)
Civil Statutes (Titles 78 to 111)
Civil Statutes (Titles 112 to Final Title)
Texas Probate Code
Constitution of the State of Texas 1876
Code of Criminal Procedure
Effective Dates of Laws
UCC Acknowledgments
Vernon's Texas Rules Annotated

Information about marriage—informal or formal—would probably be located in the Texas Family Code.[10] (And, if you read the previous pages of this book, you were already told that. Close reading pays off.)

If you were to go to the library and locate the physical copy of the Texas Family Code, below is a picture of what you would see.

TABLE OF CONTENTS

XV

As you can see, the table of contents in the book version of the statute allows you to see where the section on informal marriage is in relation to the larger code—Title 1, The Marriage Relationship, Subtitle A. Marriages, Chapter 2, Subchapter E. Marriage without Formalities. As a reader, you can then look to the surrounding sections to see if there are other provisions you should peruse because they may affect your reading of the provision that is most relevant to you. For example, in this case, the "Definitions" section located in Chapter 1 of the same title seems relevant because it may define terms in the statute at issue.

Another way to access a state statute is to use an online legal search engine, such as Westlaw or Lexis, as discussed above. Below is what you would find if you looked up the Texas Family Code on informal marriage on Westlaw Edge.

10. You will note that in Texas, as in other jurisdictions, there are both annotated and unannotated statutes. Annotated codes—like regular codes—contain the language of the official statute, but, in addition, contain summaries of important judicial decisions related to the included provision(s).

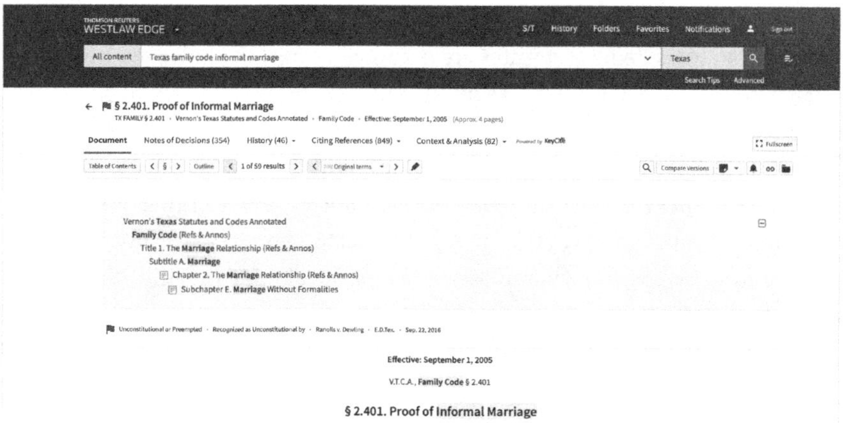

The complete index to the code does not appear automatically online the same way it would if you accessed the statute in hard copy. That said, in just a few easy clicks, you can access a table of contents and peruse the statute online just as you would in hard copy. First, click on "Family Code," and then, if you scroll down, you can click on the various chapters to reveal subchapters and sections.

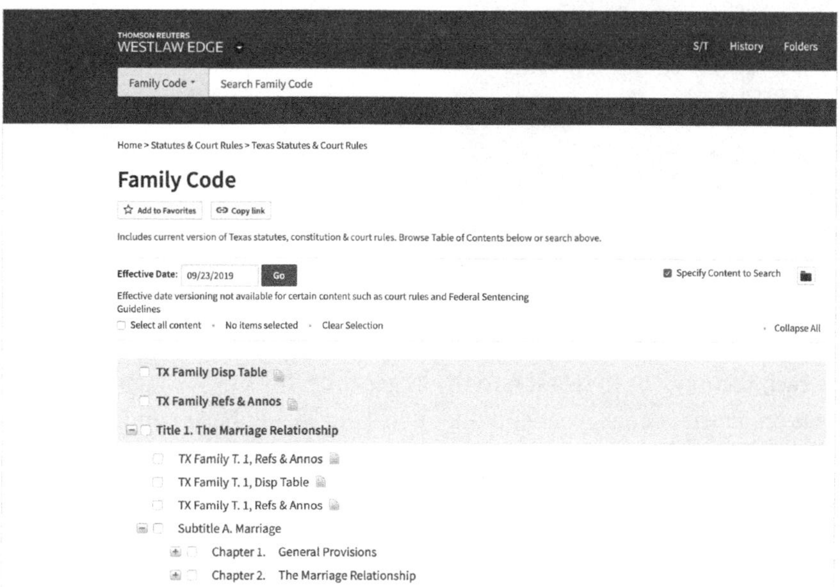

By orienting yourself in the larger Family Code—whether online or in a hard-copy version of the code—you can tell that informal marriage is just one of the ways that a couple can be considered married in Texas.

2. Organization and structure of federal statutes

Like Texas statutes, federal statutes are organized topically; however, instead of subject-matter codes, federal statutes are divided into different, subject-specific numbered titles.[11] There are 50 different titles that contain federal statutes, such as Title 11 (Bankruptcy), Title 26 (the Internal Revenue Code), and Title 49 (Transportation). Each federal title is further broken down into parts, chapters, and sections. Just as with Texas state statutes, you could go to the library and locate a hard copy of any federal statute. If you were to go to the library and locate the physical copy of Title 28 of the federal code, which contains the federal statutes related to the judiciary and judicial procedure, below is a picture of what you would see.

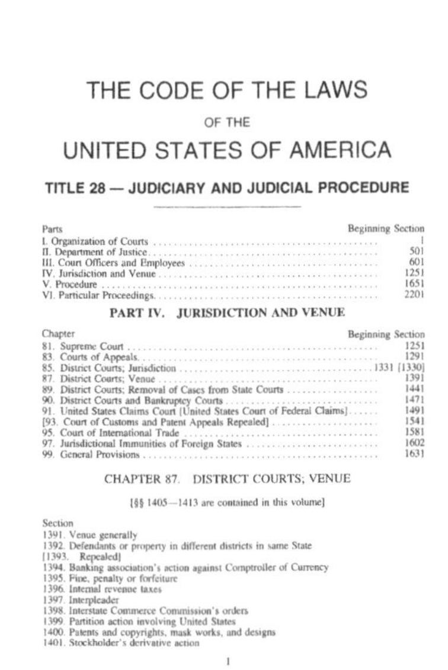

THE CODE OF THE LAWS
OF THE
UNITED STATES OF AMERICA

TITLE 28 — JUDICIARY AND JUDICIAL PROCEDURE

Parts	Beginning Section
I. Organization of Courts	1
II. Department of Justice	501
III. Court Officers and Employees	601
IV. Jurisdiction and Venue	1251
V. Procedure	1651
VI. Particular Proceedings	2201

PART IV. JURISDICTION AND VENUE

Chapter	Beginning Section
81. Supreme Court	1251
83. Courts of Appeals	1291
85. District Courts; Jurisdiction	1331 [1330]
87. District Courts; Venue	1391
89. District Courts; Removal of Cases from State Courts	1441
90. District Courts and Bankruptcy Courts	1471
91. United States Claims Court [United States Court of Federal Claims]	1491
[93. Court of Customs and Patent Appeals Repealed]	1541
95. Court of International Trade	1581
97. Jurisdictional Immunities of Foreign States	1602
99. General Provisions	1631

CHAPTER 87. DISTRICT COURTS; VENUE

[§§ 1405—1413 are contained in this volume]

Section
1391. Venue generally
1392. Defendants or property in different districts in same State
[1393. Repealed]
1394. Banking association's action against Comptroller of Currency
1395. Fine, penalty or forfeiture
1396. Internal revenue taxes
1397. Interpleader
1398. Interstate Commerce Commission's orders
1399. Partition action involving United States
1400. Patents and copyrights, mask works, and designs
1401. Stockholder's derivative action

1

As you can see, the table of contents in the book version of the statute allows you to see where each section falls in relation to the larger code. If you were looking for the federal rule on general venue, you would look in Title 28—Judiciary and Judicial Procedure, Part IV, Jurisdiction and Venue, Chapter 87, Section 1391, Venue generally.

Similar to the different ways you can access Texas statutes, you can access federal statutes using an online legal search engine, such as Westlaw or Lexis, in addition to locating them in hard copy. Below is what you would find if you were to look up section 1391 of Title 28 on Westlaw.

11. There are three versions of the federal codes: the United States Code, the United States Code Service, and the United States Code Annotated. The official version of the code is the United States Code. The other two unofficial versions of the Code contain the official statutory language of the United States Code plus summaries of judicial opinions related to the particular statutes.

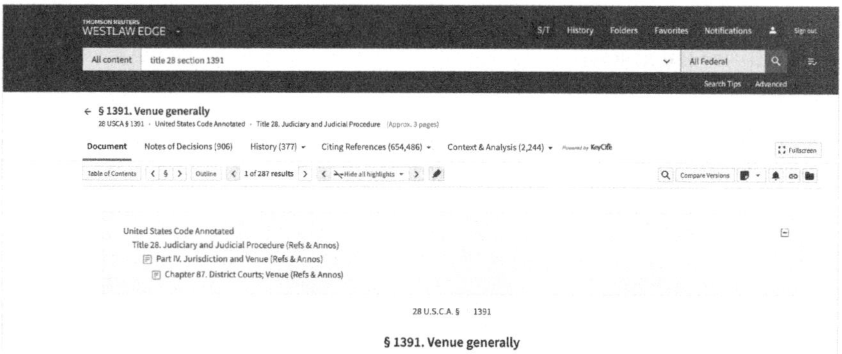

Like the Texas statutes, the table of contents for federal statutes does not automatically appear in its entirety, but by clicking "Title 28. Judiciary and Judicial Procedure," you can open up the relevant portions of the table of contents in order to orient yourself in the statute and review other nearby provisions.

3. Applying organizational structure

Now that you understand how statutes are organized, let's turn back to the hypothetical scenario from before. You have successfully located Section 2.401 of the Texas Family Code, which on its face sets forth the standard for establishing an informal marriage in Texas. Now, per step one for reading a statute, you need to "zoom out" of the specific, relevant provision and orient yourself in the Texas Family Code more generally. Doing so will give you general context for what you are reading and will help you determine which, if any, other provisions of the Texas Family Code may be relevant to your client's inquiry.

Using Westlaw, first locate section 2.401 of the Texas Family Code. Review the statute for context.

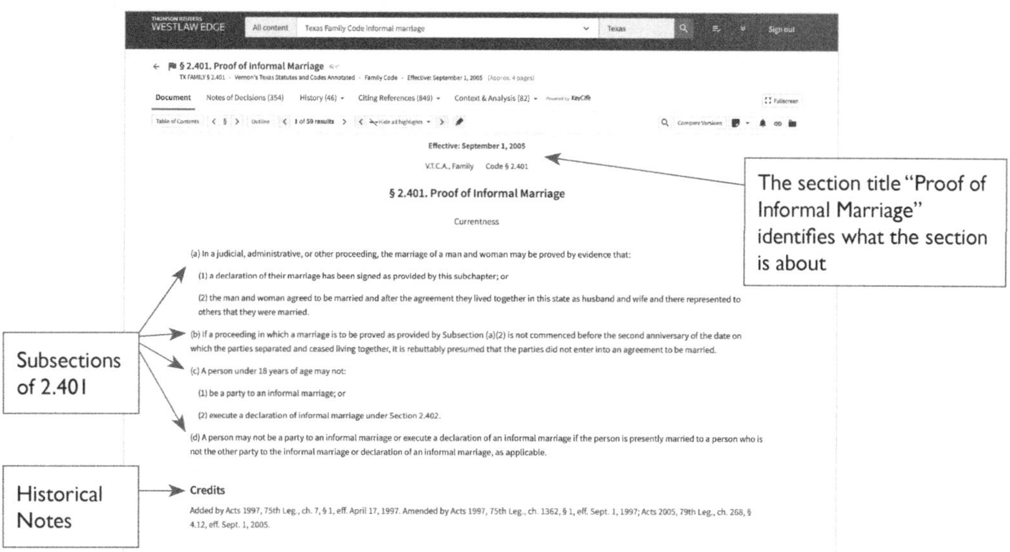

Then back out of the specific section to view the table of contents for the relevant subtitle. You will see the following.

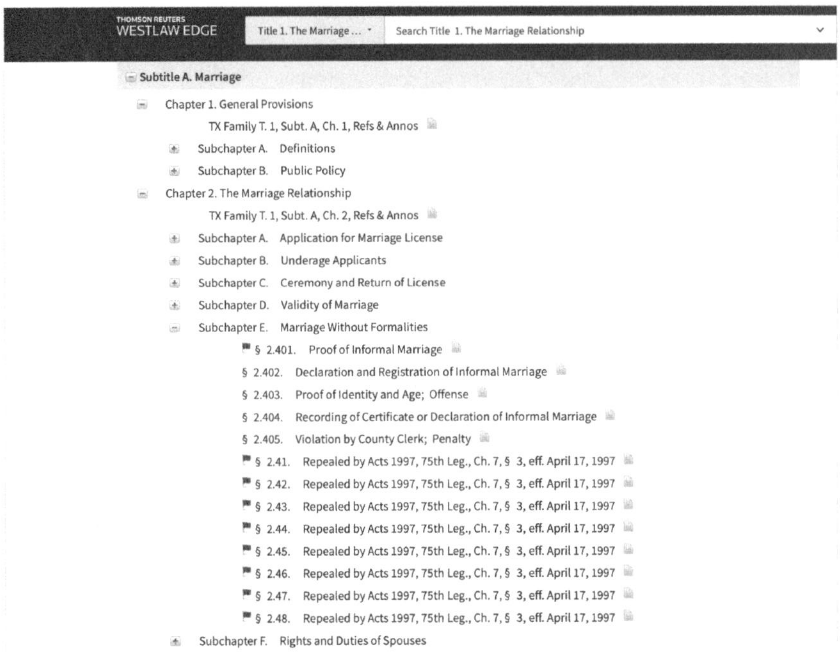

Given this context, you may decide to review the definitions in subchapter A as well as section 2.403 regarding proof of identity and age related to informal marriages. You will also note that the section you are focused on—section 2.401—contains a red flag. Westlaw's red flag system denotes that this particular provision of the code is no longer good law.[12]

12. The U.S. Supreme Court held that there was a fundamental right to marry that included homosexual couples. *See generally Obergefell v. Hodges*, 135 S. Ct. 2584 (2015). That decision impacts Texas's ability to allow only a "man and a woman" to get informally married. The statute itself is not overturned, but to the extent that it prohibits a man and a man or a woman and a woman from satisfying the requirements of informal marriage, it is unconstitutional and will likely not be enforced.

Step two: Skim the statute, paying attention to any headings and any conclusions, to get the statute's context. Make an effort to decipher how the statute operates and to whom or to what it applies. Do not use a highlighter or take notes during this step. Sit on your hands.

The second step required to read a statute is to skim the statute. Like the first step where you determine how the statute you are reading relates to the larger code, during this step, you figure out the statute's general meaning and how its different parts, subparts, sentences, and words relate to one another. You achieve this by discerning the answers to the following questions while you read: What does the statute allow, prohibit, or require? Does the statute provide any limitations or exceptions? Are there any cross-references mentioned in the statute itself? Are there any terms that need to be defined?

What does the statute allow, prohibit, or require? This inquiry mandates that you—as the reader of the statute—understand both the type of conduct or behavior the statute aims to regulate and how the statute is aiming to regulate that conduct or behavior (for example, by allowing, prohibiting, or requiring it). A statute allows conduct if it states that conduct is acceptable. A statute prohibits conduct if it forbids or disallows it. A statute requires conduct if it states that certain conduct is compulsory or mandatory.

Does the statute provide any limitations or exceptions? Statutes often provide limitations or exceptions to the rule they set forth. Limitations or exceptions are matters or conduct that is not included or covered by the general statutory language. For example, a statute may prohibit parking on the street overnight but provide an exception for local residents who have an overnight parking permit.

Are there any cross-references mentioned in the statute itself? A cross-reference is a reference to another statute or another section of the same statute. Statutes include cross-references to other statutory provisions in order to avoid restating large quantities of material in multiple locations, while signaling to the reader that they are relevant to the provision being read. When a statute contains a cross-reference, that reference effectively incorporates the cross-referenced provision into the statute. As such, it is essential that you, as a good statutory reader, review any and all other statutory provisions cross-referenced in the statute you are reading.

Are there any terms that need to be defined? Oftentimes, statutes will provide definitions of the terms used in the statute. Sometimes these definitions are in the statutory section you are reading, but sometimes they are in a different section or not defined at all within the statute. You should always look up the definitions of any terms used in the statute (either by finding the definition in the statute itself, in caselaw, or in a legal dictionary) to maximize your understanding of the statute.

Skim section 2.401 of the Texas Family Code for answers to these four questions:

<table>
<tr><th>SECTION 2.401: PROOF OF INFORMAL MARRIAGE</th><th>QUESTION</th><th>ANSWER</th></tr>
<tr><td rowspan="4">(a) In a judicial, administrative, or other proceeding, the marriage of a man and woman may be proved by evidence that:
(1) a declaration of their marriage has been signed as provided by this subchapter; or
(2) the man and woman agreed to be married and after the agreement they lived together in this state as husband and wife and there represented to others that they were married.
(b) If a proceeding in which a marriage is to be proved as provided by Subsection (a)(2) is not commenced before the second anniversary of the date on which the parties separated and ceased living together, it is rebuttably presumed that the parties did not enter into an agreement to be married.
(c) A person under 18 years of age may not:
(1) be a party to an informal marriage; or
(2) execute a declaration of informal marriage under Section 2.402.
(d) A person may not be a party to an informal marriage or execute a declaration of an informal marriage if the person is presently married to a person who is not the other party to the informal marriage or declaration of an informal marriage, as applicable.</td><td>What does the statute allow, prohibit, or require?</td><td>The statute allows an informal marriage if there is a declaration or proof of certain requirements/ elements.</td></tr>
<tr><td>Does the statute provide any limitations or exceptions?</td><td>There are three limitations:
1. If more than two years has passed, it is rebuttably presumed that there was no agreement to be married.
2. If a person is under 18, s/he cannot be informally married.
3. If a person is currently married to a third party, s/he cannot be informally married.</td></tr>
<tr><td>Are there any cross-references mentioned in the statute itself?</td><td>The statute cross-references section 2.402, which sets forth the requirements for proving an informal marriage by declaration/ registration.</td></tr>
<tr><td>Are there any terms that need to be defined?</td><td>What is an agreement?
What is a declaration of marriage?</td></tr>
</table>

In short, by skimming the statute, you can discern that it sets forth the requirements for establishing an informal marriage. The statute provides a number of limits on a party's ability to informally marry and includes a cross-reference.

Step three: Slowly read the statute with painful particularity. Look up terms you do not know, interact with the text, and note what is said, as well as what is not said, in the text. Pay close attention to "watchwords" and grammatical construction. During this step, you may take notes and highlight key text.

The third step required to read a statute is that you "zoom in" and review the statute slowly and with particularity. To do this, you need to isolate the "watchwords" in the statute, determine if the statute is setting forth elements or factors, and then break the statute into bite-sized, grammatically sensible pieces to ensure you understand what the statute is—in this case—requiring and who is required to prove what.

Watchwords are deceptively small words in a statute that, if changed, would alter the meaning of the statute entirely. Some legal writing professors refer to these words as red flag words, words of authority, or operative words. The table below highlights the most important words to watch for when reading statutes (aka "watchwords").

WATCH WORD	MEANING
And	Requires all elements or factors to be met or considered
Either/Or	Requires only one of the elements or factors to be met or considered
If... then	Creates an exception to the standard
Unless	Creates an exception to the standard
Except	Creates an exception to the standard
Should or may	Allows conduct, but does not mandate it
Should not or may not	Disallows conduct, but does not prohibit it
Will	Provides for a future event
Must or shall	Mandates conduct
Must not or shall not	Prohibits conduct
Provided that	Creates a condition or exception or adds an additional requirement

To determine whether the statute sets forth elements or factors, you must first understand the difference between the two. If a rule is made up of elements, it means that to satisfy the rule you must establish each of (read: all of) the specified elements. If a rule is made up of factors, it means that to satisfy the rule you must weigh a series of factors to determine whether you satisfy the rule, but failure to find one of the factors is not fatal. You may need to try to reorder the structure of the statute into elements or factors by placing the subject of the statute first.

For simplicity, engage in a slow reading of section 2.401(a). First, highlight the watchwords in the statute.

Section 2.401: Proof of Informal Marriage

(a) In a judicial, administrative, **or** other proceeding, the marriage of a man **and** woman **may** be proved by evidence that:

(1) a declaration of their marriage has been signed as provided by this subchapter; **or**

(2) the man **and** woman agreed to be married **and** after the agreement they lived together in this state as husband and wife **and** there represented to others that they were married.

Next, based on an analysis of the highlighted watchwords, you can quickly see that there are two ways to establish an informal marriage as set forth in subsections (a)(1) and (a)(2) of the statute. Moreover, if one is establishing an informal marriage through the avenue set forth in (a)(2), the use of the watchword "and" between the requirements demonstrates that one will need to establish three **elements** to prove an informal marriage.

Last, try to reorder the requirements of the statute to make it easier to see/understand how to establish an informal marriage in Texas.

A man and a woman can establish an informal marriage if:

(1) they sign a declaration of marriage as set forth in this subchapter;

—OR—

(1) they agree to be married; (2) after agreeing to be married, they live together in Texas as husband and wife; **and** (3) they represent to others that they were married.

Step four: Think about how this particular statute relates to other statutes or other pieces of law (cases possibly) that you have read and/or how it helps you resolve client problems.

The fourth step to reading a statute is to zoom back out again and to assess how the statute you read relates to other laws or helps you resolve your current client's and any future client's issue(s). Here, in the case your client has brought to you, there is no evidence that she or her boyfriend signed a declaration of an informal marriage. Accordingly, it seems that the validity of the boyfriend's divorce filing will turn on whether he can show evidence to support the three elements required for an informal marriage: (1) they agreed to be married; (2) after the agreement they lived together in Texas as husband and wife; and (3) they represented to others that they were married. Moreover, per the statute, your client and her boyfriend must be of different sexes and over 18. Last, if the boyfriend did not file his petition for divorce within two years of ceasing living together with your client, it is presumed they were not informally married, and the boyfriend has a greater hurdle to prove the informal marriage.

As evidenced by this exercise, statutory reading is arduous, perhaps even more arduous than reading those awful Ikea assembly instructions. Reading statutes is often like navigating a new language. To really grasp what the statute is requiring, prohibiting, or limiting, you must refrain from simply power-reading the language of the statute, and, instead, you must read the statute carefully following the four-step process. Although this process is slow going, the depth of understanding it yields will more than make up for the time spent.

B. *How to read a case*

Law students are required to read on average 450 pages a week.[13] The vast majority of this reading is comprised of judicial opinions, which lawyers, judges, professors, and law students commonly refer to as cases. Cases are written opinions or decisions authored by judges that specify the resolution of a legal dispute and the reasons for that resolution.

At first, it takes law students hours to read and comprehend cases. In fact, during the first month of law school, new law students tend to be able to read and comprehend only three pages of a case per hour.[14] As students become more familiar with the structure and language of cases, however, their reading becomes more efficient and, thus, quicker. Accordingly, although the care you give to case reading will not vary much from the process set forth in this chapter, the pace with which you can complete that process will quicken.

---

13. Sally Kane, *Tips Before Starting Law School*, The Balance Careers (June 25, 2019) https://www.thebalancecareers.com/preparing-for-your-first-year-of-law-school-2164369.

14. Lawnerds.com, *Speed Reading a Case*, http://lawnerds.com/guide/reading.html (last visited May 28, 2019).

Just as with statutory reading, the reading process required for law students and lawyers to "read" a case is much more in-depth than the process required to read a novel or even an undergraduate textbook. The four steps set forth at the beginning of this chapter should serve as your four guideposts for navigating your way through legal opinions as a new law student. In an effort to provide you with a bit more guidance as you navigate the hundreds of cases you will read in your first semester of law school alone, the steps below fine-tune the four steps recommended for legal reading generally to ensure extra care is given to the nuances of case reading.

Step one: Identify the purpose for which you are reading the case. What part of the law are you trying to understand?

Step two: Skim the case to understand the context of the case, such as which court the case comes from and the names and roles of the parties. While you skim, you should identify the different parts of the case, any headings, and any conclusions. Do not use a highlighter or take notes during this step except to indicate where the different key pieces of the case start/stop.

Step three: Slowly read the case. Look up terms you do not know, interact with the text, note what is said, as well as what is not said, in the case. Omit sections of the case that are irrelevant to the issue for which you are reading the case. During this step, you may take notes and highlight key passages of the case.

Step four: Think about how this case relates to others you have read and/or how it helps you resolve hypotheticals.

Let's run through a hypothetical to help you better understand how to read a case. Congratulations, you have passed the bar exam and are a newly sworn-in member of the Texas Bar! You are a young associate at a small law firm eager to make a good impression on the partner for whom you work. Early in the morning, the partner walks into your office, sits across from your desk, and explains that she has a client meeting later in the afternoon. She explains that she needs you to send her an email memo by noon detailing what is required in order for her client to set aside a will based on a claim of undue influence. The partner hands you a stack of cases and explains she has already done the research but has not read the cases in detail. The case on the top of the pile is *In re Estate of Fiedler*. You begin your project by reading that case.

Step one: Identify the purpose for which you are reading the case. What part of the law are you trying to understand?

The first step you should complete in order to read a case is a pre-reading step: discern why you are reading the case. At first blush, this question may seem obvious, but usually, it requires you to step back, orient yourself, and think critically about what you need/hope to get out of the case. Your purpose for reading the case will inform the sections of the case on which you focus your time. If you are reading a case for a class—say torts—the purpose for which you are reading will be dictated by the assigned chapter in which the case appears. If you skim through the table of contents of your casebook, you may see that the case you are reading falls within the part on intentional torts, the chapter on battery, and the subsection of that chapter on intent. Accordingly, in our example, the purpose for which you will be reading that particular case is to understand how you establish the intent element of battery.

Speaking frankly, however, once you complete law school, research does not arrive on your desk in a bound casebook with a table of contents to highlight the importance of each case. Instead, you will need to discern the purpose for which you are reading a case by the work assignment you have been given or the issue your client has asked you to resolve. In the hypothetical above, you have been asked to send an email memo to the partner for whom you work explaining "what is required in order for her client to set aside a will based on a claim of undue influence." Accordingly, when you read the first case in the stack of cases the partner hands you, your purpose in reading the case is to understand the requirements for establishing undue influence. With this overarching purpose noted, you can then begin to dig into the case in more detail.

Step two: Skim the case to understand the context of the case, such as which court the case comes from and the names and roles of the parties. While you skim, you should identify the different parts of the case, any headings, and any conclusions. Do not use a highlighter or take notes during this step except to indicate where the different key pieces of the case start/stop.

In order to complete the second step required to read a case, you must first understand the different parts of a case. Not all cases will look the same, and not all cases will contain all the parts described below. In addition, the source from which you get a case—the reporter, Westlaw, Lexis, or another source—also affects the appearance and contents of the case. A case from a reporter only contains the basic case information and the judicial opinion itself (including concurrences and dissents) itself. On the other hand, cases from online search engines such as Westlaw and Lexis contain research tools and summaries created by editors that precede the judicial opinion itself. These tools and summaries are not part of the case itself and, thus, are not law. Accordingly, it is critical that you are able to distinguish these research tools and summaries from actual parts of the case so that you do not mistakenly cite to or rely on them as if part of the actual case. Below is the case *In re Estate of Fiedler* from Lexis with annotations to help you begin to understand and identify the different parts of a case.

The Caption: the title of the case, which, in most instances, is made up of the last names of the two parties to the lawsuit.

Headnotes: a system for identifying the key legal topics and subtopics covered by the case (called Key Numbers in Westlaw). Headnotes are **not** law, and, as such, you should not cite them.

In the Estate of Fiedler

Court of Appeals of Texas, Thirteenth District, Corpus Christi - Edinburg

April 14, 2011, Delivered; April 14, 2011, Filed

NUMBER 13-09-00386-CV

Reporter
2011 Tex. App. LEXIS 2856 *; 2011 WL 1441888

IN THE **ESTATE** OF ERNST B. **FIEDLER**, DECEASED

Prior History: [*1] On appeal from the County Court at Law No. 1 of Jefferson County, Texas.

In re **Estate** *of* **Fiedler***, 2007 Tex. App. LEXIS 3792 (Tex. App. Beaumont, May 17, 2007)*

Core Terms

the will, undue influence, directed verdict, exerted, trial court, testament, execute, drove, pet

Case Summary

Procedural Posture
Appellant decedent's friend challenged a decision of the County Court at Law No. 1 of Jefferson County (Texas), which denied her motion for a directed verdict ***in*** this will contest case and found, as argued by appellee decedent's niece, that the decedent's will was procured by undue influence and fraud.

Overview
The friend arranged to have an attorney prepare a will for the decedent, ***in*** which he left his entire ***estate*** to the friend. A will contest was filed. The trial court denied the friend's motion for a directed verdict and a jury found that the will was procured by fraud and undue influence. The court affirmed. A jury could have found undue influence. The decedent and friend had only met 15 months prior to the execution of the will, at a time when the decedent had just experienced a frightening fall and was undergoing cancer treatment. The friend called her attorney to discuss the decedent's property, despite his desire not to create a will. The friend arranged to have the attorney meet the decedent to discuss the will, and the friend was a witness to its signing. The jury could have found that the friend influenced the decedent to her advantage. The friend represented that the State would decide how the decedent's property would be disbursed if he did not have a will. The jury could have found that the friend knew this to be false or she made the statement recklessly without any knowledge of its truth. The trial court did not err ***in*** denying the friend's motion for a directed verdict.

Outcome
The court affirmed.

LexisNexis® Headnotes

Civil Procedure > Trials > Judgment as Matter of Law > Directed Verdicts

Civil Procedure > ... > Standards of Review > Substantial Evidence > Sufficiency of Evidence

HN1[] **Judgment as Matter of Law, Directed Verdicts**

An appeal from the denial of a motion for directed verdict is essentially a challenge to the legal sufficiency of the evidence. The appellate court thus reviews the denial of a directed verdict by considering all the evidence ***in*** the light most favorable to the non-movant, disregarding all evidence to the contrary, and resolving all reasonable inferences ***in*** favor of the non-movant. To reverse the trial court's denial of a motion for directed verdict, appellant must show that the evidence conclusively proves a fact that establishes appellant's right to judgment as a matter of law and that there is no evidence to the contrary. Further, ***in*** claims or defenses supported only by meager circumstantial evidence, the

The Citation: shortly after the caption (or sometimes directly underneath it), you will find the legal citation for the case. The legal citation tells you the court that decided the opinion and the reporter.

The Case Summary (called a synopsis in Westlaw): a summary of the facts and holdings of the case. Case summaries are **not** law and are drafted by publishers, not by the actual judges who heard the case. You should never cite a case summary.

evidence does not rise above a scintilla, and thus is legally insufficient, if jurors would have to guess whether a vital fact exists.

Estate, Gift & Trust Law > ... > Will Contests > Undue Influence > Elements

HN2[] **Undue Influence, Elements**

To establish undue influence, the Texas Supreme Court has stated that the party must show: (1) the existence and exertion of influence; (2) the effective operation of an influence so as to subvert the will or overpower the mind of the grantor at the time of the execution; and (3) the execution of an instrument the maker would not have executed but for such influence. There must be some evidence to show that the influence was not only present, but was exerted with respect to making the instrument. Mere requests or efforts to execute a favorable instrument are not sufficient to establish undue influence unless the requests or efforts are so excessive so as to subvert the will of the maker.

Estate, Gift & Trust Law > ... > Will Contests > Undue Influence > Elements

Evidence > Types of Evidence > Circumstantial Evidence

HN3[] **Undue Influence, Elements**

Undue influence may be proven by circumstantial, as well as direct, evidence. More often than not, undue influence is impossible to establish by direct proof, and may only be shown by circumstances. When determining a claim of undue influence, it is proper to consider all evidence of relevant matters that occurred within a reasonable time before or after the will's execution.

Estate, Gift & Trust Law > ... > Will Contests > Undue Influence > Elements

HN4[] **Undue Influence, Elements**

Fact-finders should consider the following ten factors when determining the existence of undue influence: (1) the nature and type of relationship existing between the testator, the contestants, and the party accused of exerting such influence; (2) the opportunities existing for the exertion of the type or deception possessed or employed; (3) the circumstances surrounding the drafting and execution of the testament; (4) the existence of a fraudulent motive; (5) whether there had been a habitual subjection of the testator to the control of another; (6) the state of the testator's mind at the time of the execution of the testament; (7) the testator's mental or physical incapacity to resist or the susceptibility of the testator's mind to the type and extent of the influence exerted; (8) words and acts of the testator; (9) weakness of mind and body of the testator, whether produced by infirmities of age or by disease or otherwise; (10) whether the testament executed is unnatural ***in*** its terms of disposition of property.

Civil Procedure > Appeals > Standards of Review > General Overview

HN5[] **Appeals, Standards of Review**

When reviewing the evidence, the appellate court may not substitute its judgment for that of the jury even if it disagrees with the outcome.

Torts > ... > Fraud & Misrepresentation > Actual Fraud > Elements

HN6[] **Actual Fraud, Elements**

The elements of fraud are: (1) that a material representation was made; (2) the representation was false; (3) when the representation was made, the speaker knew it was false or made it recklessly without any knowledge of the truth and as a positive assertion; (4) the speaker made the representation with the intent that the other party should act upon it; (5) the party acted ***in*** reliance on the representation; and (6) the party thereby suffered injury.

Counsel: For APPELLANT: Thomas A. Niederhofer, Attorney at Law, Baytown, TX.

For APPELLEE: Terry Wood, Attorney At Law, Beaumont, TX.

Judges: Before Chief Justice Valdez and Justices Rodriguez and Benavides. Memorandum Opinion by Justice Benavides.

Opinion by: GINA M. BENAVIDES

The Judges: the judge(s) who heard the case, as well as the judge(s) who authored the opinion, any concurrences, and any dissents.

The Opinion: the actual decision by the judge in the case. The opinion is what you can cite to if you cite the case.

Opinion

MEMORANDUM OPINION

Memorandum Opinion by Justice Benavides

Appellant, Tammy Laurie Leger, contends the trial court erred ***in*** the underlying will contest lawsuit when it denied her motion for directed verdict because there was insufficient evidence to justify the jury's findings of undue influence and fraud. We affirm.

I. BACKGROUND[1]

Ernst B. ***Fiedler*** was born on November 16, 1926, the youngest of five siblings. A World War II veteran, ***Fiedler*** spent most of his life working on his family's farm-and-ranch homestead ***in*** Hamshire, Jefferson County, Texas. According to his niece Paula ***Fiedler***, Ernst was a frugal, taciturn man who was "forthright" and "strong-willed." He married Bessie ***Fiedler in*** 1967. Ernst and Bessie's marriage lasted for twenty years until she passed away ***in*** 1987. They had no children.

Paula testified **[*2]** at trial that, over the years, Ernst refused to prepare a will or final testament to dispose of his personal property. Paula testified that she "would explain to him that it would be to his benefit to have some sort of will that would designate what to do with his property" and "offered to take him to a lawyer." However, according to Paula, Ernst stalwartly opposed the idea:

> His response was, over all the years with the family members, including my father and myself, was that he really and truly didn't give a blankety-blank-blank about having a will and that, you know, it was going to be as it was. He didn't care about having a will. He didn't care what happened . . . .

Paula testified that Ernst's "strong-willed" disposition changed ***in*** 2002, when he fell off the roof of his garage and lay ***in*** his yard for approximately four to six hours ***in*** the dark, cold night until someone found him. At this point, Paula stated that Ernst "became quite paranoid about being alone and being sick or being injured." Ernst was taken to the Veteran's Administration ("VA") hospital ***in*** Houston to recuperate from this fall. Ernst convalesced at the VA hospital for a full year as his recovery was complicated **[*3]** by his injuries from the fall and an ongoing fight with cancer. He kept company with his brother Paul ***Fiedler***, Paula's father, who was also undergoing treatment at the VA at the same time. While at the hospital, Paula paid Ernst's bills, cared for his property, and visited him regularly.

The record shows that Ernst met Leger ***in*** July of 2002 at the VA hospital while he was still recuperating from his surgery. Leger's husband, David, was related to Ernst's late wife Bessie. Leger testified that the next time she saw Ernst was when he stopped by her home ***in*** Hamshire ***in*** May 2003. Ernst began visiting Leger regularly to have dinner and the two eventually became friends. Leger helped Ernst with his cancer medications by organizing them into a daily pill box. She also gave him occasional rides to the VA hospital for various doctor appointments.

In approximately July of 2003, Ernst and Leger drove around Jefferson County to visit Ernst's numerous properties. Ernst owned several tracts of land, both individually or jointly with other family members, throughout the Hamshire/Winnie area. Leger asked Ernst if he had a will. Ernst told Leger that "he did not have a will and did not intend to have **[*4]** a will." ***In*** fact, Ernst proclaimed that he would "just let [his family] fight over it." Leger told Ernst that if he did not prepare a will, the State of Texas would decide how his property was disbursed. Leger stated that she "did not agree" with Ernst's decision to not have a will and "thought he should decide where his property goes. He worked for [his property]; he should decide." ***In*** her words, she continued to "fuss" about Ernst getting a will, but he remained unconvinced.

Leger testified that she, of her own volition, called Thomas Niederhofer, a local attorney, to discuss the disposition of Ernst's property ***in*** approximately July 2003. Niederhofer had previously handled Leger's parents' wills, and he had also handled some child custody issues for Leger's brother. Leger testified that she discussed Ernst's properties with Niederhofer. Niederhofer told her that he would need legal descriptions of Ernst's property to prepare a will and gave Leger directions about what to look for and how to look for it. Shortly thereafter, Leger drove Ernst to the Jefferson County courthouse to research and make copies of the deeds to his properties. Leger testified that she "lifted the books" at **[*5]** the courthouse to obtain

---

[1] This case is before this Court on transfer from the Ninth Court of Appeals ***in*** Beaumont pursuant to an order issued by the Supreme Court of Texas. *See* Tex. Gov't Code Ann. § 73.001 (Vernon 2005).

The Facts: typically the first part of the body of the opinion sets forth the facts of the case that led to the filing of the suit.

The Procedural History: usually following the recitation of the facts, the opinion will set forth the procedural history of the case or how the case moved throughout the legal system (e.g., where the case was originally filed and subsequent/related decisions in the case).

the deeds, because Ernst was seventy-five years old at the time and could not do so.

Leger then scheduled a meeting between Niederhofer and Ernst at her home. The conversation regarding Ernst's will took place at Leger's kitchen table, with Leger present the entire time. After meeting with Ernst, Niederhofer prepared Ernst's will. Niederhofer later called Leger, not Ernst, to inform her that Ernst's will was ready. The record showed that Leger and Niederhofer agreed to execute the will at Prosperity Bank ***in*** Winnie, Texas. Leger drove Ernst to the bank to execute his will and witnessed him sign his will.

Ernst died on February 17, 2006, at the age of seventy-nine. When Ernst's will was probated, Paula and her father Paul discovered that Ernst had left his entire ***estate*** to Leger. Ernst had also appointed Leger as the independent executrix of his ***estate***. ***In*** the event that Leger predeceased Paula, Paula would be his independent executrix and inherit the ***estate***. Paul, Ernst's brother, contested the will and claimed that it was procured by Leger's undue influence and fraud. When Paul died, his daughter Paula assumed his position ***in*** the will contest. After Paula concluded **[*6]** her case-***in***-chief during a trial on the merits, Leger moved for a directed verdict, which the trial court denied. At the end of the trial, the jury eventually found that Ernst's will was procured by undue influence and fraud. ***In*** response, Leger filed this appeal.

II. STANDARD OF REVIEW

HN1[] "An appeal from the denial of a motion for directed verdict is essentially a challenge to the legal sufficiency of the evidence." *Fein v. R.P.H., Inc., 68 S.W.3d 260, 265 (Tex. App.—Houston [14th Dist.] 2002, pet. denied)*; *see also* *Tex. Dep't of Protective & Regulatory Servs. v. Mulligan, No. 10-03-00254-CV, 2005 Tex. App. LEXIS 2370, at *3 (Tex. App.—Waco Mar. 24, 2005, pet. denied)* (mem. op.). We thus review the denial of a directed verdict by considering all the evidence ***in*** the light most favorable to the non-movant, disregarding all evidence to the contrary, and resolving all reasonable inferences ***in*** favor of the non-movant. *Fein, 68 S.W.3d at 265*; *see also* *Mulligan, 2005 Tex. App. LEXIS 2370, at **3-4*. To reverse the trial court's denial of a motion for directed verdict, appellant must show that the evidence conclusively proves a fact that establishes appellant's right to judgment as a matter of law **[*7]** and that there is no evidence to the contrary. *Mulligan, 2005 Tex. App. LEXIS 2370 at *4*; *Fein, 68 S.W.3d at 265*. Further, "[i]n claims or defenses supported only by meager circumstantial evidence, the evidence does not rise above a scintilla, and thus is legally insufficient, if jurors would have to guess whether a vital fact exists." *City of Keller v. Wilson, 168 S.W.3d 802, 813 (Tex. 2005)*.

The Law of the Case: the legal principles that govern the case. The law may be set forth all at the beginning or sprinkled throughout various subsections of the opinion.

III. ANALYSIS

Leger, ***in*** essence, asks this Court to overturn a jury verdict based on insufficiency of the evidence. We analyze each of the issues the jury considered, undue influence and fraud, ***in*** turn.

A. Undue Influence

Client's Issue: Undue Influence

1. Applicable Law

Leger asserts that the trial court erred ***in*** denying her motion for directed verdict because there was insufficient evidence to show that she exerted undue influence over Ernst's will. HN2[] To establish undue influence, the Texas Supreme Court has stated that the party must show: (1) the existence and exertion of influence; (2) the effective operation of an influence so as to subvert the will or overpower the mind of the grantor at the time of the execution; and (3) the execution of an instrument the maker would not have executed but for such influence. *Rothermel v. Duncan, 369 S.W.2d 917, 922 (Tex. 1963)*. **[*8]** There must be some evidence to show that the influence was not only present, but was exerted with respect to making the instrument. *Id.*; *Cotten v. Cotten, 169 S.W.3d 824, 827 (Tex. App.—Dallas 2005, pet denied)*. Mere requests or efforts to execute a favorable instrument are not sufficient to establish undue influence unless the requests or efforts are so excessive so as to subvert the will of the maker. *Curry v. Curry, 153 Tex. 421, 270 S.W.2d 208, 212 (Tex. 1954)*.

HN3[] Undue influence may be proven by circumstantial, as well as direct, evidence. *See* *Rothermel, 369 S.W.2d at 922*; *see also* *Peralez v. Peralez, No. 13-09-0259-CV, 2010 Tex. App. LEXIS 4781, at **12-13 (Tex. App.—Corpus Christi June 24, 2010, pet. denied)* (mem. op.). "More often than not, undue influence is impossible to establish by direct proof, and may only be shown by circumstances." ***In re Estate** of Olsson, 344 S.W.2d 171, 173-74 (Tex. Civ. App.-El Paso 1961, writ ref'd n.r.e.)*. When determining a claim of undue influence, it is proper to consider all evidence of relevant matters that occurred within a reasonable time before or after the will's execution. *Watson v. Dingler, 831 S.W.2d 834, 837 (Tex. App.—Houston [14th Dist.] 1992, writ denied).*

HN4[↑] Fact-finders **[*9]** should consider the following ten factors when determining the existence of undue influence:

> (1) the nature and type of relationship existing between the testator, the contestants, and the party accused of exerting such influence;
> (2) the opportunities existing for the exertion of the type or deception possessed or employed;
> (3) the circumstances surrounding the drafting and execution of the testament;
> (4) the existence of a fraudulent motive;
> (5) whether there had been a habitual subjection of the testator to the control of another;
> (6) the state of the testator's mind at the time of the execution of the testament;
> (7) the testator's mental or physical incapacity to resist or the susceptibility of the testator's mind to the type and extent of the influence exerted;
> (8) words and acts of the testator;
>
> (9) weakness of mind and body of the testator, whether produced by infirmities of age or by disease or otherwise;
>
> (10) whether the testament executed is unnatural ***in*** its terms of disposition of property.

In *re* ***Estate*** *of Graham, 69 S.W.3d 598, 609-10 (Tex. App.—Corpus Christi 2001, no pet.)*; ***see also*** *Peralez, 2010 Tex. App. LEXIS 4781, at **13-14.*

2. Analysis

HN5[↑] "When reviewing the evidence, this Court **[*10]** may not substitute its judgment for that of the jury even if it disagrees with the outcome." *Mar. Overseas Corp. v. Ellis, 971 S.W.2d 402, 407 (Tex. 1998).* Here, considering all the evidence ***in*** the light most favorable to Paula, disregarding all evidence to the contrary, and resolving all reasonable inferences ***in*** favor of Paula, there is considerable evidence from which a reasonable jury could have found undue influence. *See Fein, 68 S.W.3d at 265.*

We analyze the evidence by reviewing the factors set forth ***in*** *Graham.* First, regarding the nature and type of relationship existing between Ernst and Leger, we note that the two had only met fifteen months prior to the execution of his will when Ernst was undergoing cancer treatment and had just experienced the frightening event of falling from his garage roof and laying injured and alone for several hours on a cold, dark evening. With regard to the second and fifth factors, Leger had many opportunities to influence Ernst, as he frequently had dinner at her home, she assisted him with his multiple medications, and she drove him to Houston at various times to attend doctor appointments.

According to Paula, evidence of the third *Graham* factor **[*11]** is the strongest ***in*** this case: the circumstances surrounding the drafting and execution of Ernst's will. Leger called Niederhofer, her family attorney, to discuss the disposition of Ernst's properties, even though Ernst had made clear that he did not care to devise a will. After Leger's discussion with Niederhofer, Leger took Ernst to the Jefferson County courthouse to research the legal descriptions of all of his deeds. Leger then arranged to have Niederhofer meet Ernst ***in*** her home at her kitchen table to discuss the preparation of a will. When Niederhofer completed Ernst's will, he called Leger, not Ernst, to schedule a time and place to execute the will. Leger drove Ernst to the place of the will's execution and was also a witness to its signing.

The fourth *Graham* factor, concerning fraudulent motives, is obvious: Ernst left his entire ***estate*** to Leger, a woman whom he had only met fifteen months prior to executing his will. This fact also implicates the tenth factor-"whether the testament executed is unnatural ***in*** its terms of disposition of property."

The sixth, seventh, eighth, and ninth factors are related: all deal with the testator's state of body and mind. Although Ernst was **[*12]** described as a "forthright" and "strong-willed" man, the end of his life was defined by illness and loneliness. His wife had pre-deceased him; he was suffering from cancer; and he had suffered some frightening events alone.

There was more than a scintilla of evidence to prove the elements of undue influence ***in*** this case. *See City of Keller, 168 S.W.3d at 813.* We conclude that the jury could reasonably conclude that Leger unduly influenced Ernst to devise his will to her advantage, and we will not substitute our judgment for that of the jury. *See Ellis, 971 S.W.2d at 407.*

Irrelevant Issue: Fraud

B. Fraud

Leger also asserts the trial court erred ***in*** denying her motion for a directed verdict because there was insufficient evidence to show that she procured Ernst's will by fraud.

1. Applicable Law

HN6[] The elements of fraud are: (1) that a material representation was made; (2) the representation was false; (3) when the representation was made, the speaker knew it was false or made it recklessly without any knowledge of the truth and as a positive assertion; (4) the speaker made the representation with the intent that the other party should act upon it; (5) the party acted ***in*** reliance on the representation; and (6) the party **[*13]** thereby suffered injury. *See Aquaplex, Inc. v. Rancho La Valencia, Inc., 297 S.W.3d 768, 774 (Tex. 2009)* (citing ***In*** *re FirstMerit Bank, N.A., 52 S.W.3d 749, 758 (Tex. 2001))*.

2. Analysis

Here, Leger represented to Ernst that the State of Texas would decide how his property was disbursed if he did not have a will. The record revealed that Leger believed her statement to be true, even though she did not have any legal training and was not familiar with the Texas Probate Code. A jury could have believed that Leger either knew this statement to be false or made it recklessly without any knowledge of its truth. Leger also acknowledged that she "fussed" with Ernst to obtain a will. Again, the jury was certainly within its purview to find that Leger represented that the State would decide how Ernst's property would be disbursed with the intent that Ernst would take her advice and obtain a will, which he did.

Further, there is ample evidence that Ernst relied on Leger's material representation, because he created a will after a lifetime of refusing his family's advice to do so. As his niece Paula testified, Ernst "really and truly didn't give a blankety-blank-blank about having a will . . . he **[*14]** didn't care what happened. . . ." Ernst's steadfast decision not to have a will, which he maintained for over seventy years, changed once Leger represented that his property would be disbursed by the State.

Again, we will not substitute our judgment for that of the jury. *Ellis, 971 S.W.2d at 407*. We conclude that more than a scintilla of evidence was presented at trial for a jury to conclude that fraud occurred ***in*** the procurement of Ernst's will. *City of Keller, 168 S.W.3d at 813*. We overrule Leger's issue regarding the trial court's denial of her motion for directed verdict.

IV. CONCLUSION

Having overruled Leger's issue, we affirm the decision of the trial court

GINA M. BENAVIDES,

Justice

Delivered and filed the

14th day of April, 2011.

End of Document

The Disposition: a statement setting forth the resolution of the dispute.

Step three: Slowly read the case. Look up terms you do not know, interact with the text, note what is said, as well as what is not said, in the case. Omit sections of the case that are irrelevant to the issue for which you are reading the case. During this step, you may take notes and highlight key passages of the case.

The third step you should take when reading a case is to read the case slowly, intentionally, and diligently. This step is where you finally get to dig into the content of the case—that is, where you understand the law and how the law relates to the particular facts. Although a summary of facts is often placed at the beginning of a case—and you should read it at the outset—until you dig into the law, you may not be able to understand which facts are relevant to the specific issues of law. Given this reality, you should read the statement of facts but then go back and reread the facts after you understand the legal issues. Doing so will allow you to ascertain which facts go to each legal issue that you face. That is, which facts are "trigger facts"?

After reading the facts section with a particular focus on the issues relevant to you, begin reading the case paragraph by paragraph and section by section. Typically, a case will contain headings that split its content into sections for you. However, sometimes older cases do not contain headings; in that situation, you should section the case off by creating your own headings, noting where the court begins to grapple with each new legal issue or element of a claim. In addition to sectioning the case, at the close of each paragraph, make sure you understand what the paragraph you just read means. Ask yourself: "What was the purpose of the paragraph in plain English?" Then, note that purpose in the margins. You may need to read paragraphs or even entire sections multiple times to understand the content.

When engaging in close reading, remember to look up any terms or words that you do not understand. In addition, it is smart to circle or highlight watchwords (*see* Section V.A above) when a case describes the law.

Below is an example of a section of the sample case—*In re Fiedler*—with the types of notes you might make on a case while engaging in deep reading to understand the legal requirements for an undue influence claim in Texas.

THE CASE	YOUR MARGIN NOTES
1. Applicable Law Leger asserts that the trial court erred in denying her motion for directed verdict because there was insufficient evidence to show that she exerted undue influence over Ernst's will. To establish undue influence, the Texas Supreme Court has stated	**Procedural posture:** appeal of denial of motion for directed verdict. **Motion for directed verdict:**[15] a motion made before a case is submitted to the jury and argues that no reasonable jury could find for the opposing party.
that the party must show: (1) the existence and exertion of influence; (2) the effective operation of an influence so as to subvert the will or overpower the mind of the grantor at the time of the execution; and (3) the execution of an instrument the maker would not have executed but for such influence. *Rothermel v. Duncan*, 369	Gray highlighting = three elements required to establish undue influence (UDI). NOTE: "and" means you need to show all three elements.
S.W.2d 917, 922 (Tex. 1963). There must be some evidence to show that the influence was not only present, but was exerted with respect to making the instrument. Id.; *Cotten v. Cotten*, 169 S.W.3d 824, 827 (Tex.	**Element 1 subrule:**[16] Need influence + influence must be exerted
App.—Dallas 2005, pet. denied). Mere requests or efforts to execute a favorable instrument are not sufficient to establish undue influence unless the requests or efforts are so excessive so as to subvert the will of the maker. *Curry v. Curry*, 153 Tex.	**Element 2 subrule:** Requests that a testator write a certain will that works in the requestor's favor alone is not enough to show UDI.
421, 270 S.W.2d 208, 212 (Tex. 1954). Undue influence may be proven by circumstantial, as well as direct, evidence. *See Rothermel*, 369 S.W.2d at 922; *see also Peralez v. Peralez*, No. 13-09-0259-CV, 2010 Tex. App. LEXIS 4781, at **12-13 (Tex. App.—Corpus Christi June 24, 2010, pet. denied) (mem. op.).	**Evidence needed for UDI:** UDI can be established using circumstantial or direct evidence. **Circumstantial evidence:**[17] evidence that requires reasoning or an inference to connect or prove a fact. **Direct Evidence:**[18] evidence that supports a fact explicitly.

15. Motion for directed verdict may be a term you would look up in a legal dictionary.
16. As will be discussed later, subrules define the general rule, here, the element at issue.
17. "Circumstantial evidence" may be a term you would look up in a legal dictionary.
18. "Direct evidence" may be a term you would look up in a legal dictionary.

Step four: Think about how this case relates to others you have read and/or how it helps you resolve hypotheticals.

The last step you should complete when reading a case is to think about the case. Really think about what you just read. What are the main takeaways? What rules of law can you glean from the case that might be applicable to your client's case or a future case? Are there limits on the applicability of the case?

C. *How to brief a case*

A case brief is simply a written summary of a case. There are a number of ways to format a case brief and, in all honesty, no one form is perfect. The key takeaway is that you really should brief the cases you read in some format in order to ensure you are reading actively and carefully and to have a record of the case highlights to save time in the future. When you finish law school and begin practicing law, attorneys often continue to brief cases, especially in preparation for an oral argument to help them quickly address any questions a court may have about the implications, law, or facts from any case discussed in the briefing.

Below is a simple form you may use to brief cases. It contains explanations for what each part of the brief is calling for. These explanations will help you as you work to generate your first case briefs for all your classes.

ITEM	DESCRIPTION
Case Name	The case name is located at the top of the case. It gives the last names of the parties. It is generally formatted like the following: *Plaintiff v. Defendant, Petitioner v. Respondent,* or *Appellant v. Appellee*. For example: *Roe v. Wade*. The case name is also referred to as the caption.
Court and Date	This is the court writing the opinion and the date of the opinion.
Disposition and Procedural History	The procedural history of the case is a summary of how the case got to the court it is in. The disposition is how the court decided the issue procedurally, such as remand, reverse, or affirm.
Question Presented (i.e., the issue)	The question presented is generally a legal question that the party that filed the case or the appeal wants the court to answer. Sometimes there is more than one question.

ITEM	DESCRIPTION
Trigger (Legally Relevant) Facts	Not all facts are relevant; some are relevant for one purpose but not for another. Once you find the question presented and the holding, you should have a better feel for which facts are truly important. The facts are not the court's holding or reasoning, but rather include the legally significant facts underlying the case and, specifically, the issues before the court.
Plaintiff's Argument	What did the Plaintiff argue to the court? The Plaintiff may be the appellant or appellee depending on if it filed the appeal or not.
Defendant's Argument	What did the Defendant argue to the court? The Defendant may be the appellant or appellee depending on if it filed the appeal or not.
Rule (i.e., the law)	The rule may look like three things: (1) a succinct statement of the governing legal principle that the higher court uses to decide the case (about a sentence in length); (2) a sentence or paragraph in which the higher court answers the question presented; or (3) a paragraph that describes under what circumstances a person or entity is liable. The rule may be all three. You will sometimes have to edit what the court says—without losing meaning—to shorten the rule.
Reasoning (on each issue)	The reasoning is generally several paragraphs following the rule in which the court explains *how* and *why* it answered the question presented as it did. It is a blend of facts and legal language. Pay close attention to this because you will have to show your reasoning when you answer essay questions. Take time to fully wrap your head around how the court explains itself. You will encounter both clear and well-explained reasoning and some fuzzy and hard-to-follow reasoning.
Holding (on each issue)	The holding(s) are the court's answer(s) to the question(s) presented. The holdings are not the narrow disposition of the case, for example, "case reversed and remanded," but, instead, are broader substantive holdings that deal with the interpretation of the governing rule. If the issues were stated precisely, the holding can be stated as "yes" or "no" or in short statements taken from the language used by the court. Sometimes it's: "We hold that. . . ."

ITEM	DESCRIPTION
Main Takeaway	For substantive classes, every case is in the textbook for a reason. Before you read and while you read, you should ask yourself over and over, "What is the main takeaway of this case? Why have the authors included this case in the book, and why have they placed the case in this particular section?" Find this and you are golden. But, remember that sometimes your professors will use a case for different or additional reasons beyond what the casebook author intended. Don't get nervous, just try to understand why the professor is assigning the case. In legal writing class, as you brief cases, note here how you will use the case in your written assignment (e.g., what issue you will use it for).
Other Notes	Here you should note if there is significant dicta (portion of the opinion with legal reasoning that is not essential to the resolution of the issue(s) before the court) or if there are issues discussed that are not relevant to why you are reading the case.

If you want to practice briefing a case, review *Rothermel v. Duncan* in the Appendix at page 238. Create a case brief focusing only on the issue of undue influence. Then compare your case brief with the sample also included in the Appendix.

VI. Formulaic legal writing

In math class, you use formulas. You plug numbers into the formula to get an answer. While the numbers you plug into a formula will change and the answer you get out of the formula will change, the formula itself never changes. Why? Because it works. It gets you from the problem to the answer. In legal writing, we use the CRAC formula to help us get from the problem to the answer. Why? Because it works and, more importantly, it is what your audience—whether that be a partner at a law firm or a judge—expects.

In legal analysis, we use deductive reasoning, meaning we set out our conclusion and then support that conclusion. At its most basic sense, as lawyer, we support our conclusion by applying the law to the facts of our case.

Put simplistically, to reach our conclusion we need the law and facts.

Conclusion = law + facts

Put more specifically, to reach our conclusion we need the law and then we need to apply that law to the facts:

Conclusion = Rule (law) + Analysis (law applied to facts)

Let's do a very easy example. Let's say the Conclusion we want the court to reach is that "Dan was speeding while driving in the school zone." What do we need to show our audience in order for the audience to reach that Conclusion? We need to set forth (1) what the speed limit was in the school zone (law); and (2) how fast Dan was driving (facts).

Let's say we learn that the speed limit in the school zone was 20 miles per hour (law) and that Dan was driving 35 miles per hour (facts).

Our CRAC would look like this:

Conclusion:	Dan was speeding in the school zone.
Rule:	The speed limit in a school zone is 20 miles per hour.
Analysis:	Dan was driving 35 miles per hour, which is 15 miles per hour over the speed limit.
Conclusion:	Accordingly, Dan was speeding in the school zone.

Of course, as a lawyer, the problems you solve and the legal analysis that you do to find an answer will be much more complicated than the above example. However, the formula will be the same. You will always start with your Conclusion. To show the reader how you reached your Conclusion, you will state the governing law (Rule) and then apply the Rule to the facts of your case (Analysis). You will then repeat your Conclusion. No matter how hard the problem, the formula is the same:

Conclusion + Rule + Analysis + Conclusion

Formulaic writing makes certain legal writing scholars scoff. They think that formulaic writing can stifle creativity, is not the best way to respond to every legal problem, and can lead to boring, dull legal analysis. They are right. If a lawyer spent their entire career sticking to the formulas in this book, that lawyer would never be considered an "excellent" legal writer in the leagues of the late Justice Anthony Scalia or Justice Ruth Bader Ginsberg. However, before you learn to run, you have to learn to walk. Before you learn to sing, you have to learn to talk. Formulaic writing teaches you the basics. It teaches you how to communicate like lawyers do. It breaks down complex legal analysis into small, simple steps. Formulaic writing, if followed, will cause your legal analysis to be strong and sound. Once your legal analysis is strong and sound, then, in an upper-level writing course, you can work on making it "sing."

Legal writing is difficult. It is a learned skill, is not something that comes naturally, and is unlike any other type of writing. In law school, we had a friend who was an excellent writer. He had numerous published books, columns, and articles. He had an undergraduate degree in English from a prestigious college. He was talented, smart, and experienced when it came to writing. That is why it came as such a surprise when he got a C in legal writing during his first semester of law school. Although he was a good writer and his grammar was impeccable, his legal analysis was poor. It is imperative to understand that good writing does not equal good legal writing. Good legal writing is composed of good writing plus good legal analysis. Thus, while formulaic writing can seem "boring," it will teach you how to communicate your legal analysis in a way that is proven to work. Once you have mastered how to "talk" like a lawyer through formulaic writing, you can and should improve upon the formulas and deviate from the formulas to make your writing "sing." In Parts Two and Three of this book formulaic writing is discussed in detail and in the context of both objective and persuasive writing.

A. *Macro formulaic writing: CRAC*

As already mentioned, CRAC is an acronym for Conclusion, Rule, Analysis, and Conclusion.[19] CRAC is the structure used to organize legal arguments on a macro level, whether those arguments appear in essay responses on an exam, an objective memorandum to a partner, or a persuasive motion or brief to the court. While different lawyers use different acronyms depending on how they were taught in law school,[20] the result is the same: lawyers first identify the issue by stating the conclusion or restating the question; lawyers then provide the rule/governing legal authority for the issue; lawyers next apply the rule/governing legal authority to facts that go to the problem/issue at hand; and lawyers lastly restate their conclusion on the issue.

1. Why use CRAC

A lawyer's effectiveness turns on her ability to explain and to persuade. Many law students are under the wrong impression that a lawyer's success in explaining and persuading hinges on her ability to draft eloquent sentences and complex legal analyses. Truthfully, however, a lawyer's success at its core turns on whether she logically organizes her argument.

2. How to use CRAC

You will use the CRAC structure (Conclusion, Rule, Analysis, and Conclusion) to organize each "issue" in your essay, memo, Multistate Performance Test ("MPT"), or brief. That is worth repeating: you use the CRAC structure for each "issue" in your essay, memorandum, MPT, or brief. The reason the word "issue" is in quotation marks is because what constitutes an issue varies depending on the call of the question you are answering and the type of document you are drafting. An issue might be a cause of action, a defense, or an element of a claim. A rookie law student mistake—one that professors see time and time again—is writing one giant CRAC for the entirety of the question even though the question raises more than one "issue."

---

19. When we get to persuasive writing, you will see that we add an extra "C" for "Counter-Analysis" so that your organization is CRACC (Conclusion, Rule, Analysis, Counter-Analysis, Conclusion).

20. There are dozens of variations of CRAC used by various legal writing programs across the nation. For example, some lawyers use IRAC (Issue, Rule, Analysis, Conclusion) or CREAC (Conclusion, Rule, Explanation, Application, Conclusion). The variation turns—for the most part—on the specificity each law school wants to provide via its selected acronym.

a) Using CRAC in formal legal writing

For memorandums, briefs, motions, etc., the CRACs go in the main body of the document. In memorandums, your CRACs go in the "Discussion" section (the body) under the heading for the corresponding issues. In motions and briefs, your CRACs go in the "Argument and Authorities" section (the body) under the heading for the corresponding issues. Typically, each CRAC is separated by a heading or sub-heading.

If you are writing a memorandum, to determine how many issues you have (and thus how many CRACs you need), you should look at the assignment instructions. For example, you may be asked: "Please write a memorandum analyzing whether or not our client, Ms. Piper, has a cause of action for intentional infliction of emotional distress under Texas law." The number of issues you have, which is the same as the number of CRACs you will need, will be tied to the elements of an intentional infliction of emotional distress cause of action under Texas law. You would have four CRACs because, after reading through Texas caselaw, you would find that an intentional infliction of emotional distress cause of action has four elements: "(1) the defendant acted intentionally or recklessly, (2) the conduct was 'extreme and outrageous,' (3) the actions of the defendant caused the plaintiff emotional distress, and (4) the resulting emotional distress was severe."[21]

The assignment instructions may explicitly tell you that there are certain issues that you do not need to analyze and, if that is the case, you will adjust the number of CRACs accordingly. For example, you could be asked: "Please write a memorandum analyzing whether our client, Ms. Piper, has a cause of action for intentional infliction of emotional distress under Texas law. You do not need to discuss whether Defendant's conduct caused Ms. Piper emotional distress or whether the distress Ms. Piper suffered was severe." You would, thus, only have two issues (elements) remaining and, therefore, two CRACs.

b) Using CRAC on essay exams

As discussed in more detail in Parts Two and Three, CRAC is the structure you should use when answering bar-style essay exam questions in law school as well as when answering essay questions on the essay portion of the bar exam itself.

When faced with an essay question, the first thing you must do is read all of the question and identify the issues. Because, remember, the number of issues presented in the question itself dictates the number of CRACs. Let's look at an example. On a contracts exam, you might be given a set of facts and then asked: "Did the parties form a contract?" To answer this question, you must identify and analyze the issues, which, in the example, are the elements required for contract formation. As you have (or will) learn in contracts class, a valid contract has four elements (offer, consideration, acceptance, mutuality) and, thus, you would have four issues. Because you have four issues, you would have four CRACs. Because, as always, # of Issues = # of CRACs.

---

21. *Standard Fruit & Vegetable Co., Inc. v. Johnson*, 985 S.W.2d 62, 65 (Tex. 1998).

c) Using CRAC on Multistate Performance Tests ("MPTs")

As discussed in more detail in Part Four, CRAC is useful for tackling the MPT, but given the time-pressured nature of the exam it is slightly modified and made simpler. The MPT is drafted by the National Conference of Bar Examiners and administered in most states as part of the state's bar exam. Unlike the essay questions on the bar exam, which test substantive knowledge of the law, the MPT is unique in that it does not test substantive knowledge of the law. Rather, the MPT "is designed to test an examinee's ability to use fundamental lawyering skills in a realistic situation and complete a task that a beginning lawyer should be able to accomplish."[22] While the task on any given MPT can vary, it always involves written legal analysis. Therefore, the skills you learn in legal writing class will help you succeed on the MPT. What makes the MPT different than the assignments you will do in legal writing class is that the MPT is a time-pressured exam where examinees only have 90 minutes to read the problem, the underlying facts, and the governing law, and then complete the written task—whether that be a memorandum, brief, letter, etc. This extreme time pressure is what makes the MPT difficult.

B. Micro formulaic writing: the building blocks for CRAC

We know that CRAC stands for Conclusion, Rule, Analysis, and Conclusion. We also know that in both objective and persuasive writing, each issue has a CRAC. But, none of that helps you actually write a Conclusion (first and last "C" of CRAC), a Rule ("R" of CRAC), or an Analysis ("A" of CRAC). Faced with this realization, this book's approach to writing does not end with adopting the CRAC formula; it also provides "micro formulas" within CRAC to help you draft the different parts of your CRAC.

C. Where we will use micro formulas

Within the CRAC formula, we will use "micro formulas" to help you learn how to craft Rule statements ("R") and how to do Analysis ("A"). These micro formulas are covered in excruciating detail in Part Two, Section II.F.2 and Part Three, Section II.G.3. But to foreshadow what you will learn there, let's look at a few examples. Under the "R" of CRAC, the Rule has three parts: (i) general rule; (ii) subrules; and, sometimes, but not always, (iii) case illustration(s). Thus, we will use the following micro formulas to help us as we draft our Rules.

Rule = general rule + subrules
or
Rule = general rule + subrules + case illustration

22. National Conference of Bar Examiners, Multistate Performance Test http://www.ncbex.org/exams/mpt/ (last visited June 15, 2019).

Similarly, we will use micro formulas to help you learn how to draft the most complex part of the Rule—the case illustration. For example, we use the following micro formula to draft a case illustration:

Case illustration = topic sentence + holding + trigger facts + reasoning

By using formulas beyond just the big CRAC, you will be able to break down the different parts of CRAC, better understand how the parts work individually and together, and make sure that your legal analysis is complete. As an added benefit, with these formulas in hand, you will rarely feel as if you are starting to write with an entirely blank piece of paper.

VII. Citing the law

A citation is how you attribute what you have written to its source. Proper citing requires that you master both: (1) when a citation is needed; and (2) what is the proper form of the citation. A citation serves multiple purposes.

First, a citation tells your reader the source/authority of your assertion. For example, let's say you write the following in a motion to a Texas state trial court: **In Texas, a will can be set aside on the ground of undue influence.** If you do not include a citation after that sentence, the authority/source for that assertion is nothing or maybe, at best, you (i.e., new lawyer). That sentence, without a citation, is like telling the reader (here, the trial court), "Hey, just trust me that here, in the great State of Texas, a will can be set aside on the ground of undue influence." The reader will not give much weight to what you have written because you have not told the reader that it is supported by legal authority. That is, you are missing a citation to the source for your assertion that, in Texas, a will can be set aside on the ground of undue influence. Now, let's say, in your motion to the trial court, you write this instead: **In Texas, a will can be set aside on the ground of undue influence. *Rothermel v. Duncan*, 369 S.W.2d 917, 922 (Tex. 1963).** The citation added to the end of the sentence tells the reader that the source/authority for your assertion is the Texas Supreme Court case *Rothermel v. Duncan*. No longer are you telling the reader, "Hey, just trust me!" Instead, you are telling your reader that, per a Texas Supreme Court case, the highest court on all issues of state law in Texas, a will can be set aside on the ground of undue influence. As explained above, a lower court is bound by the precedent of courts above it; accordingly, the trial court would find very authoritative your citation to a Texas Supreme Court case, which is mandatory (binding), primary authority.

Second, a citation allows the reader to find the source of your assertion. In the above example, the citation was ***Rothermel v. Duncan*, 369 S.W.2d 917, 922 (Tex. 1963)**, and this citation was written in what lawyers commonly refer to as "*Bluebook* form." *The Bluebook* provides "a systematic method by which members of the profession communicate important information about the sources and legal authorities upon which they rely in their work."[23] While a complete summary of *Bluebook* citation form is beyond the scope of this book, suffice it to say that using a citation and putting it in correct form allows a reader to find and to go to the source you are citing. For case citations, like the one in the example above, the citation consists of four parts, each of which conveys important information to the reader. First is the case name, which consists of the parties' names ***Rothermel v. Duncan*** followed by a comma. Second is the reporter volume number **369**, the reporter abbreviation **S.W.2d**, and first page of the case **917**, collectively **369 S.W.2d 917**. Third is a comma followed by the specific page(s) of the case where the assertion may be found **922**. This is called a pincite. Fourth is an open parenthesis followed by the abbreviation for the deciding court and the year of the decision followed by a closed parenthesis and period **(Tex. 1963)**.

1 2 3 4

(*Rothermel v. Duncan,***)** **(**369 S.W.2d 917**)** **(**, 922**)** **(**(Tex. 1963).**)**

Specifically, it is the second part of the citation—the reporter volume number, reporter abbreviation, and first page of the case—that is most helpful in allowing the reader to find the case by either (1) going to the book, which is Volume 369 of the Southwest Reporter Second Series on page number 917; or, more likely, (2) entering "369 S.W.2d 917" in an electronic search database like Westlaw or LexisNexis.

Third, a citation helps you avoid plagiarism by attributing what you have written to its source. Black's Law Dictionary defines plagiarism as "the deliberate and knowing presentation of another person's original ideas or creative expressions as one's own work."[24] While Black's Law definition requires intent on the part of the writer in order to constitute plagiarism, some law schools' honor codes define plagiarism as encompassing conduct that is both deliberate/intentional and conduct that is inadvertent/accidental. The quintessential example of plagiarism is taking the work of another, for example, an essay answer written by a classmate, a former student, a student at another school, etc. and passing it off as your own. Intentional plagiarism can also happen if you, for example, copy and paste from a secondary source that summarizes a rule of law and pass it off as your own summary of the rule of law in a memo or motion by failing to cite to the secondary source or failing to use quotations. Hopefully, it goes without saying that you should not ever do this in law school. Avoiding intentional plagiarism such as this is not something that should need to be taught to law students. You should never pass off the work of another as your own. Doing so will likely cause you not only to fail the given assignment, but also will likely cause you to be referred

---

23. THE BLUEBOOK: A UNIFORM SYSTEM OF CITATION (Columbia Law Review Ass'n et al. eds., 20th ed. 2015).

24. *Plagiarism*, BLACK'S LAW DICTIONARY 1335 (10th ed. 2014).

to the honor council or disciplinary board at your school and, potentially, be reported to the character and fitness section of your state bar.

However, plagiarism happens not only when you intentionally copy the entire work or large parts of the work of another, but it also can happen in more subtle ways. Plagiarism is often caused by failure to properly cite and/or failure to use quotations when taking language from another source. While failing to properly cite or use quotations can be deliberate and done with a bad motive, more often it is the result of not fully understanding the rules of attribution. Thus, learning when to cite and how to cite will help you to avoid plagiarism.

A. *Attribution: when to cite and use of quotations*

As a general matter, you should include a citation after every assertion that is taken from another source. Here is an easy rule to live by: "When in doubt, CITE!"

In the context of first-year legal writing and, specifically, in the context of CRAC, this means that you usually cite to legal authority after almost every sentence in your "R"/Rule of CRAC, and you usually cite to legal authority and/or the record (facts of your case) after almost every sentence in your "A"/Analysis of CRAC. With respect to the two "C"s/Conclusions of CRAC, you do not need a citation because your Conclusions will be something you generated as a product of applying the law to the facts such that you did not take it directly from another source.

Below is an excerpt from a CRAC. You will see that everywhere a citation is needed is indicated by the words CITE LAW (if a citation is needed to legal authority) or CITE RECORD (if a citation is needed to the underlying facts of the client's case at issue).

> This Court should grant summary judgment because Contestants cannot establish a fact issue with respect to the third element of their undue influence claim. A contestant will not meet her burden to show undue influence unless she proves the execution of a testament that the testator would not have made but for the influence. CITE LAW. The third element is not satisfied unless the testament is "unnatural." CITE LAW. A testament is unnatural only when "all reasonable explanation in affection for the devise is lacking." CITE LAW. "Circumstances that are as consistent with a will executed free from improper influence as they are with a will resulting from undue influence cannot be considered as evidence of undue influence." CITE LAW.
>
> If there is evidence of a broken relationship between the testator and a close relative, disinheriting the close relative will not be considered unnatural. In *Guthrie*, the court held that the testatrix disinheriting her son was not an unnatural disposition. CITE LAW. In that case, the testatrix completely excluded the contestant, her only living son, from her will, leaving her estate to her brothers—who took care of her and with whom she had a "close relationship." CITE LAW. The testatrix rarely spoke with her son and told people that

> she had no relationship with him. CITE LAW. The court reasoned that "[g] iven the evidence of the strained relationship," the disposition did not "seem unreasonable" such that the evidence did not raise a question of fact on the third element of undue influence. CITE LAW.
>
> Here, Testator's disposition in his will to Ms. Dieger, who Testator loved, was not unnatural. Like *Guthrie*, where the testatrix disinherited her son with whom she had a "strained relationship" in favor of the beneficiaries with whom she had a "close relationship," Testator had a strained relationship with Contestants and a more than "close relationship" with Ms. Dieger. CITE LAW; CITE RECORD. Not only did Ms. Dieger take care of Testator like the beneficiaries did in *Guthrie*, she lived with him for more than two years as both his girlfriend and de facto nurse. CITE LAW; CITE RECORD. Testator and Ms. Dieger were in love. CITE RECORD. By contrast, like the testatrix's relationship with her son in *Guthrie*, Testator's relationship with Contestants was strained. CITE LAW; CITE RECORD. They made clear to Testator that they disapproved of his relationship with Ms. Dieger and "rarely" saw Testator toward the end of his life. CITE RECORD. Indeed, the last time Contestants saw Testator they had a "heated exchange" about his new will and his relationship with Ms. Dieger. CITE RECORD. Nevertheless, unlike the testatrix in *Guthrie*, Testator did not disinherit Contestants—he particularly provided for them and for their children in his will. CITE LAW; CITE RECORD. He left each Contestant $10,000 and their children each $5,000. CITE RECORD. Thus, the facts of this case weigh more heavily against finding Testator's disposition unnatural given that Contestants were not disinherited, and it cannot be said that "all reasonable explanation in affection for the devise is lacking." CITE LAW; CITE RECORD. Rather, Testator's will and the devises therein are "reasonable" given that he was in love with Ms. Dieger, who took care of him for more than two years, and that he was at odds with Contestants, with whom he had not made "peace" before he died. CITE LAW; CITE RECORD. Accordingly, this Court should grant summary judgment because Contestants cannot establish a fact issue with respect to the third element of their undue influence claim.

You should see that almost every sentence in the Rule and Analysis of CRAC has a citation after it. The only sentences that do not include a citation in the Rule and Analysis sections are topic sentences. This is because topic sentences are kind of like "mini-conclusions" in that they introduce, summarize, and connect for the reader the information in the current paragraph. The topic sentence does not present a new rule or point of law in and of itself, but, instead, summarizes or previews what is in the sentences that follow. Therefore, a citation is usually not needed in a topic sentence. Rather, including a citation after a topic sentence can be confusing to a reader because it makes the topic sentence look like a subrule as opposed to a topic sentence. In summary, you do not need a citation after your topic sentences. "Wait," you say. "I hear what you are saying, but it is confusing me!" To that, we reply: be calm, carry on, and remember the easy rule we live by: "When in doubt, CITE!" Citing after your topic sentence is technically not wrong, rather it is simply stylistically better not to distract from your topic sentence with a citation. Therefore, if you are confused or "in doubt" about citations and topic sentences, what should you do? CITE.

We know that we need to cite after every assertion that is taken from another source. When we take an assertion from another source word for word, rather than paraphrasing that other source, we need to use quotations to indicate that we are using the exact words of another. When the material you are quoting from is more than 50 words, you should use a block quote. Otherwise, you indicate you are using the words of another by using quotation marks around the text.

The below text is copied/pasted from the case *Estate of Johnson*, 340 S.W.3d 769, 784 (Tex. App.—San Antonio 2011, pet. denied). If you were to quote the entirety of that text word for word, you would put it in block quotation format because it exceeds 50 words. Block quotations do not use quotation marks. Instead, block quotations are indicated by indenting the text on the right and left sides and using single spacing. Note that the citation follows the block quote and is left-justified, but it is not a part of the block quote.

> Accordingly, evidence of a reasonable explanation for an unnatural disposition does not prevent a jury from finding undue influence. Instead, where such evidence is preferred, the jury must determine which explanation should be given more weight and which explanation is more credible. In this case, the jury disbelieved the explanation proffered by the Appellants in finding undue influence.

Estate of Johnson, 340 S.W.3d 769, 784 (Tex. App.—San Antonio 2011, pet. denied).

Block quotes should be used sparingly, if at all, because block quotes are often skipped over by readers. Let's say, instead of using a block quote, you want to form a subrule from the second sentence above. If you want to use the exact words to create that subrule, you need to use quotes and a citation. If you alter the text in any way, you should use brackets inside the quotation to indicate the alteration.

"[T]he jury must determine which explanation should be given more weight and which explanation is more credible." *Estate of Johnson*, 340 S.W.3d 769, 784 (Tex. App.—San Antonio 2011, pet. denied).

Let's say you do not want to take the language word for word from *Estate of Johnson*, but, instead, you want to paraphrase the language to create a subrule. Here, you would not need to include quotations, but you would need to include a citation.

> Where there are competing explanations for a disposition, whether the disposition is unnatural is a question for the jury. *Estate of Johnson*, 340 S.W.3d 769, 784 (Tex. App.—San Antonio 2011, pet. denied).

B. How to cite (Bluebook, Indigo Book, state-specific citation forms)

We discussed when you need a citation and why you need a citation, but how do you properly form citations? The short answer is you look to a citation manual like *The Bluebook*, which explains (in painstaking detail) how to cite just about everything under the sun according to the Uniform System of Citation followed in the legal profession. However, *The Bluebook*, while certainly the most prominent legal citation manual, has a few drawbacks. First, if bought new, it costs $38.00. Second, the publishers keep making new editions, meaning you may be shelling out $38.00 more than once if you want to stay up to date. Third, because the vast majority of *The Bluebook* pages are devoted to constructing citations for the purpose of law review footnotes (something first-year law students will not need to worry about in their first-year legal writing class), it can be a little (a lot) confusing. Enter: *The Indigo Book*.[25] *The Indigo Book* is a (1) free, online resource; (2) that is consistent with *The Bluebook* citation style; and (3) is a whole lot less confusing. To access it, go to https://law.resource.org/pub/us/code/blue/IndigoBook.html or Google "The Indigo Book."

As law professors, we have found that *The Indigo Book* covers everything that you will need to know how to cite in first-year legal writing. And, by using lots of examples and by eliminating law review-specific details, *The Indigo Book* is also much easier for legal writing students to follow. While *The Bluebook* and *The Indigo Book* cover general citations, it is important to be aware that some states have their own state-specific citation manuals that govern citation to state-specific legal authority. For example, Texas, California, and Louisiana—just to name a few—all have their own unique citation systems. If you are writing something to be filed in state court, you should check the see if the state has its own citation form that supersedes *The Bluebook* when it comes to proper citation to state legal authorities.

Whichever legal citation manual or manuals you use, below are our "top four" citation tips. Because in first-year legal writing the most common legal authority you will cite is cases, most of these tips deal with case citations.

Tip #1: Placing long citations, short citations, and *Id.* (Bluebook Rule B10.2; Indigo Book Rule 15.2, 15.3).

The first time you cite something, you use the full citation. If you cite the same material again in your paper, you will use either "*Id.*" or a short citation, depending on where the subsequent citation is found. If you are citing to the same single source from the immediately preceding citation, you will use "*Id.*" if the subsequent citation is at the

25. Sprigman et al., The Indigo Book: A Manual of Legal Citation, Public Resource (2016), https://law.resource.org/pub/us/code/blue/IndigoBook.html (last visited June 25, 2019).

same page number (pincite), or you will use "*Id.* at ___." if you are citing to the same single source but to a different page number/pincite. If you are citing to something you have previously cited, but it is not from the immediately preceding citation, you will use the short form citation (*see* tip #2 for how to form a short citation). Look at the example below. Note that the citation in the first sentence is a full citation because, in the example, it is the first time the writer is citing *Rothermel*. The second sentence uses the citation "*Id.* at____." because it is also citing to *Rothermel*, the immediately preceding citation, but is citing to a different page of the opinion than the first sentence. The third sentence cites the *Green* case for the first time, and, therefore, it uses a full citation. The last sentence cites *Rothermel* again and uses a short citation because *Rothermel* has already been cited, but here, "*Id.*" is inappropriate because the citation immediately preceding the last sentence is not *Rothermel*.

> The first element of an undue influence claim is "the existence and exertion of an influence." *Rothermel v. Duncan*, 369 S.W.2d 917, 922 (Tex. 1963). To determine whether there was an existence and exertion of an undue influence, courts examine the *Rothermel* factors, which include: (1) "the nature and type of relationship existing between the testator, the contestants, and the party accused of exerting [the] influence"; (2) the "opportunities existing for the exertion of the type of influence or deception possessed or employed"; (3) "the circumstances surrounding the drafting and execution of the testament"; (4) "the existence of a fraudulent motive"; and (5) "whether there has been an habitual subjection of the testator to the control of another." *Id.* at 923. When a plaintiff uses circumstantial evidence to prove the first element, the "circumstances must be so strong and convincing and of such probative force as to lead a well-guarded mind to a reasonable conclusion not only that undue influence was exercised but that it controlled the will power of the testator at the precise time the will was executed." *Green v. Earnest*, 840 S.W.2d 119, 121 (Tex. App.—El Paso 1992, writ denied). Evidence showing a mere opportunity to exert an improper influence, and nothing more, is insufficient to establish the first element. *Rothermel*, 369 S.W.2d at 923.

It is inappropriate to use "*Id.*" if the preceding citation cites more than one source. In the example below, because the first sentence cites two sources, it is inappropriate to use "*Id.*" after the second sentence because it would be unclear which authority (*Rothermel* or *Estate of Johnson*) you are referring to for the source of the second sentence. Instead, you would use a short citation after the second sentence to indicate the source.

> The first element of an undue influence claim is "the existence and exertion of an influence." *Rothermel v. Duncan*, 369 S.W.2d 917, 922 (Tex. 1963); *In re Estate of Johnson*, 340 S.W.3d 769, 784 (Tex. App.—San Antonio 2011, pet. denied). To determine whether there was an existence and exertion of an

undue influence, courts examine the *Rothermel* factors, which include: (1) "the nature and type of relationship existing between the testator, the contestants, and the party accused of exerting [the] influence"; (2) the "opportunities existing for the exertion of the type of influence or deception possessed or employed"; (3) "the circumstances surrounding the drafting and execution of the testament"; (4) "the existence of a fraudulent motive"; and (5) "whether there has been an habitual subjection of the testator to the control of another." *Rothermel*, 369 S.W.2d at 923.

Tip #2: Example case citations—going from long to short.

How do you transform a full citation into a short citation? We are glad you asked. Citation manuals tell you all the different parts of a citation, what the parts mean, and how to piece them together. That is all well and good, but, if you are like a lot of law students, what you really want is an example. Below are some example case citations in long-form and short-form (and how to get from long to short). As you draft your citations, you can look back to these examples and others and "check" yourself. Do you have all your commas? Is your spacing right? Do you have a pincite?

REPORTED CASE EXAMPLE (*Bluebook* Rule B10.1, B10.2; *Indigo Book* Rule 11.1, 15.2)

Long: *Bruff v. N. Miss. Health Servs., Inc.*, 244 F.3d 495, 497 (5th Cir. 2001).

Bruff ~~*v. N. Miss. Health Servs., Inc.*~~, 244 F.3d ~~495,~~ **at** 497 ~~(5th Cir. 2001)~~.

Short: *Bruff*, 244 F.3d at 497.

Id. or *Id.* at __.

UNREPORTED CASE EXAMPLE (*Bluebook* Rule B10.1.4, B10.2; *Indigo Book* Rule 12.4, 15.2): Note that some cases are not assigned to reporters. For these cases, you include the case name, docket number, citation to either Westlaw or Lexis, star pagination, and, inside the parentheses, the court and the complete date (as opposed to just the year).

Long: *Pok Seong Kwong v. Am. Flood Research, Inc.*, No. 302CV2189-R, 2004 WL 906173, at *2 (N.D. Tex. Apr. 16, 2004).

Pok Seong Kwong ~~*v. Am. Flood Research, Inc.*~~, ~~No. 302CV2189-R~~, 2004 WL 906173, at *2 ~~(N.D. Tex. Apr. 16, 2004)~~.

Short: *Pok Seong Kwong*, 2004 WL 906173, at *2.

Id. or *Id.* at *__.

Note: When using "*Id.*" for these unreported citations, if citing to a different page, you will use the star pagination. For example: *Id.* at *3.

STATE-SPECIFIC CITATION FORM EXAMPLES: As discussed above, several states have their own citation forms. Because the problem in this book involves Texas law (one of the states with its own unique citation form), the below examples use the Texas Rules of Form from Texas's *The Greenbook*.[26]

Texas Supreme Court (*Greenbook* Rule 2.1)

Long: *Rothermel v. Duncan*, 369 S.W.2d 917, 922 (Tex. 1963).

Rothermel ~~*v. Duncan*~~, 369 S.W.2d 917, at 922 ~~(Tex. 1963)~~.

Short: *Rothermel*, 369 S.W.2d at 922.

Id. or *Id.* at __.

Texas Courts of Appeals (*Greenbook* Rule 4.1.1): It is fascinating how unique and different the Texas citation form for Texas Court of Appeals cases is from the citation form in *The Bluebook*. While what comes before the parentheses looks similar to *The Bluebook*, what comes inside the parentheses is very different. In Texas, you include the name of the court ("Tex. App."), followed by an em dash and the city where the court is located ("—San Antonio"), followed by the year ("1990"), followed by a comma and the writ history or petition history (", no writ"). What is writ or petition history? In short, for civil cases in Texas, it tells what happened after a case was decided by the court of appeals and, if applicable, the Texas Supreme Court's disposition of the case.[27]

Long: *Smallwood v. Jones*, 794 S.W.2d 114, 119 (Tex. App.—San Antonio 1990, no writ).

Smallwood ~~*v. Jones*~~, 794 S.W.2d ~~114,~~ **at** 119 ~~(Tex. App.—San Antonio 1990, no writ)~~.

Short: *Smallwood*, 794 S.W.2d at 119.

Id. or *Id.* at __.

Texas Court of Appeals "unreported" or electronic citations (*Greenbook* Rule 4.1.2) *The Greenbook* citation form to Texas courts of appeals cases that are unreported start out looking similar to the citation form for unreported cases in *The Bluebook*: it begins with the case name, followed by the case number, followed by the citation to Lexis or Westlaw, followed by star pagination. However, what is in and after the parentheses are very different. Like the reported Texas courts of appeals cases, you include the name of the court, followed by an em dash and the city where the court is located, followed by the whole date (as opposed to just the year), followed by a comma and the writ history or petition history. In addition, you must note if the

26. The Greenbook: Texas Rules of Form (Tex. Law Rev. Ass'n, 14th ed. 2018).
27. *Id.* at Rule 4.4.

case is designated as a per curium and/or memorandum opinion for cases from 2003 or after by including parenthetical information so indicating. Whew! That is intense.

Long: *In re Estate of Clifton*, No. 13-11-00462-CV, 2012 WL 3139864, at *2 (Tex. App.—Corpus Christi Aug. 2, 2012, no pet.) (mem. op.).

In re Estate of Clifton, ~~No. 13-11-00462-CV~~, 2012 WL 3139864, at *2 ~~(Tex. App.—Corpus Christi Aug. 2, 2012, no pet.) (mem. op.)~~.

Short: *In re Estate of Clifton*, 2012 WL 3139864, at *2.

Id. or *Id.* at *__.

Tip #3: Tables—some of them—are your friends.

The Bluebook has 16 tables in its white pages and two tables in its blue pages. While you will rarely, if ever, look at most of them, there are a few that you will regularly use.

ABBREVIATIONS FOR:	WHERE TO FIND:	SUMMARY/ EXAMPLE:
Court documents	*Bluebook* Bluepages Table 1	Use this table to help formulate citations to court documents in your case. For example, if you were citing to a Defendant's Motion for Summary Judgment filed in your case, you would abbreviate it "Def.'s Mot. for Summ. J."
Case names	*Bluebook* Table 6 (Indigo Table 11)	Use this table to find which words in case names are abbreviated when citing cases. For example, if your case was American Association of Restaurants v. Smith National Laboratory, when referring to the case name in a citation, the following words would need to be abbreviated: *Am. Ass'n of Rests. v. Smith Nat'l Lab.*
Court names	*Bluebook* Table 7 (Indigo Table 9)	Use this table when citing cases to determine how to abbreviate the type of court that decided the case in the citation. Note that the court is coupled with the geographical location. For example, for a citation to an administrative court case, you would use the abbreviation "Admin. Ct." to refer to the court. In a citation to a federal district court case, you would use the abbreviation "D." to refer to the court.

ABBREVIATIONS FOR:	WHERE TO FIND:	SUMMARY/ EXAMPLE:
U.S. geographical locations	*Bluebook* Table 10.1 (Indigo Table 12.1)	Use this table for geographical terms (U.S. states, cities, and territories) in case citations. For example, Alabama is "Ala."; Missouri is "Mo."; and Wyoming is "Wyo."
Months	*Bluebook* Table 12 (Indigo Table 17)	Use this table when a month is used in a citation. Every month except May, June, and July are abbreviated.
Periodicals	*Bluebook* Table 13 (Indigo Table 18)	Use this table to abbreviate periodical names in citations. For example, Harvard Law Review is abbreviated "Harv. L. Rev."

Tip #4: When to use signals (Bluebook Rule 1.2; Indigo Book Rule 4).

Signals can precede a citation to inform the reader about the relationship between the assertion and the authority cited for that assertion. *The Bluebook* and *Indigo Book* divide the signals into four categories: (1) signals that indicate support (*E.g.*, *Accord*, *See*, *See also*, *Cf.*); (2) signals for comparison (*Compare . . . with . . .*); (3) signals for contrast (*Contra*, *But see*, *But cf.*); and (4) signals for background/general information (*See generally*). Note that if no signal is used, it means that the authority cited directly states the assertion.

For a complete discussion of what each signal means, you should refer to *Bluebook* Rule 1.2 (or *Indigo Book* Rule 4). However, you should know that signals are very important in legal writing. The use or misuse of a signal can completely change the meaning of what you are saying to the reader.

To illustrate this, let's look at an example. The following is an excerpt from *In re Caruthers' Estate*, 151 S.W.2d 946, 948 (Tex. Civ. App.—Beaumont 1941, writ dism'd judgm't cor.), where the court upheld a testator's disposition of most of his estate to charities supported by the church in which the testator was a devoted member throughout his life:

> Our courts have ever been diligent to guard the right of a testator to dispose of his property as he pleases and to uphold bequests made for charitable and religious purposes. Obviously, such bequests are less apt to be the result of undue influence than those made to private individuals who might for selfish reasons be inclined to exert influence upon the testator.

Let's say you wanted to write the following:

> Whenever a disposition is made to a charitable organization, courts are disinclined to find the charitable disposition to be a product of undue influence. *In re Caruthers' Estate*, 151 S.W.2d 946, 948 (Tex. Civ. App.—Beaumont 1941, writ dism'd judgm't cor.).

If you do not include a signal, the lack of the signal signifies to the reader that *Caruthers' Estate* directly states your assertion. However, is it accurate that *Caruthers' Estate* directly states that assertion? Go back and reread the excerpt. What do you think? Not really. Rather, it would be more accurate to say that *Caruthers' Estate* "supports" that assertion or that the assertion "follows from it."[28] Accordingly, you should use a "*See*" signal before the citation.

> Whenever a disposition is made to a charitable organization, courts are disinclined to find the charitable disposition to be a product of undue influence. *See In re Caruthers' Estate*, 151 S.W.2d 946, 948 (Tex. Civ. App.—Beaumont 1941, writ dism'd judgm't cor.).

VIII. Grammar and style

Grammar is the way in which language is structured. The part of grammar that is most relevant to your work as a lawyer is known as syntax and construction. Syntax and construction provide the basic rules that allow us to understand each other, both in terms of the spoken and the written word. These rules dictate, for example, the parts of speech, the use of punctuation, the use of capitalization, and pronoun/antecedent agreement. Style, on the other hand, is the gray area among the rules of grammar. Style is a set of preferences and often imposes arbitrary rules affecting voice and tone. Style has nothing to do with syntax. Both grammar and style are central to becoming a successful legal writer. Rules of grammar are 100 percent learnable. Style, however, as you can imagine, is a bit more squirrelly, especially given that style preferences may vary depending on your audience. Below we have captured the top eight—widely accepted—rules of grammar and style for legal writers. Be mindful that while grammar rules are black and white, proper style may vary from situation to situation.

A. *Why grammar and style are important*

Grammar matters. It is that simple. First, the use of improper grammar affects a law student's grades in legal writing. Second, the use of improper grammar impacts a lawyer's credibility to her clients, peer lawyers, and judges. Moreover (and probably more importantly), the use of improper grammar affects both law students' and lawyers' abilities to communicate effectively and precisely.

---

28. THE BLUEBOOK, *supra* note 23, Rule 1.2.

The last thing you want as a law student or as a new lawyer is for someone to focus on your poor grammar rather than on the arguments you are making on your client's behalf. If you think we are creating an issue that does not exist, think again. Recently, a federal judge in the Eastern District of Kentucky commented on the lawyer's grammar: "Once again [] counsel is reminded that he should at least make a pretense of having proofread his documents before filing them in federal court. The Court was hesitant to even cite to [counsel's] brief here, given the poor quality of counsel's writing."[29]

Moreover, improper or unintended grammatical issues can affect the substance of what law students and lawyers are trying to communicate. For example, an inadvertently omitted or a misplaced comma can completely change the meaning of a sentence in a brief, a clause in a contract, or a provision in a municipal code. A recent judicial opinion out of Ohio illustrates the ramifications of improper grammar. A local ordinance in West Jefferson, Ohio, was drafted to read as follows: "it is illegal to park on a village street '**any motor vehicle camper**, trailer, farm implement and/or non-motorized vehicle for a continued period of twenty-four hours.'" A local woman woke up at 5:30 pm (she works nights) and discovered that her green pickup truck had been towed and the local police issued her a citation for violation of the ordinance. In assessing whether it was improper to tow the resident's motor vehicle, the Ohio court noted: "[b]y utilizing rules of grammar and employing the common meaning of terms, 'motor vehicle camper' has a clear definition that does not produce an absurd result. If the village desires a different reading, it should amend the ordinance and insert a comma between the phrase 'motor vehicle' and the word 'camper.' As written, however, legislative intent is clear from looking at the language used in the ordinance itself."[30] This lack of a comma worked to the local woman's advantage, but is that what the drafters meant?

B. *Quick review: the top eight most important grammar and style rules for legal writing*

There are countless grammar rules crucial to a law student's or a young lawyer's ability to draft articulate, clear, and accurate sentences. Unfortunately, given curricular shifts in undergraduate and high school education, there is an ever-increasing number of college graduates who are unfamiliar with the rules of grammar and style that form the basis for how we speak and write. The purpose of this section is not to teach or re-teach you English grammar in its entirety. Instead, this section aims to highlight the top eight rules of grammar and style most critical to a lawyer's work. As such, if as you navigate writing courses in law school, you realize that you are deficient in your understanding of the rules of English grammar, we encourage you to seek additional help to shore up your grammar abilities.[31]

---

29. *Colyer v. Speedway, LLC*, 981 F. Supp. 2d 634, 641 n.5 (E.D. Ky. 2013).

30. *W. Jefferson v. Cammelleri*, 12th Dist. No. CA2014-04-012, 2015-Ohio-2463, 2015 WL 3824456, ¶ 18.

31. There are a number of resources available to law students to help them shore up their understanding of English grammar. A few of our favorite resources are listed here: WILLIAM STRUNK & E.B. WHITE, THE

1. Rule one: plain language

Using bigger words does not make you seem smarter. How about we repeat that for emphasis: using multisyllabic, thesaurus-found words does not make you (or make you appear) smarter. Instead, the smartest lawyers are those who can take the law—which is necessarily complex on its own—and make it easy to understand. One of the primary ways law students and young lawyers begin to do this is by constantly reminding themselves to use plain, simple English in their writing. How do you do this? Follow these few failsafe tips.

Tip #1: When possible, leave Latin where it originated—in ancient times—and prefer simple words over complex ones.

To utilize arcane phraseology to expound on the state of jurisprudence is, well, absurd. For whatever reason, many entering law students are under the impression that to be a lawyer they have to "sound" like one and that to sound like a lawyer they need to use complex and multisyllabic words. Truthfully speaking, however, what clients pay lawyers to do is to take the law and to make it understandable. So, the reality is that using plain English is the best way to communicate orally and in writing because, simply put, it is the best way to ensure that others are understanding what you are saying or writing.

What does this mean for lawyers in particular? At times as a lawyer, you will need to use terms of art; after all, there are some terms that cannot be simplified without introducing inaccuracies (for example, "battery" cannot be replaced with "hit" and "family violence" cannot be replaced with "abuse"). However, aside from terms of art, lawyers should avoid legalese and Latin phrasing in their writings. Brian Garner has written a number of books dedicated to helping lawyers simplify their language; below is a sampling of legal and "stuffy" terms he suggests you avoid using and some suggested alternative phrasing for each.[32]

GARNER SAYS INSTEAD OF THIS	TRY THIS
Ab initio	From the start
Forthwith	Now
Herein	Here
Sui generis	Unique
To wit	Namely
Inter alia	Among other things

ELEMENTS OF STYLE (Pearson, 4th ed. 2014); BRYAN GARNER, THE REDBOOK (West, 3d ed. 2013); ANNE ENQUIST ET AL., JUST WRITING: GRAMMAR, PUNCTUATION, AND STYLE FOR THE LEGAL WRITER (Wolters Kluwer, 5th ed., 2017).

32. GARNER, *supra* note 31, at 219.

Tip #2: Use (parallel) lists.

Legal readers think in terms of factors and elements. As a result, legal readers appreciate and easily comprehend information when it is presented in numerated or bulleted lists. Given this reality, when the content you are explaining lends itself to it, create a numerated or bullet-pointed list to help your reader navigate the elements, factors, or conditions you are explaining. In addition, when using lists in your legal writing, be mindful to make your lists parallel in terms of construction. What does that mean? Make sure that each item in the list follows the same grammatical structure. For instance, if the first item in the list begins with a past participle, all listed items should begin with a past participle. This parallel structure will make it easier for your reader to see how the different listed items relate to one another.

NON-PARALLEL LIST

There are three elements required to establish an informal marriage in Texas:

1. the couple must agree to be married;
2. cohabitation as husband and wife after the agreement; and
3. representation to others that they were married.

PARALLEL LIST

To establish an informal marriage in Texas, a couple must show that they:

1. agreed to be married;
2. cohabitated as husband and wife after the agreement; and
3. represented to others that they were married.

Tip #3: Keep your sentences concise and easy to follow.

Generally speaking, your sentences should average around 20 words in length. You should have some sentences that are far fewer than 20 words and some others woven in that hover around 30 words. The variation in length helps keep your reader engaged and focused (too many similarly constructed sentences risks lulling your reader to sleep). Sentence length is important not only for ease of reading, but also because it affects your reader's comprehension. We recommend that you discipline yourself to highlight any sentence that is more than 30 words in your legal writing. Once you have identified a long sentence, ask yourself whether the long sentence can be improved by splitting it into two sentences or removing unnecessary words or phrases.

In addition to length, draft your sentences in a way that makes it easy for your reader to identify the subject, verb, and object of the sentence. This aim is typically accomplished by locating the subject and verb near the front of your sentences and avoiding writing in the passive voice (see grammar Rule Two for more on passive voice).

Tip #4: Make sure your writing passes the readability test.

The best way to test the readability of your document is to read it aloud and make sure you—as both the reader and the writer—can follow the content you drafted. Obviously, this readability test is somewhat inaccurate because you drafted the text and are at an advantage in trying to understand it as you read it aloud. Given this reality, there are two other ways to ascertain the readability of your legal writing. The first is to listen to it as Google Docs reads it aloud. This approach will highlight long, complex sentences so that you can go back and fix them after the read-through. The second option is to run readability statistics in Microsoft Word. The generally accepted rule is that all writings—including legal writings—should have a readability score around a 40 or 50 and be within a middle or high school range. You can review the readability statistics of any document you draft in Microsoft Word by selecting "show readability" as an option (File menu > Options > Proofing tab)[33] and then running a grammar and spell check of your document. Below you will see the readability results from the Objective Memorandum and Opposition to the Motion for Summary Judgment that are in the Appendix.

Objective Memorandum Readability Statistics:

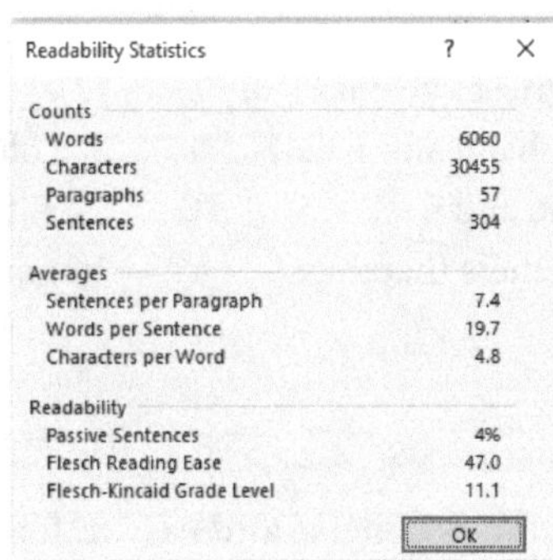

Readability Statistics	? ×
Counts	
Words	6060
Characters	30455
Paragraphs	57
Sentences	304
Averages	
Sentences per Paragraph	7.4
Words per Sentence	19.7
Characters per Word	4.8
Readability	
Passive Sentences	4%
Flesch Reading Ease	47.0
Flesch-Kincaid Grade Level	11.1
	OK

Opposition to Motion for Summary Judgment Readabilty Statistics:

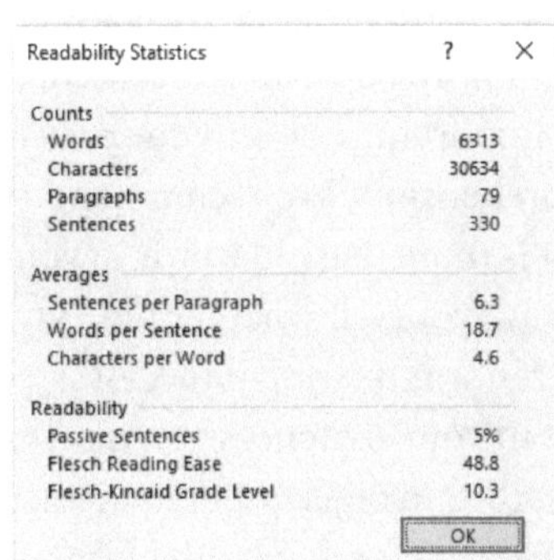

Readability Statistics	? ×
Counts	
Words	6313
Characters	30634
Paragraphs	79
Sentences	330
Averages	
Sentences per Paragraph	6.3
Words per Sentence	18.7
Characters per Word	4.6
Readability	
Passive Sentences	5%
Flesch Reading Ease	48.8
Flesch-Kincaid Grade Level	10.3
	OK

33. On a Mac computer, go to Word > Preferences > Spelling and Grammar > Show readability statistics.

Tip #5: Omit any extra words.

Mark Twain nailed it when he said, "If I had more time, I would have written a shorter letter." Deadlines, which are constant for lawyers, often leave little time for editing. Moreover, working against the clock often results in less time to edit and, thus, longer writings.

Truth be told, it is not **hard** to get rid of extraneous words and tighten your writing, but it does take time and diligence. Given that a lawyer's success is tied directly to her ability to communicate ideas in writing, clarity of communication is crucial. This reality means that it will behoove you to carve out the time Twain did not have to shorten your writings and tighten the language you use to express your ideas. To get the most bang for your buck when working to omit extra words, focus on the following areas.

- **Replace common but compound phrases with single words meaning the same thing**. Some examples are below.

COMPOUND	SIMPLE
With reference to	About
With regard to	Regarding
By virtue/means/reason of	By
In connection with	With
In order to	To
With respect to	About
With the exception of	Except for
Until such time as	Until
As a consequence of	Because of
As a matter of	In fact
Despite the fact that	Although
In spite of the fact that	Although
Due to the fact that	Because

- **Replace weak verbal phrases that contain adverbs + verbs with a better, stronger verb**. For example, instead of writing "the general counsel walked slowly home after his full workday," you could write "the general counsel plodded home after his full workday." Similarly, instead of writing, "the Defendant quickly ate the bag of gummy bears before anyone could see," you would write, "the Defendant devoured the bag of gummy bears before anyone could see."

- **Avoid redundant phrases**, such as "null and void," "whether or whether not," "peace and quiet," "free and clear," or "true and correct."
- **Remove extra intensifiers and qualifiers.** New legal writers often fall into the trap of adding in intensifiers or qualifiers because they are insecure about their ability to communicate the law effectively. Locate such words in your writing, and simply put, remove them. Some examples of words to search for and remove include: clearly, extremely, somewhat, very, essentially, generally, perhaps, really, and highly.

2. Rule two: passive voice

In grammar-speak, the "voice" of a verb refers to the relationship of the subject to the action expressed by the verb. When a sentence is written in the active voice, the subject of the sentence is doing the action of the verb. When a sentence is written in passive voice, the subject of the sentence is the one on whom the action is being done. In other words, in a sentence written in passive voice the subject is passive. Let's look at a sentence drafted in passive voice and then redrafted in active voice to help you understand the difference between active and passive voice. In both sentences the subject of the verb is underlined and the verb is bolded and italicized.

> **Passive voice:** Texas law ***was studied*** by first-year <u>students</u> from UNT Dallas College of Law.
>
> **Active voice:** First-year <u>students</u> from UNT Dallas College of Law ***studied*** Texas law.

Why does it matter whether a sentence is active or passive? The voice of a sentence matters because legal writing should be primarily written in active voice. There are a number of reasons why legal writers should use active voice instead of passive voice when they write. First, active voice is more concise and impactful than passive voice. In a profession that values clarity, precision, and efficiency, the clearer and more concise, the better. Second, text written in active voice is easier for the reader to understand because it clearly identifies the subject of the sentence and the doer of the action. Third, because legal writing often focuses on evaluating an actor's conduct, legal writers should employ active voice because it emphasizes the actor. Despite the general preference for writing in active voice, legal writers may write in passive voice when the actor of the verb is unknown or when the writer wants to hide or de-emphasize the actor. For example, if a lawyer represents someone in a criminal case, he may not want to say "Defendant brandished a knife." Instead, in such an instance, the lawyer may prefer to write "A knife was brandished." Reframing the sentence in this way—by using the passive voice—allows the lawyer to de-emphasize the proximity of her client, the Defendant, to the knife and tries to prevent a reader from associating her client with a weapon.

Given the preference for writing in active voice, a significant challenge for law students and young lawyers is identifying the "voice" employed in their writing and, then, converting any sentences written in passive voice into active voice. So how do you identify passive voice?

> **Option one:** Look for sentences that contain a "to be" verb plus the word "by." A "to be verb" includes is, was, were, be, or has been.
>
> The law ***was*** overturned ***by*** the U.S. Supreme Court. = Passive Voice
>
> **Option two:** Look for sentences that contain a "to be" verb plus an implicit version of the word "by" that can be identified using the "by zombies" trick. If you can insert "by zombies" after the verb in a sentence and the sentence still makes sense, then the sentence is probably passive voice.
>
> The law ***was*** overturned [***by zombies***]. = Passive Voice
>
> The law ***was*** devastating to the farmers. = Active Voice (adding "by zombies" would not make sense)

Once you have identified sentences that are drafted in passive voice, your next job is to convert those sentences to active voice. You can do this in three easy steps:

Step one: Identify the subject, verb, and object of the sentence. The verb is the action word in the sentence that describes what the subject is doing. The subject is what or who the sentence is about. The object is the person or thing that receives the action of the verb.

Step two: Make the subject do the action of the verb.

Step three: Make sure the verb matches the subject in terms of singularity/plurality.

Let's practice these three steps with the following sentence, currently drafted in passive voice: **The battery was committed by the boy when he hurled his phone at his teacher.**

Step one: **Identify the subject, verb, and object of the sentence.**

The battery was committed by **the boy** when he hurled his phone at the teacher.

Object **Verb** **Subject**

Step two: **Make the subject do the action of the verb.**

The boy committed the battery when he hurled his phone at his teacher.

Subject **Verb** **Object**

Step three: **Make sure the verb matches the subject in terms of singularity/plurality.**

Here, the boy and battery were both singular, so shifting the organization of the sentence does not require a change to the singularity/plurality of the verb.

3. Rule three: commas

Commas are punctuation marks used to separate various parts of a sentence. Use of commas can provide clarity to writing and can help communicate the content of a sentence more effectively. Unfortunately, commas are frequently misused. This misuse may stem from failure to learn the rules related to commas or it may stem from learning inaccurate rules—for example, the rule often espoused by grade school teachers telling you to place a comma wherever you would pause if you read your sentence aloud. As a result of this dearth of knowledge and/or application of incorrect rules, we have a mix of overuse of commas and then—possibly in overreaction to the previously mentioned erroneous rule—an equal amount of missed comma usage.

There is, however, hope. Although there are more uses for and rules related to commas than there is space in this book, there are a handful of key comma rules that can improve your usage exponentially. To help, below you will find the top ten most commonly missed/misapplied comma rules, each with an example or two.

Comma rule #1: Use a comma to separate each item in a series (the Oxford comma).

There have been hot debates over the necessity of the Oxford comma—the comma that precedes the final item in a multi-item list. Some believe that the Oxford commas is superfluous. Others believe that the Oxford comma should be placed as a matter of course. Through debate, what has become clear is that the absence of the Oxford comma does not always affect the meaning of a sentence. However, at times, failing to include the Oxford comma will change the meaning of what is written.

Legal writers and legal readers prefer consistency and predictability. Because of this tendency for consistency, we recommend that, as a matter of course, you include the Oxford comma even where it is not absolutely necessary. Including it where unnecessary does not change the meaning of the sentence, but omitting it in some circumstances can upend what is written. Err on the side of inclusion.

Comma rule #2: Use commas to set off quotations.

The comma serves as a signal to the reader that you are starting or ending a quote. Accordingly, you should use commas in the following instances: (1) when you have a statement before your quote, use the comma to signal a quote is coming; (2) when you start with a quote, use the comma to signal the quote has ended; and (3) when a statement interrupts your quote, do both—use a comma to let your reader know the first part of the quote has ended and a comma to let your reader know the rest of the quote is coming. Below you will find an example of each type of quote-based comma.

> **When introducing a quote:** Ygritte said, "You know nothing, John Snow."
>
> **When following a quote:** "I am the one who knocks," Walter White said.
>
> **When interrupting a quote:** "Clear eyes, full hearts," Coach Taylor yelled, "can't lose."

Comma rule #3: Use commas after introductory words or phrases.

An introductory word (here, first, finally, etc.), a phrase (a phrase does not have its own subject and verb), and a clause (a clause has its own subject and verb), all set the stage for the main part of the sentence. Use a comma after the introductory word, phrase, or clause to let your reader know the introduction is over and you are moving on to the main part of the sentence.

> **Introductory word:** Loudly, she explained her position to the judge.
>
> **Introductory phrase:** Typing quickly, Meredith finished the brief before the deadline.
>
> **Introductory clause:** After they finished the final, Brian's study group went out for dinner.

Comma rule #4: Use commas to join independent clauses joined by a coordinating conjunction.

When a sentence is made up of two separate, independent clauses, you should use a comma together with a coordinating conjunction to separate each independent clause. An independent clause is a clause that could stand alone as a sentence (it has a subject and a verb). Students often remember coordinating conjunctions through the mnemonic FANBOYS (for, and, nor, but, or, yet, so).

> Jeff won the moot court competition, **and** he submitted the best brief.
>
> vs.
>
> Jeff won the moot court competition and submitted the best brief.

Comma rule #5: Use commas to set off nonessential information in a sentence.

When a sentence contains a nonrestrictive phrase or clause—meaning a phrase or clause that adds nonessential information to the sentence—the nonrestrictive clause should be set off by commas. A phrase or clause is nonrestrictive if when removed from the sentence, the sentence retains its meaning. The nonrestrictive clause is in bold below.

> Several law students, judges, and attorneys attended the speech, **which began at 1 p.m.**, regarding how to reduce pollution.

Some students deeply struggle to figure out whether a clause is restrictive or nonrestrictive. Generally speaking, a clause that is framed by "that" is typically restrictive and a clause that is framed by "which" is generally nonrestrictive.

> **Correct:** Cars that are manual are difficult to drive.
>
> **Incorrect:** Cars, which are manual, are difficult to drive.

The fact that the cars are manual is essential to the meaning of the sentence. Therefore, it should be a restrictive clause using "that." If it is put in a non-restrictive clause ("which"), removing the clause changes the meaning of the sentence. The writer is not saying that all cars are difficult to drive. Rather, the writer is saying that cars with a manual transmission are difficult to drive.

The problem with using that general rule to determine the type of clause you are dealing with is that many students and lawyers use "which" and "that" incorrectly. Truthfully, the category a clause falls into will depend on the context and meaning. The illustration below is a way to visualize the example sentence to determine whether it is restrictive or non-restrictive.

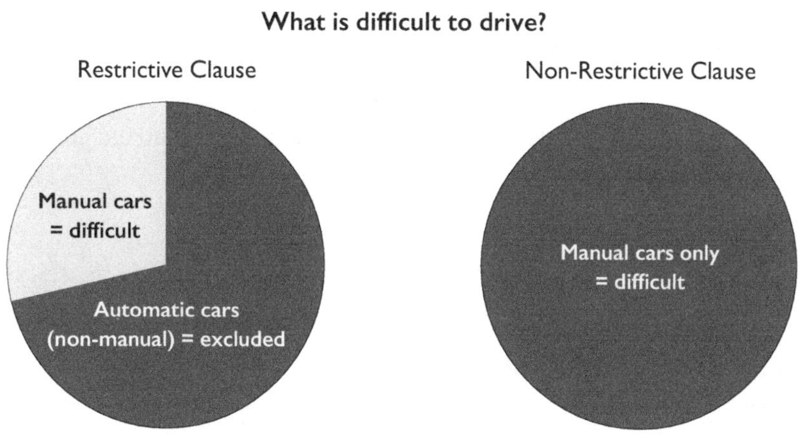

Comma rule #6: Do not use a comma to offset a restrictive phrase.

If a sentence contains a phrase or clause that is restrictive—that is essential to the sentence for its meaning to be clear—you should NOT set the restrictive clause off with commas.

> Lawyers who work hard will receive a raise.

If you remove the phrase "who work hard" you still have a complete sentence, but you have lost the meaning—that only lawyers who work hard get raises. We are not trying to say every lawyer will get a raise. Because it is essential to the meaning of the sentence, you **do not** need a comma.

> The podcast that covered Adnan Syed's case has become very popular.

Similarly, if you remove the phrase "that covered Adnan Syed's case" you would have a complete sentence, but it would not be clear which podcast you were describing.

Comma rule #7: Use commas between adjectives that describe the same noun.

When multiple adjectives describe the same noun, you should separate those adjectives with a comma. Hint: If you can put *and* or *but* between the adjectives, a comma will probably belong there.

The judge is a tall, distinguished man.

Because you could write "tall and distinguished," you need a comma.

When I was in law school, I lived in a tiny old house near campus.

Because you probably would not say that you lived in a "tiny and old house," you do not need a comma between the adjectives.

Comma rule #8: Use a comma to separate a direct address from the rest of the sentence.

Use a comma when you are directly addressing someone or something. If the direct address comes at the beginning or end of a sentence, use one comma to set it off. If the direct address comes in the middle of the sentence, use a pair of commas to set it off.

Elle Woods, your LSAT score is impressive!

Get the confession, Perry Mason, or you could lose the case!

Comma rule #9: Use a comma with numbers, dates, addresses, and titles.

Dates: Set off the year from the rest of the sentence with a pair of commas.

On June 13, 1966, the U.S. Supreme Court issued its opinion in *Miranda v. Arizona*.

Addresses: Separate out the elements of an address with a comma. The exception is the zip code.

Judge Learned Hand was born in Albany, New York, in 1872.

Please send a copy of the brief to the Dallas County Clerk at 1201 Elm Street, Dallas, TX 75270.

Titles: Where a title follows a name, separate out the name with a pair of commas.

Johnnie Cochran, J.D., helped defend O.J. Simpson.

Numbers: If writing a number more than three digits, use commas to separate the numbers into groups of three (e.g., 200,000).

Comma rule #10: Do not put a comma where a period should go.

Do not run two independent clauses together by using a comma instead of a period. This use of a comma creates what is called a comma splice or a run-on sentence. There are a few options for fixing this. You could split the sentence at issue into two separate sentences; you could create an introductory phrase and use a comma; or you could add a coordinating conjunction and a comma.

> **Incorrect:** He forgot to study, he failed the test.
>
> **Correct:** He forgot to study. He failed the test.
>
> **Correct:** After he forgot to study, he failed the test.
>
> **Correct:** He forgot to study, and he failed the test.

4. Rule four: semicolons vs. colons

The default rule you should follow is that you should use semicolons and colons sparingly. In fact, the best advice for new legal writers is to avoid using them at all unless you must. Why? Because more often than not, writers misuse and/or overuse semicolons and colons. If you decide to employ a colon or semicolon, the rules below will help you ensure your usage is proper.

a) Semicolons

Semicolons have two common uses. First, you should use a semicolon (instead of a comma) to separate listed items or items in a series when there are internal commas in the list or series.

Compare the following:

> **Series separated with commas:** The judge ruled on three motions in court today: a motion to dismiss, a motion in limine, and a *Daubert* motion.
>
> vs.
>
> **Series separated with semicolons:** The judge heard three cases today: *In re Adams*, an undue influence case; *Tom v. Phill*, a battery case; and *United States v. Erie.*

Second, you can (but need not) use a semicolon instead of a period to separate two independent clauses. Often writers will use a semicolon in lieu of a period when the reader wants to highlight the deep connection between the two clauses by tying them together. Another alternative to using a semicolon to separate two independent clauses is to add a coordinating conjunction (a FANBOY as explained in Comma rule #4) and then use a comma to separate the independent clauses.

Compare the following:

> **Two independent clauses separated with a period:** The attorney argued passionately. He was disappointed when the judge denied his motion for summary judgment.
>
> vs.
>
> **Two independent clauses separated with a semicolon:** The attorney argued passionately; he was disappointed when the judge denied his motion for summary judgment.
>
> vs.
>
> **Two independent clauses separated by a comma and a coordinating conjunction (FANBOY):** The attorney argued passionately, and he was disappointed when the judge denied his motion for summary judgment.

b) Colons

Colons, like semicolons, have multiple uses. In most instances, the use of a colon is a stylistic choice because there are other, grammatically correct punctual marks that you could use in place of the colon. There are a few central ways to use the colon.

> **Use #1:** Use colons to introduce an item or a series of items. When using a colon in this way, you do not capitalize the first item after the colon (unless for some other reason it should be capitalized).
>
>> In law school you are required to read many things: statutes, cases, textbooks, and even regulations.
>
> **Use #2:** Use colons between two sentences if the second sentence emphasizes or illustrates the first.
>
>> Reflecting back, the first year of law school was incredibly hard: we had to read hundreds of cases, attend long lectures, take regular quizzes, and sit for long exams.
>
> **Use #3:** Use colons to introduced bulleted or numbered lists.
>
>> Undue influence requires proof of three elements:
>>
>> 1. the existence and exertion of an influence;
>> 2. the influence overpowered the mind of the testator; and
>> 3. the execution of the will only occurred because of the influence.

5. Rule five: punctuation in quotations

Quotation marks designate words, phrases, or sentences that are quoted. In Section VII.A, above, we discussed the importance of quotations, how and when to use them, and the different ways to express quoted material in your writing (inline quotations or block quotations). Once students master where to use quotations, they often struggle with the placement of punctuation in and around quoted material. The rules that dictate where punctuation goes in relation to quotations are not hard, but many students are not introduced to the proper rules before law school.

> **Periods:** Final periods go inside quotation marks. It does not matter whether the period is part of the original quotation or whether you are adding it as the final period.
>
> **Commas:** Commas go inside quotation marks. It does not matter whether the comma is part of the original quotation or whether you are adding it as a final comma before the quote ends.
>
> **Semicolons and colons:** Semicolons and colons go outside the quotation marks, even if there was a semicolon or colon included as part of the quotation at the end of the material quoted.
>
> **Question marks and exclamation marks:** Question marks and exclamation marks go inside the quotation marks if they are included as part of the original quotation, but they go outside the quotation marks if they were not part of the original quotation.

Another quotation-related grammar rule that often throws law students off is the use of single versus double quotation marks. In legal writing, you only use single quotation marks for nested quotations (or quoted materials within quoted material). When you refer to terms of art, unless those terms are part of a nested quotation, you should use traditional double—not single—quotation marks. Similarly, if you are indicating that a phrase is odd, informal, or ironic, you should also use traditional double quotation marks around that phrase.

6. Rule six: subject-verb agreement

Singular verb

The law student studies hard.

Singular subject because one student

Plural verb

UNT Dallas College of Law students study hard.

Plural subject because refers to more than one student

This rule is not complicated. The subject of a sentence must agree with the verb. This means that if the subject of a sentence is singular, the verb of the sentence must be singular. On the other hand, if the subject of the sentence is plural, the verb must also be plural.[34]

Although the rule itself is simple, there are a handful of pronouns (called indefinite pronouns) that when used as subjects make it hard to discern whether to use a singular or plural verb. For indefinite pronouns, you will need to memorize whether they take a singular or plural verb.

INDEFINITE PRONOUNS THAT ALWAYS TAKE A SINGULAR VERB	INDEFINITE PRONOUNS THAT ALWAYS TAKE A PLURAL VERB	INDEFINITE PRONOUNS THAT CAN TAKE EITHER A SINGULAR OR PLURAL VERB (DEPENDING ON USAGE)
Anyone	Both	All
Everyone	Few	Any
Someone	Many	More
Anybody	Others	Most
Somebody	Several	Some
Nobody		
Each		
One		
Either		
Neither		

34. An oddity of English grammar is that to make a verb singular you have to add an "s," and to make a verb plural, typically you omit the "s." On the other hand, to make a noun (or subject) singular you omit the "s," while to make a noun or subject plural you have to add an "s."

For the third category, to determine whether the particular pronoun requires a singular or plural verb, you need to identify whether the subject is singular or plural. When the pronoun is acting as a singular subject, use a singular verb; otherwise, use a plural verb.

7. Rule seven: hyphens, en dashes, and em dashes

Hyphen -

En dash –

Em dash —

Although similar in appearance, the hyphen, the en dash, and the em dash are punctuation marks distinct from one another in terms of appearance and purpose.

The **hyphen** is the most commonly used type of dash, and it is also the shortest in terms of its length. Unfortunately, because many people do not know there are different types of dashes, the hyphen (the most easily accessible dash) is often misused where an en dash or em dash would be appropriate. A hyphen should not be used as punctuation but, instead, should be used to combine different types of compound words and adjectival phrases. One of a hyphen's main purposes is to combine modifiers with nouns they modify. In particular, one should hyphenate certain compound modifiers that come before nouns, such as "well-established rule" or "little-known fact." Second, one should also hyphenate the modifiers "all," "ex," and "self" when they come before nouns, such as "all-time," "ex-spouse," or "self-doubt." Third, one should use a hyphen before elect, such as a "president-elect." Fourth, one should hyphenate compound numbers that modify a noun, such as "twenty-two cases" or "twenty-two-year-old judge." Fifth, one should hyphenate two parties who are combined to modify a noun, such as "attorney-client privilege." Sixth, one should use a hyphen between "e" and any other word when "e" is meant to abbreviate electronic, such as "e-mail" or "e-commerce." The hyphen is easily inserted into text by using the hyphen key on the keyboard.

An **en dash** is the least frequently used dash. An en dash means "to" and is used to connect numbers and occasionally words. For example, an en dash should be employed in the following sentence: **The salary for first-year public defense attorneys, $50,000–$60,000, is more than enough for a young lawyer to live on.** You also use en dashes between page ranges, including page ranges in citation sentences. To insert an en dash in Microsoft Word, under the "Insert" tab, one must click "Symbol," click "More Symbols," then under "Special Characters" click "En Dash."

An **em dash** is the longest of the dashes. Like a comma, colon, or parenthetical, the em dash is a mark of separation that tells the reader that what follows bears some relation to what it preceded. Em dashes should be used (1) to signal the beginning and end of the list; (2) to set off an introductory list containing commas; (3) to show abrupt shifts; (4) to cue the reader to shocking or surprising information; or (5) as a punctuation in place of parentheses or to set off a non-restrictive clause. To insert an em dash in Microsoft Word, follow the instructions above for "en dash" but select "Em Dash" from the "Special Characters."

8. Rule eight: capitalization

Let's be honest, most law students have mastered basic capitalization rules by the time they begin high school. That said, there are a few capitalization rules that are either tricky or specific to legal writing. These capitalization rules are worth a quick review.

CATEGORY	RULE	EXAMPLE
Titles/job/ roles	Capitalize official titles or roles if they come before and are attached to the name. But do not capitalize the title if it comes after the name.	Judge Emily Miskel Emily Miskel, judge
Geography	Capitalize specific geographical regions but not points of the compass or directions.	North America Let's travel north.
Acronyms	Use capital letters for every letter of almost all acronyms.	SCOTUS (acronym for Supreme Court of the United States)
Court	The word court is ***only*** capitalized in the following instances: (1) when referring to the United States Supreme Court; (2) when the name of the court is spelled out, e.g., the United States District Court for the Northern District of Texas; (3) when referencing the specific court that you are before or the one that will rule on your case.	The Court may overturn its own decision rendered in *Roe v. Wade.* We ask the Court to grant summary judgment. vs. The court in *Rothermel* reviewed the elements of undue influence.
Defendant/ Plaintiff	The plaintiff and defendant are capitalized only when referring to the parties in your particular case.	Defendant moved for summary judgment, and, in response, Plaintiff appealed. vs. The defendant in *Rothermel* had two children.
Order/ Motion	Titles of documents (such as motions or orders) are capitalized when they are referring to a document that has been filed in the same matter in which you are filing your document.	Defendant requests that the Court grant her Motion for Summary Judgment. vs. Drafting a motion for summary judgment is a hard skill to master.

2 | Objective Legal Writing

Before reading this part of the book, you should skim through the objective memoranda in the Appendix on page 239.

Students often suffer from so-called "Law and Order" syndrome. Misled by the often-watched (and idolized) television lawyers, students mistakenly believe that a lawyer's job turns on his or her ability to engage in oral advocacy and argument. As alluded to in Part I of this book, however, a lawyer's primary job is not oral advocacy but writing. Lawyers write, and they write a lot. To make this more difficult, the type of writing that lawyers do varies. There are two primary types of writing that lawyers do: objective legal writing and persuasive legal writing. This section of the book focuses on objective writing.

I. What is objective writing?

Objective writing is often referred to as predictive writing. No matter what you call it—objective or predictive—the purpose of this type of legal writing is to present a balanced analysis of the law, given the facts presented. In other words, objective legal writing does not take a position and then design an argument to further or support that position. Instead, objective writing answers a question and then sets forth and applies legal authority to explain that answer to the reader. There is a small twist here that can be confusing to students. Objective writing, while neutral and balanced in its approach and analysis of the law, is not devoid of persuasion. After all, once you have neutrally analyzed the law, the purpose of your memorandum is—in many ways—to show your reader how you reached your result and, implicitly, to have them agree with your ultimate prediction. This nuanced persuasion is decidedly different than the persuasion at the core of persuasive writing; however, it is disingenuous to suggest objective writing does not have any desire to persuade its reader, given that you want to show the reader your prediction is correct.

A. *Types of objective writing*

Objective writing itself can take a few different forms. The most common type of objective writing, especially in the first year of law school, is a formal objective legal memorandum ("objective memo") drafted for internal office purposes or for clients. An objective memo—regardless of its audience—involves the presentation of a question, a brief answer, and then an often lengthy, detailed analysis explaining how the lawyer-author arrived at his or her answer based on the law and facts at hand.

Law students—you included—are often introduced to objective memos during the first semester of their first year of law school. The reason for this early introduction is that an objective memo is a great mechanism for assessing and then fine-tuning a developing lawyer's ability to write and engage in deep legal analysis. In addition, objective memos are often assigned to summer legal interns and junior lawyers. Accordingly, it is important to have exposure to the form and content of such documents before a potential employer uses that written product to assess your potential as a future employee.

Truth be told, however, objective memos are becoming less common in practice, at least in their formal and lengthy form. Instead, clients and lawyers alike are relying more on abbreviated versions of objective memos to cut client costs and to account for the quicker pace of the practice of law. After all, to draft lengthy analysis necessarily requires a lawyer's time and, thus, requires a client's money. As a result, students and young lawyers will often be asked to draft abbreviated e-mail memos, in lieu of formal objective memos.

In addition to objective memos and e-mail memos, there are other forms of objective writing that students and young lawyers will likely encounter during practice. For example, when serving as a clerk or intern for a court, a student may be asked to draft a bench memorandum ("bench memo"). A bench memo is a form of objective writing drafted by a judicial intern or clerk to advise a judge on how to decide a case (or an issue in a case) by offering an objective review of both sides of the case (or issue). Unlike the briefs that the parties submit to the court in a case—where each party presents its side of the argument (with brief discussion of counterarguments)—a bench memo summarizes and develops both sides' arguments, recognizes the strengths and weaknesses of those arguments, and recommends a course of action. Another common form of objective writing is a client letter. Client letters vary in terms of form based on the content they aim to cover. Some client letters will be longer and contain deeper analysis, while others may be shorter and more conclusory.

Although you will likely encounter all of these types of objective writing in practice, this part of the book will focus on introducing you to the two primary forms of objective writing that most students and summer interns encounter: the objective memo and the e-mail memo.

B. *Understanding and identifying the purpose, audience, length, and tone for objective writing*

Each form of objective writing and, in fact, each assignment itself, regardless of form, will vary in terms of length, audience, tone, and purpose. Some objective memos, for example, are simply requests for legal research, while others require legal research plus an analysis of how that research is likely to apply to a specific scenario or a specific set of facts. In other words, although two assignments may both call for an objective memo, the ultimate product for each assignment may look and sound different depending on what the particular issue or assignment demands.

So how do you determine the form, audience, length, and purpose of whatever objective writing you have been asked to draft? Well—wait for it—**it depends**. You need to take time to understand what you are being asked to do and what product you are being asked to produce. You need to assess who the reader or readers of what you are drafting will be. After all, who your reader is will affect both the content and the tone of your objective writing. Last, you need to assess the expected length of the writing. The length of any piece of objective writing will depend, in part, on who your reader is, but it may also be informed by time and cost constraints.

Although each assignment will vary depending on its specific assigned task, below is a chart that should help you think through issues of purpose, audience, length, and tone for the various types of objective writing.

	FORMAL OBJECTIVE MEMORANDUM	E-MAIL MEMORANDUM	CLIENT LETTER	BENCH MEMORANDUM
PURPOSE	Formal memorandums objectively inform a reader about what the law is and then suggest what the outcome will likely be when the law is applied to a particular set of facts.	E-mail memorandums communicate the crux of legal research or basic legal analysis in a streamlined e-format, which is easily read on a phone, computer screen, or tablet.	A client letter summarizes legal analysis, often originally captured in a formal objective memorandum, in a way that the client can understand and that focuses on the bottom line more than on the process of getting to the bottom line.	Bench memorandums objectively inform the reader what the law is, summarize what the parties' arguments are, and then convey what the outcome should be when the law is applied to the facts of the case.

	FORMAL OBJECTIVE MEMORANDUM	E-MAIL MEMORANDUM	CLIENT LETTER	BENCH MEMORANDUM
AUDIENCE	A supervising lawyer or a client	A supervising lawyer or a client	A client	A judge or judicial clerk
LENGTH	Length depends on issues covered but is typically more than ten pages.	Length is typically one screen, but if longer, the email should be easily readable and digestible in e-format (on a phone, computer screen, or tablet).	Length is limited to a few pages, often single-spaced.	Length depends on issues covered but is typically more than ten pages.
TONE	Tone is professional and formal and presents a deep but balanced view of the law and facts.	Tone remains professional, but often the content and language are streamlined.	Tone is professional but is adjusted if the client is a non-lawyer to explain the law in layperson terms and to clearly communicate the bottom-line recommendation.	The tone of a bench memo is decisive, and it is clear in its assessment of the strengths and weaknesses of each party's case.

II. Objective memos

Objective memos remain—for better or worse—a type of document that all lawyers are expected to be able to draft. As alluded to above, objective memos can vary in terms of content and exact format, depending on the specific assignment given and the audience for whom you are drafting the memo. Despite these potential differences, however, at their core, all objective memos are expected to answer a specific question and are designed to explain the basis for that answer—in terms of law and fact—in a clear and organized fashion. This section of the book will introduce you to the basic format and content of an objective memo. Once you enter practice, you may need to tweak the form, content, and/or style of your objective memo to comply with the particular nuances of your office, your supervisor, or your practice area. This introduction, however, will ensure you have the basic constructs to succeed when tasked with drafting an objective memo in law school or in practice.

A. *Overview of the organization of an objective memo*

Objective memos are rigid in terms of their macro structure and the order in which that macro structure appears in the memo itself. While the particular formatting may vary somewhat from law firm to law firm, practice area to practice area, or classroom to classroom, readers expect to find the basic six sections of an objective memo in, generally speaking, the same predictable order: (1) the heading; (2) the question(s) presented; (3) the brief answer(s); (4) the statement of facts; (5) the discussion; and (6) the overall conclusion. The discussion section of objective memos is the core of the legal analysis of the memo. Each of the six parts of the memo, however, is important and plays a distinct role. The following sections will provide you with guidance regarding how to format and draft each of the six sections of an objective memo. The picture below captures the framework of the six sections of your objective memo.

MEMORANDUM

TO:

FROM:

DATE:

SUBJECT:

QUESTION PRESENTED

BRIEF ANSWER

STATEMENT OF FACTS

DISCUSSION

CONCLUSION

B. *The heading*

The heading provides basic information regarding the subject, the audience, and the author of the objective memo. It allows the author to give the memo's reader macro context regarding what she is about to read. The heading also provides future readers (maybe colleagues in the law firm who are grappling with a similar case) with client and subject matter context for the memo. Importantly, the heading also identifies the date on which a memo was drafted. The date is important because it tells the reader—both current and future—that it sets forth the law as of the date of its drafting, and thus it may not capture changes to the law that occurred after the memo was drafted. Below is an example of what a heading should look like.

MEMORANDUM

TO:	Alex B. Partner
FROM:	Savi Adams
DATE:	October 1, 2018
SUBJECT:	John Bell, Client 0001.555456: Undue Influence

As illustrated by the example, your heading should identify the product as a memo and then contain "To," "From," the "Date" of the memo, and the "Subject" of the memo. The label "Memorandum" should be highlighted using boldface, all-caps, and underlining and should be centered on the page. In addition, the heading should be easy to read, and the tabbing should be evenly spaced.

C. *The question(s) presented*

Nearly every objective memo has the primary purpose of answering a legal question or multiple legal questions for the reader (and then explaining that answer). The question grappled with in an objective memo is written out immediately following the objective memo's heading and is called "Question Presented." Obviously, if there is only one question at issue, there will be only one question presented, whereas if there are multiple questions addressed in the memo, there will be multiple questions presented, and, in that case, the heading will be "Questions Presented."

1. The purpose of question(s) presented

The question presented tells the reader the exact legal problem that will be answered and explained in the objective memo. Moreover, because the question presented appears at the opening of an objective memo, the statement of the question provides a framework for the reader to navigate the rest of the objective memo.

2. The number of question(s) presented needed

This may seem self-evident, but you need the same number of questions presented as the number of macro issues addressed in the objective memo. Typically, this means that you will have one question presented for each cause of action or affirmative defense at issue. Note that you should not draft a question presented for each element of a claim for a couple of reasons. First, if you draft multiple, separate questions presented asking whether each element is satisfied, you never ask (or answer) the real question at issue—whether a party is likely to be successful in establishing the larger cause of action. Second, if—trying to avoid the problem just mentioned—you pose multiple element-based questions each in the context of the larger cause of action, the answer to each question posed will necessarily be no! For example, you necessarily cannot establish undue influence by satisfying just element one (because undue influence requires all three elements).

3. Formulas for drafting question(s) presented

There are lengthy articles and entire book chapters dedicated to different formats to use to draft a question presented. Despite the many options, there are two universally accepted formats for drafting a question presented, and these are the two formats you should master and (at least in your legal writing course) use. The first—and the most traditional—is the under/can-does-is/when approach. The second—and more modern—is the multi-sentence approach. Below you will find a formula for and an example of each format. Regardless of which format you ultimately decide to use, a good question presented will identify the governing law and set forth the legally relevant ("trigger") facts on which the issue will turn.

UNDER/CAN-DOES-IS/WHEN FORMULA

Under	+	Controlling jurisdiction and law governing the question presented	+	**Can/ Does/ Is**	+	Legal question being asked	+	**When**	+	Trigger facts (or the facts that will determine the outcome of your client's case)?

UNDER/CAN-DOES-IS/WHEN EXAMPLE

Under Texas law, **can** Mr. Bell prove that Ms. Bell's Revised Will was a product of the undue influence of Ms. Welsh **when**, after suffering a head injury and after five months of regular contact with Ms. Welsh and her mushroom tea, Ms. Bell used an attorney-friend of Ms. Welsh to change her will to leave the majority of her estate to Ms. Welsh's non-profit rather than to her husband?

MULTI-SENTENCE FORMULA

Sentence stating the general law. + Sentence (or two or three sentences) stating the trigger facts. + Sentence asking about the legal issue?

MULTI-SENTENCE EXAMPLE

Sentence stating the general law.

Under Texas law, a contestant can get a will set aside based on the ultimate beneficiary's undue influence if the prior beneficiary can establish the "existence and exertion of an influence"; the "effective operation" of such influence to "subvert or overpower" the mind of the testator at the time of the execution of the testament; and the execution of a will that the testator[1] would not have executed "but for" such influence. *Rothermel v. Duncan*, 369 S.W.2d 917, 922 (Tex. 1963).

A handful of sentences stating the trigger facts.

Ava Bell executed a will that left the majority of her estate to her husband, John Bell ("Original Will"). After suffering a head injury that left her with mild memory lapses and depression (for which her doctor prescribed her an antidepressant), Ms. Bell met Anna Welsh and became inspired by and involved in Ms. Welsh's non-profit, Happiness of Life ("HOL"). During the next five months, Ms. Welsh and Ms. Bell were in regular contact. Ms. Welsh suggested changes to Ms. Bell's medical and lifestyle practices, and Ms. Welsh advised Ms. Bell that the quickest way for her to achieve her desired happiness and to gain an honorary title through HOL was to financially provide for HOL in her will. After consuming a cup of mushroom tea, Ms. Bell met with Ms. Welsh's attorney-friend and changed her previously executed will to leave the majority of her estate to HOL, rather than to her husband ("Revised Will").

Sentence asking about the legal issue.

Under Texas law, can Mr. Bell prove that Ms. Bell's Revised Will was a product of the undue influence of Ms. Welsh?

4. Top tips for drafting question(s) presented

As you draft your question presented, keep the following tips in mind:

Tip #1: Try to keep your question presented as brief as possible so it is easy for your reader to comprehend.

Tip #2: Phrase your question presented in a way that has a definitive yes or no (or likely yes or likely no) answer.

1. I have used the term testator throughout for simplicity's sake. That said, the term testator is typically used to refer to a male testator, and the term testatrix is typically used to refer to a female testator.

> **Tip #3: In objective writing, your question presented should be neutral rather than conclusory; in other words, the question presented should be a real question rather than a rhetorical one (or one that by design mandates an answer).**

D. The brief answer(s)

The brief answer provides the bottom-line answer to the question presented and a few critical reasons for that conclusion. The brief answer appears near the beginning of the objective memo, and it immediately follows the question presented.

1. The purpose of brief answer(s)

The purpose of the brief answer is to provide the reader with a succinct answer to the question presented without the reader being forced to wade through the entire objective memo. In addition to simply providing an answer up front, the brief answer serves to provide the reader with a framework as he navigates the entirety of the memo.

2. The number of brief answer(s) needed

You need a brief answer for each question presented in your objective memo. In other words, # of questions presented = # of brief answers.

3. Formula for drafting a brief answer

BRIEF ANSWER FORMULA

Pick one of the following answers that indicate the appropriate degree of certainty of your conclusion: 1. Yes. 2. Likely, yes. 3. Likely, no. 4. No.	+	State the answer linked to the question presented.	+	Discuss the presence or absence of any elements/components in the same order they are addressed in the discussion section of the memo.

BRIEF ANSWER EXAMPLE

> Likely, no. Although Mr. Bell can probably establish the first two elements required to set aside a will based on undue influence, he is unlikely to succeed in establishing the third element because of the charitable nature of the bequest. Accordingly, it is unlikely that a court would set aside Ms. Bell's Revised Will based on Ms. Welsh's undue influence.

Notice that in the brief answer you do not need citations. You do not need citations because your brief answer is your summary of what follows in the discussion section of your objective memo. Notice also that the brief answer is—wait for it—brief. You should keep your brief answer to no more than a paragraph in length because the reader will ultimately get the complete explanation in the body of the discussion section of your objective memo.

E. *Statement of facts*

The statement of facts is the section of your memo where you explain the factual foundation for your client's legal question. In other words, this is where you tell the story. A statement of facts should not include legal conclusions or legal argument; instead, it should include only the facts. Therefore, you should not say in your statement of facts "Defendant was recklessly driving" because that is a legal conclusion. Instead, you would show by the facts that the Defendant was reckless. For example, "Defendant was driving 25 miles above the speed limit in a school zone." That is, your statement of facts should show, not tell. The facts in your statement of facts will be used again in your Analysis. In an Analysis of the above example, you would apply the law to the fact provided and conclude that the defendant was recklessly driving.

1. What facts you should include in your statement of facts

The statement of facts should include the facts of the case on which the resolution of the question(s) presented turns. Generally speaking, you should include the following three categories of facts in your statement of facts:

> **Legally Significant Facts (or trigger facts):** These facts are determinative, key, critical, trigger facts; these are facts in your client's case that will affect a court's analysis.
>
> **Background or Procedural Facts:** These are facts that provide **context** for understanding your client's situation, the roles of the people involved in the legal issue, and the current status of the pending question.
>
> **Emotional Facts:** These are facts that are not necessary to resolve the legal issues but that help the reader understand what motivated the parties to act or react in a particular way.

You may find it hard at the beginning to determine which facts are legally significant. You cannot understand this until you have a firm grasp of the law. Typically, the best way to determine legal significance is to review the facts in relation to the elements of the cause of action at issue. For example, if you were to draft a statement of facts for the memo assessing whether Mr. Bell is likely to succeed in getting his wife's Revised Will set aside based on Ms. Welsh's undue influence, you would review the facts that you know and try to discern which known facts are relevant to each element of an undue influence claim. You might begin by creating a chart to help you link the facts to the law and, thus, to help you figure out which facts are legally significant. Below is an example table that sets forth the elements and notes some key facts related to the third element. You can practice identifying legally significant facts by filling in facts relevant to the first two elements of undue influence.

ELEMENT OF UNDUE INFLUENCE	RELEVANT FACT(S)
Existence and exertion of an influence.	
Effective operation of such influence to subvert or overpower the mind of the testator at the time of the execution of the testament.	
The execution of a will that the testator would not have executed "but for" such influence.	Ms. Bell's Original Will provided only for her relatives. Ms. Bell's Revised Will lessened her allotted inheritances to her family members and identified a charity—HOL—as the primary beneficiary of her estate. Ms. Bell has a connection to HOL (she participated in it, and it motivated her to find happiness).

When you have completed the chart, you will then draft the statement of facts (usually in chronological order, not by element) being mindful to include each of the facts identified in your chart.

In addition to the legally significant facts, your objective memo's statement of facts should also include background facts and, possibly, a select number of emotional facts. You should be judicious when including background and emotional facts; in other words, be careful not to include too many emotional or background facts. Including too many will make it harder for your reader to identify those facts that affect the outcome of the case—the legally significant or trigger facts. Emotional facts, in particular, are a powerful tool when you are engaging in persuasive writing (Part Three). They also have an important role in objective writing because the power of certain emotional facts may affect the weight a particular fact is given or how the fact may be viewed later by a judge, jury, client, or opposing party.

Once you have drafted your entire objective memo, you should go back and review your statement of facts. Compare the facts that you used in the discussion section (which will be in the Analysis) and make sure that each of those facts is also included in your statement of facts. In addition, make sure to note the facts that you include in your statement of facts that you do not use in your discussion. Do you need them to provide background or to show your reader potential emotional facts that may come up if the case goes forward? If so, you can leave them. However, if not, you should you omit them from your statement of facts so as not to distract your reader.

2. How to tell a story objectively in your statement of facts

Remember the purpose of the objective memo: to predict the likely outcome of the law's application to the facts of your client's case. You, as the drafter of an objective memo, need to maintain a neutral perspective and to objectively set forth the law and the facts. Maintaining this neutral perspective is often one of the hardest parts of drafting an objective memo, especially for new legal writers. The already mentioned "Law and Order Syndrome" is typically to blame; after all, students have grown up watching lawyers creatively "spin" and frame facts in order to win cases. But you must resist the temptation. You must present the facts on both sides and present them in a neutral way. When you write persuasively (Part Three) you will get to select facts to highlight and facts to diminish in order to advocate and to persuasively frame your case.

In order to ensure your statement of facts is objective in nature, ask yourself the following questions:

> **Question one:** Do you include facts from both sides' perspectives? That is, do you include the facts that are in favor of finding a particular element, cause of action, or defense, as well as those that might cut against finding a particular element, cause of action, or defense?
>
> **Question two:** Do you characterize facts or state them in neutral terms? Often a signal that you are characterizing facts is the use of adverbs or adjectives in your statement of facts. Highlight adjectives and adverbs in your statement of facts and then ask yourself whether they are part of the facts or, instead, your characterization of the facts. Omit them if they are your characterization (or opinion).

3. How to organize your statement of facts

There are a number of ways you can organize your statement of facts. As you grow as a legal writer and as you grapple with more complex problems, you will have flexibility in how you present the story—by the order in which the events took place (in chronological order), by each element of a claim, by each claim, or by each event or actor. How you organize your facts will be dictated by how best to explain what happened in the context of the legal question at issue. That said, for now (and always as a default), you should organize your statement of facts chronologically.

To order your statement of facts chronologically, you will often have to create a timeline on which you record the events and facts collected from various documents, interviews, and e-mails. After all, facts—even in an interview—are often not given to you in perfect chorological order. As a lawyer, one of your main jobs will be to become the master of the facts of your case. Learning how to organize facts from various sources into a timeline or chronology will help you with this task. There are a number of tools available that will help you create a chronology, including Microsoft Office's Timeline, Chronology Marker, or Timeline-Diary and Notes. Below is an example of the beginning of a factual chronology for the events giving rise to Mr. Bell's contest of Ms. Bell's Revised Will.

FEBRUARY 2016	Ava Bell executed her Original Will that left $10,000 to each of her parents, $5,000 to her brother, and the residual of her estate to her husband, Mr. Bell.
AUGUST 2017	Ms. Bell suffered severe head trauma as a result of a car accident. Following the accident, Ms. Bell's doctors reported that she fully recovered, but she continued to suffer from lapses in memory. She returned to her job at a furniture store, but was prescribed medication to treat her lingering depression.
SEPTEMBER 2017	Ms. Bell's brother died, and her doctor increased her antidepressant dosage.
JANUARY 2018	Ms. Bell met Ms. Welsh, who was the head of the non-profit organization HOL.
JANUARY – MARCH 2018	Ms. Welsh was assigned as Ms. Bell's "Happiness Mentor." Ms. Welsh kept in close contact with Ms. Bell, including texting her ten times a day. Ms. Bell began dressing in hemp clothing (rather than her business-professional attire), stopped watching television, stopped wearing makeup, and grew distant from her friends. Ms. Bell stopped taking her prescribed antidepressant and, instead, substituted mushroom tea.

4. Use of headings in your statement of facts

It is often helpful to use headings in your statement of facts to help guide your reader through the events. In persuasive writing, factual headings are an additional opportunity to frame the facts in your client's favor. In objective writing, headings can improve readability and comprehension of your statement of facts, making it easier for your reader to follow the events that are at the center of the question(s) presented. For example, think about the facts related to Mr. Bell's potential will contest. After you order the facts chronologically, can you insert headings to help your reader follow the events? Below are sample headings that you might employ to help break up the statement of facts in Mr. Bell's case and guide your reader from event to event. Note the sample headings are topical in nature but chronologically ordered.

> **Heading one:** Ms. Bell's Original Will left the majority of her estate to her husband, Mr. Bell.
>
> **Heading two:** After executing her Original Will, Ms. Bell suffered head trauma and was treated for depression.
>
> **Heading three:** Ms. Bell met Ms. Welsh and joined HOL.
>
> **Heading four:** After suffering head trauma and joining HOL, Ms. Bell's behavior changed.
>
> **Heading five:** Ms. Bell desired to achieve happiness and promotion within HOL.
>
> **Heading six:** Ms. Bell revised her Original Will.

5. Tips for drafting your statement of facts

When drafting your statement of facts keep the following tips in mind:

- **Tell your reader the story of the case.** A story is easier to follow than a series of facts not woven together for the reader.
- **Use the past tense.** The events you are detailing in your statement of facts already happened. As a result, you should use the past tense.
- **Use role designations, in addition to names.** A role designation identifies the role of the person in the cause of action (not his role in the case procedurally but factually). For example, in the objective memo you are drafting related to Mr. Bell, you should refer to the key actors in terms of their names and their factual roles in the case—Mr. Bell, the contestant; Ms. Bell, the testator; Ms. Welsh, the alleged influencer. Using such role designations will allow your reader to better relate the key players in your case to the players involved in the legal precedent you will rely on in the discussion section of your memo.
- **Provide context.** Begin your statement of facts by providing the context of your client's story and end your statement of facts reminding your reader what your memo will address.
- **Vary your sentence and paragraph length.** Employ both short and long sentences to keep your reader interested. Related to this, make sure to divide your statement of facts into digestible paragraphs—not too long or too short—that are organized topically.

- **Organize your thoughts intentionally and use chronological order.** It is much easier for a reader to follow a story if it is presented in chronological order because this way the readers are used to hearing stories—from beginning to end.
- **Describe trigger facts (the legally relevant facts) with precision and detail.** Trigger facts are the facts on which your case will turn. It is critical that your reader is able to identify and understand these critical facts.
- **CITE after every sentence.** In the "real" world, sometimes you will not need to include citations to the record (factual documents) in your statement of facts (especially where the facts on which you are relying come primarily from interviews of your own client). That said, it is important to get in the habit of citing, and it is critical to master correct and consistent citation form.

F. Discussion

The discussion section of your objective memo is the heart of your memo in terms of substance and length. The discussion section is where you set forth the law in detail, explain the law, and then apply the law to your client's facts to show your reader how you reached your conclusion or predicted outcome.

The discussion section itself can (and usually should) be broken into multiple parts. For example, in the objective memo drafted for Mr. Bell, the discussion section begins with an introduction in the form of an introductory roadmap, and then, the remainder of the discussion is divided into three sections. Each of the three sections sets forth a CRAC for one of the three elements of an undue influence claim. The outline below (extracted from the objective memo drafted for Mr. Bell) shows you how to set up the macro organization of a discussion section of an objective memo.

DISCUSSION

[Introductory Roadmap Goes Here]

I. ELEMENT 1 HEADING GOES HERE.
[CRAC for Element 1 Goes Here]

II. ELEMENT 2 HEADING GOES HERE.
[CRAC for Element 2 Goes Here]

III. ELEMENT 3 HEADING GOES HERE.
[CRAC for Element 3 Goes Here]

1. Introductory roadmap

A discussion section of an objective memo rarely, if ever, covers only a single issue. Instead, although there may be a single question presented, that single question typically requires an analysis of multiple elements or factors to determine the answer. In light of this underlying complexity, your objective memo should begin with an introductory roadmap. This roadmap is exactly what it sounds like: it provides a map outlining the organization of your discussion section. It reminds your reader of the question presented and the answer reached, but more importantly, it provides a very broad overview of the analytical steps required to get from the question presented to the answer. In addition, your introductory roadmap should mention any otherwise relevant elements or defenses that your discussion may not cover so that, in addition to what is forthcoming, your reader also knows what not to expect in the discussion ahead.[2]

a) Purpose of an introductory roadmap

To understand the purpose of an introductory or overall roadmap, remove yourself from the law for a minute. Think about the following two ways in which your mom can give you the same instructions to meet her at Buc-ee's[3] in Terrell, Texas.

> **Alternative 1:** Your mom tells you to leave the law school and meet her at Buc-ee's in Terrell, Texas.
>
> **Alternative 2:** Your mom tells you to leave the law school and meet her at Buc-ee's in Terrell, Texas, by taking the following steps: (1) take I-30 East; (2) stay right onto US-80 E; (3) keep straight on TX-557 E Spur; (4) take ramp right and follow signs for FM-148; (5) turn right onto FM-148; and (6) arrive at Buc-ee's on the right (if you reach Medical Drive you have gone too far).

Which alternative will better help you understand how to get from the law school to Buc-ee's to meet your mom? Obviously, the second alternative is much easier to follow because it tells you how to get there.

An introductory roadmap in an objective memo should do essentially what alternative two in the Buc-ee's scenario above does: it reminds the reader of the issue and the conclusion, and then outlines the exact path that the objective memo will take to get there. After all, readers absorb what they are reading better when they first understand the purpose and organization of what they are reading. Compare two alternative introductory roadmaps for the discussion section of the objective memo for Mr. Bell.

2. At times, an element, claim, or defense may be omitted from a lawyer's analysis by instruction (stated in the assignment itself) or because the parties have stipulated to it.

3. Do not know what Buc-ee's is? It is only THE greatest gas station Texas has to offer.

Alternative 1 (poorly drafted roadmap):

> **DISCUSSION**
>
> Mr. Bell is unlikely to establish that Ms. Welsh unduly influenced Ms. Bell in the execution of her Revised Will. Although Mr. Bell will likely be able to show evidence sufficient to establish the first two elements required to set aside a will based on undue influence, he will likely not be able to establish the third element and, thus, will not be able to set aside Ms. Bell's Revised Will.

Alternative 2 (roadmap that shows analytical process):

> **DISCUSSION**
>
> Mr. Bell is unlikely to establish that Ms. Welsh unduly influenced Ms. Bell in the execution of her Revised Will. In Texas, a court will set aside a will for undue influence when the plaintiff proves three elements: "(1) the existence and exertion of an influence; (2) the effective operation of such influence so as to subvert or overpower the mind of the testator at the time of the execution of the testament; and (3) the execution of a testament which the maker thereof would not have executed but for such influence." *Rothermel*, 369 S.W.2d at 922. Undue influence may be shown by direct or circumstantial evidence. *Id.* Mr. Bell will likely be able to show evidence sufficient to establish the first two elements required to set aside a will based on undue influence; however, he will likely not be able to establish the third element and, thus, will not be able to set aside Ms. Bell's Revised Will.

The first alterative introductory roadmap is not terrible, but it does not help the reader forecast the three elements of undue influence that the memo will set forth and analyze. On the other hand, the second alternative, which details how the reader will get from the issue to the conclusion, provides the reader with a better understanding for how the objective memo will analytically get from the question to its answer by setting forth the three elements in the order they will be discussed and then explaining which elements are and are not satisfied.

b) Formula

Unfortunately, there is no single, precise formula for drafting an introductory roadmap. The reason for this is because the structure of each roadmap will depend, in large part, on the complexity of the issues covered in the objective memo. How many claims does it address? How many elements or factors are required for each claim? Are there any affirmative defenses?

Generally speaking, however, a roadmap usually follows the following formula.

ROADMAP FORMULA

Conclusion on objective memo's cause of action.	+	List of elements or factors and any overarching subrules that apply to all elements.	+	Conclusion on objective memo's cause of action with a brief explanation tying the conclusion to the elements or factors.

c) Mini-roadmaps under subheadings

Now that you understand the purpose of an introductory roadmap—to forecast the basic steps of analysis necessary to get from the memo's question presented to its brief answer—do you think there are other places that you might want to use roadmaps in your discussion? Of course! Generally speaking, any time you have a large section of your memo that is subdivided into multiple smaller sections you will insert a mini-roadmap between the larger section heading and the first subdivision heading. This is called a mini-roadmap, and its purpose is to forecast the steps involved in the analysis of that subdivision.

For example, the first element required to establish undue influence is the existence and exertion of an influence. In order to determine whether a contestant can satisfy this element, a court will consider multiple factors. Thus, when you begin drafting that section, you may decide to do a large section heading for element one followed by multiple subheadings, one for each relevant factor. If you decide to use such a structure, include a mini-roadmap forecasting why the text below is divided into multiple subsections and telling your reader the result of the analysis of the totality of those separate subsections. Below is an example of a mini-roadmap for element one and then the subheadings (text omitted) that would follow. Note, in the example below (and in the sample memo itself), the mini-roadmap and subsequent subdivisions occur after the rule and thus only divide the factor-based analysis of the element.[4]

4. Please note, to save space we have only included the actual headings for each subdivision rather than the heading and the text that follows. In the sample memo (and for any subheadings in your memo), each heading is followed by text.

A. **On balance, the five factors used to analyze the first element of undue influence weigh in favor of finding that Ms. Welsh both wielded and exerted undue influence over Ms. Bell.**

Unlike in *Estate of Steed*, where the evidence established only an opportunity to influence, the evidence in Mr. Bell's case is more like that in *Estate of Johnson*, where there was evidence of a number of the factors employed to assess the first element of undue influence. *Estate of Steed*, 152 S.W.3d at 811; *Estate of Johnson*, 340 S.W.3d at 783. Accordingly, like the contestant in *Estate of Johnson*, Mr. Bell will likely be able to demonstrate circumstantial evidence of enough factors to establish the first element of undue influence.

1. <u>The first factor—the nature and type of relationship between the parties—likely weighs against finding that Ms. Welsh both wielded and exerted undue.</u>

2. <u>The second factor—the opportunity to exert influence—weighs in favor of finding that Ms. Welsh both wielded and exerted undue influence over Ms. Bell.</u>

3. <u>The third factor—the circumstances surrounding the drafting of the will—weighs in favor of finding that Ms. Welsh both wielded and exerted undue influence over Ms. Bell.</u>

4. <u>The fourth factor—fraudulent motive—weighs against finding that Ms. Welsh both wielded and exerted undue influence over Ms. Bell.</u>

5. <u>The fifth factor—habitual subjection—weighs in favor of finding that Ms. Welsh both wielded and exerted undue influence over Ms. Bell.</u>

If you are still struggling to understand when or where you include a mini-roadmap in your discussion, understand that they are not always necessary. That said, if your discussion section includes a heading on top of a subheading with no text in between the two (like Heading II on the next page), it is a good indication that you may need to insert a mini-roadmap between the two headings.

DISCUSSION

[Introductory Roadmap Goes Here]

A. HEADING ONE

B. HEADING TWO

[Mini-Roadmap Goes Here]

1. SUBHEADING ONE

2. SUBHEADING TWO

C. HEADING THREE

2. CRAC: objective writing

After your introductory roadmap, what comes next in your discussion is the substantively hard work of an objective memo: your legal analysis drafted in the form of issue-based CRACs. Remember, your legal analysis should, generally speaking, always take the form of CRAC because this is the organizational structure that lawyers use to frame their arguments. While the CRAC structure is somewhat malleable once you master the basic skills of legal reasoning, during your first year of law school you should employ it religiously. Before you begin drafting the CRACs in your discussion section, you have to figure out how many issues you have to address in your discussion and, thus, how many CRACs you need to draft.

When you are writing your objective memo, you will need the same number of CRACs as the number of issues you have been asked to address. That is, # of issues = # of CRACs. In other words, the number of CRACs will be dictated by the assignment itself and by how many issues the assignment asks you to address. However—and here is the important part—you may need additional CRACs because, as we discussed in Part One, Section VI.A, macro issues often contain elements or factors. If an issue requires the analysis of three separate elements, you then need a CRAC not just for the macro issue, but instead for each element you must address in order to assess the macro issue.

For example, in the e-mail assigning you the work on Mr. Bell's case, Alex B. Partner writes: "Please draft a formal memorandum that I can share with Mr. Bell analyzing whether he is likely to succeed in establishing the three elements required to show undue influence." Based on the assignment, you might think that you need one CRAC for undue influence. However, Mr. Partner has helped you out by forecasting in his e-mail that a claim of undue influence requires that the contestant prove three elements (and, even if he had not told you this, you would have figured it out by yourself when you started your research). Because an undue influence claim requires three elements,

DISCUSSION

[Introductory Roadmap Goes Here]

I. MR. BELL WILL LIKELY ESTABLISH THE EXISTENCE AND EXERTION OF AN UNDUE INFLUENCE OVER MS. BELL.

[CRAC for Element 1 Goes Here]

II. MR. BELL PROBABLY CAN ESTABLISH THAT THE UNDUE INFLUENCE OF MS. WELSH OVERPOWERED MS. BELL'S MIND AT THE TIME SHE EXECUTED HER REVISED WILL.

[CRAC for Element 2 Goes Here]

III. MR. BELL CAN PROBABLY NOT ESTABLISH THAT MS. BELL WOULD NOT HAVE EXECUTED HER REVISED WILL BUT FOR MS. WELSH'S INFLUENCE.

[CRAC for Element 3 Goes Here]

you now know you really have three separate "issues"[5] and you will, thus, need three separate CRACs in the discussion section of your objective memo. Using this information, you now know the basic structure of the discussion section of your memo (that is, the outline of your legal analysis and each issue you need to tackle using the CRAC analytical structure).

In some instances, the number of elements of a claim may not precisely reflect the number of CRACs in your discussion because the assignment instructions may explicitly tell you that there are certain issues that you do not need to analyze. If that is the case, you will adjust the number of CRACs needed accordingly. For example, you could be asked: "Please draft a formal memorandum analyzing whether Mr. Bell is likely to succeed in getting Ms. Bell's Revised Will set aside based on Ms. Welsh's undue influence. At this time, you do not need to discuss the third element required for undue influence." You would, thus, only have two issues (elements) remaining and, therefore, two CRACs.

Once you determine the number of CRACs and what issues are at the core of each CRAC, you then need to begin the hard work: analyzing each issue following the CRAC formula. The sections that follow will walk you through precisely how to do this, starting with "C" (Conclusion), then "R" (Rule), then "A" (Analysis), and then the final "C" (Conclusion).

5. A word of caution: because your discussion section contains three issues and, thus, has three CRACS, it does not mean that you should have three separate questions presented. This seeming disconnect can be confusing for new law students.

a) CRAC: Creating objective opening and closing Conclusion sentences

Every issue in your memo will begin **and** end with a Conclusion—a statement of the conclusion or result of your legal analysis of that issue. Unlike John Grisham novels that build for hundreds of pages to a surprise ending, good legal analysis gives away the ending up front. The reason that all legal analyses begin with the conclusion is that readers absorb more if they understand—in advance—the significance of what they are about to read. Thus, by leading with the conclusion of your analysis, you are helping your reader better comprehend your argument. In addition, by beginning your legal analysis with your Conclusion, you will keep your analysis better organized and focused. Given these benefits, you should begin each separate legal analysis by stating the conclusion for the issue you are addressing and then closing out that issue's legal analysis by restating that same, substantive conclusion.[6]

i. How to write objective Conclusions

Conclusion sentences in your objective memo tell your reader the resolution of the legal issue being addressed. While there are only two Conclusions (two "C"s) in each CRAC, you will have three forms of conclusions for each issue you are addressing because, in addition to your opening and closing conclusion sentences, you will also include a conclusory heading before your CRAC on each issue. Conclusory headings orient the reader (by clearly dividing the larger discussion section into smaller issue-based sections) and, just like opening and closing conclusion sentences, give away the result of the legal analysis to come on that particular issue. Typically, at least one of the three conclusions (often the closing conclusion) will include a key reason or key fact to explain the basis for the conclusion.

In objective writing, conclusion sentences can be qualified. In other words, your conclusion need not be 100 percent certain but, instead, can include some finessing language such as "likely" or "unlikely." For example, in the memo for Mr. Bell, there are conclusion sentences for each element and each conclusion is qualified as opposed to certain. Below is the opening conclusion for element one.

> Mr. Bell will likely be able to prove the first element required to set aside a will based on undue influence.

6. It is important to note that conclusory-based headings do not serve as the "C" or Conclusion required at the beginning of each CRAC. Instead, you will have a conclusion-based heading, and then, following that heading, the first sentence of your text will restate the conclusion of your analysis. For many law students, the repeated conclusions (the heading, the opening Conclusion and the closing Conclusion) seem overly repetitive. However, headings and the text of an argument itself serve entirely different roles. In fact, a reader may only read the headings or, alternatively, may skip the headings altogether and just dig into the text of the argument. Given the different roles of headings and the text, it is helpful for readers to have the conclusion provided in both places. That said, for stylistic purposes, you should vary the length and content of the conclusion-based headings and your opening and closing conclusion sentences so they are not identical in form, as discussed in Part Two, Section II.F.2.a.ii.

Notice how this conclusion forecasts to the reader the result of the lawyer's analysis on the first element. Moreover, rather than the lawyer guaranteeing the result, the lawyer qualifies her conclusion by noting that the result is "likely" rather than certain. Lawyers qualify their answers in objective memos because, at the early stages of a case (typically when objective memos are drafted), a lawyer likely does not have all the facts of the case, and additional facts discovered later may affect the lawyer's conclusion. In other words, using qualified conclusion language gives a lawyer some "wiggle room" to adjust her analysis later if/when she learns new or different information that affects the outcome of a particular issue or the case more generally.

ii. How to vary your different objective Conclusions

In addition to the general struggle law students have adjusting to the substantive redundancy of legal writing (and legal analysis), many law students have difficulty figuring out how to elegantly vary their conclusion sentences to communicate the same substantive conclusion in all the places an experienced reader expects it, while avoiding linguistic redundancy. Generally speaking, there are a few techniques you can use to vary your different conclusion sentences.

> **Technique one:** Conclude once setting forth the details of the issue or element on which you conclude.
>
> **Technique two:** Conclude in a broad, non-specific way (in relation to the named element or issue, omitting the detail).
>
> **Technique three:** Conclude in a way that also explains the primary reason or reasons for the conclusion.

The examples below, based on the objective memo drafted for Mr. Bell, illustrate how to vary conclusion sentences to avoid redundancy.

CONCLUSORY HEADING FOR ELEMENT ONE (TECHNIQUE ONE)

> Mr. Bell will likely establish the existence and exertion of an undue influence over Ms. Bell because the relelvant factors weigh in favor of the first element.

OPENING CONCLUSION FOR ELEMENT ONE (TECHNIQUE TWO)

> Mr. Bell will likely be able to prove the first element required to set aside a will based on undue influence.

CLOSING CONCLUSION FOR ELEMENT ONE (TECHNIQUE THREE)

> Accordingly, the second, third, and fifth factors related to element one weigh in favor of finding the exercise and exertion of an influence, while the first and fourth factors weigh against. Given that the factor analysis requires weighing rather than that "all factors be present," on balance, a court is likely to find that Mr. Bell can establish the first element of his undue influence claim.

You will notice that, as illustrated by the three examples above, by making even slight variations in the drafting of your conclusion sentences, you are able to minimize the redundancy that your reader might otherwise experience, especially when the section or element being addressed is a fairly simple or brief one.

b) CRAC: Creating objective Rules

Your Rule is the second part of your CRAC, and as such, it directly follows the opening Conclusion. Rule statements are the scaffolding of all legal analysis. Without clearly articulated rules, there would be nothing to apply facts to and no standard to use to try to discern or predict a resolution of the legal problem presented. In other words, pay attention because this section of the book is especially important.

Objective rule statements are generally comprised of three parts: the general rule, subrules, and one or more case illustrations. Given the importance of rule statements to the success of your legal analysis, it is critical that you learn to identify and draft all parts of a legal rule. Moreover, it is important while you are still mastering legal analysis that you always include all three parts of a rule (with one exception discussed in the section on case illustrations *infra*) and that you do so in the required order—from the general rule to the subrules to the case illustrations.

Each part of an objective rule plays a unique role. First, the general rule is the part of the rule where you state the law governing the element or claim at issue. Subrules are specific rules that explain the general rule. Second, subrules often define terms from the general rule, identify how courts determine whether the general rule is satisfied (e.g., factors), and/or identify evidence that is needed to satisfy the general rule. Third, case illustrations demonstrate how that general rule (and its subrules) have been applied in prior cases.

These three parts of a legal rule—the general rule, subrules, and case illustrations—work together to explain the law at issue to the reader. Moreover, these three parts of a rule help define the parameters of the legal standard at issue from its broadest application (the general rule) to its narrowest (the case illustration). A well-drafted and complete Rule is central to your reader's understanding of the legal standard at issue and, thus, his ability to follow how you apply the law to the facts to arrive at your predicted outcome.

Let's look at an example of a rule statement that contains all three parts of a Rule to better understand what these parts look like in action. Below is the rule statement for element three from the objective memo for Mr. Bell. The three parts of the rule statement are labeled for you.

General Rule

The third—and final—element of undue influence requires that a plaintiff show that the testator would not have executed her will but for the alleged influence. *Rothermel*, 369 S.W.2d at 922. This element turns on whether the will provided for an unnatural disposition of property. *Estate of Davis*, 920 S.W.2d 463, 467 (Tex. App.—Amarillo 1996, writ denied). In deciding whether a disposition is unnatural, courts look to evidence that a "testator unexpectedly disinherited close family members previously provided for." *Estate of Luthen*, 2014 WL 6632952, at *7. Although an alleged influencer's reasonable explanation for an unnatural disposition is not dispositive, *Estate of Johnson*, 340 S.W.3d at 784, a reasonable explanation as to the otherwise unnatural disposition can result in a court finding no but-for causation, *Estate of Luthen*, 2014 WL 6632952, at *8. Complicating the legal analysis involved in this element, well-settled Texas public policy favors leaving one's estate to charity because such bequests are less susceptible to undue influence given the "selfish reasons" for exerting undue influence are presumed absent for charitable institutions. *Caruthers' Estate*, 151 S.W.2d 946, 948 (Tex. App.—Beaumont 1941, writ dism'd judgm't cor.) ("Our courts have ever been diligent to guard the right of a testator to dispose of his property as he pleases and to uphold bequests made for charitable and religious purposes. Obviously, such bequests are less apt to be the result of undue influence than those made to private individuals who might for selfish reasons be inclined to exert influence upon the testator.").

Subrules: From Broad to Narrow

Absent a reasonable explanation, a disposition that disinherits close relatives and charities previously provided for is evidence of an unnatural disposition and, thus, undue influence. In *Estate of Reno*, the court held that the testator would not have made the dispositions in his revised will, which disinherited family members and charities previously provided for, but for the influence of the alleged influencer. 443 S.W.3d 143, 154 (Tex. App.—Texarkana 2009, no pet.). In that case, the testator executed an original will bequeathing the estate to the testator's children, grandchildren, and multiple non-profits, such as hospitals and churches. *Id.* After execution, one daughter severed all ties with the testator and

Case illustration

Case illustration

> the alleged influencer assisted the testator in preparing a revised version of the will. *Id.* The revised will was "completely different" from the testator's original will because it disinherited certain family members and charities for which the original will had provided. *Id.* The court reasoned that, because there was no reasonable explanation for the revisions to the will and the revisions made were "self-serving" to the alleged influencer, the revised will was unnatural and without a reasonable explanation. *Id.* Accordingly, the court determined that the testator would not have executed the revised will but for the influence of the alleged influencer. *Id.*

With practice, all law students and lawyers alike should be able to master drafting excellent legal rules by following the guidelines provided in this book. The next few sections will walk you through how to draft each of the three parts of an objective Rule.

i. CRAC: general rule, the first part of an objective Rule

The general rule is the first part of your three-part rule statement in objective writing. A general rule is a succinct statement of the law that governs the legal element at issue in the subsection you are drafting. General rules are not hard to identify because they are usually explicitly set forth in a case or a statute.

In addition, general rules are also not terribly hard to draft because, most often, they are the specifically stated elements of a claim. In objective writing, which is neutral in perspective, you should usually draft your general rules using the same language used in the source for the rule. In fact, if you do not mirror the general rule language provided by the source but, instead, paraphrase that general rule language, you risk introducing unintended inaccuracy or persuasive spin into your supposedly neutral statement of the law. You should draft all general rules in the present tense (because the general rule is currently the law) and follow your general rule statement by a citation to the case or statute from which it came.

Let's practice finding and drafting general rules by turning to Mr. Bell's case. In the memo for Mr. Bell, we know that the core issue is whether Mr. Bell is likely to succeed in getting Ms. Bell's will set aside based on Ms. Welsh's "undue" influence. If we look at the seminal Texas Supreme Court case on undue influence, *Rothermel v. Duncan*,[7] what are the general rule(s) for an undue influence claim? See if you can find them in the excerpt below that was copied and pasted directly from *Rothermel*.

> [1, 2] Undue influence in the procurement of a testament is a ground for its avoidance separate and distinct from the ground of testamentary

7. 369 S.W.2d 917 (Tex. 1963).

> incapacity; for while testamentary incapacity implies the want of intelligent mental power, undue influence implies the existence of a testamentary capacity subjected to and controlled by a dominant influence or power. . . . Thus, before a testament may be set aside on the grounds of undue influence the contestant must prove: (1) the existence and exertion of an influence; (2) the effective operation of such influence so as to subvert or overpower the mind of the testator at the time of the execution of the testament; and (3) the execution of a testament which the maker thereof would not have executed but for such influence. . . . .

We know that general rules are the statement of the law that governs the issue and that general rules often take the form of an element or elements of a claim. Here, *Rothermel* identifies three elements required for undue influence.

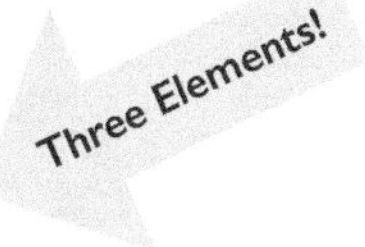

> . . . contestant must prove: (1) the existence and exertion of an influence; (2) the effective operation of such influence so as to subvert or overpower the mind of the testator at the time of the execution of the testament; and (3) the execution of a testament which the maker thereof would not have executed but for such influence. . . .

Because there are three elements, there are three separate general rules (each of the three elements). As previously discussed, because there are three elements of the claim, you will have three separate CRACs (one for each of the three elements). The general rule for the Rule of each CRAC is actually the element you are addressing.

If you look to element three, what is the general rule for element three? The general rule for element three is the element itself. Easy enough, right? See the sample general rule for the third element of undue influence from the memo for Mr. Bell.

> The third—and final—element of undue influence requires that a plaintiff show that the testator would not have executed her will but for the alleged influence. *Rothermel*, 369 S.W.2d at 922.

This general rule, as discussed above, objectively restates the element set forth in *Rothermel* without paraphrasing terms of art such as "executed" and "but for." Instead, the language from the general rule's source—*Rothermel*—is used. In addition, as discussed above, this sample general rule is written in present tense and is followed by a citation to the case from which the general rule was taken—*Rothermel.*

If you step back for a minute and take a look at the macro organization of the discussion section of Mr. Bell's memo, you will notice that the general rule for each of the three elements is written in parallel structure or, in other words, with the same introductory language and using the same basic grammatical structure. By using parallel structure across your various general rules, you can help your reader see the similarities between the different sections (here, each general rule or section is a required element of the claim) and, thus, help your reader follow and relate the different general rules to one another. For your convenience and to help you easily discern this parallelism, you can see the general rule for each of the three sections or elements taken from the objective memo in the table below.

ELEMENT	GENERAL RULE
Element 1	The first element of undue influence requires that a plaintiff prove the existence and exertion of an influence. *Id.*
Element 2	The second element of undue influence requires that a plaintiff prove that the improper influence overpowered the testator's mind at the time of the will's execution. *Rothermel*, 369 S.W.2d at 922.
Element 3	The third—and final—element of undue influence requires that a plaintiff show that the testator would not have executed her will but for the alleged influence. *Rothermel*, 369 S.W.2d at 922.

ii. CRAC: subrules, the second part of an objective Rule

Subrules are the second part of your three-part rule statement in objective writing. Subrules are short excerpts from cases that explain the parameters and meaning of the general rule. Subrules ensure that your reader understands the general rule at issue and how that general rule is (or is not) satisfied. You should draft subrules, like the general rule, in present tense. In addition, just like for general rules, each subrule should be followed by a citation to the legal authority where the subrule was found.

As discussed above, identifying and drafting general rules is not a difficult task. You review the seminal case or a statute and locate the general rule; then, you insert it into your CRAC after your opening Conclusion. But, for your reader, simply reading a general rule does not really help him understand the legal standard at issue. For example, if you step back and read the general rule for undue influence's element three—"the third element of undue influence requires that a plaintiff show that the testator would not have executed her will but for the alleged influence"—do you understand what it means? Do you understand how to figure out whether a particular will "would not have been executed but for" the influence? Not really.

This is where subrules come into play. The main purpose of subrules is to **explain** the general rule. Subrules define terms in the general rule, set forth tests that courts use to determine whether the general rule is satisfied (for example, the factors a court weighs in considering a general rule), and identify what evidence does or does not satisfy the general rule. Subrules are typically woven together using the bridging technique. Bridging occurs when you pull language from the general rule into your subrules and, also, when you build on your subrules by pulling language from one subrule and repeating it in the next subrule. Using this bridging technique improves the flow of your subrules, while simultaneously reducing the need for artificial transition words, such as "next," "then," or "in addition," which can distract your reader. Subrules are also drafted in a particular order—from the most general to the narrowest.

Let's look at the memo for Mr. Bell again to better understand how to draft subrules. Below are the general rule and the subrules for element three from the objective memo for Mr. Bell.

General Rule

The third—and final—element of undue influence requires that a plaintiff show that the testator would not have executed her will but for the alleged influence. *Rothermel*, 369 S.W.2d at 922. This element turns on whether the will provided for an **unnatural** disposition of property. *Estate of Davis*, 920 S.W.2d 463, 467 (Tex. App.—Amarillo 1996, writ denied). In deciding whether a disposition is **unnatural**, courts look to evidence that a "testator unexpectedly disinherited close family members previously provided for." *Estate of Luthen*, 2014 WL 6632952, at *7. Although an alleged influencer's reasonable explanation for an **unnatural** disposition is not dispositive, *Estate of Johnson*, 340 S.W.3d at 784, a reasonable explanation as to the otherwise **unnatural disposition** can result in a court finding no but-for causation, *Estate of Luthen*, 2014 WL 6632952, at *8. Complicating the legal analysis involved in this element, well-settled Texas public policy favors leaving one's estate to **charity** because such bequests are less susceptible to undue influence given the "**selfish** reasons" for exerting undue influence are presumed absent for **charitable** institutions. *Caruthers' Estate*, 151 S.W.2d 946, 948 (Tex. App.—Beaumont 1941, writ dism'd judgm't cor.) ("Our courts have ever been diligent to guard the right of a testator to dispose of his property as he pleases and to uphold bequests made for **charitable** and religious purposes. Obviously, such bequests are less apt to be the result of undue influence than those made to private individuals who might for **selfish** reasons be inclined to exert influence upon the testator.").

Subrules: From Broad to Narrow

This example does a nice job demonstrating the use of bridging. The bold and underlined terms use repetitive language to bridge or transition from one subrule to the next. Similarly, the highlighted terms are repeated from the general rule into the subrules to help create cohesion in the larger rule statement. This example also illustrates the proper way to order subrules—from broad to narrow. The image below is a pictorial illustration of that order.

GENERAL RULE

- **The third—and final—element of undue influences requires that a plaintiff show that the testator would not have executed her will but for the alleged influence.**

SUBRULES

- **This element turns on whether the will provided for an unnatural disposition of property.**
  - **In deciding whether a disposition is unnatural, courts look to evidence that a "testator unexpectedly disinherited close family members previously provided for."**
    - **Although an alleged influencer's reasonable explanation for an unnatural disposition is not dispositive, a reasonable explanation as to the otherwise unnatural disposition can result in a court finding no but-for causation.**
    - **Complicating the legal analysis involved in this element, well-settled Texas public policy favors leaving one's estate to charity because such bequests are less susceptible to undue influence given the "selfish reasons" for exerting undue influence are presumed absent for charitable institutions.**

The general rule is the broadest of the rules in the rule statement. Then, following that broad general rule, is the first subrule, which broadly identifies the factor that courts use to assess the third element. Thereafter, the subrules get narrower—first defining the terms (e.g., unnatural) and then identifying the evidence that satisfies or does not satisfy the terms.

[a] How to find objective subrules

For practicing lawyers, mining cases for subrules is a relatively quick, easy, and—some lawyers would even say—fun task. Finding subrules, however, is difficult for law students. It is difficult because law students—beginning ones especially—do not know where to look or what to look for when trying to find subrules. In terms of what to look for, subrules are, at their core, snippets of law that define or explain the larger rule at issue. In terms of where to look, subrules usually come from statutes or caselaw. In caselaw, subrules typically follow the statement of the general rule. Some cases will have all the general rules and subrules grouped together, while other cases will break each general rule out and follow each general rule with subrules that explain that particular general rule. While some cases are subrule gold mines (meaning they contain subrule after subrule), others may have no relevant subrules.

Let's continue working with the third element of undue influence to practice finding subrules. You should begin your search for subrules by reviewing caselaw that discusses the third element required for undue influence (there may, in fact, be some cases that do not grapple with the third element at all—you can set those cases aside for purposes of finding element three subrules). Based on your prior, careful reading of the general rule for element three, you can probably spot a few terms of art that need defining. "But for," for example, is at the core of the element and is a phrase that jumps out because you probably do not know what it means. Using this term as an example, you will look in the relevant caselaw to find out how courts have interpreted "but for" or, in other words, you will look for subrules to help explain this part of the general rule. As you search, keep in mind that typically an entire case will not address a single element of a claim. So, if you are looking for subrules related to a particular element (here, element three), usually the best place to start looking is in the part of a case that specifically addresses the element or factor at issue.

Below is an excerpt from *Estate of Luthen*.[8] This excerpt is from the part of *Estate of Luthen* that deals with the third element of undue influence. Because this case includes headings in its opinion, it is very easy to determine which part of the opinion addresses which element.

> The last element is "predicated upon" the last factor: "whether the testament executed is unnatural in its terms of disposition of property." *Rothermel*, 369 S.W.2d at 923. Whether the testament unnaturally disposes of property is, to a certain extent, directed by the preceding factors. We consider the testator's stated desires and actions, *see In re Estate of Johnson*, 340 S.W.3d 769, 784 (Tex. App.—San Antonio 2011, pet. denied), and whether the testator unexpectedly disinherited close family members previously provided for, *see In re Estate of Russell*, 311 S.W.3d 528, 535 (Tex.App.—El

8. No. 13-12-00576-CV, 2014 WL 6632952, at *4 (Tex. App.—Corpus Christi–Edinburg Nov. 24, 2014, no pet.) (mem. op.).

> Paso 2009, no pet.). "[I]t is only where all reasonable explanation in affection for the devise is lacking that the trier of facts may" conclude the devise is an "unnatural disposition." *Id.* at 923–24.... The presentation of an explanation does not foreclose competing evidence or explanations, and whether an explanation is reasonable hinges on surrounding facts and credibility. *See In re Estate of Johnson*, 340 S.W.3d at 784. In *In re Estate of Johnson*, the appellants challenged the jury's undue-influence finding using the same contention advanced by Ley. *See id.* at 783. The appellants argued that "the evidence could not support a finding of undue influence because evidence was presented establishing a reasonable explanation for B's disposition of his estate." *Id.... In re Estate of Johnson* recognized the inescapable principle that the mere offering of an explanation is not dispositive of this factor and element. *See id.* at 784.... We hold that when, as here, competing explanations are advanced by the parties, "the jury must determine which explanation should be given more weight and which explanation is more credible." *Id.* This factor and this element weigh in favor of finding a fact issue. *See Nixon*, 690 S.W.2d at 548–49.

What, if any, parts of the excerpt from *Estate of Luthen* help the reader better understand the meaning of the "but for" term we identified above? What parts help the reader better understand any other aspect of the third element required for undue influence? This excerpt has many potential subrules—for example, one that defines but-for as unnatural; one that then defines unnatural; and one that then explains what is not unnatural. It is a goldmine of sorts.

As you read and find potential subrules in cases like this one, you should keep track of those subrules in an organized way (and usually by element). When you have finished reviewing all the relevant caselaw, you may have a handful of subrules that appeared in multiple cases. This repetition is a sign that a particular subrule is likely important to understanding the general rule. In other words, if there are certain repeated subrules, you will likely want to include those as subrules in your Rule. In addition, by keeping track of all subrules, including recording similar subrules that appear across cases, it will position you to select the best (in objective writing the best subrule means the one that is the clearest) version of the subrule to use in your Rule.

The table below is an example of one method you can use to record subrules while you read caselaw. Note that because the citations are not in final form, the subrules captured in the table are in pre-writing format and are not final work product.

Subrules for Element 3

ESTATE OF LUTHEN	ESTATE OF JOHNSON	ESTATE OF DAVIS
In deciding whether a disposition is unnatural, courts look to evidence that a "testator unexpectedly disinherited close family members previously provided for." *Luthen* at *7.		
"[I]t is only where all reasonable explanation in affection for the devise is lacking that the trier of facts may conclude the devise is an unnatural disposition." *Luthen* at * 7 (quoting *In re Estate of Russell*).		
A reasonable explanation as to the otherwise unnatural disposition can result in a court finding no but-for causation. *Luthen* at *8.		

Many of the key subrules related to element three are filled in from *Estate of Luthen*. For practice, you should review *Estate of Johnson*[9] and *Estate of Davis*.[10] Based on your review, you should then identify and record any additional subrules from those cases that help explain further the third element of undue influence.

[b] How many subrules do you need to find?

Law students always ask how many subrules they need for each element. Unfortunately, there is no universal number. Instead, the number of subrules needed will depend on the complexity of the general rule that the subrules aim to explain and on how much legal precedent there is interpreting that particular general rule. Generally speaking, if you have fewer than three subrules, you should critically reflect on whether the subrules you rely on are truly sufficient to explain the general rule to your reader. On the other hand, if you have, say, ten subrules, you should reflect on whether each subrule adds to your reader's understanding of the general rule or whether some of the subrules are redundant or should be modified and converted to case illustrations.

iii. CRAC: case illustrations, the third part of an objective Rule

Case illustrations are the third and final part of your three-part rule statement. Case illustrations provide examples of the general rule and subrules "in action." People

9. 340 S.W.3d 769 (Tex. App.—San Antonio 2011, pet. denied).
10. 920 S.W.2d 463 (Tex. App.—Amarillo 1996, writ denied).

learn by example, and that is what case illustrations do—they provide specific examples of the application of the rule at issue to a set of past facts and the result that followed.

For purposes of understanding case illustrations, let's look back at the memo for Mr. Bell and, in particular, at the second element of undue influence, which turns on whether the improper influence overpowered the testator's mind at the time of the will's execution. The general rule and an abbreviated version of the subrules for this element are below.

> The second element of undue influence requires that a plaintiff prove that the improper influence overpowered the testator's mind at the time of the will's execution. *Rothermel*, 369 S.W.2d at 922. To establish the second element, courts look at four factors: (1) "the state of the testator's mind at the time of the execution"; (2) "the testator's mental or physical incapacity to resist or the susceptibility of the testator's mind to the type and extent of the influence exerted"; (3) "the words and acts of the testator"; and (4) the "weakness of the mind and body" of the testator. Id. at 923. Susceptibility to influence alone is insufficient to establish this element; instead, evidence must demonstrate that "efforts actually overwhelmed [the testator's] free agency" or, put another way, "overpowered [the testator's] ability to decide for [her]self." *Matter of Kam*, 484 S.W.3d 642, 653 (Tex. App.—El Paso 2016, pet. denied); *Mackie v. McKenzie*, 900 S.W.2d 445, 449 (Tex. App.—Texarkana 1995, writ denied) (quoting *Rothermel*, 369 S.W.2d at 922) ("Not every influence exerted on a person is undue. It is not undue unless the free agency of the testator was destroyed and the will produced expresses the wishes of the one exerting the influence."). To demonstrate that the testator's mind was, in fact, overpowered or subverted, courts look at the "testator's mental or physical incapacity to resist or the susceptibility of the testator's mind to the type and extent of the influence exerted." *Rothermel*, 369 S.W.2d at 923.

You may think after reading this rule and subrule: "That's all well and good, but give me an example. Give me an example of a case where the court held conduct met that standard or an example of a case where the court held conduct did not meet that standard."

In response to this need for more precision in your explanation of the rule, you may decide to illustrate a case to establish what sort of evidence or conduct in precedent (past) cases has been held to be sufficient to establish the "overpowering" required by the second element of undue influence. After all, this is the role of case illustrations—they provide the reader with examples of the rule being applied to a factual scenario and the result of that application.

In some instances, however, one case illustration alone may still not be "enough" for your reader to understand the Rule. This happens most often when the rule requires the assessment of the parameters of behavior. In such a scenario, you may decide to use two case illustrations to show the reader an example of the type of evidence that has been held to satisfy and not satisfy the rule (that is, to establish "parameters of behavior"). For example, for "overpowering" a testator's mind, you may decide to illustrate two cases: one on each end of the spectrum, i.e., one where the court held that the testator's mind was overpowered (element two was satisfied) and one where the court held that the testator's mind was not overpowered (element two was not satisfied).

By having a case illustration from each end of the spectrum (standard met vs. standard not met), later in your Analysis (CRAC), you will be able to compare or contrast your client's facts to the facts of the illustrated cases to objectively predict where your client's facts fall on the spectrum. Using two case illustrations—where such caselaw is available—is especially important in objective writing.

As a matter of qualification, now that you understand how helpful case illustrations can be, it is important to note that case illustrations are not always needed. Sometimes, the rule and subrules are so straightforward that no one would ask: "Can you give me an example of that?" In these situations, a case illustration is not necessary.

For example, let's say the issue is who can recover damages under the bystander doctrine. Below is the general rule (first sentence) and subrule (second sentence) you would find for the third element of the bystander doctrine.

> Under the third element of the bystander doctrine, the bystander must show that they are "closely related" to the victim of the accident in order to recover damages. *Freeman v. City of Pasadena*, 744 S.W.2d 923, 924 (Tex. 1988). A bystander is "closely related" if the bystander is one of the "parents, siblings, children, [or] grandparents of the victim." *Garcia v. San Antonio Housing Auth.*, 859 S.W.2d 78, 81 (Tex. App.—San Antonio 1993, no writ).

Do you need a case illustration to help you determine if someone is "closely related" to the victim, such that she can recover damages? No, it is straightforward! You do not need an example to explain the rule. When this is the case, Rule = general rule + subrules. In other words, when this is the case your Rule will only have two, instead of three, parts.

Having provided this qualification, it is worth repeating that, generally, in objective writing you will use a case illustration. In fact, generally, in objective writing you should use two case illustrations per issue or element—one that holds the element is satisfied and one that holds the opposite.

[a] Parts of a case illustration

Each case illustration has four parts: (1) a topic sentence; (2) the holding of the case on the element or issue for which you are illustrating it; (3) the trigger facts related to the element or issue for which you are illustrating the case; and (4) the court's reasoning or how the court applied the facts to the law to reach its holding. That is, case illustration = topic sentence + holding + trigger facts + reasoning. Case illustrations should be drafted in past tense,[11] and every sentence of your case illustration (except for your topic sentence) should be followed by a citation to the illustrated case.

Let's work through *Estate of Steed* to draft each of the four parts of a case illustration related to the second element of undue influence.

Part one: Topic sentence stating the reason you are illustrating the case.

The first sentence of your case illustration is the topic sentence of the paragraph. This topic sentence highlights the importance of the illustrated case for the reader. Many students find it easier to draft these topic sentences after they back up and ask themselves the following questions: "Why am I illustrating this case" and "What principle do I want my reader to take away from this case illustration?" Many find it easier to leave a place holder for the topic sentence and to fill in the topic sentence after completing the entire case illustration. This is because the topic sentence is one that summarizes the key reason you included the case in your Rule.

> Evidence that a testator suffers from depression is insufficient to satisfy the second element of undue influence as long as the testator is able to conduct her affairs and is physically capable.

Part two: The holding of the illustrated case on the issue for which you are illustrating it.

In the second sentence of your case illustration, you will state the court's holding with respect to the specific element at issue (as opposed to the holding of the court with respect to the entire cause of action).

> In *Estate of Steed*, the court overturned the jury's finding that the testator's mind was overpowered and, accordingly, the jury's finding of undue influence. 152 S.W.3d at 811.

---

11. Case illustrations are drafted in past tense because the cases you are illustrating were decided in the past (i.e., are past examples of the law being applied).

Part three: The trigger facts related to the issue for which you are illustrating the case.

After stating the specific holding of the case, next you will set forth the facts underlying the court's holding. These facts are called the trigger facts—they are the facts that were essential to the court's holding with respect to the element at issue.

> In that case, although the testator suffered from depression and anxiety and was taking Prozac, he was able to conduct his business affairs (for example, he worked as an attorney) and was a physically able person. *Id.*

Part four: The court's reasoning or how it got from the trigger facts to its holding on the issue for which you are illustrating the case.

Finally, after you state the trigger facts, you will set forth the court's reasoning. The court's reasoning consists of how/why the court reached its holding based on the trigger facts before it. What was the court's reasoning in holding that the defendant's conduct you just described met the standard? The reasoning is what connects the trigger facts to the holding—it shows why the court reached the result it did.

> The court reasoned that it was "clearly wrong and unjust" for the jury to find that the wife overpowered the testator's mind because the testator was "a meticulous, detail[ed] person" who "worked regularly to the date of his death" and was "not physically or mentally impaired from performing his daily tasks." *Id.*

As you advance in your legal writing career, you will see that there are other effective ways to illustrate cases. However, a strong case illustration will always include a topic sentence, the holding, the trigger facts, and the court's reasoning. Therefore, as a legal writing beginner, employing the case illustration formula (set forth below) is a failsafe way to make sure your case illustrations are strong and complete.

[b] Formula for case illustrations

<u>CASE ILLUSTRATION FORMULA</u>

Topic Sentence	+	<u>In</u> [insert case name], <u>the court held</u> [insert conclusion for element or issue you are illustrating the case for]	+	<u>In that case</u>, [insert trigger facts from case related to element or issue you are illustrating the case for]	+	<u>The court reasoned that</u> [insert court's reasoning for issue or element you are illustrating the case for]

[c] Pulling it together

Turning back to Mr. Bell's case, the objective memo's Rule for the second element of undue influence contains two case illustrations. These two illustrations not only provide the reader with examples of how courts have applied the legal standard in the past, but as discussed above, their polarity defines the parameters of the legal standard—in one illustration the court held that the testator's mind was overpowered and in the other the court held there was insufficient evidence to establish that the testator's mind was overpowered.

Evidence that a testator suffers from depression is insufficient to satisfy the second element of undue influence as long as the testator is able to conduct her affairs and is physically capable. In *Estate of Steed*, the court overturned the jury's finding that the testator's mind was overpowered and, accordingly, the jury's finding of undue influence. 152 S.W.3d at 811. In that case, although the testator suffered from depression and anxiety and was taking Prozac, he was able to conduct his business affairs (for example, he worked as an attorney) and was a physically able person. *Id.* The court reasoned that it was "clearly wrong and unjust" for the jury to find that the wife overpowered the testator's mind because the testator was "a meticulous, detail[ed] person" who "worked regularly to the date of his death" and was "not physically or mentally impaired from performing his daily tasks." *Id.*

Evidence that a testator was using drugs or alcohol around the time of the will's execution is sufficient to prove that the testator was susceptible to an undue influence overpowering her mind. In *Estate of Johnson*, the court held the testator's alcohol abuse coupled with his memory dysfunction made him increasingly susceptible to undue influence such that the second element of the *Rothermel* test was satisfied. 340 S.W.3d at 778. In that case, the testator was an alcoholic and had an ongoing drinking problem. *Id.* In addition to the alcohol use, there was also evidence that the testator suffered memory dysfunction. *Id.* The court reasoned that drinking had an adverse effect on his reasoning and left him less capable of resisting the undue influence brought on by the beneficiary to change his will. *Id.* Furthermore, the court reasoned that due to the testator's alcohol abuse and the effect it had on his mental capacity to resist, the testator was susceptible to undue influence and that ample opportunity existed for the beneficiary to unduly influence the testator while he was drinking. *Id.*

By having this complete picture (an understanding of when a court has held the second element is satisfied and when the court has held the second element is not satisfied), the reader is best positioned to understand the parameters of the rule at issue. In addition, with this lay of the land, the reader is ready to understand the Analysis (CRAC) that will follow the Rule.

c) CRAC: Drafting objective Analysis

The "A" of CRAC or the Analysis is arguably the most important part of CRAC because it is where the law meets your client's facts. After you have set forth the basic rule (the general rule) and explained that rule (subrules and case illustrations), you will apply the law to the facts of your case in the Analysis. That is, you take the Rule and apply it to the facts of your client's case to support your predicted outcome—the Conclusion—on the issue.

Remember in math class when your teacher told you that you must "show your work"? Your middle school math teacher made clear that it was not sufficient to simply say 712 divided by 8 = 89. Instead, you had to show your teacher how you got from the problem to the answer. You did this by showing your teacher your long division in a step-by-step manner rather than by just showing your teacher the answer.

```
      89
8 | 712
    -64
      7↓
     72
```

Think of the Analysis section of your CRAC as the place in your legal analysis where you "show your work." In your Analysis, you are showing your reader your work for the following equation: Rule + client's facts = your conclusion on the issue.

In the Analysis section, you should not add any new legal authority for the issue. Instead, all legal authority for the issue should be in your Rule. In the Analysis section, you should also not add any new facts. Instead, all facts for the issue should be in your statement of facts. When you think about it, as you write your Analysis, it is really just a mixing and matching of what is already in your Rule (legal authority for the issue) with what is already in your statement of facts (facts for the issue). If you have a well-written, complete Rule and a well-written, complete statement of facts, then the Analysis should be the easiest part of your memo to write.

In practice, however, students struggle with the Analysis. The main reason for this struggle ties back to a fear of redundancy. Law students mistakenly think that because they have already drafted the rule in the Rule section (and the reader has read it) and set forth the facts in the statement of facts (and the reader has read it) they can just tie them together with a conclusion or conclusory analysis—facts + Rule = Conclusion (voila!). This is wrong. You **must** show your reader how to take the facts and apply them to the rule. The reader is not in your head. Thus, to show your reader how you got to your Conclusion, you must show them, step by step. Failing to do so leaves the reader to do the work and risks that the reader does not apply the right (or the most significant) facts to the rule and, thus, does not, in the end, understand or agree with your predicted conclusion.

In order to show your work in your Analysis, make sure your Analysis section has two parts:

Part one: You will start your Analysis section of CRAC with a sentence predicting what happens when the Rule is applied to the facts.

Part two: Then, you will prove the prediction (part one) through either pure rule-based reasoning (if it is a straightforward application) or a combination of analogical reasoning and rule-language bridging (if it is not a straightforward application).

i. Part one of an objective Analysis

As described below, in your Analysis, you will use either rule-based reasoning or analogical reasoning with rule-language bridging. Regardless of which you use, you will start your Analysis in the same way. The first sentence of your Analysis will predict what happens when you compare the facts of your case to the Rule. This first part can be described as a topic sentence or mini-conclusion. Indeed, because it serves as a topic sentence/mini-conclusion, it is the only sentence in your Analysis that will not need a citation.

(ex. 1) Here, a court will likely hold that the Defendant's conduct was "extreme and outrageous."

(ex. 2) Mr. Bell's case is distinct from *Estate of Reno* and akin to *Cook*; accordingly, a court is likely to follow *Cook* and find that Mr. Bell cannot satisfy the third element.

Next, in part two, you will prove your prediction in part one.

ii. Part two of an objective Analysis

After you state your prediction as to what happens when you compare your facts to the Rule (part one), you will prove why that result occurs by using either (1) pure rule-based reasoning; or (2) analogical reasoning and rule-language bridging.

A note about citations: in part two of your Analysis, you will be discussing both the law and the facts of your client's case. Therefore, after each sentence in part two of your

Analysis, you will need a citation. Depending on the subject of the sentence, that citation may be to the law, record, or both.

[a] Pure rule-based reasoning

Rule-based reasoning is used when the application of the rule to your facts is straightforward. You use rule-based reasoning in your Analysis when your Rule is so straightforward that you did not need an example (case illustration). That is, if you did not include a case illustration in your Rule, you will use pure rule-based reasoning in your Analysis because there will be no example case with which you can compare and/or contrast.

RULE

> Under the third element of the bystander doctrine, the bystander must ← **General Rule** show that they are "closely related" to the victim of the accident in order to recover damages. *Freeman v. City of Pasadena*, 744 S.W.2d 923, 924 (Tex.1988). A bystander is "closely related" if the bystander is one of the "parents, siblings, children, [or] grandparents of the victim." *Garcia v. San* ← **Subrule** *Antonio Housing Auth.*, 859 S.W.2d 78, 81 (Tex. App.—San Antonio 1993, no writ).

You conduct rule-based reasoning by tying language from the rule to your facts to predict an outcome. Using the bystander doctrine example from earlier, let's say that the facts of your case were that the victim of an accident was Martha and the bystander who witnessed the accident was Paula, Martha's daughter. Your Analysis using rule-based reasoning might look like the example below.

ANALYSIS

> Paula will satisfy the third element of the bystander doctrine. Because ← **Analysis Part 1** Paula is Martha's daughter, she is "closely related" to the victim Martha ← **Analysis Part 2** and, as such, can recover damages. *Freeman*, 744 S.W.2d at 924; *Garcia*, 859 S.W.2d at 81; Mem. from A. Partner to File (Nov. 30, 2019).

You see that the Analysis using rule-based reasoning is straightforward. Here, the facts of our client's case are that Paula, the bystander, is the victim's, Martha's, daughter. Applying the law in the Rule (a bystander is closely related if they are a child of the victim) to the facts of this case (Paula, the bystander, is a child of the victim, Martha), is a straightforward application.

Here is another example using a statute. In many states, an establishment, like a bar or restaurant, that sells alcohol can be liable under the state's Dram Shop Act if the establishment's employees over-serve a patron and that patron's intoxication causes a plaintiff's injury. An affirmative defense to an establishment's liability is called the "safe harbor" provision. In Texas, for example, the statute provides that an employee's actions that violate the Dram Shop Act are not attributable to the employer-establishment if (1) the employer-establishment required its employees to attend a Texas Alcohol and Beverage Commission ("TABC")-approved "seller training program"; (2) the employee actually attended the program; and (3) the employer did not directly or indirectly encourage the employee to violate the Dram Shop Act.[12]

The first two elements of the affirmative defense are straightforward. The employer-establishment either did or did not require employees to attend TABC-approved training, and the employees either did or did not attend. Thus, the Rule for each of these elements will be straightforward. There is nothing really to explain and, thus, a case illustration is not needed. Therefore, the application of the Rule to the facts in the Analysis will also be straightforward and will use rule-based reasoning.

Let's say that the evidence showed that the establishment, Chip-Home Bar & Grill, as a condition of employment, required its employees to attend TABC-training, and the evidence showed current training certifications for all employees. Below is what the Rules and Analysis (rule-based) may look like for the first two elements.

Rule → The first element of the safe harbor provision is satisfied when the employer-establishment "requires its employees to attend a commission-
Analysis Part 1 → approved training program." Tex. Alco. Bev. Code Ann. § 106.14(a)(1). Here, Chip-Home satisfies the first element. Chip-Home's training
Analysis Part 2 → manual contains a section that requires all employees to attend TABC-training as a condition of employment. Mem. from A. Partner to File (Nov. 30, 2019).

Rule → The second element of the safe harbor provision is satisfied when it is shown that "the employee has actually attended such a training pro-
Analysis Part 1 → gram." Tex. Alco. Bev. Code Ann. § 106.14(a)(2). Here, Chip-Home satisfies the second element. Chip-Home has evidence of training certifi-
Analysis Part 2 → cates that show all employees had attended TABC-training and had a current TABC certification. Mem. from A. Partner to File (Nov. 30, 2019).

You see that rule-based reasoning is a simple, straightforward application of the Rule to the facts of the client's case.

[b] Analogical reasoning + rule-language bridging

Most often, however, the rules and the application of your client's facts to them are not so straightforward. Therefore, pure rule-based reasoning is insufficient. Instead, you will need to use a combination of analogical reasoning and, what we will call, rule-language bridging.

---

12. Tex. Alco. Bev. Code Ann. § 106.14(a).

When the Rule is not straightforward, in order to fully explain the law in the Rule, you must include case illustrations to provide the reader with examples of when the Rule was satisfied and was not satisfied. If you included case illustrations in your Rule, you will need to conduct analogical reasoning in your Analysis. Analogical reasoning means reasoning by analogy. You will use analogical reasoning to compare the facts of your case to the precedent cases that you have illustrated. You will show that your case is either like the precedent case such that your case requires the same result or that your case is unlike the precedent case such that your case requires a different result. When applying analogical reasoning, you should compare discrete facts from the case you illustrated to the corresponding discrete facts in your case. When you use analogical reasoning in your Analysis, you are conducting fact-to-fact comparisons to show that the facts of your case are either like or unlike the facts of the precedent case.

Just because you included case illustrations in your Rule and are doing analogical reasoning in your Analysis to compare and contrast your facts to those cases, it does not mean that you get to simply ignore the general rules and subrules from your Rule in your Analysis. You will still apply the general rule and subrules to your facts; however, that application is less straightforward than pure rule-based reasoning. Instead, you will "bridge" the language from the rules and subrules to your facts in your Analysis. This rule-language bridging is used in combination with analogical reasoning to comprise your Analysis.

Let's first start with a non-legal example to understand how analogical reasoning works.

JAKE'S EXPERIENCE

> Jake is a college student. He is taking English Literature 101 with Professor Plum. In Professor Plum's syllabus, he includes a provision that provides: "Late assignments will not be accepted unless there are extraordinary circumstances. Extraordinary circumstances include circumstances that were unforeseeable and that could not with proper planning have been avoided."
>
> Jake had a paper due on May 15 by 8 a.m. He was supposed to submit a hard copy of the paper to Professor Plum's office by that time. He left his apartment at 7 a.m. on May 15 to drive to the college, which was only 20 minutes away. On his way, Jake got a flat tire after hitting a nail. He stopped to change the tire as fast as he could and immediately went to the college. He did not arrive to the college until 8:30 a.m., and as a result, the paper he submitted was late.
>
> Jake is wondering whether his late paper will be accepted. He hires you to do some research and predict an outcome for him.

The first thing you do is look at the syllabus and find the written rule in the syllabus governing late submissions of assignments in Professor Plum's class. The "rule" provides:

"Late assignments will not be accepted unless there are extraordinary circumstances. Extraordinary circumstances include circumstances that were unforeseeable and that could not with proper planning have been avoided."

From the rule language alone, can you predict whether Jake's late paper will be accepted? Not really. The rule is not very straightforward. What would be helpful, you think, are examples of when Professor Plum applied the rule either to accept or to reject submissions of other students. It would also be helpful, you think, to figure out for these past examples what the circumstances were that caused the student's paper to be late, what decision Professor Plum made with respect to the late paper, and what reasoning he applied to make his decision. That is, to further explain the rule, you need past examples of when the rule was met and was not met. You need case illustrations!

You walk around campus and find two students who had similar experiences regarding late assignments and Professor Plum.

SARA'S EXPERIENCE

Sara tells you that she had a paper due for Professor Plum and submitted it 23 hours late. Sara tells you that she left her house at 7:30 a.m. to submit the paper by 8 a.m. because the college is only 15 minutes away from her house. While she was driving to the college to submit the paper, her car was hit by a student on a bicycle. While Sara was uninjured, the student on the bicycle was severely injured. Sara had to wait with him until the ambulance arrived and then rode in the ambulance with him to the hospital. When she got to the hospital, the (very scared) student asked Sara to stay with him until his parents arrived because he had no friends. His parents did not arrive until 10 p.m. When Sara left the hospital, the building housing Professor Plum's office was locked. She turned in the paper the next morning at 7 a.m. as soon as the building was open. Professor Plum accepted the paper because he said that (1) being hit in a car by a bicycle is not something that happens normally or could have been easily avoided; and (2) Sara was not at fault. Professor Plum said it was important to his decision that Sara acted as a Good Samaritan by staying at the hospital with the injured student and that Sara was diligent in submitting the paper as soon as the building opened the next day.

MOLLY'S EXPERIENCE

Molly tells you that she had paper due for Professor Plum and left her house to submit it an hour before it was due (even though the college was only five minutes away). A police officer stopped Molly on her way to submit the paper. Molly said she had never in her life received a ticket and was only going four miles over the speed limit. The police officer eventually let Molly go with a warning. But the stop caused Molly to not arrive at the college to submit her paper until 8:05 a.m.—five minutes after it was due. Professor Plum did not accept the paper because he said that (1) it is foreseeable that one will get a ticket if driving too fast; and (2) Molly was at fault and proper planning (in the form of not speeding) could have avoided the situation and resulting late paper.

These "case illustrations" give you more insight into the meaning of the rule and into when Professor Plum (the authority) has held the rule to have been satisfied and not satisfied. Now that you have a full explanation of the rule, you need to apply it to Jake's facts to predict an outcome.

To do so, you should use analogical reasoning to predict whether Jake's case is more like Sara's, where the late paper was accepted, or more like Molly's, where the late paper was rejected. That is, where does Jake fall on the Molly/Sara spectrum?

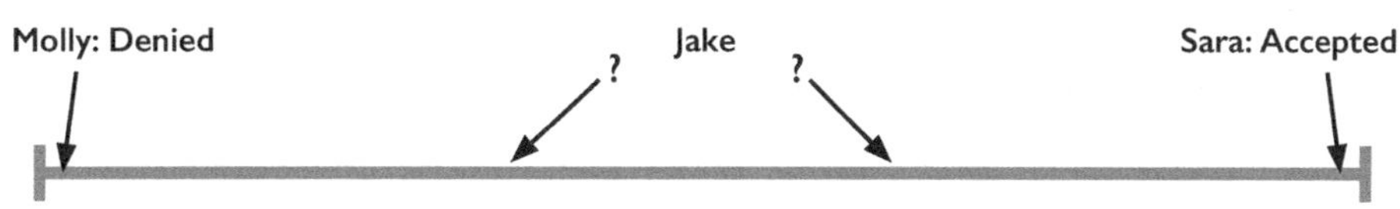

Analogical reasoning is an unnecessarily fancy word for comparing and contrasting. We must compare the facts of Jake's case to the facts of Molly's case and to the facts of Sara's case to predict whether Professor Plum will find that Jake's late submission was caused by extraordinary circumstances, like Sara's, or not, like Molly's. We must take similar facts from Jake's experience and put them side by side with similar facts from Sara's experience and Molly's experience to reach our prediction.

So, what's your prediction? Will Professor Plum likely accept Jake's late paper like he did Sara's late paper? Or, will Professor Plum likely reject Jake's late paper like he did Molly's late paper? Where did you put the facts of Jake's case on the Molly–Sara spectrum?

Let's say you predict that Professor Plum will accept the late assignment. While Jake's facts are not as strong as Sara's, you conclude Jake's facts are more like Sara's facts than Molly's facts.

Part one of your Analysis would be: "While Jake's case is not as strong as Sara's case, it is likely that Professor Plum will accept Jake's late assignment." Then, you would need to show your work in part two through analogical reasoning and rule-language bridging. Specifically, you need to tie Jake's facts to the rule in the syllabus and compare and contrast Jake's facts with Sara's and Molly's. You must show how you reached your prediction, why you reached your prediction, and what your thought process was.

> **Not showing your work.** Similar to Sara's case, Jake's flat tire was unforeseeable. Unlike Molly's case and like Sara's case, Jake was not at fault for his flat tire. Like Sara, he could not have prevented his flat tire.
>
> **Showing your work.** Like Sara, who was in a car accident that was not caused by her own fault, Jake had a flat tire, which Professor Plum will likely find is not caused by his own fault. Similar to being hit by a bike, running over a nail is not something that can be avoided. However, unlike being hit by a bicycle, it is far more common to get a flat tire. While getting a flat tire is likely more foreseeable than being hit by a bike, it is likely that Professor Plum will still find that getting a flat tire is unforeseeable because there is nothing Jake could have done to avoid it. Unlike Molly, whom Professor Plum found could have avoided getting pulled over by not speeding, Jake could not have avoided getting a flat tire. What makes Jake's case weaker than Sara's is that, unlike Sara, whom Professor Plum found acted like a Good Samaritan, Jake did not do anything to help another person. However, like Sara who submitted her late paper as soon as feasible, Jake submitted his late paper as soon as he could. Jake's paper, which was submitted 30 minutes late, was closer to being submitted on time than Sara's paper, which was submitted 23 hours late.

You see how the two examples differ. In the first example, you do not show your thought process. You do not show the reader step by step how you got to your prediction. It is much like not showing your work in math class. In the second example, you show the reader how and why you got to your prediction. You are comparing and contrasting fact to fact with the examples (precedents) and you are connecting your facts with the rule language through rule-language bridging (foreseeable, unforeseeable, could have avoided, etc.)

[c] Analogical reasoning formula

If you are using analogical reasoning in your Analysis, you will have had one or more case illustrations in the Rule of your CRAC. You must compare and contrast the facts of your case to the precedent cases you illustrated. If you have cases on both ends of the spectrum—one where the element at issue is met and one where the element at issue is not met—you must show the reader where your case falls on the spectrum between the two precedent cases.

For example, in the objective memo, the writer illustrates two cases for the second element of undue influence in the Rule: *Estate of Steed*, where the court held the second element was not satisfied, and *Estate of Johnson*, where the court held the second element was satisfied. In the Analysis, you start with part one, which is your prediction as to whether a court will find the facts of your client's case more like *Estate of Steed* or more like *Estate of Johnson*.

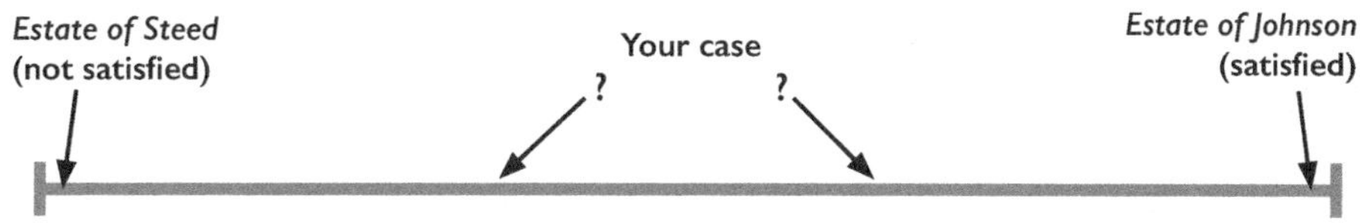

Then you must prove part one through the analogical reasoning set forth in part two. To do analogical reasoning, you must do two things. First, you must take a trigger fact from your case and put it next to a similar trigger fact from a precedent case and compare or contrast the two facts. You should repeat this for each trigger fact or set of trigger facts. That is, you must do a fact-to-fact comparison and/or contrast with both your illustrated cases. Second, as you do your fact-to-fact comparison and/or contrast, you must tell the reader why that comparison or contrast matters. That is, you must bring it full circle for the reader. Why should the reader care that your facts are similar to or different from a precedent case? What does that mean? Why and how is that significant?

To help you engage in fact-to-fact comparisons and contrasts, you can use and repeat the following "formula" sentences.

> **To compare:** Like [precedent case], where [trigger fact from precedent case], here [similar trigger fact from your case].
>
> **To contrast:** Unlike [precedent case], where [trigger fact from precedent case], here [different trigger fact from your case].

By using this formula, it will force you to show your work and to use a parallel structure. Take a look at the example below from the objective memo for Mr. Bell.

> Like the testator in *Estate of Johnson*, who abused alcohol, Ms. Bell was under the influence of mushroom tea provided to her by Ms. Welsh during the execution of her Revised Will.

You will see that the sentence takes a discrete trigger fact from the illustrated case *Estate of Johnson* in the Rule (abused alcohol) and compares it to a similar discrete trigger fact from your client's case (drank mushroom tea).

To do fact-to-fact comparisons and contrasts, you need not strictly adhere to the formula. It is okay to deviate from the exact words of the formula as long as you are comparing and contrasting between your case and the precedent case on a fact-to-fact level. In the example below from the objective memo for Mr. Bell, while the rigid formula is not used, the writer is contrasting the facts of the client's case to those of one of the illustrated cases. The differences are explained side by side and are obvious to the reader. Next, you see that the last sentence is where the reader is told why the contrast between the facts of your client's case and the case *Estate of Steed* matters. The last sentence brings full circle the purpose of the fact-to-fact analysis.

> Moreover, although depression alone is insufficient to establish the second element required for undue influence, Ms. Bell did not suffer only from depression like the testator in *Estate of Steed*. 152 S.W.3d at 811. In contrast, Ms. Bell battled depression coupled with lingering effects of head trauma. Mem. from A. Partner to File (Sept. 22, 2018). Additionally, the testator in *Estate of Steed* was depressed but otherwise capable of handling his own affairs; in fact, he was a "detailed person" who "worked daily" and was not "mentally impaired from performing his daily tasks." 152 S.W.3d at 811. In contrast, although there is some evidence that Ms. Bell, like the testator in *Estate of Steed*, was independent and capable (i.e., after her head trauma the doctors reported that she "fully recovered," and she "returned to work") Ms. Bell's story is not as simple as that of the practicing attorney in *Estate of Steed*. Mem. from A. Partner to File (Sept. 22, 2018). Ms. Bell suffered a brain trauma shortly before meeting Ms. Welsh, and, after her trauma, she suffered from depression and memory lapses. *Id.* Given this distinction, the reasoning of *Estate of Steed* does not squarely apply to Ms. Bell's situation, and, instead, a court in Mr. Bell's case is likely to find that the "pivotal" second element of undue influence is satisfied. *See Matter of Kam*, 484 S.W.3d at 653.

[d] Using rule-language bridging with analogical reasoning

In your Analysis, even though you are using analogical reasoning to compare your facts to the illustrated cases, it does not mean that you get to ignore rule-based reasoning. Rather, you should still be connecting your facts with the language of the general rule and subrules for the issue. However, because the application of the rule-language to your facts is not straightforward or sufficient in and of itself, the term we like to use for incorporating the rule language in this instance is rule-language bridging.

In part two of your Analysis, in addition to doing analogical reasoning, you should take "soundbites" or terms from the general rule and subrules and tie those soundbites to your facts and analysis of the issue. That is, you pull language from your general rule and subrules into your Analysis and incorporate such language throughout. In this way, you are making sure that your Analysis is using everything in your Rule—not just the case illustrations. Below is an example from the objective memo's Analysis for the first element. Notice how both analogical reasoning (comparing facts to *Estate of Steed*) and rule-language bridging (taking language from a subrule from *Estate of Clifton*) are used together.

> Moreover, like in *Estate of Steed*, where the court did not find fraudulent motive when the alleged influencer and the testator shared a business, here, Ms. Bell and Ms. Welsh shared in an organization—HOL—about which they were both passionate. *Estate of Steed*, 152 S.W.3d at 809; Mem. from A. Partner to File (Sept. 22, 2018). This shared interest in HOL gave them a mutual interest in the organization's success, including its financial success. Accordingly, at most, Ms. Welsh made a "[m]ere request[]" which is "not sufficient to establish undue influence." *Estate of Clifton*, 2012 WL 3139864, at *2 (citing *Curry*, 270 S.W.2d at 212).

G. *Overall conclusion*

The overall conclusion to your objective memo is where you tie together the pieces of your discussion to state a more global conclusion. The overall conclusion of your memo restates the conclusion articulated in the brief answer(s) and then sets forth the central reason(s) for that core conclusion. The overall conclusion does **not** summarize your entire memo. On the other hand, the conclusion also does **not** simply set forth a single conclusion sentence for the claim or cause of action at issue. Instead, typically a paragraph in length, the overall conclusion reminds the reader of the brief answer(s) and briefly restates the reasons for that conclusion. Below is a sample conclusion from the memo drafted for Mr. Bell.

> Mr. Bell can probably establish the first two elements required to set aside a will based on undue influence—the existence and exertion of an influence on Ms. Bell and the overpowering of Ms. Bell's mind at the time of the execution of her will. However, because Ms. Bell's Revised Will effectively disinherits Mr. Bell for the benefit of a charitable institution to which Ms. Bell had strong ties, Mr. Bell is unlikely to succeed in establishing but for causation as required by the third element. Accordingly, Mr. Bell is unlikely to be able to set aside Ms. Bell's Revised Will on the ground of undue influence.

Note that this conclusion restates the answer to the ultimate question—will Mr. Bell be successful in getting Ms. Bell's Revised Will set aside based on Ms. Welsh's undue influence—and then explains its answer in terms of the elements analyzed in the discussion.

III. E-mail memos

As mentioned previously, with the increasing pressure from clients to reduce legal costs and the increasing demand for instantaneous or real-time communication, lawyers often find themselves drafting abbreviated legal analysis in e-mail memos rather than drafting more lengthy and formal objective memos. In many ways, the heart of the analysis in an e-mail memo looks much like that in a more formal objective memo; however, the formalities are often fewer, and the length is often abbreviated. Yet, it is crucial to understand the art of drafting e-mail memos in the legal profession.

A. The realities of e-mail[13]

E-mail is the most common method of communication that lawyers use today.[14] Despite the frequency of its use, however, the reality is that e-mails are dangerous. Yes, that is right, using e-mail to communicate is as fraught with risk when used as part of your job as it is when it is used as part of your personal life. Why? In all honesty, there are countless reasons that e-mailing is dangerous, but there are four reasons specifically worth mentioning here.

First, e-mail is effectively unerasable. Even though you may delete an e-mail from your computer, it still exists on the sender's device, and more poignantly, it likely remains in a technology "cloud" just waiting to be uncovered. Second, e-mail is discoverable. This means—setting aside issues of privilege—one side to a lawsuit can force the other side to hand over old, even seemingly erased, e-mails as part of litigation. Third, e-mail often lacks the context to properly determine the tone in which it should be read. This reality means that e-mails are subject to multiple interpretations and, thus, are subject to massive misinterpretation. Fourth, e-mail is forwardable to anyone and publicly postable with just a single click. This means that e-mails are not private.

These realities do not mean we should not use e-mails. But these realities do mean that we should be mindful of the content, style, and tone we use when e-mailing. As lawyers, e-mails should not be off-the-cuff communications. Instead, lawyers, in particular, need to be diligent and careful about what they say in an e-mail.

B. The parts of an e-mail memo

Given the realities of e-mail, you need to err on the side of formality whenever communicating electronically. Part and parcel to this, you should be mindful to include the typical parts of an e-mail.

Salutation: The salutation is the opening greeting of your e-mail. When selecting an

---

13. You should also apply the realities related to e-mail communication and the risks and dangers associated therewith to text-based communications with other lawyers, clients, or opposing counsel. In fact, communication by text is arguably more risky because there is little litigation related to the application of the attorney-client privilege and text messages.

14. *See* Kristen Konrad Robbins-Tiscione, *From Snail Mail to E-Mail: The Traditional Legal Memo in the Twenty-First Century*, 58 J. LEGAL EDUC. 32, 32 (2008).

appropriate salutation, pick a salutation that reflects the formality of the relationship you as the sender have with the recipient. Always err on the side of being too formal and always use a person's highest title when addressing him or her. For example, if Samantha Smith is a judge and a professor, you should address her as Judge Smith because being a judge is a higher honor than being a professor. Generally, the following are acceptable salutations (which should be followed by a colon or comma at the outset of an e-mail): Dear Mr. Smith, Dear Robert (used only if a close relationship), Dear Professor Smith, Dear Director Smith, Mr. Smith, or Ms. Smith.

As a general practice, try to determine the recipient's gender by doing outside research before you send him or her an e-mail. If, even after research, you remain uncertain of a person's gender, you may use "Mx." as a gender-neutral way to address him or her.

Similarly, you should avoid using Mrs. or Miss when addressing women. In many states and countries, it is offensive to use Miss or Mrs. because doing so defines a woman in terms of her marital status; in fact, the European Union has banned the use of both terms as sexist.

Last, despite the fact that *you* may associate the terms with respect, you should avoid using the terms Ma'am and Sir to address an e-mail recipient. Many people find these terms facially offensive. Others find the fact that the writer did not do the requisite research to determine his or her actual name before sending an e-mail offensive.

Subject line: Select a subject line that tells the reader what to expect in the e-mail and is specific enough to differentiate it from his/her millions of other e-mails.

First sentence: The first sentence of your e-mail should restate the question asked or the issue that you are addressing in your e-mail.

Body: The body of your e-mail should be brief but should answer the question asked in detail. The content of the body of an e-mail will vary depending on the type of question being addressed in the e-mail. For multi-paragraph e-mails, you should not forget to employ normal paragraphs with the first line indented just as you would in a formal letter. The body of an e-mail may present a good opportunity to use bullet points. Although bullet points are sometimes considered too informal for a letter, bullets or lists often allow an e-mail author to more clearly and succinctly cover multiple issues without the need for extensive transitions.

Closing sentence: The closing sentence of an e-mail, especially an e-mail from a junior lawyer to his supervisor, often takes the form of a sentence offering to answer any further questions and to do additional follow-up work.

Signature block: A signature block includes a closing that is appropriately formal followed by one's full name and contact information. Often students and other professionals include favorite quotations or shout-outs to their favorite sports' teams. Such add-ons to one's signature block should be omitted because they may be offensive, or they may create an unintended tone to the e-mail. A few universally accepted closings include "Best Regards," "Sincerely," or "Respectfully."

Privileged notation: Use the same confidentiality and privilege warnings on an e-mail that you would use on a paper document.

C. E-mail etiquette

Aside from being careful to draft your e-mail with the requisite parts as described above, there are a few rules of e-mail etiquette that you should keep in mind whenever you draft (and ultimately send) an e-mail.

- Take the same care when you draft an e-mail that you would when drafting a written letter. What does this mean? It means use good grammar, be mindful of the tone of your e-mail, and print out your e-mail and proofread it before you hit send.
- Draft the e-mail "to" yourself rather than drafting it to the person to whom you are actually writing the e-mail. This method provides protection in case you accidently hit send before the e-mail is complete. In such an instance, it will simply send to you rather than sending an unfinished e-mail to a client, supervising lawyer, opposing counsel, or judge.
- Think before you write. Is the subject you are writing about appropriate for an e-mail communication, or would it be better to draft a formal letter, handle it by phone, or maybe even address it in person?
- Use the subject line. Make the subject line of the e-mail specific enough so that your audience knows what the e-mail addresses and so that you can find it later if you need to search for it in your e-mail outbox.
- Use the attachment function. Consider attaching documents that support your analysis in your e-mail, such as cases, statutes, or affidavits. In addition, name any attachments so that the reader knows what they are.
- Be mindful of length. Although the old "one screen" rule for an e-mail does not strictly apply anymore (especially now that most of us are accustomed to reading on screens of varying sizes), be aware that an e-mail is intended to be succinct. If the communication you need to send is longer than a standard size computer screen, think about converting it to a word document and attaching it as a more formal communication to a summary e-mail.

D. Sample e-mail memo

So, what do all of these parts of an e-mail look like when properly put together? In advance of asking you to write a formal objective memo assessing whether Mr. Bell will likely get Ms. Bell's Revised Will set aside based on undue influence, Alex B. Partner calls you and requests a quick e-mail memo identifying the requirements to set aside a will based on undue influence in Texas. He explains that he needs the e-mail in advance of his meeting with Mr. Bell in two hours. Faced with this task, you do some preliminary research and turn up the *Rothermel* case (located in the Appendix). After reading the case, you draft the following professional e-mail with all the necessary parts.

From: Adams, Savi
Sent: Monday, June 24, 2018 8:15:32 AM
To: Partner, Alex B.
Subject: John Bell, Client 0001.555456: Elements Required for Undue Influence

Specific Subject

Professional Salutation

Dear Mr. Partner:

First Sentence Restates Assignment

The purpose of this email is to identify the legal requirements for Mr. Bell to set aside Ms. Bell's Revised Will based on Ms. Welsh's undue influence.

In Texas, a contestant is required to prove three elements to set aside a will based on undue influence:

Succinct E-mail Body

1. The "existence and exertion of an influence";
2. The "effective operation" of such influence to "subvert or overpower" the mind of the testator at the time of the execution of the testament; and
3. The execution of a will that the testator would not have executed "but for" such influence.

Rothermel v. Duncan, 369 S.W.2d 917, 922 (Tex. 1963). For your convenience, I have attached the *Rothermel* case to this email and have highlighted the relevant language.

Closing Sentence offers follow-up assistance

Please let me know if I can provide you with any additional help on this case or any future cases.

Best Regards,

Savi

Professional Closing and Signature Block

Savi P. Adams
Partner & Partner LLC
1212 Moon Court, Suite 1400
Dallas, Texas 75219
(214) 555-1234 (telephone)
(214) 555-6709 (facsimile)

Privileged Notation

PRIVILEGED AND CONFIDENTIAL: Communication Subject to the Attorney-Client Privilege and the Attorney-Work-Product Doctrine

3 | Persuasive Legal Writing

Before reading this part of the book, you should skim through the Motion for Summary Judgment and Opposition to the Motion for Summary Judgment in the Appendix.

When you were younger, you may have had a relative say something to the effect of, "You are so good at arguing! You should be a lawyer!" Generally, when people hear the term lawyer, their minds go to the lawyers in a courtroom in a television drama. These lawyers are glamorous. They stand before a judge and jury in an old-fashioned looking courtroom that is necessarily filled with mahogany. These lawyers give lengthy speeches, arguing their client's position with furor and passion. They wave their arms. They pound their fists. And, with the carefully scored musical background, they persuade you—the audience—to feel something.

When you came to law school, you might have thought that right out of the gate you would be passionately arguing like the lawyers on television. We call this the "Law and Order" effect. Instead, in your doctrinal courses, you found yourself reading case after case after case. There was no arguing, but, instead, there was learning the law and learning about the way judges make decisions. In your legal writing course, you did not get to argue either. Instead, you started with objective writing, where you were told to not take a position but, instead, to give a balanced analysis of the law.

This part of the book focuses on transitioning from objective writing to persuasive writing. "Hooray," you say. "I finally get to argue?" Yes and no. Lawyers do not simply argue: they persuade. In this part of the book, we will tackle persuasive writing, and you will learn how to make persuasive legal arguments. By using the same problem as you used in the objective writing section of the book, you will be able to see the difference between objective and persuasive writing.

When doing this reading, you will often turn back to Part Two of this book to refresh your memory on the foundational skills introduced when you learned objective legal writing. In this part of the book, you will build on these foundational skills to transform your writing from objective to persuasive.

I. What is persuasive writing?

The reason most legal writing programs start with objective writing and then move to persuasive writing is that you must understand the law before you can apply it persuasively. Persuasive writing should start with an objective analysis of the law and an objective analysis of your client's case. You need to look at the law and facts objectively so that you know the strengths of your case, the obstacles you must overcome, and, therefore, your best plan of attack to "win." While the tools you learned in objective writing will help you as you turn to persuasive writing, there are key differences between the two.

	OBJECTIVE WRITING	PERSUASIVE WRITING
GOAL	To provide a predictive/ informative analysis of how the law will be applied to a set of facts	To advocate for your client's position by persuasively arguing for a desired outcome
AUDIENCE	Supervising attorney or clients	Court (judge, judicial staff, judicial clerks)
DOCUMENT	Objective memo or e-mail	Motion or brief
FORMULA	CRAC (Conclusion, Rule, Analysis, Conclusion)	CRACC (Conclusion, Rule, Analysis, Counter-analysis, Conclusion)

A. *Goal of persuasive writing*

In objective writing, your goal is to predict an outcome. You do not have a side. You do not have a position. You do not have a bias. Instead, you are charged with conducting an even-handed and balanced analysis of the law as applied to the facts. In objective writing, you do not advocate for a certain outcome but, instead, predict which outcome is most likely based on the legal authority. You must inform your audience.

In persuasive writing, your goal is very different. Your goal is to persuade your audience. You have a side. You have a position. You have a bias. You are charged with advocating for your client's position. You do this by framing the law in a way that best suits your client, framing your client's facts in the light most favorable to her, and persuasively applying the law to your client's facts to argue for a specific outcome. You must persuade your audience to agree with your position.

B. *Audience in persuasive writing*

In order to write persuasively, you must know your audience and, specifically, the needs of that audience. In persuasive writing, your audience is the court, which is comprised of the judge (or judges), the judicial staff, and the judicial clerks. What do courts need? A trial court's biggest "need" is sufficient information to make a decision that is in line with legal precedent because a trial court does not want to be overturned on appeal. Therefore, in order to meet this need, you must persuade the trial court judge that a decision in your client's favor is in line with legal precedent. Trial courts do not make law, but they apply the law. Moreover, in persuading a trial court, your focus needs to be on precedent. Argument of what the law "should be" or policy arguments will not be as persuasive to a trial court as arguments focused on what the law is.

On the other hand, if your audience is the highest court in your state (e.g., the Texas Supreme Court) or the United States Supreme Court (SCOTUS), the needs of your audience are different. Because these are courts of discretionary review, oftentimes there is no legal precedent that governs the issue, and, instead, the court must effectively make the law. Thus, the highest courts need you, as an advocate for your client, to tell them what the law should be and why that law is in line with public policy. The needs of an intermediate appellate court fall in between the needs of a trial court and the needs of the highest court. Intermediate appellate courts must make decisions in line with the binding precedent of the state supreme court or SCOTUS. However, intermediate appellate courts will also be persuaded by what the law should be and by policy arguments, unlike trial courts.

Importantly, regardless of which court you are before, it is crucial to remember that your audience is a judge—not a jury. Persuading a judge is very different than persuading a jury. While a jury might be persuaded by appeals to emotion, a judge expects a sound and logical legal argument. That is not to say judges are devoid of human emotion or that emotion has no place in persuading a judge, but any appeal to a judge's emotion should be subtle (normally through how you frame your client's facts) and secondary to an appeal to the judge's logic.

C. *Types of persuasive writing*

Persuasive writing can take many different forms. The form your persuasive writing will take depends on the procedural posture of your case and the issue being addressed.

1. Trial court motions

In the trial court, documents that contain legal arguments and ask the court to take action are called "motions." The party filing the motion (the party asking the court to take action) is called the movant. When the movant files a motion, the other side (the non-movant) will often file a "response" or "opposition" to that motion, asking the court to deny the action or relief requested by the movant. Oftentimes, the moving party, after having been served with the non-movant's opposition, will get an opportunity to file a written response to the non-movant's opposition, which is called a "reply."

There are a variety of different motions that come up in a trial court, and the format of these motions depends on the trial court you are before and the type of motion you are filing. For example, some trial courts require you to file a "motion," which is usually one or two pages asking for the relief you want, and an accompanying "memorandum of law," which is where you make your legal arguments in detail. Other trial courts simply require you to file only a single document that is a "motion," which includes the requested relief and the legal arguments in support. Thus, before writing a motion, it is important to check the local rules of procedure.

Pre-trial motions are motions that are filed after the case is filed and before the start of the trial. Pre-trial motions range from generally non-controversial (e.g., a motion for an extension of time to file something) to controversial but not dispositive (e.g., a motion to transfer the case to a different venue or a motion to compel discovery) to dispositive (e.g., a motion to dismiss or a motion for summary judgment). Dispositive motions are arguably the most important pre-trial motions because they can result in the final resolution of a specific issue in the case (e.g., a single cause of action is dismissed) or the final resolution of the case in its entirety (e.g., all causes of action are dismissed).

In addition to pre-trial motions, there are motions that arise both during trial (trial motions) and after trial (post-trial motions). For example, during trial, after the plaintiff has presented its case in chief, a defendant may file a motion for directed verdict (or judgment as a matter of law) asking the court to enter judgment in favor of the defendant without allowing the case to go to the jury. Some common post-trial motions include motions for judgment notwithstanding verdict (asking the court to disregard the jury's verdict and enter a contrary one because no reasonable jury could have reached the verdict issued) or a motion for new trial (asking the court for a new trial because of significant error or insufficient evidence to support the jury's verdict).

2. Appellate briefing

If a party wants to challenge a decision of a trial court, it can file an appeal to an appellate court. The party filing the appeal is called the appellant, and the party on the other side responding to the appeal is called the appellee or respondent. In the typical intermediate court of appeals case, the appellant first files an opening brief setting out the issues to be resolved on appeal and the legal arguments in support. The appellee/respondent then files a brief responding to the appellant's opening brief. Then, the appellant has the opportunity to file a reply brief.

After the intermediate court of appeals decides the case on appeal, the losing party may choose to file a petition for review to the highest appellate court (either a state supreme court or SCOTUS) asking the highest appellate court to review the decision of the intermediate appellate court. Because the highest appellate courts are courts of discretionary review, the highest appellate court may or may not decide to review the intermediate appellate court's decision. If the highest appellate court decides to review the case, it will grant the petition for review. If review is granted, the petitioner (party asking for relief) will file an opening brief on the merits; the respondent (other party) will file a responding brief on the merits; and the petitioner will be given an opportunity to file a reply brief. As you can see, this process is much like the process of an intermediate appellate court.

D. *Formula for persuasive writing*

The good news is that the formula you will use for persuasive writing is almost identical to the CRAC formula that you used for objective writing. In persuasive writing, you will use the formula CRACC. The new "C" following the Analysis stands for Counter-analysis, which is introduced in Part Three, Section II.G.3, below. The other parts of CRAC (Conclusion, Rule, Analysis, Conclusion) remain, but you will learn how to make these parts persuasive rather than objective.

II. Motion writing

This book focuses on trial court motions, as opposed to appellate briefs, to teach you persuasive writing because, throughout your career as a lawyer, you are far more likely to write or respond to trial court motions than to write or respond to appellate briefs. While most lawyers will regularly write and respond to motions in trial courts, only a small percentage of lawyers who specialize in appellate law will regularly write appellate briefs.

A. *What is a motion for summary judgment*

In this book, we use a motion for summary judgment as our vehicle to learn persuasive writing. Before we dive into motion writing, it is important that you understand the vehicle we are using as an example and how it comes into play in the life cycle of a civil case. We try to explain the concept of summary judgment as simply as possible given that this is not a book on civil procedure. However, it is important that you understand how summary judgment works so that you will be able to give context to and not be confused by the persuasive writing example we use in this book.

A motion for summary judgment is a pre-trial motion that is filed in the vast majority of civil cases. To understand a motion for summary judgment, let's look at *Randall's Food Markets v. Johnson.*[1]

FACTS OF THE CASE: *RANDALL'S FOOD MARKETS V. JOHNSON*

Mary Johnson was a manager at the grocery store Randall's. One day, she was shopping at the Randall's store where she worked. She brought several

1. *Randall's Food Markets, Inc. v. Johnson*, 891 S.W.2d 640 (Tex. 1995).

> items to the checkout counter. As the cashier was ringing up her items, he saw that Ms. Johnson had a wreath she was holding around her arm. The cashier rang up all the other items and asked if there was anything else, and Ms. Johnson said there was nothing else. Ms. Johnson paid for the rung-up items, but she left without paying for the wreath. The cashier reported to the store's director and district manager that Ms. Johnson took the wreath without paying.
>
> A couple of days later, Ms. Johnson came back to Randall's and the store's director questioned her about the wreath in an office at the back of the store. Ms. Johnson admitted she forgot to pay for the wreath. The store's director asked that Ms. Johnson wait for the district manager to arrive so that Ms. Johnson could meet with him. He asked that she not go on the store floor but, instead, wait in the office or go to the employee lounge in the back of the store. Ms. Johnson waited in the office, leaving once to use the bathroom and again to pay for the wreath and visit a friend working at the store.
>
> When the district manager arrived, he questioned Ms. Johnson further, causing her to cry. Ms. Johnson was suspended without pay for 30 days and told she would be transferred to a different store.

What does Ms. Johnson do next? She files a civil lawsuit. Ms. Johnson (Plaintiff) sued Randall's (Defendant) for, among other things, intentional infliction of emotional distress and false imprisonment. Below is a basic chart showing where summary judgment usually fits into a civil lawsuit.

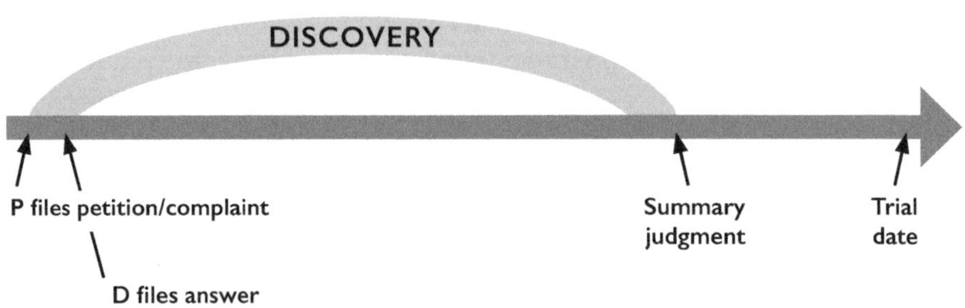

After a plaintiff files a lawsuit by filing either a petition or a complaint with the causes of action (terms vary depending on the jurisdiction), the defendant will file an answer denying the plaintiff's allegations. The parties will then conduct discovery. Discovery, simply put, is where the parties gather evidence and information related to the case. Motions for summary judgment are usually brought after discovery is well underway or even complete (although, technically, motions for summary judgment do not have to be brought after discovery) and before trial.

Summary judgment is a procedural device whereby a court can dismiss and eliminate unmeritorious claims or defenses. Below is the standard for summary judgment in Texas, where the *Randall's Food Markets v. Johnson* case was decided. The standard, however, is similar in most jurisdictions across the United States.

> **STANDARD FOR SUMMARY JUDGMENT FROM *RANDALL'S FOOD MARKETS V. JOHNSON***
>
> A trial court shall grant summary judgment if the moving party meets its burden to prove that the evidence shows "there is no genuine issue as to any material fact and the moving party is entitled to judgment as a matter of law on the issues expressly set out in the motion."[2]

What does that standard mean? It means that the moving party, usually the defendant, must show that the admissible evidence establishes that there is no genuine issue of material fact as to the plaintiff's causes of action such that the defendant is entitled to judgment (the defendant wins) as a matter of law. Put another way, if the defendant conclusively disproves one or more of the plaintiff's causes of action, then summary judgment must be granted.

You can think of summary judgment as a screening device or filtering mechanism. If a plaintiff has brought a cause of action, and there is no genuine issue of material fact with respect to that cause of action such that the defendant is entitled to judgment as a matter of law, then the plaintiff's cause of action does not deserve to go to trial. In fact, a trial would be a waste of time and resources because there are no fact issues, and, as such, there is nothing for a jury to decide. Granting summary judgment, however, is a big deal because it takes away a plaintiff's case (or a part of a plaintiff's case) and a plaintiff's right to have that case (or that part of his case) decided by a jury. Therefore, when deciding a motion for summary judgment, the court will exercise caution by putting the thumb on the scale in favor of the non-movant (plaintiff), in whose favor all doubts, evidence, and inferences will be made.

Back to Ms. Johnson's case. One of the claims Ms. Johnson brought against Randall's was for false imprisonment. Randall's moved for summary judgment on Ms. Randall's false imprisonment claim. The elements required to prove a false imprisonment claim are (1) willful detention; (2) without consent; and (3) without authority of law.[3]

Let's get a few things straight as we work through this summary judgment example.

- **At trial, who has the burden to prove the elements of false imprisonment?** Ms. Johnson, because it is her cause of action.

- **At trial, how many elements of the false imprisonment claim must Ms.**

2. Tex. R. Civ. P. 166a(c).
3. *Randall's Food Markets*, 891 S.W. 2d at 644–45.

Johnson prove to succeed? All three of them. If she cannot prove one, she will lose.

- **In Randall's motion for summary judgment, how many elements of Ms. Johnson's false imprisonment claim must Randall's conclusively disprove to get its motion granted?** Just one. If Randall's can show there is no genuine issue of material fact with respect to at least one element of Ms. Johnson's false imprisonment claim, then summary judgment will be granted because if Ms. Johnson cannot prove one element, she cannot prove her cause of action.

When Defendant Randall's moved for summary judgment with respect to this claim, Randall's argued that there was no genuine issue of material fact with respect to the first element of willful detention. How do you think the court ruled? How would you rule?

Looking at the evidence (even in the light most favorable to Ms. Johnson), is there a fact issue with respect to whether she was willfully detained in the office at the back of the store during the questioning by the Randall's district manager or store director? No way! She was not restrained physically or otherwise. In fact, she left twice.

EXCERPT FROM *RANDALL'S FOOD MARKETS V. JOHNSON*

Johnson does not contend that her detention was effected by actual physical force; rather, she alleges that Simmons detained her by sternly insisting that she stay put, which caused her to fear that he would physically prevent her from leaving had she attempted to leave. In effect, Johnson alleges that Simmons impliedly threatened her person. This allegation is conclusively negated by the fact that Johnson left the area that she was allegedly confined to twice, and no one tried to stop her from doing so. Neither Simmons nor anyone else guarded Johnson. Simmons never stated that he would physically restrain Johnson if she attempted to enter the floor of the store. Simmons did not even attempt to confine Johnson to a particular place; he merely suggested that she avoid one area of the store. In short, no threat was made to detain Johnson.

Simmons' request that Johnson not work in one area of the workplace does not constitute false imprisonment. When an employer supervises its employees, it necessarily temporarily restricts the employees' freedom to move from place to place or in the direction that they wish to go. Without more, however, such a restriction is not a "willful detention." An employer has the right, subject to certain limited exceptions, to instruct its employees regarding the tasks that they are to perform during work hours. Johnson was compensated for the time that she spent waiting for Seals, and Simmons gave her the choice of passing this time working on a volunteer project or sitting and waiting in the office. In order to effectively manage its business, an employer must be able to suggest, and even

> insist, that its employees perform certain tasks in certain locations at certain times. As a matter of law, Randall's did not falsely imprison Johnson.[4]

Ms. Johnson's claim was unmeritorious and did not deserve to go to trial because there would have been nothing for the jury to decide with respect to her claim given that the evidence conclusively showed Ms. Johnson was not detained. Therefore, Randall's sustained its burden to prove it was entitled to summary judgment.

As you can see, summary judgment is an important procedural device. It would have been a waste of resources to allow Ms. Johnson's claim to proceed to trial. By granting summary judgment, the court dismissed Ms. Johnson's false imprisonment claim.

In the summary judgment context, a party moving for summary judgment (the movant) is always arguing that there is no genuine issue of material fact such that the movant is entitled to judgment as a matter of law. The party opposing the motion for summary judgment (the non-movant) is always arguing the opposite: there is, at a minimum, a genuine issue of material fact such that the case deserves to move forward.

Refer to the sample motion for summary judgment (Happiness of Life's Motion for Summary Judgment on Plaintiff John Bell's Claim of Undue Influence ("Defendant's MSJ")) and sample opposition (Plaintiff John Bell's Opposition to Defendant Happiness of Life's Motion for Summary Judgment on Plaintiff's Claim of Undue Influence ("Plaintiff's MSJ Opposition")) in the Appendix of this book. Can you find the standard for summary judgment in both documents? How do they differ?

B. *Overview of the formal parts of motion*

When filing a motion or opposition (for simplicity's sake, we use the term "motion" to refer to both), as a general matter, it will include the following sections:

- **Caption and Title:** The caption and title include general information about the case (court, document number, party names, and title of the document being filed) and are located at the top of the first page of the document.
- **Introduction:** The introduction is the first thing the court will read and is a summary of the arguments made in the document.
- **Statement of Facts:** The statement of facts provides the relevant facts that the court must know to decide the issue before it.
- **Governing Legal Standard:** The governing legal standard provides an overview of the standard that governs the court's decision when deciding the motion. Depending on the type of motion, the standard will vary.

---

4. *Id.* at 645–46.

- **Argument and Authorities:** The argument and authorities contains the meat of the argument (the CRACCs).
- **Conclusion:** The conclusion consists of one to two sentences restating the relief requested in the motion.
- **Signature Block:** The signature block contains the signature and contact information for the author of the motion or opposition.

These sections will be discussed in more detail, *infra*. While these sections can generally be found in any trial court motion, regardless of the specific type of motion, some jurisdictions require additional or different sections. Therefore, it is always wise to check the local rules of your jurisdiction to see if any additional or different sections are needed. For example, as you see in the example set forth in the appendix of this book, in Texas state court a motion for summary judgment usually includes a section called "Summary Judgment Evidence," where the evidence relied upon in the motion for summary judgment is listed.

C. *Caption and title*

The caption appears on the top part of the first page of a motion. It identifies the court where the case is pending, the docket number, and the parties. The caption is the same on any trial court filing for a particular case, regardless of which party files it or what type of case document is filed. Under the caption is the title of the document in ALL CAPS. While the caption stays the same regardless of what type of document is being filed, the title changes depending on whom the document belongs to and what the document is regarding. Below are a couple of examples.

NO. 2019-55555

	'	IN THE PROBATE COURT
	'	
	'	OF DALLAS COUNTY, TEXAS
ESTATE OF AVA BELL, Deceased.	'	
	'	
	'	PROBATE COURT NO. 2

HAPPINESS OF LIFE'S MOTION FOR SUMMARY JUDGMENT ON
PLAINTIFF JOHN BELL'S CLAIM OF UNDUE INFLUENCE

NO. 2018-55555

PAUL VITOR,	'	IN THE DISTRICT COURT
	'	
Plaintiff,	'	
	'	
VS.	'	OF DALLAS COUNTY, TEXAS
	'	
CHIP-HOME CORP.,	'	
	'	
Defendent.	'	
	'	14TH JUDICIAL DISTRICT
	'	

DEFENDENT CHIP-HOME CORP.'S MOTION FOR SUMMARY JUDGMENT

D. *Introduction*

Following the caption and title is the introduction. The introduction is the first part of your motion that the court will read. Given this, the introduction is your first opportunity to persuade the court. Because your introduction is your first impression to the court on the issue, it is incredibly important.

An introduction should give the court a preview or summary of your argument. After reading the introduction, the judge should know the main points of your argument and the relief you are requesting. You should think of the introduction like this: if a judge were to have only two minutes to read your motion or opposition, what you would have her read is the introduction because it would contain the overall relief you request and the key reasons for granting or denying that relief. Put another way, the introduction is the "CliffsNotes" version of your motion or opposition.

1. Why you should write the introduction last

Your introduction is a preview or summary of the content of your argument (which is contained in the argument and authorities section of your motion or opposition). Even though the introduction is the first thing the court reads, we recommend that you write it last for a couple of reasons. First, it is much easier to write a summary of your argument after you have written the full content of your argument. Indeed, if you wait to write your introduction until after the content of your argument is finalized, you will often save time by cutting and pasting portions of your argument into your introduction. Second, if you write your introduction before finalizing the content of your argument, and the content of your argument changes, you will then have to go back and edit your introduction. Save time and write your introduction last.

2. How to organize your introduction

There is not one way to organize an introduction, and approaches to introductions vary greatly among lawyers. However, a theme of this book is simplicity. Rather than showing you dozens of sample introductions done every which way, we will provide you with an organizational structure that works and can be applied to write an introduction for any motion or opposition. As you progress through law school and into practice, you may adjust this approach to fit your particular style.

FORMULA FOR AN INTRODUCTION WITH ONE CAUSE OF ACTION OR ONE BIG ISSUE

Part one: First, persuasively state the overall conclusion you want the court to reach.

Part two: Next, incorporating the legal standard, persuasively state the overarching rule.

Part three: Then, preview your arguments regarding the issue in the order that they will be discussed. This "preview" should include an application of the law to the facts.

Part four: Last, persuasively restate the overall conclusion you want the court to reach.

The below example is taken from the sample opposition in the Appendix on page 306. You will see that there is only one big issue/cause of action: undue influence. As annotated below, the example contains all four parts of an introduction.

Part 1 → This Court should deny summary judgment on Plaintiff/Contestant John Bell's claim of undue influence. Happiness of Life ("HOL" or "Defendant") **Part 2** → fails to meet its burden to prove that there is no genuine issue of material fact as to any of the three elements of undue influence: "(1) the existence and exertion of an influence; (2) the effective operation of such influence so as to subvert or overpower the mind of the testat[rix] at the time of the execution of the testament; and (3) the execution of a testament which the maker thereof would not have executed but for such influence." *Rothermel v. Duncan*, 369 S.W.2d 917, 922 (Tex. 1963). First, Defendant fails to prove **Part 3** → the absence of a genuine issue of material fact with respect to whether HOL exerted an undue influence on Mrs. Bell when it poisoned Mrs. Bell against her husband; alienated Mrs. Bell from her friends and hobbies; controlled Mrs. Bell's daily decisions, had access to Mrs. Bell's finances; solicited Mrs. Bell to change her will in exchange for an honorary title; and assisted Mrs.

Bell with the drafting and execution of her new will. Second, Defendant fails to prove the absence of a genuine issue of material fact with respect to whether HOL overpowered Mrs. Bell's mind at the time of the new will's execution when the evidence shows that Mrs. Bell was under the influence of mind-altering magical mushroom tea, given to her by HOL's founding member Anna Welsh, at the time of the will's execution. Third, Defendant fails to prove the absence of a genuine issue of material fact as to the third element when the evidence supports that Mrs. Bell made an unnatural disposition when she left the bulk of her estate to a 12-member, cult-like organization joined only four months prior instead of her husband.

Because the Defendant fails to meet its burden of negating Mr. Bell's undue influence claim, and because there exists, at a minimum, a fact issue as to each element of undue influence, this Court should deny summary judgment. ← **Part 4**

FORMULA FOR AN INTRODUCTION WITH MORE THAN ONE CAUSE OF ACTION OR MORE THAN ONE BIG ISSUE:

Part one: First, persuasively state the overall conclusion you want the court to reach.

Part two: Next, repeat the following for each cause of action or big issue:

i. Incorporating the legal standard, persuasively state the conclusion you want the court to reach.

ii. State the overarching rule.

iii. Preview your arguments in the order they will be discussed.

Part three: Last, persuasively restate the overall conclusion you want the court to reach.

The example below contains two causes of action, defenses, or big issues. As annotated pictorially, the example illustrates all parts and subparts of a multi-issue introduction.

This Court should grant summary judgment as to Plaintiff's cause of action under the Texas Dram Shop Act because Plaintiff cannot prove one or more elements of its claim. Alternatively, this Court should grant summary judgment because Defendant can prove the affirmative defense that it complied with the Dram Shop Act's safe harbor provision as a matter of law, and Plaintiff has no evidence to rebut such defense. ← **Part 1**

First, Plaintiff cannot meet its "onerous burden" to establish a prima facie case with respect to two of the three elements of his Dram Shop Act ← **Part 2.i**

cause of action. To sustain a Texas Dram Shop Act claim against Defendant
Part 2.ii. → Chip-Home Corporation, Plaintiff has the burden to prove that: (1) Chip-Home was a "provider"; (2) it was "apparent" to Chip-Home that it was serving an "obviously intoxicated" patron who presented a "clear danger" to herself and others; and (3) the patron's intoxication was a proximate cause of Plaintiff's injuries. Tex. Alco. Bev. Code Ann. §2.02(b). With re-
Part 2.iii. → spect to the second element, Plaintiff cannot prove that at the time Chip-Home served patron Karen Stevenson—as opposed to after the time of service—a reasonable person would have considered her "obviously intoxicated." With respect to the third element, Plaintiff's injury—which he sustained when a flying tree branch from a third-party vehicle struck him following a car accident with patron Ms. Stevenson—was not a foreseeable danger from the patron's intoxication. As such, this "new and independent" cause broke the causal chain and negates the third element of Plaintiff's cause of action.

Part 2.i. → Second, even if Plaintiff could prove the prima facie elements of his Dram Shop Act cause of action, which he cannot, this Court should grant summary judgment because Chip-Home complied with the safe harbor provision—i.e. the affirmative defense contained in the Dram Shop Act.
Part 2.ii. → Under the safe harbor provision, an employee's actions that violate the Dram Shop Act are not attributable to the employer if: (1) the employer required its employees to attend a TABC-approved "seller training program"; (2) the employee actually attended the program; and (3) the employer did not directly or indirectly encourage the employee to violate the Dram Shop Act. *Id.* § 106.14(a)(1). Chip-Home has the burden to prove the first two elements, and it has conclusively proved compliance. Plaintiff has the burden to negate the third element to rebut the affirmative defense. Plaintiff
Part 2.iii. → cannot rebut such defense because there is no evidence that suggests Chip-Home affirmatively encouraged its employees to over-serve patrons. Accordingly, this Court should grant summary judgment because the safe harbor provision protects Chip-Home.

Part 3 → Because Plaintiff cannot establish a prima facie cause of action under the Dram Shop Act or, in the alternative, because Chip-Home proves its affirmative defense under the safe harbor provision, this Court should grant summary judgment.

E. *Statement of facts*

After your introduction, you will include a statement of facts. Much like your statement of facts in objective writing, your statement of facts should include the legally relevant facts that go to the issue or issues before the court. However, in persuasive writing, you are not just telling a story—you are telling a story from a point of view. Do not underestimate the power and importance of a statement of facts in persuasive writing. As Justice Louis Brandeis said: "Let me write the statement of facts, and I care not who writes the law."[5]

1. How a persuasive statement of facts differs from an objective one

In objective writing, your statement of facts objectively sets forth both sides of whatever story you are telling. You do not have a point of view; instead, your goal is to tell a neutral, complete story. You include background facts, trigger facts, and emotional facts, but as an objective writer, you are not trying to frame the facts in a way that makes the reader feel one way or another.

It is well known that there are two sides to every story. In persuasive writing, you want the court to agree with your client's side of the story. Therefore, the way you frame your statement of facts will be in the way that is most favorable to your client. You will not mislead the court, omit facts, or make up facts to tell your client's story, but, instead, you will frame the facts in a way that emphasizes the facts that are "good" for your client and de-emphasizes the facts that are "bad."

Let's say that the facts are as follows: Plaintiff, Mary Miller, 83, was walking home from church when an unleashed Rottweiler rescued and owned by Defendant, Michael John, ran up to Ms. Miller and bit her leg. This bite caused Ms. Miller's leg to bleed. Ms. Miller immediately went to an urgent care center, where she was given 25 stitches in her leg. At the time of the bite, Ms. Miller was on a small stretch of grass on Mr. John's property that sits between the sidewalk and the street.

Ms. Miller plans to bring a cause of action under California Civil Code Section 3342, which provides, "The owner of any dog is liable for the damages suffered by any person who is bitten by the dog while in a public place or lawfully in a private place, including the property of the owner of the dog, regardless of the former viciousness of the dog or the owner's knowledge of such viciousness."

The statute can be broken down into three elements: (1) the owner's dog bit the plaintiff; (2) the plaintiff was injured; and (3) the bite occurred while in a public place or lawfully in a private place. Therefore, the trigger or legally significant facts are the facts that go to each element.

---

5. Michael R. Fontham & Michael Vitiello, Persuasive Written and Oral Advocacy in the Trial and Appellate Courts 37 (Wolters Kluwer Law & Business 2012).

Compare how the facts may be stated objectively, as opposed to persuasively for each side.

> **OBJECTIVELY**
>
> While Plaintiff was walking home, Defendant's dog bit and injured Plaintiff. The injury occurred on a small stretch of grass on Mr. John's property that sits between the sidewalk and the street.
>
> **PERSUASIVELY FOR PLAINTIFF**
>
> Ms. Miller, who is 83, was walking home from church on the public sidewalk. While resting on a patch of grass between the public sidewalk and the public street in front of Defendant's home, Defendant's Rottweiler—who was not on a leash—attacked her. The Rottweiler's teeth sank into Ms. Miller's leg, causing a three-inch gash. To stop the bleeding, Ms. Miller had to have 25 stitches sewn into her leg.
>
> **PERSUASIVELY FOR DEFENDANT**
>
> Plaintiff was bitten by Mr. John's rescue dog. At the time of the injury, Plaintiff was sitting on Mr. John's private property without permission.

Note how the same story is told differently for the Plaintiff and for the Defendant. The trigger facts are only those included in the objective version: (1) Defendant's dog bit Plaintiff; (2) Plaintiff was injured; and (3) the location of the injury. In the persuasive versions, each story includes these same trigger facts, but the story is different for each side. For starters, each side is personalizing himself/herself and de-personalizing the other side. Plaintiff refers to herself as Ms. Miller and refers to Defendant as generic "Defendant." Whereas, Defendant does the opposite. Notice how, if you are telling the story from the Plaintiff's side, you are including background facts and emotional facts that paint a picture favorable to your client. Does it legally matter that the Plaintiff was walking home from church or that she was 83 years old? No. Does it legally matter for the strict liability statute that the dog was a Rottweiler or that it was unleashed? No. However, these facts are favorable to the Plaintiff and help tell her side of the story. If you represent the Defendant, you would not include these facts, and omitting them would not be "dishonest" because they are not legally significant. Rather, the trigger fact is that a dog bit the Plaintiff. No more. And, you will notice that Defendant points out that the dog was a rescue animal, which is an emotional fact favorable to the Defendant.

Notice that, with respect to the bite, the Plaintiff's side of the story is told actively and with strong verbs like "attacked" and "sank." On the other hand, the Defendant's side of the story is told passively and generally. With respect to the injury, the Defendant simply states that there was an injury, while the Plaintiff goes into detail about the injury. Finally, with respect to the location, the Plaintiff emphasizes that the place of injury was between two public places to set up the Plaintiff's argument: that the location of the injury was public. In contrast, the Defendant emphasizes that the location was on his private property.

In persuasive writing, it is your job to tell a truthful, complete story but to tell it in a way that is framed favorably for your client.

2. Telling your client's "side of the story" through emphasis and de-emphasis

In persuasive writing, your statement of facts must, like objective writing, include all legally significant or trigger facts. You must tell a complete story. Also, like objective writing, in persuasive writing, your statement of facts should not contain legal argument or legal conclusions. So, how do you make your statement of facts persuasive? First, let's talk about what not to do. Do not omit "bad" facts or fabricate "good" facts. This will not make your statement of facts persuasive. Instead, omitting bad facts (or making up good facts) is both counterproductive and destructive because the other side will include the omitted facts, which will bring to the court's attention your lack of candor and cause you to lose credibility with the court.

Rather, to make your statement of facts persuasive, you should present the same facts as the other side (the legally significant facts) but do so in a way that is most favorable to your client by emphasizing good facts and de-emphasizing bad facts.

Use the following eight techniques to emphasize and de-emphasize:

Technique one: Space. Spend more space/words on facts that you want to emphasize than on facts that you want to de-emphasize.

Consider the following example from the briefs in the case *Morse v. Frederick*,[6] which involved whether a school district had violated a student's First Amendment rights when the school district punished the student for displaying a banner reading "Bong Hits 4 Jesus" at an Olympic Torch Relay, which students attended as part of a school-sanctioned event.

EXCERPT FROM SCHOOL DISTRICT'S STATEMENT OF FACTS

Joseph Frederick, a Juneau-Douglas High School student, and several of his schoolmates positioned themselves on the sidewalk opposite the campus to await the torch relay. Pet. App. 25a. Before the torch arrived, Principal Deborah Morse approached this group to investigate the throwing of snowballs and beverage bottles that originated from their vicinity. J.A. 24, 41, 43. As the torchbearers and television camera crews approached, Frederick and his friends unfurled a large banner emblazoned with the phrase "BONG HiTS 4 JESUS." Pet. App. 25a. Frederick's banner—which measured (by his estimation) 14 feet long—was clearly visible to the large

6. *Morse v. Frederick*, 551 U.S. 393 (2007).

number of students assembled on campus. J.A. 24; Pet. App. 70a; Opp'n to Pet. at 1 n.1.1[7]

EXCERPT FROM STUDENT'S STATEMENT OF FACTS

Frederick, an eighteen-year-old resident of Juneau, Alaska, stood among a crowd of students and adults on a public sidewalk in front of private homes and awaited the arrival of the Olympic Torch Relay. J.A. 9–10, 15–16. When the Olympic torch neared, he and several others held up a banner that read "Bong Hits 4 Jesus" in the hopes of attracting the attention of television crews covering the event. J.A. 27–28, 67.[8]

Notice how the school district is giving more space to the details about the displaying of the banner (a good fact for the school district), whereas the student is giving it less space.

Technique Two: Location. You can de-emphasize bad facts by "hiding" them in an introductory clause. For example, "Although Ms. Jones had a D.W.I. last year, since that time she has stopped drinking alcohol; attended Alcoholics Anonymous meetings twice a week; and started volunteering for Mothers Against Drunk Driving." The bad fact (D.W.I.) is de-emphasized by its location in the introductory clause, and the reader's focus is on the good facts (sobriety, meetings, and volunteering).

Technique Three: Passive Voice. While, generally speaking, you want your writing, including your statement of facts, to be written in active voice, passive voice can and should be used when it has the purpose of de-emphasizing the actor. For example, if you represent the defendant in a criminal case for murder, which sounds better for your client?

Passive voice: The victim was shot.

Active voice: Defendant shot the victim.

Passive voice allows you to state the legally significant fact without emphasizing the actor.

Technique Four: Noun and Verb Choice. You can persuade in your statement of facts through your choice of words, specifically your choice of nouns and verbs. In the earlier dog-bite example, notice how the Defendant dog owner used the generic noun "dog," while the Plaintiff used the specific noun

7. Br. of Pet'r at 4, *Morse v. Frederick*, 551 U.S. 393 (2007) (No. 06-278), 2007 WL 118979, at *4.

8. Resp't Br. at 1, *Morse v. Frederick*, 551 U.S. 393 (2007) (No. 06-278), 2007 WL 579230, at *1.

"Rottweiler," and how the Defendant used the weak verb "was bitten," while Plaintiff used the strong, vivid verb "attacked." These word choices were made deliberately to tell the story in the light most favorable for each side.

Technique Five: Labeling. You can subtly persuade in your statement of facts by how you refer to parties or players in your case. Notice how in the Defendant's MSJ (Appendix F), Defendant Happiness of Life refers to itself as "Happiness of Life" or "HOL" and refers to Plaintiff John Bell as only "Plaintiff." In this way, Defendant is personalizing itself, but de-personalizing the other side. Plaintiff does the opposite in his MSJ Opposition (Appendix G): Plaintiff personalizes himself by referring to himself as "Mr. Bell" and de-personalizes Defendant Happiness of Life by simply referring to it as "Defendant." Also, each side "labels" Ava Bell (the testatrix) in a slightly different way. Plaintiff refers to her as "Mrs. Bell," to emphasize the fact that she was married to Mr. Bell, while Defendant refers to her as "Ms. Bell" to de-emphasize the marriage. These are subtle differences, but they help tell each side's story in a persuasive way.

Technique Six: Show. Don't Tell. Your statement of facts should be free from your "opinions" or your legal conclusions. You should be telling a story that allows the reader to reach his or her own opinions and conclusions—one that is favorable for your client. Consider the following in a statement of facts: "Mary's academic performance was poor." That sentence is really the writer's opinion. That is, the writer is essentially telling the reader to "trust me" that Mary's academic performance was "poor" (whatever that adjective "poor" means in the mind of the writer). Now consider the following in a statement of facts: "Mary's grade point average was a 1.5 out of 4.0." This is a fact, and from this fact, the reader will draw her own conclusion that Mary's academic performance was poor. The second example is showing the reader. The first example is only telling the reader. Do you see how the second example is more powerful? If you see an adjective or an adverb in your statement of facts, it should be a red flag causing you to pause and ask yourself whether you need to revise the sentence to show, not to tell.

Just as you should not include opinions in your statement of facts, you should also not include legal conclusions or argument. In your statement of facts, it would be improper to say, "The doctor committed malpractice by leaving a sponge in Plaintiff's stomach during the operation." The first part of the sentence is a legal conclusion and argument. While this sentence would be fine in your argument and authorities section, it is improper in your statement of facts. Instead, in your statement of facts, you would simply say, "The doctor left a sponge in Plaintiff's stomach during the operation." From this, the reader would draw her own conclusion that the doctor committed malpractice.

Technique Seven: "Good" Absent Facts Should Be Included. Depending on the facts of your case, it might be that the absence of a fact or facts is, in and of itself, a good fact for your client. You should include absent facts in your statement of facts. For example, let's say you represent the plaintiff in a defamation cause of action, and you are trying to prove that the defendant acted with negligence in publishing a false, defamatory story. To show this negligence, you might include absent facts or facts showing what the defendant did **not** do. For example, "Defendant did not reach out to Plaintiff for comment. Defendant did not run a fact check on the story. Defendant did not check the background of his one anonymous source." Things the defendant failed to do—absent facts—can be "good" facts for your client and should be included in your statement of facts.

Technique Eight: Soundbites Can Be Powerful. In persuasive writing, your factual record may include party or witness depositions, letters, sworn discovery responses, or other "quotable" documents. You can and should selectively quote from these documents if it will help you to persuasively tell your client's side of the story.

For example, Defendant's MSJ in the Appendix of this book selectively quotes the depositions to describe Ms. Bell's marriage to Mr. Bell:

> Ms. Bell told Ms. Welsh that her marriage to Plaintiff was "miserable," and her home life was "difficult." *Id.* at 7:6–21. Mr. Bell did not support Ms. Bell's membership in HOL or her choices to stop taking prescription drugs, stop drinking, and stop being materialistic. *Id.* Indeed, Plaintiff admitted that his marriage to Ms. Bell was "rocky." Ex. 2, John Bell Dep. 8:16–23.

You should see how these quotes help Defendant to persuasively present its side of the story: that Ms. Bell had good reason for reducing her husband's share in her will. Note that it is okay to use adjectives in the statement of facts when they are part of a quote from the factual record because, in this context, the adjectives are not the writer's opinion but, instead, part of the facts of the case.

3. How to organize your statement of facts

Just like in objective writing, your statement of facts should, in the vast majority of cases, be organized chronologically. Chronological order is the easiest for the reader to follow; therefore, unless you have a reason to stray from chronological order, it should be your default organizational structure for your statement of facts. To organize your statement of facts chronologically, you should start by creating a timeline and then, using this timeline, pull in your legally significant facts (trigger facts).

Why might you stray from chronological order? Let's say that your facts deal with two different sets of parties. For example, let's say you have a case against a product manufacturer and a retailer of the product for an injury caused by the product. You might choose to group your facts as follows: (1) facts related to the injury, (2) facts related to the manufacturer, and (3) facts related to the retailer. Using strict chronological order might be confusing as there are really three different "timelines."

To keep your statement of facts organized, you should always use descriptive subheadings to keep your reader on track and to break up your facts. See how the statement of facts subheadings in Defendant's MSJ versus those in Plaintiff's MSJ Opposition tell two sides of the same story:

DEFENDANT'S MSJ

II. STATEMENT OF FACTS

A. After executing her first will, Ms. Bell suffered an accident, lost her brother, and became depressed.

B. Ms. Bell met Ms. Welsh, joined HOL, and became "the most happy she had been in years."

C. Plaintiff did not support Ms. Bell's newfound happiness through HOL, and their marriage became "miserable."

D. Ms. Bell executed a new will, decreasing Plaintiff's share and leaving the residuary of her estate to the non-profit HOL, of which she was an avid member.

PLAINTIFF'S MSJ OPPOSITION

II. STATEMENT OF FACTS

A. Mrs. Bell's 2016 Will left the bulk of her estate to her husband, Mr. Bell.

B. Mrs. Bell suffered severe head trauma and was treated for depression.

C. Mrs. Bell met Anna Welsh, joined HOL, and became brainwashed.

D. After brainwashing Mrs. Bell, Ms. Welsh told Mrs. Bell the "quickest way" to gain an honorary title in HOL was to change her will to leave HOL a substantial sum of money.

4. Citing to the record

Your statement of facts should include citations to the factual "record," i.e., the evidence of the case. In trial court motions, the factual record is usually attached to the motion or opposition as a number of exhibits. Just as when you cite to legal authority, your citations to the factual record in your statement of facts should be in *Bluebook* form. Refer to *Bluebook* Bluepages B17.1.1 and B17.2, and Bluepages Table 1 for how to formulate citations to the factual record.

> **Long cite:** John Bell Dep. (Jan. 9, 2019) 4:3–6, attached as Ex. 2.
>
> **Short cite:** Ex. 2, John Bell Dep. 8:16–23.

F. Legal standard

After the statement of facts and before you get into the meat of your argument, you will include a section on the legal standard according to which the court will decide the specific type of motion before it. A legal standard is different than a rule. A legal standard is the lens through which a court reviews the issue based on the procedural posture of the case. It is not cause of action specific; rather, it is specific to the procedural posture of the case and the type of motion before the court. For example, whenever a trial court is deciding a motion for summary judgment, regardless of whether it is a motion for summary judgment regarding a negligence cause of action, defamation cause of action, premises liability cause of action, breach of contract cause of action, or so forth, it will use the same legal standard to decide the motion. That uniform legal standard for motions for summary judgment is as follows: a motion for summary judgment will be granted only when there is no genuine issue of material fact, and the movant is entitled to judgment as a matter of law.

1. Where to find the legal standard

Legal standards for trial court motions are set forth in both the rules of procedure and caselaw. For example, the standard for summary judgment in federal court is set forth in Federal Rule of Civil Procedure 56: "The court shall grant summary judgment if the movant shows that there is no genuine dispute as to any material fact and the movant is entitled to judgment as a matter of law."[9] The standard is elaborated on by caselaw, which provides that "[o]n summary judgment the inferences to be drawn from the underlying facts ... must be viewed in the light most favorable to the party opposing the motion."[10] Whenever a federal trial court decides a motion for summary judgment, this legal standard or summary judgment "lens" is used. In contrast to a motion for summary judgment, when a motion to dismiss is filed, which is at a different procedural posture in the case, the court uses a different lens. The standard for a motion to

---

9. Fed. R. Civ. P. 56.
10. *United States v. Diebold, Inc.*, 369 U.S. 654, 655 (1962).

dismiss filed in federal court is set forth in Federal Rule of Civil Procedure 12(b) and states that a motion to dismiss will be granted if a plaintiff's complaint "fail[s] to state a claim upon which relief can be granted."[11] The standard is elaborated on in caselaw, which provides a motion to dismiss for failure to state a claim will be granted only if "it appears beyond doubt that the plaintiff can prove no set of facts in support of his claim which would entitle him to relief."[12] Regardless of what type of claim the defendant moves to dismiss (negligence, breach of contract, etc.), the lens the court will use to decide the motion to dismiss is the same.

2. How to state the legal standard of review persuasively for your client

You should state the standard of review that governs your motion in a way that is favorable to your client. Both the motion and the opposition will include the same standard, but each will frame it differently. One side (the movant) wants the standard to be met, while the other side (the non-movant) does not. The standard itself will not change, but how it is framed and explained will. After all, each side needs to state the standard in the way that is persuasive for her client.

Compare how the movant (Defendant Happiness of Life) states the summary judgment standard compared to how the non-movant (Plaintiff John Bell) states the standard.

> SUMMARY JUDGMENT STANDARD FROM MSJ
>
> Texas Rule of Civil Procedure 166a(c) provides that summary judgment must be granted if "there is no genuine issue as to any material fact," and "the moving party is entitled to judgment as a matter of law." Tex. R. Civ. P. 166a(c). Summary judgment provides a means to eliminate "patently unmeritorious claims," and it should be granted if the record establishes the right of the defendant to judgment as a matter of law. *Swilley v. Hughes*, 488 S.W.2d 64, 68 (Tex. 1972). When a defendant moves for summary judgment on a plaintiff's cause of action, it does not need to disprove all elements; instead, it must only disprove one. *Henkel v. Norman*, 441 S.W.3d 249, 251 (Tex. 2014).
>
> SUMMARY JUDGMENT STANDARD MSJ OPPOSITION
>
> Under Texas Rule of Civil Procedure 166a(c), a court must deny summary judgment unless the movant establishes that there is no genuine issue of material fact, and, therefore, the movant is entitled to judgment as a matter of law. Tex. R. Civ. P. 166a(c). In deciding whether there is a genuine issue of material fact precluding summary judgment, evidence favorable to the non-movant will be taken as true. *Nixon v. Mr. Prop. Mgmt. Co., Inc.*, 690

---

11. Fed. R. Civ. P. 12(b)(6).
12. *Gibson v. United States*, 781 F.2d 1334, 1337 (9th Cir. 1986), *cert. denied*, 479 U.S. 1054 (1987).

> S.W.2d 546, 548–49 (Tex. 1985). Every reasonable inference must be indulged in favor of the non-movant, and any doubts must be resolved in the non-movant's favor. *Id.* at 549.

Both sides present and cite the same standard, but the movant states the standard positively because the movant wants the standard to be met (summary judgment *must be granted* when), whereas the non-movant states it negatively because the non-movant does not want the standard to be met (a court *must deny* summary judgment unless). After stating the standard, each side explains it in a way that is favorable to his or her client. The explanations of the standard are both correct, but the movant explains the standard in a way that emphasizes the parts more favorable to the standard being met (framing the standard as less difficult to meet), whereas the non-movant explains the standard emphasizing parts favorable to the standard not being met (framing the standard as difficult to meet).

G. Argument and authorities

The meat of your legal argument will go in a section titled "Argument and Authorities" or "Argument," depending on the style in your jurisdiction. The argument and authorities section is like the discussion section of an objective memo, except it is persuasive. That is, it is an argument, not a neutral discussion. In persuasive writing, you should give some thought as to how you organize the issues in your argument and authorities section in order to maximize your persuasion. If you have multiple causes of action or defenses that you need to address, you should start with your strongest argument first. For example, let's say as the defendant you are moving for summary judgment on the plaintiff's cause of action and on your own affirmative defense. You "win" whether summary judgment is granted as to either. Therefore, you should start with whichever—the cause of action or the affirmative defense—you believe gives you the strongest chance of winning the motion.

Similarly, within a single cause of action or defense, in persuasive writing, you may choose to start with your "best" element, even if that element is the last element of the cause of action. For example, if a defendant is moving on a plaintiff's cause of action, the defendant will win if it meets its burden to show no genuine issue of material fact with respect to only one of the elements of plaintiff's cause of action. While the defendant may choose to argue there is no genuine issue of material fact on all of the elements, it only needs to disprove one in order to win. Therefore, the defendant may choose to start with the element on which the court is mostly likely to find there is no genuine issue of material fact and address the remaining elements in the order of their strength. However, if all of the elements are equally "strong," it probably makes sense to address them in the order in which they typically appear so the motion is the most logical.

When responding to a motion, you need not adopt the other side's organization. Rather, you can organize your arguments in the order of their strength. The exception to this rule is that it may make sense to simply follow the other side's organization as the non-movant where you must "win" on all issues and are not raising any new issues not covered by the movant's motion. For example, in a motion for summary judgment where the defendant has moved on all three elements of a plaintiff's three-element claim, to "win" the plaintiff must "win" on all three elements. That is, the plaintiff must show the court all three elements are equally strong such that the order of them does not matter and re-ordering the elements will simply make the opposition harder for the court to follow.

1. Overall roadmap

Just as in the discussion section of an objective memo, in the argument and authorities section of your motion you begin with an overall, introductory roadmap. Because, in your motion, you already have an introduction section that summarizes and previews the arguments in the body of your motion, the overall roadmap at the beginning of the argument and authorities section is a little more "bare bones" than the one in the discussion section of an objective memo.

The overall roadmap should state the overall conclusion you want the court to reach and then list the arguments you will make in the order that they will be discussed. If there is anything that will not be discussed, you should dispose of that issue in the roadmap. Additionally, if there are any favorable "subrules" that apply generally to all of the issues or elements addressed in your motion, you can include those in the overall roadmap as well.

DEFENDANT'S MSJ OVERALL ROADMAP

> V. ARGUMENT AND AUTHORITIES
>
> There is no genuine issue of material fact as to Plaintiff's claim of undue influence. To set aside a will on the ground of undue influence, the Plaintiff has the burden to prove: "(1) the existence and exertion of an influence; (2) the effective operation of such influence so as to subvert or overpower the mind of the testator at the time of the execution of the testament; and (3) the execution of a testament which the maker thereof would not have executed but for such influence." *Rothermel*, 369 S.W.2d at 922. Because there is no genuine issue of material fact as to any of these elements, this Court should grant summary judgment.

Notice how the Defendant begins with the overall conclusion it wants the court to reach in the first sentence. Then, Defendant lists the three elements in the order they will be discussed and argues that there is no genuine issue of material fact as to any of the elements.

PLAINTIFF'S MSJ OPPOSITION ROADMAP:

> V. ARGUMENT AND AUTHORITIES
>
> There are genuine issues of material fact as to Mr. Bell's claim of undue influence. A will must be set aside when the plaintiff proves: "(1) the existence and exertion of an influence; (2) the effective operation of such influence so as to subvert or overpower the mind of the testat[rix] at the time of the execution of the testament; and (3) the execution of a testament which the maker thereof would not have executed but for such influence." *Rothermel*, 369 S.W.2d at 922. No two cases of undue influence are exactly alike. *Id.* at 921. When examining an undue influence claim, this Court should consider "all of the circumstances shown or established by the evidence . . . even though none of the circumstances standing alone would be sufficient to show the elements of undue influence," and, "if when considered together they produce a reasonable belief that an influence was exerted that subverted or overpowered the mind of the testat[rix] and resulted in the execution of the testament in controversy, the evidence is sufficient" to establish an undue influence claim. *Id.* at 922. While undue influence may be shown by direct or circumstantial evidence, it is usually established by circumstantial evidence. *See id.* The facts in this case raise genuine issues of material fact as to each element of Mr. Bell's undue influence claim, and this Court should, therefore, deny Defendant's Motion for Summary Judgment in its entirety.

Notice how Plaintiff's roadmap looks similar to the Defendant's, but also includes rules favorable to the Plaintiff that go to all three elements of the undue influence claim.

2. Mini-roadmaps under subheadings

Just as in objective writing, any time you have a large section of your argument and authorities section that is subdivided into multiple small sections, you will insert a mini-roadmap between the larger section heading and the first subdivision heading. The mini-roadmap will simply list your arguments for that subdivided section. In the below argument and authorities example (text omitted), large sections A and B are subdivided into small sections so there is a mini-roadmap immediately under those headings. Section C is not subdivided and, therefore, does not need a mini-roadmap.

V. ARGUMENT AND AUTHORITIES

[*Overall Roadmap*]

A. [Cause of action A]

[*Mini-Roadmap*]

1. Element 1
2. Element 2

B. [Cause of action B]

[*Mini-Roadmap*]

1. Element 1
2. Element 2
3. Element 3

C. [Cause of action C]

3. CRACC: Persuasive writing

For persuasive writing, you will use the formula CRACC to present your legal arguments for each issue. CRACC stands for Conclusion, Rule, Analysis, Counter-analysis (new "C"), and Conclusion. Other than Counter-analysis, which is new, the other parts of CRAC are, in terms of other titles, the same in persuasive writing as in objective writing. However, in this section of the book, you will learn how to make those parts persuasive. In order to transform the parts of CRACC into a persuasive argument, you must have first mastered stating the parts of CRAC objectively. Therefore, it may be helpful to review the corresponding objective CRAC sections in Part Two of this book as you read through this part.

a) CRACC: Creating persuasive opening and closing Conclusion sentences

Just as in objective writing, in persuasive writing, every issue in your motion or opposition will begin and end with a conclusion sentence (first and last "C" of CRACC)—a statement of the conclusion or desired result of your legal analysis of that issue. The purpose for these conclusions is slightly different in persuasive writing than in objective writing. Although persuasive conclusions—like objective conclusions—help the reader to better understand the significance of what she is about to read, persuasive conclusions also serve the purpose of advocating for a client's desired outcome. In other words, instead of concluding by telling the reader what you **think** the outcome may be, in persuasive writing you conclude to tell the reader (the court) what you **want** the outcome to be.

Conclusion sentences in your motion tell the court your desired outcome of the legal issue being addressed. Although there are two "C"s or Conclusions in CRACC (the opening conclusion sentence and closing conclusion sentence), you will actually have three forms of Conclusions for each issue you are addressing—the third being the conclusory subheading that goes above each CRACC.

Unlike in objective writing where the conclusion states the predicted outcome based on a neutral assessment of the law and facts, in persuasive writing the conclusion requests that the court make a determination in favor of your client on the issue. Thus, you can see the conclusion sentences in Defendant's MSJ are polar-opposite those in Plaintiff's MSJ Opposition. This is because each party wants opposite outcomes: the Defendant wants summary judgment to be granted and the Plaintiff wants summary judgment to be denied. The Defendant wants the court to hold there is no genuine issue of material fact on the elements, and the Plaintiff wants the court to hold the opposite. The chart below shows these opposing conclusions for each of the elements of undue influence addressed in the motion and opposition.

	DEFENDANT (MSJ)	PLAINTIFF (OPPOSITION)
Conclusory heading for element 1	Plaintiff cannot prove the existence and exertion of an undue influence.	There is substantial evidence that HOL exerted undue influence on Mrs. Bell.
Opening Conclusion for element 1	This Court should grant summary judgment because Plaintiff cannot prove the existence and exertion of an undue influence by HOL on Ms. Bell.	This Court should deny summary judgment because there is, at a minimum, a fact issue as to whether there was an existence and exertion of undue influence by HOL.
Closing Conclusion for element 1	Each of the five *Rothermel* factors weighs against a finding of the existence and exertion of an undue influence by Ms. Welsh over Ms. Bell. Accordingly, Plaintiff will be unable to meet his burden to prove the first element, and this Court should grant summary judgment.	Ms. Welsh/HOL's influence—like most undue influence—involved an "extended course of dealings and circumstances" that dramatically influenced every area of Mrs. Bell's life and this Court—considering "all evidence of relevant matters that occurred within a reasonable time before or after the will's execution"—should hold there exists, at a minimum, genuine issues of material fact as to the existence and exertion of undue influence such that summary judgment should be denied.

b) CRACC: Creating persuasive Rule statements

Just as in objective writing, after your opening conclusion sentence ("C") is your Rule ("R" of CRAC). Rules are the basis of all legal analysis—regardless of whether that legal analysis is objective or persuasive. In fact, in persuasive writing, courts (and their judges and clerks) do not decide cases based on what you as a lawyer think but, rather, on what the law is (that is, the legal rules applicable to your case). Just like in objective writing, in persuasive writing, Rules have three parts: the general rule, subrules, and the case illustration(s). These three parts—from a macro standpoint—look the same in persuasive writing and in objective writing. First, the general rule is where you state the law governing the element or claim at issue. Second, the subrules explain the general rule by defining key terms from the general rule and identifying how courts determine whether the general rule is satisfied. Third, case illustrations explain (or illustrate) how that general rule (and its subrules) have been applied in prior cases involving similar facts. In other words, just like in objective writing, in persuasive writing, the three parts of the Rule—the general rule, subrules, and case illustrations—work together to explain the law to the court and to define the parameters of the legal standard from its broadest application (the general rule) to its narrowest (the case illustration).

However, unique to persuasive writing, the Rule serves as a persuasive tool in a lawyer's toolbelt. Sometimes this is confusing to students. "I do not understand," they say. "How can the law be persuasive? The law is the same for both sides, right?" Yes, the governing law for the issue will be the same for both sides. That is, for example, element one of an undue influence is the same for both sides: element one is the existence and exertion of an influence. You do not make the law persuasive by changing it or misstating it. Rather, how you make the law persuasive is through how you frame it. Unlike in objective writing, in persuasive writing you must be intentional in how you frame the general rule, how you select and frame subrules, and how you select case illustrations. So, although the content and the structure of the persuasive Rule is, generally speaking, similar to that of the objective Rule, in the end (as you will learn in detail below) the persuasive Rule's substance and style are unique.

i. CRACC: general rule, the first part of a persuasive Rule

Just as in objective writing, in persuasive writing the general rule is the first of the three parts of your Rule and is drafted in the present tense. Moreover, just as in objective writing, in persuasive writing the purpose of the general rule is to provide a succinct statement of the law for the issue. This is important because courts are not persuaded by what **you** think. Rather, courts want to follow the law and the legal precedent that governs the issue. Therefore, while you want to state your general rule in the way that is most persuasive for your client, you cannot, in an attempt to make the general rule persuasive, "change" the law to make it better for your client than it really is. Instead, to make the general rule persuasive, you must state it from the point of view or angle that is most favorable to your client in relation to the issue.

Let's work through an example together. The seminal case *Rothermel v. Duncan* sets forth the general rule for element three of undue influence as follows: "Thus, before a testament may be set aside on the grounds of undue influence the contestant must prove: . . . (3) the execution of an instrument that the maker thereof would not have executed but for such influence."[13]

In objective writing, it would be okay to simply copy *Rothermel*'s statement of the third element as your general rule for the third element. In persuasive writing, like in objective writing, what is quoted above from *Rothermel* is the general rule for element three. The general rule does not change. However, in persuasive writing, you would not want to simply state the general rule exactly as it is written in *Rothermel* in your motion or opposition. Rather, you need to frame the general rule in a way that is favorable to your client. To figure out how to frame the general rule persuasively, follow these four steps:

Step one: Figure out what your client wants in relation to the general rule.

To frame the general rule persuasively, you must first ask yourself: what does my client want in relation to this issue (here, element three)? If you represent the Plaintiff, he wants this element to be satisfied. If you represent the Defendant, it does not want this element to be satisfied. Both sides want the opposite outcome. Therefore, while the general rule for both sides will be the same law, the way the parties frame the general rule will be opposite.

Step two: Present the general rule in a way that supports what your client wants.

Now that you know what you client wants in relation to the general rule, you will emphasize the rule in way that supports your client's desired outcome. When you are learning to emphasize and de-emphasize parts of a general rule, consider the following two questions: (1) does my client benefit if I start the rule positively or negatively; and (2) does my client benefit if I state the rule narrowly or broadly? Beginning a rule statement by stating the outcome you want for your client will lead the reader toward that position (these are called Jedi mind tricks).

The party that wants the element to be satisfied (here, Plaintiff) will frame the general rule positively and broadly. Positively because the party wants the element to be satisfied—that is, the party wants the court to hold the element has been met. Broadly because the party wants to frame the element in a way that makes it seem easier to meet, as if a broader array of facts will satisfy the element. On the other hand, the party that wants the element to **not** be satisfied (here, Defendant) will frame the general rule negatively and narrowly. Negatively because the party wants the element to

13. 369 S.W.2d 917, 923 (Tex. 1963).

not be satisfied, and narrowly because the party wants the element to seem more difficult to satisfy such that it narrows its perceived application.

The chart below provides examples of positive, broad language and negative, narrow language that can be used to frame general rules.

Positive and broad	"The element is satisfied whenever . . ." "A party meets the element anytime . . ." "A party only need to show . . . to satisfy element . . ."
Negative and narrow	"The element is not satisfied unless . . ." "A court will not hold the element is satisfied except when . . ."

Step three: Emphasize or de-emphasize the burden of proof in the general rule.

Whichever side does not have the burden of proof on the element will, when framing the general rule, emphasize the burden of the other side. The party that does have the burden of proof will de-emphasize the heaviness of the burden. Looking again at the example here, because undue influence is Plaintiff's cause of action, Plaintiff has the burden of proof and, as such, Plaintiff will de-emphasize his burden, while Defendant will emphasize it.

Step four: Make sure your general rule is accurate and complete.

Your general rule, while persuasive, must remain accurate. Make sure your general rule remains true to the actual legal standard.

In summary, unlike in objective writing where the general rule is often—in essence—cut and pasted into the memo from its source, in persuasive writing you should not just cut and paste the general rule into your motion or opposition. Instead, you need to think about framing the general rule in a way that is most persuasive for your client. Below is an example of a general rule written three ways: objectively, persuasively in favor of the Defendant, and persuasively in favor of the Plaintiff.

OBJECTIVE MEMO

> The third element required before a testament may be set aside on the grounds of undue influence is "the execution of an instrument that the maker thereof would not have executed but for such influence." *Rothermel v. Duncan*, 369 S.W.2d 917, 923 (Tex. 1963).

This sample general rule for element three from the objective memo is, in essence, the statement of the rule as it appears in the caselaw with little adjustment and no spin.

PLAINTIFF'S MSJ OPPOSITION

> The third element of undue influence is satisfied whenever the evidence shows the execution of a testament which the testator would not have executed but for the influence. *Rothermel v. Duncan*, 369 S.W.2d 917, 923 (Tex. 1963).

This sample general rule for element three from Plaintiff's MSJ Opposition is written positively ("element is satisfied") and broadly ("whenever"), thus, maximizing the chances that a reader will find the element satisfied. Additionally, the burden of proof is de-emphasized.

DEFENDANT'S MSJ

> A contestant will not meet her burden to show undue influence unless she proves the execution of a testament that the testator would not have made but for the influence. *Rothermel v. Duncan*, 369 S.W.2d 917, 923 (Tex. 1963).

This sample general rule for element three from Defendant's MSJ is written negatively ("will not meet her burden to show") and narrowly ("unless") and, thus, lessens the chances that the reader will find the element satisfied. Defendant's framing of the general rule also emphasizes that the Plaintiff has the burden to satisfy this element.

ii. CRACC: subrules, the second part of a persuasive Rule

Subrules perform the same role in persuasive writing as they do in objective writing: they explain the general rule. Also, just like in objective writing, persuasive subrules are drafted in the present tense. Unique to persuasive writing, subrules are another persuasive tool in a lawyer's toolbelt that support your legal position and persuade your reader that your requested outcome is the right one.

Generally speaking, the art of generating a persuasive rule statement turns on your selection of subrules that support your argument and emphasize or frame the law in a way that supports the result your client wants. There are a few things to keep in mind when making subrules persuasive. First, as was noted in the discussion of general rules, you cannot misrepresent the law. You must accurately state the law and cannot change the law by only including subrules to favor your client. Second, the key to making subrules persuasive is through your framing of subrules with your client's desired outcome in mind. Unlike in objective writing, where you want to provide the court with a complete, neutral picture of the law, in persuasive writing you want to present the court with an accurate picture of the law that is framed in favor of your client's position.

Therefore, when it comes to subrules, you need not include all subrules that define the general rule. Rather, you must include, what we will call, "crucial subrules"—subrules that define key terms in the general rule. With respect to other subrules, you should only include ones that are favorable for your client.

In the chart below, the first subrule is a crucial one because it defines the third element. You see that, because it is a crucial subrule, both sides will include it in their subrules; however, they will frame it differently. Similar to general rules, you see that the Plaintiff, who wants the standard satisfied, frames the subrule positively, whereas the Defendant does the opposite. The framing of your subrules (in addition to the perspective from which they are written) deeply affects their persuasion. With respect to the other subrules, you will see that the ones the Plaintiff includes and the ones the Defendant includes are not the same. Rather, the parties pick and choose the subrules that are favorable in order to frame the law persuasively for their sides.

OBJECTIVE SUBRULES FOR ELEMENT THREE	PLAINTIFF'S MSJ OPPOSITION'S PERSUASIVE SUBRULES FOR ELEMENT THREE	DEFENDANT'S MSJ'S PERSUASIVE SUBRULES FOR ELEMENT THREE
Finally, the establishment of the fact that the testament executed would not have been executed but for such influence is generally predicated upon a consideration of whether the testament executed is unnatural in its terms of disposition of property. *Rothermel v. Duncan*, 369 S.W.2d 917, 923 (Tex. 1963).	If the testament executed is "unnatural," the third element is satisfied. *Rothermel v. Duncan*, 369 S.W.2d 917, 923 (Tex. 1963).	The third element is not satisfied unless the testament is "unnatural." *Rothermel v. Duncan*, 369 S.W.2d 917, 923 (Tex. 1963).
Whether the testament unnaturally disposes of property is, to a certain extent, directed by the preceding factors. We consider the testator's stated desires and actions, [] and whether the testator unexpectedly disinherited close family members previously provided for, . . . *In re Estate of Luthen*, 13-12-00576-CV, 2014 WL 6632952, at *7 (Tex. App.—Corpus Christi Nov. 24, 2014, no pet.) (internal citations and quotations omitted).	A court will consider "the testator's stated desires and actions, [] and whether the testator unexpectedly disinherited close family members previously provided for" in determining whether the testament is unnatural. *In re Estate of Luthen*, 13-12-00576-CV, 2014 WL 6632952, at *7 (Tex. App.—Corpus Christi Nov. 24, 2014, no pet.) (internal citations and quotations omitted).	Do not include because it highlights law in unfavorable way for client's position.

(cont.)

(cont.)

OBJECTIVE SUBRULES FOR ELEMENT THREE	PLAINTIFF'S MSJ OPPOSITION'S PERSUASIVE SUBRULES FOR ELEMENT THREE	DEFENDANT'S MSJ'S PERSUASIVE SUBRULES FOR ELEMENT THREE
[I]t is only where all reasonable explanation in affection for the devise is lacking that the trier of facts may conclude the devise is an unnatural disposition. *In re Estate of Luthen*, 13-12-00576-CV, 2014 WL 6632952, at *7 (Tex. App.—Corpus Christi Nov. 24, 2014, no pet.) (internal citations and quotations omitted).	Do not include because it highlights law in unfavorable way for client's position.	A testament is unnatural only when "all reasonable explanation in affection for the devise is lacking." *In re Estate of Luthen*, 13-12-00576-CV, 2014 WL 6632952, at *7 (Tex. App.—Corpus Christi Nov. 24, 2014, no pet.) (internal citations and quotations omitted).

iii. CRACC: case illustrations, the third part of a persuasive Rule

Persuasive case illustrations are designed to, like case illustrations in objective writing, provide an example of how another court has applied the rule at issue in a different case. Persuasive case illustrations—just like with persuasive general rules and persuasive subrules—also serve as another tool in the persuasive lawyer's toolbelt because they help persuade the reader to give the lawyer the outcome she seeks.

Persuasive case illustrations contain the same four parts as objective case illustrations: (1) a topic sentence; (2) the holding of the case on the element or issue for which you are illustrating it; (3) the trigger facts related to the element or issue for which you are illustrating it; and (4) the court's reasoning or how it applied the facts to the law to reach its holding. Moreover, just like in objective writing, persuasive case illustrations should be drafted in the past tense.

Unlike in objective writing, where you select cases to illustrate in order to provide your reader with an accurate and full picture of the law, in persuasive writing, you select cases to illustrate that will help you persuade the court to reach the outcome your client wants. To do this, you should select cases to illustrate that are "good law" (meaning they have not been overturned), have facts similar to the facts of your case, and reach the outcome that your client wants on the issue for which you are illustrating the case. That is, unlike in objective writing where you illustrate factually similar cases on both ends of the spectrum (one where the element was satisfied and one where it was not), in persuasive writing you generally illustrate only factually similar cases that reach the same outcome that you want. For example, if you represent the Plaintiff and you are looking for cases to illustrate for element one of your cause of action, you would be looking for cases that are factually similar to your case **and** that held element one was satisfied. (You would not want to illustrate a case that was factually similar to your case but held that element one was not satisfied because that is not the outcome you want.) Then, in your Analysis ("A"), you would argue to the court that your case is so like the favorable illustrated case(s) that the court should reach the same outcome as the court(s) reached in the illustrated case(s) on that element.

Thus, the difference between case illustrations in objective and persuasive writing is less about changing the illustration on a sentence level but more about which cases you pick to illustrate. In persuasive writing, case illustrations look the same in that you are still including a topic sentence (although the topic sentence should be stated persuasively for your client), the court's holding, the trigger facts, and the court's reasoning. However, in persuasive writing, you are only illustrating cases that reach the same outcome that you want the court to reach on the issue. That is, the biggest difference between objective case illustrations and persuasive case illustrations is the cases that you pick.

Below are three case illustrations related to the second element of undue influence that demonstrate how the selection of a case or cases to illustrate affects the potential outcome and the persuasive effect of the case illustration.

OBJECTIVE EXAMPLE

The first example contains two case illustrations that are drafted objectively to provide a complete and neutral picture of the parameters of the element at issue (here, element two).

Evidence that a testator suffers from depression is insufficient to satisfy the second element of undue influence as long as the testator is able to conduct her affairs and is physically capable. In *Estate of Steed*, the court overturned the jury's finding that the testator's mind was overpowered and, accordingly, the jury's finding of undue influence. 152 S.W.3d at 811. In that case, although the testator suffered from depression and anxiety and was taking Prozac, he was able to conduct his business affairs (for example, he worked as an attorney) and was a physically able person. *Id.* The court reasoned that it was "clearly wrong and unjust" for the jury to find that the wife overpowered the testator's mind because the testator was "a meticulous, detail[ed] person" who "worked regularly to the date of his death" and was "not physically or mentally impaired from performing his daily tasks." *Id.*

Evidence that a testator was using drugs or alcohol around the time of the will's execution is sufficient to prove that the testator was susceptible to an undue influence overpowering her mind. In *Estate of Johnson*, the court held the testator's alcohol abuse coupled with his memory dysfunction made him increasingly susceptible to undue influence such that the second element of the *Rothermel* test was satisfied. 340 S.W.3d at 778. In that case, the testator was an alcoholic and had an ongoing drinking problem. *Id.* In addition to the alcohol use, there was also evidence that the testator suffered memory dysfunction. *Id.* The court reasoned that drinking had an adverse effect on his reasoning and left him less capable of resisting the undue influence brought on by the beneficiary to change his will. *Id.* Furthermore, the court reasoned that due to the testator's alcohol abuse and the effect it had on his mental capacity to resist, the testator was susceptible to undue influence and that ample opportunity existed for the beneficiary to unduly influence the testator while he was drinking. *Id.*

PERSUASIVE DEFENDANT EXAMPLE (FROM DEFENDANT'S MSJ)

Defendant illustrates Estate of Steed—*a case where the court held the second element of undue influence was not satisfied—because Defendant wants the court in its case to reach the same outcome as the court in* Estate of Steed *with respect to element two (holding it is not satisfied).*

The fact that a testatrix suffers from depression is insufficient to meet the second element of undue influence when the testatrix is still able to conduct her business affairs and is physically capable. In *Estate of Steed*, the court overturned the jury's finding that the testator's mind was overpowered and, as such, the jury's finding of undue influence. 152 S.W.3d at 811. In that case, although the testator suffered from depression and anxiety and was taking Prozac, he was able to conduct his business affairs and was a physically able person. *Id.* The court reasoned that it was "clearly wrong and unjust" for the jury to find that the wife overpowered the testator's mind because the testator was "a meticulous, detailed person" who "worked regularly to the date of his death" and was "not physically or mentally impaired from performing his daily tasks." *Id.*

PERSUASIVE FOR PLAINTIFF EXAMPLE (FROM PLAINTIFF'S MSJ OPPOSITION)

Plaintiff illustrates Estate of Johnson—*a case where the court held the second element of undue influence was satisfied—because Plaintiff wants the court in his case to reach the same outcome as the court in* Estate of Johnson *with respect to the element two (hold it is satisfied).*

Evidence that a testatrix was using drugs or alcohol around the time of the will's execution is sufficient evidence to prove that a testatrix was susceptible to an undue influence overpowering her mind. In *Estate of Johnson*, the court held the testator's alcohol abuse, coupled with his memory dysfunction, made him increasingly susceptible to undue influence such that the

> second element was satisfied. 340 S.W.3d at 778. In that case, the testator was an alcoholic. *Id.* There was evidence that the testator suffered memory dysfunction as well. *Id.* The court noted that drinking had an adverse effect on his mind and cognitive reasoning, leaving him "vulnerable to undue influence." *Id.* The court reasoned that due to the testator's alcohol abuse and the effect it had on his mental capacity to resist, the testator was "susceptible to undue influence" and that "ample opportunity" existed for the beneficiary to unduly influence the testator while he was drinking. *Id.*

If you compare each example, you can see that, unlike in objective writing, parties in persuasive writing are usually only illustrating cases that reach the result they want on the issue or element. In the next section—the Analysis ("A")—the parties will argue that their case is like the illustrated (favorable) cases such that the same outcome is warranted in their case.

c) CRACC: Creating persuasive Analysis

Just as in objective writing, after your Rule is your Analysis ("A" of CRACC). In your Analysis, you will apply the law for the issue, which you have just stated persuasively in the Rule for the issue, to your facts for the issue, which you have stated persuasively in the statement of facts, to argue for the outcome you want the court to reach on the issue.

We tell students that if you have a persuasive Rule for the issue and you have all the facts stated persuasively for the issue in your statement of facts, then writing an Analysis is a little like copying, pasting, and matching. Your Analysis is really just a combination of your Rule and facts on that issue, both of which you have already stated persuasively elsewhere in your motion before you get to the Analysis of the issue. We recommend not writing the Analysis for any issue until you have finalized the statement of facts and Rule for the issue. Obviously, you may need to go back and edit or tweak those sections after you have written your Analysis, but, because the Analysis is the product of these two parts, it makes sense to write your Analysis after those parts are completed.

In persuasive writing, the organization of your Analysis is similar to that in objective writing, except you are arguing—not predicting.

i. Part I made persuasive

In part one of your Analysis, you will argue what happens when you apply the Rule for the issue to the facts for the issue or, put another way, you will argue what result the court should reach when applying the Rule for a particular issue to the facts for that same issue. Compare part one of the Analysis stated objectively, stated persuasively for the plaintiff, and stated persuasively for the defendant on the same issue.

> **Part 1 stated objectively**: It is likely that a court would find that HOL overpowered Mrs. Bell's mind.

Part 1 stated persuasively for the defendant: Here, there is no genuine issue of material fact as to whether HOL overpowered Ms. Bell's mind because the evidence demonstrates that Ms. Bell was physically and mentally capable, such that she was not susceptible to influence.

Part 1 stated persuasively for the plaintiff: Here, the Court should also find that there is sufficient evidence to create a fact issue as to whether Mrs. Bell had her mind subverted or overpowered by HOL.

ii. Part 2 made persuasive

In part two, you will support or prove your argument in part one. If the application of the Rule to the facts for the issue is straightforward, you will use pure rule-based reasoning. Otherwise you will use a combination of analogical reasoning and rule-language bridging.

[a] Pure rule-based reasoning made persuasive

Pure rule-based reasoning is simple and covered in detail when we discussed objective writing in Part Two. Because pure rule-based reasoning is only used when the application of the rule to the facts is straightforward, there is really nothing to "argue." In a sense, "it is what it is." Thus, the difference between pure rule-based reasoning in objective writing and persuasive writing is really only a change in tone. You simply change your tone from predictive to persuasive. Review the bystander example. Below is a comparison of the Analysis using pure rule-based reasoning both objectively and persuasively. You will see the difference is subtle because the Analysis is so straightforward that "it is what it is."

OBJECTIVE EXAMPLE

Part 1 ⟶ Paula will satisfy the third element of the bystander doctrine.

Part 2 ⟶ Because Paula is Martha's daughter, she is "closely related" to the victim Martha and, as such, can recover damages. *Freeman*, 744 S.W.2d at 924; *Garcia*, 859 S.W.2d at 81; Mem. from A. Partner to File (Nov. 30, 2019).

PERSUASIVE EXAMPLE

Part 1 ⟶ It is undisputed that Paula satisfies the third element of the bystander doctrine.

Part 2 ⟶ Because Paula is Martha's daughter, this Court should find that she is "closely related" to the victim Martha and, as such, can recover damages. *Freeman*, 744 S.W.2d at 924; *Garcia*, 859 S.W.2d at 81; Mem. from A. Partner to File (Nov. 30, 2019).

[b] Analogical reasoning and rule-language bridging made persuasive

Just like in objective writing, it is essential that you "show your work" in persuasive writing. Imagine this conversation:

You: "Judge, you should reach the result we want because our case is like the precedent case that reached the result we want."

Judge: "Okay, why?"

You: "Because our case is exactly like the precedent case."

Judge: "Okay, but how?"

You: "Because it is just like the precedent case and is on all fours with the facts of that case."

Judge: "Okay . . . why?"

Total nightmare! You are arguing, but there is no meat. You are not showing the court why your argument is correct. You must show your work. Here is what lawyers sometimes do when writing before a court. They write beautiful Rule statements for a particular issue, and, then, in the Analysis, they simply write something like, "Accordingly, because the facts in this case meet the standard, this Court should deny summary judgment." As said by one court, there "is the duty to cite evidence and authority **and explain why [the] same mandates the result desired by the [party] . . . . One does not satisfy this burden by merely uttering conclusions**."[14] You cannot merely utter the conclusion that you want the court to reach, you must show the court that the conclusion you want the court to reach is the correct one.

In persuasive writing, you will normally use a combination of analogical reasoning and rule-language bridging in your Analysis.

[c] Analogical reasoning: arguing your case is like precedent case such that same result is warranted

Because, in your Rule, you will have only illustrated cases that reach the same result you want the court to reach (favorable cases), in your Analysis when you do analogical reasoning you are arguing that your case is similar to, or better than, the favorable illustrated cases such that the court should reach the same result as the illustrated cases. Unlike in objective writing, in persuasive writing you are not comparing and contrasting but arguing that your case is so like the illustrated case that the same result is warranted. Therefore, the "formula" you will use to do your fact-to-fact analysis (analogical reasoning) is one of comparison, not contrast: "**Like [favorable precedent case], where [trigger fact from precedent case], here [similar trigger fact from our case]**."

---

14. *Foster v. Westinghouse Elevator Co.*, No. 07-96-0322-CV, 1997 WL 360948, at * 2 (Tex. App.—Amarillo June 27, 1997, writ denied) (emphasis added).

Similarly, if your case is "better" or "stronger" than the illustrated case on the issue, you will argue that.

> "More than *Estate of Johnson*, where there was no direct evidence of the testator drinking on the day of the will's execution, here, there is direct evidence that, immediately before executing the Revised Will, Mrs. Bell drank mushroom tea with Ms. Welsh."

Plaintiff's MSJ Opposition illustrated *Estate of Johnson* for element two—a case where the court held the second element was satisfied, which is what the Plaintiff wants the court to hold in the present case. Using analogical reasoning, the Plaintiff compares the facts of his case to the illustrated case to show that the two are similar such that the same result is warranted in the present case as was reached by the court in *Estate of Johnson*. Additionally, the Plaintiff not only compares, but argues why this comparison matters throughout. The example below uses the two-part analysis formula **and** explicitly tells the court why the comparison matters (*see* bold sentences below).

Part 1 →

> Here, the Court should also find that there is sufficient evidence to create a fact issue as to whether Mrs. Bell had her mind subverted or overpowered by HOL.

Part 2 →

> Like in *Estate of Johnson*, where the testator was under the influence of alcohol around the time of the will's execution such that there was "ample opportunity" for undue influence, here, **because Mrs. Bell drank the magic mushroom tea every day, which had the effect of altering her mental state, there was "ample opportunity" for Ms. Welsh/HOL to unduly influence her.** *Estate of Johnson*, 340 S.W.3d at 778; Ex. 2, John Bell Dep. 7:4–16; Ex. 3, Welsh Dep. 8:10–9:5. More than *Estate of Johnson*, where there was no direct evidence of the testator drinking on the day of the will's execution, here, there is direct evidence that, immediately before executing the Revised Will, Mrs. Bell drank mushroom tea with Ms. Welsh. *Estate of Johnson*, 340 S.W.3d at 778; Ex. 3, Welsh Dep. 11:9–13. Additionally, like the testator in *Estate of Johnson*, who had memory deficiencies around the time of the will's execution, here, there is evidence that Mrs. Bell lost 20 percent of her memory capacity few months before executing the Revised Will. *Estate of Johnson*, 340 S.W.3d at 778; John Bell Dep. 4:8–16. Moreover, given her recent traumatic car accident and the abrupt stop to her prescribed depression medication, like *Estate of Johnson*, **there is, at a minimum, a fact issue that Mrs. Bell was uniquely "susceptible" to undue influence given her weakened mental capacity to resist.** *Estate of Johnson*, 340 S.W.3d at 778; Ex. 2, John Bell Dep. 7:4–16; Ex. 3, Welsh Dep. 8:10–9:5. **Accordingly, like in *Estate of Johnson*, this Court should hold that Mrs. Bell was susceptible to undue influence and that ample opportunity existed for HOL to unduly influence Mrs. Bell such that summary judgment should be denied.**

[d] Rule-language bridging in persuasive writing

Just as in objective writing, in persuasive writing you will connect the persuasive language in your Rule for the issue to the facts in your Analysis. By connecting the language of the general rule and subrules to the facts, you are showing the court how the facts satisfy (or fail to satisfy) the Rule. That is, you are showing your work.

Look at the example from Defendant's MSJ. The bold text is rule-language bridging (i.e. language that the Defendant has carried down from the Rule for the issue into the Analysis):

> Here, Plaintiff will be unable to prove that Ms. Bell's disposition to the charitable organization HOL was unnatural. Like the testator in *Mackie*, who left the bulk of his estate to charities that he was proud of and closely associated with, it is undisputed that Ms. Bell was proud of and closely associated with the charitable organization HOL such that Ms. Bell's leaving money to HOL was not unnatural. *Mackie*, 900 S.W.2d at 450; Ex. 3, Welsh Dep. 8:5–9. Following Texas policy, this Court should **"diligent[ly]"** protect the right of Ms. Bell **"to dispose of h[er] property as [s]he pleases"** and leave money to charity. *See Caruthers' Estate*, 151 S.W.2d at 948. Any argument that it was **"unnatural"** for Ms. Bell to reduce her husband's share should be rejected because, like *Guthrie*, where the testatrix had a **"strained relationship"** with her son, here, Plaintiff admitted his relationship with Ms. Bell was "rocky," and Ms. Bell confided that she was "miserable" in her "difficult" marriage. *Guthrie*, 934 S.W.2d at 832; Ex. 3, Welsh Dep. 7:6–21; Ex. 2, John Bell Dep. 8:16–23. Given that Mr. Bell was not supportive of Ms. Bell's newfound happiness or her membership in HOL, like the testatrix in *Guthrie*, it was not unreasonable for Ms. Bell to reduce her husband's inheritance. *Guthrie*, 934 S.W.2d at 832; Ex. 3, Welsh Dep. 7:6–21; Ex. 2, John Bell Dep. 8:16–23. Moreover, unlike *Guthrie*, where the testatrix excluded her son from the will, it is undisputed that Ms. Bell did not exclude her husband—rather she left him $5,000, which is not an insignificant amount of money. *Guthrie*, 934 S.W.2d at 832; Ex. 5, Revised Will at 1. Accordingly, this Court should hold there is no genuine issue of material fact as to the third element of undue influence.

Part 1

Part 2

Notice also that, in addition to using soundbites from the law, Defendant has incorporated soundbites from its statement of facts into the Analysis. Recall that when we discussed making your statement of facts persuasive, we discussed that it was smart to use soundbites to tell your client's side of the story. Because the facts in the Analysis should match the facts for the issue in your statement of facts, you will often have soundbites in your Analysis from the facts of your case.

iii. Example of objective versus persuasive Analysis on same element

Now that you know how to make an Analysis persuasive, closely examine the complete Analysis sections for element two taken from Appendices D, F, and G. As you compare the three different Analysis sections, label the two parts of each Analysis section, underline where analogical reasoning is used, circle where rule-language bridging is used, and highlight the parts of the Analysis where the writer tells the reader why the comparison (and contrast for the objective Analysis) matters.

OBJECTIVE ANALYSIS EXAMPLE

Mr. Bell will likely be able to establish that Ms. Welsh overpowered Ms. Bell's mind because (1) like the testator in *Estate of Johnson*, who abused alcohol, she was under the influence of mushroom tea provided to her by Ms. Welsh during the execution of her Revised Will; and (2) although Ms. Bell was generally capable like the testator in *Estate of Steed*, she suffered from depression coupled with other cognitive limitations that distinguished her situation from that presented in *Estate of Steed*. In *Estate of Johnson*, the testator suffered from alcohol abuse that, the court found, rendered him less able to resist the influence of others. 340 S.W.3d at 778. Like the testator in *Estate of Johnson*, Ms. Bell was under the influence of an unknown allegedly psychotropic drug (the mushroom tea) during the months before and at the time of her will's execution. Mem. from A. Partner to File (Sept. 22, 2018). After Ms. Bell met Ms. Welsh, Ms. Welsh substituted Ms. Bell's antidepressant prescription for HOL's mushroom tea. *Id.* This tea was designed specifically to bring the drinker into a state of intense calm and spiritualism. *Id.* Given the psychotropic effects of the mushroom tea, a court is likely to draw a parallel to the alcohol use in *Estate of Johnson* and find that Ms. Bell, like the testator in Estate of Johnson, was especially susceptible to influence given her use of the tea.

Moreover, although depression alone is insufficient to establish the second element required for undue influence, Ms. Bell did not suffer only from depression like the testator in *Estate of Steed*. 152 S.W.3d at 811. In contrast, Ms. Bell battled depression coupled with lingering effects of head trauma. Mem. from A. Partner to File (Sept. 22, 2018). Additionally, the testator in *Estate of Steed* was depressed but otherwise capable of handling his own affairs; in fact, he was a "detailed person" who "worked daily" and was not "mentally impaired from performing his daily tasks." 152 S.W.3d at 811. In contrast, although there is some evidence that Ms. Bell, like the testator in *Estate of Steed*, was independent and capable (i.e., after her head trauma the doctors reported that she "fully recovered," and she "returned to work") Ms. Bell's story is not as simple as that of the practicing attorney in *Estate of Steed*. Mem. from A. Partner to File (Sept. 22, 2018). Ms. Bell suffered a brain trauma shortly before meeting Ms. Welsh, and, after her trauma, she suffered from depression and memory lapses. *Id.* Given this distinction, the reasoning of *Estate of Steed* does not squarely apply to Ms. Bell's situation, and, instead, a court in Mr. Bell's case is likely to find that the "pivotal" second element of undue influence is satisfied. See *Matter of Kam*, 484 S.W.3d at 653.

PERSUASIVE FOR PLAINTIFF ANALYSIS EXAMPLE

Here, the Court should also find that there is sufficient evidence to create a fact issue as to whether Mrs. Bell had her mind subverted or overpowered by HOL. Like in *Estate of Johnson*, where the testator was under the influence of alcohol around the time of the will's execution such that there was "ample opportunity" for undue influence, here, because Mrs. Bell drank the magic mushroom tea every day, which had the effect of altering her mental state, there was "ample opportunity" for Ms. Welsh/HOL to unduly influence her. *Estate of Johnson*, 340 S.W.3d at 778; Ex. 2, John Bell Dep. 7:4–16; Ex. 3, Welsh Dep. 8:10–9:5. More than *Estate of Johnson*, where there was no direct evidence of the testator drinking on the day of the will's execution, here, there is direct evidence that, immediately before executing the Revised Will, Mrs. Bell drank mushroom tea with Ms. Welsh. *Estate of Johnson*, 340 S.W.3d at 778; Ex. 3, Welsh Dep. 11:9–13. Additionally, like the testator in Estate of Johnson, who had memory deficiencies around the time of the will's execution, here, there is evidence that Mrs. Bell lost 20 percent of her memory capacity a few months before executing the Revised Will. *Estate of Johnson*, 340 S.W.3d at 778; John Bell Dep. 4:8–16. Moreover, given her recent traumatic car accident and the abrupt stop to her prescribed depression medication, like *Estate of Johnson*, there is, at a minimum, a fact issue that Mrs. Bell was uniquely "susceptible" to undue influence given her weakened mental capacity to resist. *Estate of Johnson*, 340 S.W.3d at 778; Ex. 2, John Bell Dep. 7:4–16; Ex. 3, Welsh Dep. 8:10–9:5. Accordingly, like in *Estate of Johnson*, this Court should hold that Mrs. Bell was susceptible to undue influence and that ample opportunity existed for HOL to unduly influence Mrs. Bell such that such that summary judgment should be denied.

PERSUASIVE FOR DEFENDANT ANALYSIS EXAMPLE

Here, there is no genuine issue of material fact as to whether HOL overpowered Ms. Bell's mind because the evidence demonstrates that Ms. Bell was physically and mentally capable, such that she was not susceptible to influence. Like the testator in *Estate of Steed*, who suffered from depression but was able to conduct business affairs and was physically able, here, although

Ms. Bell may have suffered from depression, there is no evidence that the depression hindered her business affairs or physical capability. *Estate of Steed*, 152 S.W.3d at 811; Ex. 2, John Bell Dep. 4:17–19, 4:23–5:10. To the contrary, Ms. Bell received strong performance reviews at her job, and her husband described her as "really smart," "a strong woman," and "physically really good." Ex. 2, John Bell Dep. 4:17–19, 4:23–5:10. Additionally, unlike the testator in *Estate of Steed*, who was still on depression medication at the time he executed his will, here, at the time of the will's execution, Ms. Bell was no longer in need of depression medication because she was no longer depressed. *Estate of Steed*, 152 S.W.3d at 811; Ex. 3, Welsh Dep. 8:5–9. Moreover, there can be no dispute that Ms. Bell's mental condition—even at her worst after her brother died—fell grossly short of that of the testatrix in Guthrie, whose condition the court held did not meet the second element of undue influence, even though she was unable to care for herself, was constantly confused, and suffered a lobotomy. *Guthrie*, 934 S.W.2d at 827–28; Ex. 2, John Bell Dep. 5:24–6:6. Ms. Bell did not have a weakened physical or mental state, and, even if she did, such is "is only indicative of her susceptibility to influence; it is no evidence that such influence exists in fact." *Guthrie*, 934 S.W.2d at 832. Nothing in the record proves that Ms. Welsh's "efforts actually overwhelmed [Ms. Bell's] free agency" or that Ms. Bell lost the "ability to decide for [her]self"—to the contrary, it was Ms. Bell who initiated a new will, and the day Ms. Bell executed her Revised Will was "very normal." Ex. 3, Welsh Dep. 10:13–15; Ex. 4, Duke Dep. 3:3–7.

d) CRACC: Creating persuasive Counter-analysis

As mentioned above, the organization of persuasive writing shifts from CRAC to CRACC. Although the added letter "C" (which stands for Counter-analysis) is new, the concept of counter-analysis is not. Rather, while it was not called counter-analysis, in objective writing you did a form of counter-analysis in your objective Analysis ("A" of CRAC) when you contrasted the facts of an illustrated case from the facts of your case.

For example, review the objective memorandum in Appendix D. For the CRAC on element two, the writer predicted that the element would be satisfied as her "C" or Conclusion. The writer then illustrated two cases as part of the Rule ("R"): *Estate of Johnson* and *Estate of Steed*. In the Analysis ("A"), the writer supported her Conclusion (that element two would be satisfied) by comparing the facts of the client's case to the facts of *Estate of Johnson* (where the court held element two was satisfied) and by contrasting the facts of the client's case to the facts of *Estate of Steed* (where the court held element two was not satisfied). This contrasting is a form of counter-analysis. To support her prediction that element two would be satisfied, the objective writer had to deal with a case—*Estate of Steed*—that was somewhat factually similar but came to a different outcome than the objective writer's prediction. Look at this excerpt from the Analysis in the objective memo:

> At first blush, the opportunity Ms. Welsh had to influence Ms. Bell may seem similar to *Estate of Steed* because, like the alleged influencer in *Estate of Steed*, Ms. Welsh did not live with Ms. Bell. *Estate of Steed*, 152 S.W.3d at 809; Mem. from A. Partner to File (Sept. 22, 2018). However, the fact that the couple in *Estate of Steed* did not live together was only important because it meant that they were not in daily contact. 152 S.W.3d at 809. Here, unlike in *Estate of Steed*, Ms. Welsh was in regular contact with Ms. Bell, even though they did not live in the same home. Mem. from A. Partner to File (Sept. 22, 2018). As Ms. Bell's HM, Ms. Welsh texted her ten times a day. *Id.* This regular contact between Ms. Welsh and Ms. Bell echoes the regular contact between the testator and alleged influencer in the *Estate of Johnson* case. *Id.*; *see Estate of Johnson*, 340 S.W.3d at 779–83. In *Estate of Johnson*, the alleged influencer imbedded herself in the testator's life such that her regular presence affected the testator's decisions. *See* 340 S.W.3d at 779–83. Similarly, once Ms. Welsh came into Ms. Bell's life, not only was she in constant contact with Ms. Bell, but Ms. Bell's behavior and preferences began to shift after this constant contact started—for example, she changed her clothing, her medications, and her interactions with friends. Mem. from A. Partner to File (Sept. 22, 2018). This consistent and daily contact, dissimilar from the not-daily contact between the testator and alleged beneficiary in *Estate of Steed*, created an opportunity to exert influence, weighing in favor of finding undue influence. *Id.*; *Estate of Steed*, 152 S.W.3d at 811.

You can see that to support her prediction that element two was satisfied, the objective writer needed to show the reader why and how *Estate of Steed* could be distinguished or overcome. This is a form of counter-analysis because the objective writer is addressing and overcoming an obstacle or counterargument that could be seen to potentially weigh against her prediction.

Now, of course, this type of objective counter-analysis is different from persuasive counter-analysis. The objective writer is not advocating for a certain outcome but is, instead, predicting the outcome that is most likely after a neutral analysis of the law. In persuasive writing, in your Analysis as discussed above, you are advocating for a specific outcome in favor of your client. You are illustrating cases in your Rule that are similar to the facts of your case and arguing that your case is like the illustrated case such that the same outcome is warranted. However, there may be cases out there that are arguably similar to the facts of your case but come to the outcome opposite of the one you want. It is likely that the other side will rely on those cases and bring them to the court's attention. If the other side brings to the court's attention cases that are arguably factually similar to your case but that reach an outcome that is the opposite of the one you want for your client, then you must deal with those cases and the arguments that the other side makes regarding them. In persuasive writing, you do so in the Counter-analysis.

i. What is Counter-analysis?

The Counter-analysis (the new "C") will usually come in a new paragraph directly after your Analysis ("A") and before your final conclusion sentence (the last "C"). In your Counter-analysis, you will respond to the other side's strongest arguments and overcome potential weaknesses in your case that the other side has attempted to expose to the court.

The reason why the Counter-analysis is separate from the Analysis in persuasive writing is because you want to make your argument on the issue first (Analysis) and then separately deal with any weaknesses in your argument exposed by the other side (Counter-analysis). That is, you want to play offense before you play defense. In objective writing, any counter-analysis (contrasting) is mixed with your Analysis because as an objective writer you are not trying to persuade. In objective writing, it does not matter that you use "prime real estate" in your memo to discuss a case that comes to the opposite conclusion of your prediction. However, in persuasive writing, you do not want to spend a lot of space—much less prominent space—in your motion or opposition on cases that are "bad" for your client. Instead, you want to first and foremost focus the court on the good: the strongest cases in favor of your position and arguments that highlight the strengths of your position. This is your Analysis. Then, separately, in your Counter-analysis, you briefly, but forcefully, address and overcome the bad.

You may be wondering why you need a Counter-analysis at all. Can you not just ignore the weaknesses of your case? It is important to include Counter-analysis because you do not make potential weaknesses "go away" by ignoring them. Instead, you make potential weaknesses in your case go away by addressing them head-on and overcoming them. But, while you want to address your weaknesses head-on, you also do not want to dwell on them or emphasize them. How do you address weaknesses without highlighting them? This Catch-22 (of sorts) is what makes Counter-analysis one of the most difficult persuasive-writing skills to master.

ii. When do I need to include Counter-analysis?

You will notice that in the persuasive writing examples in this book, only the Plaintiff's MSJ Opposition has Counter-analysis in its CRACCs. The Defendant's MSJ does not include Counter-analysis. Why is that? As you will recall, in trial court, a moving party files a motion, the non-moving party files an opposition, and then the moving party will usually get the opportunity to file a reply to the opposition. Thus, oftentimes, the motion does not have Counter-analysis because the Counter-analysis will be housed in the reply to the opposition. Indeed, at the time the motion is filed, the movant may not know what the other party's arguments will be or what weaknesses the other party will bring to the court's attention that need to be addressed. It will not be until the other party files his opposition that the movant will know, for example, which case(s) it needs to distinguish. Therefore, as a general rule, the motion will not contain Counter-analysis, but the movant will engage in Counter-analysis in the movant's reply. However, the opposition or response will contain Counter-analysis addressing the "best" legal authority and arguments in the movant's motion.

However, all rules have exceptions. Sometimes the movant will know exactly what the non-movant will argue. For example, in a post-trial motion, the movant may be able to predict the arguments the non-movant will make (and the legal authority he will rely on for such arguments) with respect to a particular issue because the same issue was briefed and argued at an earlier procedural stage. In this case, it can be powerful for the movant to include counter-analysis in its motion so it can get out in front of and inoculate itself from the other party's arguments. This happens oftentimes in appellate briefs. Because the issues have been fully briefed and argued at the trial court level, both sides already know what the other will argue and, thus, appellants often include Counter-analysis in their opening briefs.

iii. Counter-analysis structure and formulas

In your Counter-analysis, you will argue why the other side's analysis of the law and facts is wrong or, at least, less persuasive than the other side suggests. In order to draft Counter-analysis follow these steps.

Step one: Critically analyze the other side's arguments and figure out what you need to address in your Counter-analysis.

Before you can write your Counter-analysis, you need to figure out which of the other side's legal authority needs to be addressed. That is, which of the other side's arguments with respect to their legal authority appear "bad" for your position such that they need to be addressed head-on? You will find the other side's arguments with respect to the law and the facts in the other side's Analysis of each issue. Therefore, before writing your Counter-analysis, you should closely re-read the opposing side's Analysis of the same issue and figure out which, if any, of the other side's cases need to be distinguished. The cases (and corresponding arguments) you will need to distinguish will likely be the ones that are most prominently referred to in the other side's Analysis of the issue. Often, the cases you need to address in your Counter-analysis are the same ones that the other side illustrated in its Rule.

Let's say that you represent Plaintiff John Bell and you want to draft a Counter-analysis for the third element. First, you should read Defendant HOL's Analysis for the second element, which is set forth below. As you are reading it, ask yourself which of Defendant's cases you need to distinguish and which of Defendant's arguments you need to address.

> Here, there is no genuine issue of material fact as to whether HOL overpowered Ms. Bell's mind because the evidence demonstrates that Ms. Bell was physically and mentally capable, such that she was not susceptible to influence. Like the testator in *Estate of Steed*, who suffered from depression but was able to conduct business affairs and was physically able, here, although Ms. Bell may have suffered from depression, there is no evidence that the depression hindered her business affairs or physical capability. *Estate of*

> *Steed*, 152 S.W.3d at 811; Ex. 2, John Bell Dep. 4:17–19, 4:23–5:10. To the contrary, Ms. Bell received strong performance reviews at her job, and her husband described her as "really smart," "a strong woman," and "physically really good." Ex. 2, John Bell Dep. 4:17–19, 4:23–5:10. Additionally, unlike the testator in *Estate of Steed*, who was still on depression medication at the time he executed his will, here, at the time of the will's execution, Ms. Bell was no longer in need of depression medication because she was no longer depressed. *Estate of Steed*, 152 S.W.3d at 811; Ex. 3, Welsh Dep. 8:5–9. Moreover, there can be no dispute that Ms. Bell's mental condition—even at her worst after her brother died—fell grossly short of that of the testatrix in *Guthrie*, whose condition the court held did not meet the second element of undue influence, even though she was unable to care for herself, was constantly confused, and suffered a lobotomy. *Guthrie*, 934 S.W.2d at 827–28; Ex. 2, John Bell Dep. 5:24–6:6. Ms. Bell did not have a weakened physical or mental state, and, even if she did, such is "is only indicative of her susceptibility to influence; it is no evidence that such influence exists in fact." *Guthrie*, 934 S.W.2d at 832. Nothing in the record proves that Ms. Welsh's "efforts actually overwhelmed [Ms. Bell's] free agency" or that Ms. Bell lost the "ability to decide for [her]self"—to the contrary, it was Ms. Bell who initiated a new will, and the day Ms. Bell executed her Revised Will was "very normal." Ex. 3, Welsh Dep. 10:13–15; Ex. 4, Duke Dep. 3:3–7.

From reading Defendant's Analysis, you should recognize that the legal authority and corresponding arguments you need to address in your Counter-analysis are comprised of *Estate of Steed* and *Guthrie*. The bulk of Defendant's Analysis is spent comparing the facts of Mr. Bell's case to these two cases and arguing that, like these two cases, element two is not satisfied. Therefore, in your Counter-analysis, you will need to address and overcome these cases head-on.

Step two: Carefully read the legal authority you need to distinguish and ask yourself five questions.

After you have identified the legal authority you need to distinguish and overcome, you should read that legal authority closely. You cannot rely on what the other side represents the legal authority to stand for in its motion; instead, you must read it yourself. For example, you cannot "trust" Defendant's case illustrations of *Estate of Steed* and *Guthrie*. You must read both cases yourself.

While you are reading the cases, you are trying to identify how you are going to distinguish and overcome them in your Counter-analysis. To figure this out, ask yourself the following five questions when reading the opposing side's cases:

1. **Is the case relied upon by the opposing side no longer "good law"?** If the answer to this question is "yes," then it is your lucky day. If a case cited by the other side

is no longer good law—meaning that it has been overturned or superseded—then you will present this in your Counter-analysis and can quickly move on. If the case is no longer good law, it need not be distinguished any further because the court will not follow a case that is no longer good law. Usually the other side will not cite cases that have been overturned or superseded; therefore, oftentimes the answer to this question is "no" and you will have to work a bit harder in your Counter-analysis to distinguish the case in a different way.

2. **Did the opposing side misstate or misrepresent a holding from the case?** If, after reading the case, you find that the other side misstated or misrepresented the court's holding on the issue, you should state this in your Counter-analysis. For example, perhaps the other side said the court granted a motion for summary judgment because it held the second element was not satisfied, when in actuality the court granted summary judgment because it found the third element was not satisfied. If you look at the example of the Counter-analysis with respect to *Guthrie, infra*, you will see an example of Counter-analysis when the other side misrepresented the court's holding.

3. **Did the opposing side misstate or mispresent the reasoning from the case?** Sometimes the other side will misrepresent the reasoning of an illustrated case—how the court got from the trigger facts to the holding. For example, let's say the court granted a motion for summary judgment (holding), and the facts were similar to your case, but the reason the court granted it was in large part based on the fact that the other side did not file an opposition to the motion for summary judgment. If the other side omitted this reason, you would present this omission in your Counter-analysis to argue the case is less persuasive and should not be followed.

4. **Did the opposing side omit or misstate trigger facts from the illustrated case to make it seem more like your case?** After reading the case, you may note that the other side's illustration of the case is not complete. Rather, the other side omitted facts or misstated facts that were important to the court's holding and that make the illustrated case less like the facts of your client's case. Importantly, you are looking for omitted trigger facts—facts that affected the court's analysis—not simply omitted facts. No case illustration is going to include every fact, but if the other side omitted trigger facts or misstated trigger facts, you should present this in your Counter-analysis as a way to argue to the court that the case is less persuasive than presented by the other side.

5. **When comparing the illustrated case to your case, did the opposing side omit or misstate trigger facts from your case to make it seem more like the illustrated case than it actually is?** Sometimes the other side will perfectly illustrate a case but will then, in its Analysis, misrepresent the facts of your case to make it seem more like the illustrated case than it actually is. If this is the case, you

should present in your Counter-analysis how the actual facts of your case (not those misrepresented by the other side) differ from the illustrated case.

Step three: Write your Counter-analysis using the formula.

Now that you know how you are going to distinguish and overcome the opposing side's case(s), you can write your Counter-analysis. In your Counter-analysis you are going to have to acknowledge this unfavorable legal authority, but you want to be careful not to emphasize or repeat the other side's legal arguments. First, you do not want to inadvertently restate the other side's position in a better or clearer way than it was stated in the other side's motion. Second, you do not want to waste the precious real estate of your opposition restating the other side's arguments such that the court gets to read the other side's argument twice: once in the other side's motion and once in your opposition.

As previously noted, addressing the other side's arguments and legal authority without emphasizing them is difficult. It takes practice and experience to master. To help you get started, consider using the following formula.

COUNTER-ANALYSIS FORMULA

First sentence: Identify the legal authority relied on by the other side that you are addressing in your Counter-analysis.

- Defendant's reliance on [precedent case] is misplaced/misguided/not persuasive.

Middle sentences: Show why the legal authority is distinguishable and/or not as persuasive as represented by the other side. This is where your answers to the five questions in step two above come in handy. Repeat and mix these sample sentences as needed.

- The [legal authority] Defendant relied on is [no longer good law] because _____.
- In [its] motion, Defendant [omits/misstates] key facts that were important to the court's holding _______.
- Unlike [precedent case], where [trigger fact from precedent case], here [different trigger fact from our case].
- Defendant [misstates/misrepresents/omits] the court's holding because ________.
- Defendant [misstates/misrepresents/omits] the court's reasoning because ________.

> **Last sentence**: Bring it all together and state why the middle sentences (distinguishing the legal authority) should matter to the court's decision.
>
> - Accordingly, this Court should [not follow/not find persuasive/find distinguishable] [precedent case].

Note that the formula may (read: will) need to be tweaked as you tailor it to the particular case(s) you are distinguishing, and, as such, it need not be followed exactly. However, this formula will provide you with a starting-off point as you begin writing your Counter-analysis.

The example below is written using the Counter-analysis formula. Notice that because there are two cases that need to be distinguished, the Counter-analysis is in two paragraphs. Sometimes, you can distinguish multiple cases in a single paragraph, but, to begin, it is smart to separate it out so that you ensure that you fully address and distinguish each case.

First sentence

> HOL's reliance on *In re Estate of Steed,* 152 S.W.3d 797 (Tex. App.— Texarkana 2004, pet. denied), to support that HOL did not overpower Mrs. Bell's mind is incorrect. Def.'s M. for Summ. J. 11–13. Unlike in *Estate of Steed,* where the testator suffered from depression but was actively taking his prescribed medication, Mrs. Bell was not taking her prescribed medication and was, instead, drinking "magic" tea. *Estate of Steed,* 152 S.W.3d at 811; Ex. 2, John Bell Dep. 7:4–16; Ex. 3, Welsh Dep. 8:10–9:5. Moreover, unlike *Estate of Steed,* where there was no evidence that the testator was "emotionally dependent" on the beneficiary, and, instead, there was ample evidence that he was independent, here there is evidence that Mrs. Bell was extremely dependent on Ms. Welsh and HOL for all life decisions, whether big or small, making her more susceptible to undue influence. *Estate of Steed,* 152 S.W.3d at 811; Ex. 2, John Bell Dep. 6:18–7:16; Ex. 3, Welsh Dep. 8:10–9:5. Accordingly, this Court should not follow *Estate of Steed.*
>
> Likewise, HOL's reliance on *Guthrie v. Suiter,* 934 S.W.2d 820 (Tex. App.—Houston [1st Dist.] 1996, no writ) is unpersuasive because HOL misleads the Court as to the *Guthrie* court's holding. Def.'s M. for Summ. J. 12–13. In *Guthrie,* the will contestant relied on evidence that the testator had a lobotomy and the appearance of an Alzheimer's patient in order to demonstrate the existence and exertion of an undue influence—the first element of *Rothermel.* 934 S.W.2d at 832. The *Guthrie* court held that, while such evidence of a weakened mental condition rendered the testator susceptible to undue influence (the second element of *Rothermel*), it was insufficient to prove the first element. *Id.* Thus, *Guthrie's* holding lends no support to HOL and, instead, at most, supports that Mrs. Bell's weakened mental condition "rendered her susceptible to undue influence." *See id.*

Middle sentences

Last sentence

H. Overall conclusion

The overall conclusion will be the last heading or section in your motion or opposition. And, here is the good news: it is the easiest part of your motion or opposition to write. While it is labeled a "conclusion," it is more of a prayer for relief asking the court to take a specific action. Normally, the conclusion in a motion or opposition is only one or two sentences long.

> VI. CONCLUSION
>
> HOL respectfully requests that this Court grant its Motion for Summary Judgment on Plaintiff's Claim of Undue Influence.

I. Signature block

After your overall conclusion, you will include a signature block with the information required by your jurisdiction (normally, your name, bar number, law firm, and contact information, such as address, phone number, fax number, and email). Before your signature, you should include "Respectfully submitted."

> VI. CONCLUSION
>
> For the foregoing reasons, this Court should deny Defendant's Motion for Summary Judgment.
>
> Respectfully submitted,
>
> Partner & Partner LLC
1212 Moon Court, Suite 1400
By: Dallas, Texas 75219
(214) 555-1234 (telephone)
(214) 555-6709 (facsimile)
>
> *Alex B. Partner*
>
> ALEX B. PARTNER
Texas State Bar No. 910111213

4 | Editing and Polishing

Editing and polishing do not mean the same thing, nor do they take place at the same point in time. However, both are essential to all writing, including legal writing. After you have finished writing, you may think you are finished, but your work is not complete. Instead, you must begin the editing and polishing process. Editing is where you review what you have written for organization, content, flow, and overall readability. Editing can be a bit of a misnomer because, during the editing phase, you are still writing. For example, you are making additions, deletions, or changes to your paper. After you complete editing, once again you may think you are finished, but again your work is not complete. Instead, you must begin the polishing or proofreading process. Polishing or proofreading is the final step in the writing process. Unlike editing, where you are reviewing the content of what you have written and making any necessary changes, when you begin the polishing phase of writing, the content should be finalized. That is, you should be polishing a final draft. In the polishing phase, you are working to make the content of your paper error free. You are proofreading for typos, misspellings, and grammar mistakes.

I. Editing process

"There is no such thing as good writing. There is only good rewriting."[1] After you have finished writing the first draft of your paper (whether it

1. Richard K. Neumann Jr., Legal Reasoning and Legal Writing: Structure, Strategy, and Style 61 (4th ed. 2001) (quoting Justice Louis Brandeis, Associate Justice of the U.S. Supreme Court).

be an e-mail, an objective memo, a motion, or a brief), you will begin editing what you have written for organization, content, flow, and overall readability. The term "editing" can be seen as synonymous with rewriting because, in the editing phase, you will often be rewriting portions of what you have already written.

One of the hardest parts about editing can be the fact that you are editing your own work. Often it can be difficult to look at what you have written and ascertain what needs to be rewritten or edited. That is, it is easier to rewrite others' work than your own. Therefore, it is necessary to approach editing your paper in a systematic way.

Step one: Zoom out and edit on a macro level

After you have finished writing the first draft of your paper, the first thing you should do is ensure that what you have written is complete and correctly organized on a macro level. In other words, check to make sure you have all the right parts in the right places. To complete this macro-level editing, you must make sure your paper follows procedural and substantive instructions.

Following procedural instructions sounds easy, but it is important because failure to do so can have dire consequences. In law school, the cost of failure to follow assignment instructions is lost points. In real life, the failure to follow instructions can result in a court not accepting your non-conforming motion or brief. As a student in a first-year legal writing class, it is likely that your professor has given you assignment instructions that specify how your paper should be formatted. If you are practicing before a court, local rules will specify how your motion or brief should be formatted. You must follow these instructions and rules. To ensure you have followed your law school formatting instructions, consider using the following formatting instruction checklist:

FORMATTING INSTRUCTION EDITING CHECKLIST

- ☐ Are you within the page limit?
- ☐ Are you using the correct font and font size?
- ☐ Are your margins correct?
- ☐ Do you need page numbers?
- ☐ Are your headings and subheadings correctly formatted and numbered?
- ☐ Are you abiding by any special instructions? (For example, we instruct our students that they should not put their names on their papers, but should, instead, use their anonymous exam IDs).

Making sure your paper follows substantive instructions is also critical. This stage of the macro edit is where you will check to make sure that your paper has all the required parts in the correct places (macro organization) and addresses all the issues. What parts are required will depend on what you are writing and the instructions given to you, but you must make sure that you have them all. You should be able to do this by scanning your headings. For example, for an objective memo, do you have a question presented, brief answer, statement of facts, discussion section, and overall conclusion? You also must look to see if you have addressed all required issues and if you have done a CRAC for each of those issues. At this point, you should also make sure that you have addressed the issues in the correct sequence and have included a proper heading for each. You are checking for "holes" in your paper. If you have any holes, you will need to fill them. To ensure that you have followed your law school's substantive formatting instructions, consider using the following substantive instruction checklist:

SUBSTANTIVE INSTRUCTION EDITING CHECKLIST

- ☐ Do you have all the formal parts of your paper and corresponding headings?
- ☐ Have you addressed all required issues?
- ☐ Do the number of issues = the number of CRACs?
- ☐ Do issues include subheadings where needed?

Step two: Zoom in and edit on a micro level

Now that you have ensured that you followed instructions (both the procedural and substantive instructions) and have all the required parts of your paper, you need to zoom in and edit each part. You should begin your micro-editing with the heart of your paper: the issues and their CRACs. Then, you should move to the other formal parts of the objective memo (i.e., question presented, brief answer, statement of facts, roadmaps, and conclusion) or motion (i.e., introduction, statement of facts, standard of review, and conclusion). The reason for starting with your CRACs is that other parts of your paper are dependent on them. For example, your statement of facts is derived by the facts used in the Analysis section of your CRACs for each issue.

Each issue should have a CRAC (objective) or CRACC (persuasive) and that CRA(C)C should be a complete argument for that issue. To make sure that your CRA(C)Cs are complete and strong, we recommend going through the following CRA(C)C checklist.

CRA(C)C EDITING CHECKLIST

Conclusion sentences CRA(C)C

- ☐ Highlight each conclusion sentence for each issue in blue.
    - ☐ Does each CRA(C)C begin and end with your conclusion on the specific issue?

CRA(C)C EDITING CHECKLIST, CONT.

Rule C<u>R</u>A(C)C

- ☐ Highlight your general rules in green.
  - ☐ After your beginning Conclusion for the issue, do you include your general rule with a citation to the leading authority for that rule?
  - ☐ For persuasive writing, is the general rule stated in a way that is favorable to your client? Either positively and broadly or negatively and narrowly?
- ☐ Highlight your subrules in purple.
  - ☐ After your general rule, do you include subrules that explain the general rule?
  - ☐ Do you include a citation to the law after each subrule?
  - ☐ Do your subrules bridge to one another?
- ☐ Highlight your case illustrations in pink.
  - ☐ For each case illustration, do you have all four parts?
  - ☐ Do you start with the topic sentence stating why the case is important?
  - ☐ Do you next state the holding for the specific issue?
  - ☐ Do you next include only the trigger facts that go to that issue?
  - ☐ Do you include the reasoning (how the court got from the facts to the holding)?
  - ☐ Do you avoid proper names in case illustrations and instead refer to the parties in case illustrations by using plaintiff, defendant, and/or another consistent and generic term (i.e., testator, establishment, employer, etc.)?
  - ☐ Do you cite after all parts of your case illustrations with the exception of the topic sentence?

Analysis CR<u>A</u>(C)C

- ☐ Highlight your Analysis in yellow. Within your analysis, underline in red facts from your case and underline in blue parts of your rule you are using in your analysis. You should see significant amounts of both red and blue intermixed in your analysis.
  - ☐ Do you start your Analysis with your Ingredient One sentence?
  - ☐ Does the Rule for the issue (C<u>R</u>A(C)C) match with the Analysis for the issue (CR<u>A</u>(C)C)?

- ☐ Are you doing rule-language bridging by incorporating "soundbites" from your general rules and subrules into your Analysis?
- ☐ Are you doing analogical reasoning for your illustrated case or cases for the issue? Are you comparing the facts of your case side by side with the similar facts from the precedent case? Are you making sure you explain in your Analysis why that comparison/contrast with the illustrated case matters?
- ☐ Are you incorporating all of your client's facts that go to the issue in your Analysis? Put another way, are there any facts that you need to add for the issue?

☐ If your Rule and Analysis for the issue do not match, do you need to trim your Rule, beef up your Analysis, or do both in order to make them match?

☐ In your Analysis, do you make sure you do not introduce any "new" law that was not included in your Rule for the issue?

☐ In your Analysis, do you include citations to the law and the record?

Counter-Analysis CRA(<u>C</u>)C (in persuasive writing only)

☐ Highlight your Counter-analysis for the issue in orange.

- ☐ Do you include a Counter-analysis for the opposing side's best authority on the issue?
- ☐ For each case you distinguish, do you tell the court the case relied upon by the other side is not persuasive?
- ☐ Do you include citations to the case you are distinguishing, the record, and/or the other side's paper in your Counter-analysis?

Make sure the other formal parts of your paper are complete—after you have checked each CRA(C)C, you need to examine the other parts of your paper. Below are checklists for an objective memo's formal parts and a motion's formal parts:

OBJECTIVE MEMO EDITING CHECKLIST

Question(s) Presented

☐ Do you use either under/does/when or the multi-sentence approach?

☐ Do you incorporate the relevant law and trigger facts that go to the legal question at issue?

OBJECTIVE MEMO EDITING CHECKLIST, CONT.

Brief Answer(s)

- ☐ Do you begin with your brief one- to two-word answer?
- ☐ Do you explain your answer concisely and without repeating what is in the question presented?

Statement of Facts

- ☐ Is your statement of facts in chronological order?
- ☐ Do the facts in your statement of facts match the facts used in your Analysis of the issue(s)?
- ☐ Do you state facts objectively?
- ☐ Do you include citations to the record throughout?

Discussion Roadmaps

- ☐ Do you begin your Discussion section with an introductory roadmap?
- ☐ Does the first sentence of your roadmap state your overall conclusion?
- ☐ Do you next set forth the overarching rule for the cause(s) of action at issue?
- ☐ Do you set forth any overarching subrules that apply to all elements of the cause(s) of action?
- ☐ Do you list your conclusions for each element at issue in the order they will be discussed?
- ☐ If there are multiple distinct issues or multiple causes of action, do you include mini-roadmaps for each distinct issue or cause of action that (1) states your overall conclusion for that distinct issue or cause of action and (2) lists the elements or issues in the order they will be discussed for that distinct issue or cause of action?

Conclusion

- ☐ Do you include an overall conclusion paragraph to end your memo that restates your predicted outcome?

MOTION EDITING CHECKLIST

Introduction

- ☐ Do you start by stating the overall relief you want the court to grant or deny?

- ☐ Do you, incorporating the legal standard for the motion, argue the conclusion you want the court to reach on each issue?
- ☐ For each issue, do you persuasively set forth the overarching rule and cite to the governing law?
- ☐ For each issue, do you preview the arguments to come in the order they will be addressed?
- ☐ Do you dispose of any issues that will not be addressed?

Statement of facts

- ☐ Is your statement of facts in chronological order?
- ☐ Do the facts in your statement of facts match the facts used in your Analysis (CRACC) of the issue(s)?
- ☐ Do you state facts persuasively by highlighting favorable facts and de-emphasizing unfavorable facts?
- ☐ Do you include citations to the record throughout?

Legal standard

- ☐ Do you include the governing legal standard with a citation to the governing law?
- ☐ Is the governing legal standard stated persuasively for your client (either positively and broadly or narrowly and negatively)?
- ☐ Do you include favorable subrules for your client to explain the legal standard?

Argument roadmaps

- ☐ Under the argument and authorities heading, do you include an overall roadmap that (1) argues the overall conclusion you want the court to reach; (2) outlines the arguments you will make in the order you will make them; and (3) if applicable, disposes of any issues that will not be addressed?
- ☐ If there are multiple distinct issues or multiple causes of action, do you include mini-roadmaps for each distinct issue or cause of action that (1) states your overall conclusion for that distinct issue or cause of action and (2) lists your arguments in the order they will be discussed for that distinct issue or cause of action?

Conclusion

- ☐ Do you include a simple conclusion sentence restating the overall relief you want the court to grant?

Step three: Zoom in more and edit on a sentence level

Through the macro and micro editing steps one and two, you have edited for organization and content. Now, you will edit on a sentence level for flow and readability. Here is a checklist to help you edit on a sentence level:

SENTENCE-LEVEL EDITING CHECKLIST

- ☐ Do you use transition words (first, second, then, next, last, etc.) to explain the relationship between ideas?
- ☐ Do you include topic sentences before your case illustration paragraphs? (If you use the formulas in this book, topic sentences are sometimes "built in" to the other parts of CRA(C)C.)
- ☐ Do you use mostly active voice? Any time you use passive voice, do you make sure it is a conscious choice? To help find passive voice, you can do a search for the word "by." This search will not catch every instance of passive voice, but it will catch many.
- ☐ Do you minimize your use of adjectives and adverbs? If you use an adjective or adverb, can you eliminate it by using a stronger noun or verb instead?
- ☐ Do you use the correct dash each time you use an en dash, em dash, or hyphen?
- ☐ Look for any sentences that are longer than 25 words. Are these sentences, when read aloud, confusing or bulky because they contain too many ideas? If so, separate the sentence or add clarifying punctuation.
- ☐ Do you employ parallelism when "listing" things?

Step four: Check your citations to the law and factual record

The last items on your editing checklist are your citations to the law and to the factual record. It is helpful to check citations separately from the content of your paper. To edit citations, you should use the following checklist:

CITATION EDITING CHECKLIST

- ☐ Print a fresh copy of your objective memo, motion, or brief. Highlight all your long citations in one color and your short citations in another color.
- ☐ Do your citations conform to *The Bluebook* or your state's local citation manual?

- ☐ Do your citations include pincites throughout?
- ☐ Do you include the full citation the first time you cite an authority? Thereafter, do you use the short citation form or *id.*?
- ☐ Do you include citations after almost every sentence in your CRA(C)Cs (excluding your Conclusions and topic sentences)?

II. Polishing process

After you have completed editing you should have a "final draft." It is from this "final draft" that you will begin polishing. The reason the words "final draft" are in quotations is because this final draft that you are polishing is not actually your end work product. Instead, only after you finish polishing, will you have your end work product—that is your "final, final draft" or the error-free version of your "final draft."

In the polishing phase, you are not rewriting. Rather, you are catching errors such as typos, misplaced commas, inconsistent spacing, etc. As you are polishing your work, it is important to know that catching your own errors—as opposed to the errors of others—is objectively difficult. The reason for this difficulty is that, when you read your own work product, your brain "autocorrects" or "generalizes" the small parts (individual words) so that it can focus on the complex parts (combining sentences to make ideas). When it comes to your own work product, your brain is so familiar with and aware of the ultimate content that your brain becomes blind to the errors in front of it: "The reason we don't see our own typos is because what we see on the screen is competing with the version that exists in our heads."[2] To fix this annoying (and amazing) autocorrect function that your brain performs when reading your own work, you must "trick" your brain into thinking that what it is proofreading is not something that it has seen hundreds of times, but is something that is brand new.[3] With this in mind, to catch errors, we recommend that you do the following when polishing to "trick" your brain into thinking it is reading your paper for the first time.

1. **Sleep on it:** Try to polish on a different day than you edit and, ideally, after a full night's sleep. You want to approach polishing with "fresh eyes."
2. **Change the look of the paper:** When polishing, use a hard copy that is in a different font type and font size from what you are used to seeing. For example, if you typed your paper in Times New Roman, size 12 font, when you print out your paper to polish, change your font to Ariel, size 28 font. Notice how much

---

2. Nick Stockton, *What's Up With That: Why It's So Hard to Catch Your Own Typos*, WIRED MAGAZINE (Aug. 12, 2014, 11:21 AM), https://www.wired.com/2014/08/wuwt-typos/.

3. *Id.*

easier it is to spot errors in the below example when you change the font. (Hint: you should see six errors.)

> Like *Primera*, where the evidence showed the a establishment trained its employees to be "vigilant' against serving intoxicated patrons, here, the evidence show that "Chip-Home takes training very seriously." *Primera*, 349 S.W.3d at 169.; Ex. 4, Morgan Dep. 2:14-18..

> Like *Primera*, where the evidence showed the a establishment trained its employees to be "vigilant' against serving intoxicated patrons, here, the evidence show that "Chip-Home takes training very seriously." *Primera*, 349 S.W.3d at 169.; Ex. 4, Morgan Dep. 2:14-18..[4]

3. **Focus on small sections:** Proofread in small sections and out of order. We recommend using a colored piece of paper or a ruler to isolate what you are proofreading line-by-line. Alternatively, you can use a highlighter to highlight proofread words one-by-one as you go down the page. You can also proofread out of order by starting at the end and reading to the beginning or randomly reading paragraphs out of order.
4. **Set the mood:** Proofread while listening to classical music, chewing gum, and sitting under non-florescent lighting. All of these things have been shown to potentially help make your brain focus.
5. **Read it aloud:** Proofread by reading the document aloud or use the text-to-speech function on Google Docs or Microsoft Word to read your document aloud to you.

4. The sentence with errors fixed should read as follows:

Like *Primera*, where the evidence showed the establishment trained its employees to be "vigilant" against serving intoxicated patrons, here, the evidence shows that "Chip-Home takes training very seriously." *Primera*, 349 S.W.3d at 169; Ex. 4., Morgan Dep. 2:14–18.

5 | Oral Presentations and Hearings

In this section of the book, we discuss how to present your written arguments in oral form. In many legal writing classes, your second semester will culminate in an in-class oral argument, where you will orally argue your persuasive work product (whether that be a motion, opposition, or brief) before a panel of "judges" (your professors, members of your school's mock trial or moot court teams, and/or lawyers and/or judges from the community). As a practicing lawyer, you will also have the opportunity to orally argue your written work product to the court.

The skills needed to be a successful oral advocate are somewhat different from the skills needed to be a successful legal writer, although not wholly unrelated. In this section, you will learn how to present a persuasive oral argument, how to prepare for an oral argument, and, specifically, how to transform your written arguments into an oral argument.

I. Purpose of oral presentations and hearings

After submitting a written motion or brief, you may be given the opportunity to orally argue your position before the court. At the trial court level, orally arguing your case is often simply called an oral hearing, whereas at the appellate level orally arguing your case is called an oral argument. For purposes of this book, we will use the terms interchangeably. An oral hearing or an oral argument provides you with an additional opportunity to persuade the court of your position and, most importantly, to answer any questions or address any doubts the deciding judge or judges have about your case. An oral argument, unlike a written motion or brief, is interactive and allows you to clarify issues in real-time, to highlight your most important points, to eliminate any misconceptions held by the judge or judges, and to respond to the other side's arguments.

At the appellate level, most judges and lawyers agree that the oral argument is important, but they also argue that it is of secondary importance to a well-written brief. As explained by Justice Ruth Bader Ginsburg: "As between briefing and argument, there is a near-universal agreement among federal appellate judges that the brief is more important—certainly it is more enduring."[1] As explained by another judge: "Appellate advocacy comes in two parts, briefs and oral arguments, and its sole object is the persuasion of appellate judges. The brief is the more important part of appellate advocacy, because judges have it in hand both before and after oral argument. It is physically with us long after the argument evaporates and is forgotten."[2] Although not as significant as the written brief, an oral argument is important and can make a difference in the outcome of the issue or the entire case. In their book *Making Your Case*, Justice Antonin Scalia and Bryan Garner note that while an oral argument "rarely" will change a well-prepared judge's mind, oral argument can make a difference when the judge, after reading the briefs, is still undecided.[3] At the trial court level, where judges are busier and have less time to read the motions or briefs, an oral argument may have an even greater effect on a judge's decision.[4]

You should note that an oral argument is not guaranteed at either the trial or appellate level. While the rules vary, as a general matter, at the appellate level, oral argument must be requested. Often, as an appellant (the party bringing the appeal), it is in your best interest to request an oral argument, especially if the legal issue before the court is complex. However, recent data suggests that the frequency with which federal courts of appeals grant oral arguments is declining. According to a recent report, oral arguments were held in only 20 percent of federal courts of appeals cases decided on the merits at the end of the 2017 fiscal year.[5] Likewise, at the federal district court level, the rarity of oral arguments is also a chief complaint among some lawyers.[6]

1. Ruth Bader Ginsburg, *Remarks on Appellate Advocacy*, 50 S.C. L. Rev. 567, 567–68 (1999).

2. Roger J. Miner, *Froessel Award Acceptance Address Confronting the Communication Crisis in the Legal Profession*, 34 N.Y.L. Sch. L. Rev. 1, 8–9 (1989).

3. Antonin Scalia & Bryan A. Garner, Making Your Case: The Art of Persuading Judges 139 (2008).

4. David C. Fredrick, The Art of Oral Advocacy 4 (2019).

5. Todd Ross, *Quiet Time? Oral Arguments Disappear in Federal Appeals Courts*, Nat'l L.J., June 1, 2018, at 16.

6. Mark R. Kravitz, *Written and Oral Persuasion in the United States Courts: A District Judge's Perspective on Their History, Function, and Future*, 10 J. App. Prac. & Process 247, 255 (2009) ("Of course, oral argument in many federal district courts is even more rare than in the federal courts of appeals. Indeed, at a recent hearing of the Judicial Conference's Civil Rules Advisory Committee on proposals to amend Rule 56, which governs summary judgment, a chief complaint of practitioners—plaintiffs' and defendants' lawyers alike—was that district court judges rarely, if ever, provide an opportunity for oral argument on summary judgment motions. There appears to be a widespread belief among both court of appeals and district court judges that oral argument is inefficient and consumes too much court time, without attendant benefit. This rejection of

Thus, while oral argument is certainly important, the opportunity for oral argument is not guaranteed, and, even when granted, it is of secondary importance to your written motion or brief. That said, oral advocacy is an important skill for law students to learn. Often, as noted above, in the first-year legal writing program, students will present an oral argument based on their persuasive motion or brief.

II. Structure and content of an oral argument

The general structure and content of an oral argument will depend on your audience, specifically, whether that audience is a trial court judge or an appellate court panel of judges. For example, you can imagine that arguing a motion before a state trial court judge is very different than arguing before the nine justices of the United States Supreme Court.

Generally, in an oral argument, the moving party (the party asking for relief) argues first, next the responding party argues, and last the moving party argues a short rebuttal. At the appellate level, the moving party that argues first is the appellant, and the responding party is the appellee. At the trial court level, the party that argues first is the moving party (whichever party filed the motion), and the party that goes second is the responding party (whichever party filed the response/opposition to the motion).

However, at the outset, it is important to discuss the main differences between trial court hearings and appellate court oral arguments. First, unlike trial court hearings, which are done before a single judge, appellate court oral arguments are done before a panel of judges, ranging from three at the Circuit Courts of Appeals to nine at the United States Supreme Court. Second, appellate court judges are generally more prepared than trial court judges. At the appellate court level, judges will have carefully read your briefing and will be very familiar with the issues. At the trial court level, judges have busier dockets and, as a result, may or may not have had enough time to carefully read and digest the issues in your motion. Third, appellate court oral arguments are generally more formal than trial court hearings. At an oral argument before an appellate court, you will be strictly timed, argue standing behind a lectern, and begin with the phrase "May it please the court." At a trial court hearing, the format of the oral argument will vary greatly depending on the court before which you are arguing. A trial court argument may be done sitting or standing. It may be done in open court or in the judges' chambers. The argument may be timed, with each side getting a certain number of minutes like in an appellate court, or it may be an untimed back-and-forth discussion between you, opposing counsel, and the judge. Thus, before arguing before a trial

oral argument has also been accompanied by a movement away from oral judgments and opinions."); Suzanne Ehrenberg, *Embracing the Writing-Centered Legal Process*, 89 Iowa L. Rev. 1159, 1162 (2004) ("Over the past 150 years, appellate courts [and more recently, trial courts] have increasingly limited the role of oral argument, and have relied more heavily on written briefs in their decision-making processes.").

court judge, it is especially important to talk with a lawyer who has previously argued before that judge so that you know what to expect.

Regardless of whether you are arguing at the trial court or appellate level or whether you are representing the moving party or the responding party, generally speaking, your oral argument can be broken into five "parts": (1) the opening; (2) the statement of facts; (3) the body of the argument; (4) responding to questions; and (5) the closing.

As noted above, if your argument is in an appellate court or in a more formal trial court, the argument will be timed (often 20 minutes total per side) and proceed in the following order:

- Moving party/appellant argument;
- Responding party/appellee argument; and
- Rebuttal by moving party/appellant, if requested.

The moving party/appellant's time for rebuttal will be reserved at the start of the oral argument and will be subtracted from the total 20-minute time period allotted.

Because the focus of this book is writing at the trial level as opposed to the appellate level, the examples in this chapter will originate from an argument on a motion for summary judgment in a trial court. However, during first-year legal writing, whether the document being argued is a trial court document or an appellate court document, you should expect that the oral arguments will be conducted with the formality of an appellate oral argument. This means you will stand in front of a podium, you will be strictly timed, and you will likely argue in front of a panel of well-informed judges.

A. Opening

After the court gives you permission to proceed with your argument, you will begin your argument with an opening. Because your opening will be your first impression, you want to start with confidence. To do this, it is important that you script your opening, memorize it, and recite it with ease. Your opening can be broken into three subparts: (1) introduce yourself; (2) state your overall position or theme; and (3) give a roadmap or overview of what you will discuss during your oral argument.

1. Introduce yourself (and reserve time for rebuttal if movant or appellant)

At the appellate level, the first words out of your mouth at an oral argument are "May it please the court." At the trial court, these formal words are not required. Rather, you start by introducing yourself, your client, your client's position in the case (plaintiff/defendant), and your client's position on the issue (movant/respondent or appellant/appellee). In trial court, your introduction may look like this:

> Good morning, Your Honor. My name is Alex B. Partner, and I represent the Plaintiff-Respondent Mr. John Bell.

In appellate court, your introduction will be similar. However, if you are the appellant, you should, immediately after introducing yourself, reserve time for rebuttal. An example introduction for an appellant may look like this:

> May it please the court. My name is Adele Smith, and I represent the appellant in this case Defendant Happiness of Life. At this time, I would like to reserve two minutes for rebuttal.

If you are in a court that gives each side 20 minutes to argue, you will have 18 minutes for your argument and then two minutes for rebuttal. If your trial court is formal and the judge has given you a set amount of time, you should also, as movant, reserve time for rebuttal in a similar manner as above.

2. State your overall position or theme

After introducing yourself, you should state your overall position or theme. Figuring out your overall position or theme is simple. Just ask yourself: what do you want the outcome of the hearing to be? Using the problem in the Appendix of this book, if you represent the Defendant/Movant Happiness of Life, what outcome do you want? You want your motion for summary judgment to be granted! How do you get the court to grant the motion? By showing that the Plaintiff cannot establish a fact issue with respect to at least one element of his undue influence claim. Defendant/Movant might state its overall position/theme like this:

> This Court should grant summary judgment as to Plaintiff's undue influence claim because Happiness of Life has shown that Plaintiff cannot establish any of the elements of his claim.

Alternatively, if you represent the Plaintiff, Mr. Bell, what do you ultimately want from the court? You want Defendant Happiness of Life's motion for summary judgment to be denied. Why? Because there are, at a minimum, genuine issues of material fact regarding the undue influence claim. Therefore, you could state your overall position like this:

> This Court should deny Defendant's Motion for Summary Judgment because Defendant fails to meet its burden of proof to show that there are no genuine issues of material fact with respect to Mr. Bell's claim of undue influence.

3. Give a brief roadmap or overview of what you will discuss

After stating your overall position or theme, you should briefly give the court an overview of what you will discuss in the order that you plan to discuss it. This should be similar to what your "roadmap" looks like in your written motion or brief. However, you may or may not hit all of the points made in your written motion or brief in your oral argument. If that is the case, you will need to adjust your oral argument roadmap to reflect only those issues you plan to cover during your oral argument. For example, let's say you represent Defendant/Movant Happiness of Life. In your motion, you discuss how there is no genuine issue of material fact for all three elements of Plaintiff's undue influence claim. But, how many elements do you need to disprove to win/have the court grant your motion for summary judgment? Just one! It may be that you make the strategic decision to argue only your strongest element or elements during oral argument as opposed to arguing all three. For example, your roadmap could look like this:

> While, as set forth in our motion, Happiness of Life proves there is insufficient evidence to establish any of the three elements of Plaintiff's undue influence claim in order for this Court to grant summary judgment, Happiness of Life must only disprove one element of Plaintiff's claim. Therefore, for purposes of our time today, Defendant will focus first on the second element of Plaintiff's claim: that there is no evidence that an alleged influence by Happiness of Life overpowered the mind of Ms. Bell. If time remains, Defendant will show there is no genuine issue of material fact as to the other two elements as well.

If representing Plaintiff Mr. Bell, you need to establish all three elements to survive summary judgment. Accordingly, your planned roadmap or overview might sound like this:

> There is sufficient evidence to create a fact issue for all three elements of Mr. Bell's undue influence claim. First, the evidence shows the existence and exertion of an undue influence by Defendant Happiness of Life on Ms. Ava Bell. Second, the evidence shows that Defendant's influence overpowered the mind of Ms. Bell at the time she changed her will. Third, the evidence shows that, but for Defendant's influence, Ms. Bell would not have changed her will to effectively disinherit her husband and leave the vast majority of her estate to the Defendant.

However, as non-movant, you must be flexible even in the "scripted" opening section of your argument. As non-movant, you will have had the benefit of already hearing the movant's argument and the court's questions such that you have a better idea of the main issues that need to be confronted. For example, if the Defendant/Movant spent its entire oral argument time on the second element of the undue influence claim, it might be smart to rework your roadmap to start with the second element and then address the remaining two elements. In that case, your revisited roadmap or overview may look like this:

> There is sufficient evidence to create a fact issue for all three elements of Mr. Bell's undue influence claim. First, because Defendant spent the bulk of its time on element two, I will start with it and show that the evidence proves Defendant's influence overpowered the mind of Ms. Bell at the time she changed her will. Second, the evidence shows the existence and exertion of an undue influence by Defendant Happiness of Life on Ms. Ava Bell. Third, the evidence shows that, but for Defendant's influence, Ms. Bell would not have changed her will to effectively disinherit her husband and leave the vast majority of her estate to the Defendant.

4. Pulling your opening together

Put together, your opening should take less than one minute. Here is an example of a complete opening, with all three parts, for the lawyer representing Plaintiff John Bell:

> Good morning. My name is Alex B. Partner, and I represent the Plaintiff-Respondent Mr. John Bell. This Court should deny Defendant's motion for summary judgment because Defendant fails to meet its burden of proof to show that there are no genuine issues of material fact with respect to Mr. Bell's claim of undue influence. There is sufficient evidence to create a fact issue for all three elements of Mr. Bell's undue influence claim. First, because Defendant spent the bulk of its time on element two, Mr. Bell will show the evidence proves Defendant's influence overpowered the mind of Ms. Bell at the time she changed her will. Second, the evidence shows the existence and exertion of an undue influence by Defendant Happiness of Life on Ms. Ava Bell. Third, the evidence shows that, but for Defendant's influence, Ms. Bell would not have changed her will to effectively disinherit her husband and leave the vast majority of her estate to the Defendant.

Remember, you should have your opening down cold. When you get up to argue, your nerves will be high. Being extremely comfortable and confident in your opening will help calm you.

B. *Statement of facts*

The statement of facts differs for the movant and the non-movant.

1. Movant

After your opening, the movant should be prepared to provide the court with a brief overview of the facts of your case that pertain to the issues before the court. Often, if the court is familiar with the facts, it will interrupt your recitation of the facts and say something like "Counsel, move on. I am familiar with the facts." However, sometimes the court will allow you to give a brief overview of the facts before diving into the bulk of your argument. Note, given that you only have a limited amount of time, your recitation of the facts should be brief. Some lawyers, especially those arguing before appellate courts that are likely familiar with the parties' briefs, skip over the statement of facts and go straight to the argument. In a trial court, a brief overview of the facts may be helpful, especially if you think the judge may not be familiar with the facts underlying your motion.

Here is an example of what the lawyer representing Defendant Happiness of Life's statement of facts could look like during oral argument:

> Ava Bell was described by her own husband as "really smart" and "strong." In January 2018, after the recent death of her brother, Ms. Bell was looking for happiness and found that happiness in the charitable organization, Happiness of Life. However, her husband, Plaintiff John Bell, was not supportive of Ms. Bell's involvement in Happiness of Life, and their marriage became, as labeled by Ms. Bell, "miserable." In May 2018, with the assistance of an attorney, Ms. Bell executed a will leaving $5,000 to Mr. Bell, $10,000 to her parents, and the residuary of her estate to the charitable organization in which she was intimately involved, Happiness of Life. Ms. Bell died in June 2018. Mr. Bell alleges that Ms. Bell's will is the product of undue influence.

2. Non-movant

The non-movant's statement of facts largely depends on what the movant did or did not do. If the movant began by giving a statement of facts and the court indicated to the movant that it was familiar with the facts, the non-movant should not give a statement of facts. Why? The court said it was familiar with the facts! If the movant omitted a statement of facts, you should also probably omit a statement of facts and simply incorporate the important facts in the body of your argument.

On the other hand, if the movant gave a statement of facts, the non-movant may also want to give a short statement of facts. However, the non-movant should be careful not to waste the court's time repeating the facts of the case, but instead limit its facts to correcting only important omissions, misstatements, or mischaracterizations of the facts presented by the movant. In their book *Making Your Case*, Justice Scalia and Bryan Garner recommend that the non-movant when providing a statement of facts use an approach like the following:

> Plaintiff Mr. Bell's description of the facts is obviously quite different from those stated by Defendant Happiness of Life. But, for the sake of time, I will rest on the facts in our written opposition and make the following corrections to Defendant's statement . . . .[7]

7. SCALIA & GARNER, *supra* note 6, at 168–69.

C. Body of planned argument

The bulk of your oral argument time will be spent in the body of your planned argument. The body of your argument is where you will set forth the points you need to make in the order provided in the roadmap you gave in your opening. In the body of your argument, you should not read from or recite your motion or brief. Not only would this be boring and redundant, there is simply not time to cover everything in your motion or brief in an oral argument. Instead, you will argue the main points or, put another way, the highlights of your argument. As a general matter, you should limit yourself to no more than three points for your oral argument, even if there are more than three points in your written motion or brief.

For each point, you will do an oral version of "CRACC." The oral version of "CRACC" is, however, quite a bit different than the written version. So instead of calling it "CRACC," we prefer to call it "C-R/A-C." For each point, you will start with your conclusion ("C") and then state why the conclusion is supported with both the law (Rule) and facts as applied to the law (Analysis). However, unlike a written motion or brief, where you fully explain the law (Rule) before applying it (Analysis), in an oral argument, presumably the court has read your motion or brief and, as such, you can mix the Rule and Analysis. Moreover, depending on the issue, and, especially if you are in trial court, you may spend significantly more time on the facts than on the law. Why? Often the judge is painfully familiar with the law.

For example, if you have a negligence case, you do not need to waste time explaining the definition of causation in great detail to the judge. Instead, you need to focus on the topic with which the judge is less familiar: why causation is or is not established in your case. Why causation is or is not established in your case will be a mix of the law with the facts, but the bigger focus will be on the facts of your case. This is especially true with a motion for summary judgment because the governing legal standard is whether there is a genuine issue of material **fact**. If you have time, after your "R/A," you will briefly restate your conclusion for the issue and simultaneously transition to the next issue. If you are running short on time, it is okay to skip the last Conclusion and simply transition to the next issue. Note that transitions are especially important in oral arguments because it is imperative that at all times the court knows what point you are addressing and can recognize when you are moving on from one issue to another. Therefore, use words like "first," "second," or "third" and phrases like "moving to the second issue" to signpost your argument.

To understand what the body of a planned argument looks like in C-R/A-C form, it is most helpful to take it out of the abstract and use an example. For the second element of undue influence, Defendant/Movant Happiness of Life's planned argument might look like the below. The Conclusion sentences are underlined and what is in the middle is the "R/A."

Conclusion

First, Plaintiff cannot prove the second and what precedent says is the "pivotal" element of his undue influence claim: that Happiness of Life overpowered Ms. Bell's mind. To establish the second element, courts have held it is insufficient to show simply that a testator had a weakened physical or mental condition. Instead, Plaintiff must show that Ms. Bell's free agency was destroyed such that she lost the ability to decide for herself. Plaintiff cannot show this. Indeed, Plaintiff admits that Ms. Bell was, and I quote, "really smart," "a strong woman," and "physically really good." While the evidence shows Ms. Bell suffered from depression in late 2017, the evidence also shows that at the time she executed her will in May 2018, she was no longer depressed, no longer taking depression medication, and was in no way hindered by depression in her personal or business affairs. Moreover, per *Estate of Steed*, even if Ms. Bell had depression at the time of the will's execution, which she did not, the second element cannot be established because there is zero evidence that she was in any way impaired from doing her daily tasks. Moreover, while Plaintiff will undoubtedly argue that her mind was overpowered because she drank mushroom tea, this is insufficient to establish that Ms. Bell's mind was overpowered. In the *Guthrie* case, the testator had a lobotomy, and, still, the court held that the second element was not established because, although the lobotomy may have rendered the testator susceptible to influence, it could not be proven that the testator's mind was overpowered. Drinking mushroom tea is hardly comparable to a lobotomy. Because Plaintiff cannot show Ms. Bell's free agency was destroyed or her mind was overpowered, summary judgment should be granted. Moving to the second element . . .

RULE/ ANALYSIS

Conclusion

Compare what is written above to this portion of Defendant Happiness of Life's Motion for Summary Judgment in the Appendix. What is different? For one, the argument is much shorter than the motion. There simply is not time to read what you have written in your motion. Second, you will notice that the legal rules (Rule) is combined with the facts of the case. By doing this, you are always persuading, and you are moving forward more efficiently (i.e., covering more material in less time). This efficiency is important because, in oral argument, time is of the essence, especially when you are "interrupted" with questions by the court, which you will be (as we will discuss in the next section). Third, you will notice that there are no citations. You do not need to cite the law or the record in your oral argument. If asked during oral argument by a judge for a citation or case name, you should be familiar enough with the case law and the record to provide such information, but, as a general matter, you do not need to "cite" in oral argument. Repeatedly "citing" the law, even just by case name, can be distracting and will slow down your argument. As put by one judge: "[I]t is almost certain that not a single case cited in argument by either name or volume and page will have been remembered."[8]

1. Being flexible in the body of your planned argument

The body of your argument is where you will spend the bulk of your time. The most important rule to live by as you prepare and deliver the body of your argument is: be flexible. In most instances, you will not be able to present a "canned" argument, and, as a result, writing and memorizing a detailed script is useless. Rather than a script, you need an outline of points you plan to make in the body of your argument, in the order you plan to make them. However, you must be mindful that "plans change," and you must be prepared for the reality that your plans **will** change. The reason is that you will be interrupted with questions. The questions may move your argument on the issue forward or they may move you to a totally a different issue. The questions may take so much time that you do not have time for your planned argument or only have time for a small portion of it. While arguing an issue, you may realize that the judges agree with you on that issue; therefore, your time will be better spent on other issues. Or, it may be that you realize that the judges disagree with you on an issue and are unlikely to change their minds so you should move on to an issue you can win.

If you are the responding party or appellee (the party that goes second), you must be especially flexible. You will have the benefit of having heard the other side's argument and the judges' questions to the other side. Therefore, you know where the judges' concerns lie, and you need to address those or use those concerns in your argument. As the responding party, you cannot give your planned argument in a vacuum. Instead, you must give your argument in the context of what has already happened—namely, what the other side argued and how the judges questioned the other side. If possible, you should incorporate the judges' comments or questions into your own argument. For example: "As commented by Judge Smith, all five factors need not be present to establish the first element . . . ." Also, in your argument as the responding party, you should respond to specific points raised by the other side in its oral argument. This is not to say that your oral argument should be "Defendant argued that . . . . Plaintiff responds that . . . ." No, instead, the responding party should incorporate its response to the other side's arguments within the responding party's *own* planned structure. For example, Plaintiff John Bell (responding party) might respond to the oral argument by Happiness of Life on page 206 by incorporating the following within Plaintiff's own discussion of element two: "Defendant argued that Ms. Bell's free agency was not destroyed because she did not have a lobotomy, however, that is not the standard."

---

8. BRYAN A. GARNER, THE WINNING ORAL ARGUMENT 138 (2009) (quoting Judge George R. Currie, who was on the Washington Supreme Court).

2. Keep calm by being prepared

In addition to being flexible, you must keep calm. The best way to keep calm is to be prepared. It is easy to get flustered when you planned to address three issues, but with three minutes left, you are still on issue one. To combat the feeling of panic you might have, you need to prepare yourself for any scenario that could be thrown at you. You should go into the argument expecting anything and everything. You should go in expecting to hit all of your points with minimal questions, expecting to change the order of your issues, expecting to devote most of your time to one issue to the exclusion of the others, expecting to be interrupted with so many questions that you do not reach any of your planned argument, and so forth. If you only have three minutes left for your remaining two issues, what would you say? You need to have a plan for this. It may be that you have a short version of the argument for both issues that you are ready to present. It may be that you skip to the third issue for your remaining three minutes and rest on your briefing for the second issue. Being prepared for whatever scenario is thrown your way will keep you calm.

D. Responding to questions from the bench

The most important part of any oral argument is the questions asked by the judge or judges and the answers given by the lawyers. Questions allow you to understand and respond to the judges' concerns about your case, clarify issues, and persuade the judges of your position. You may initially think, "I hope I am not interrupted with too many questions." However, questions should not be looked at as a burden but rather as a welcomed opportunity. A question, though an interruption to your planned argument, is not an interruption as we usually think of the word. To answer a judge's question is ultimately why you are there. The more questions, the better. Questions also give you insight into what the court is thinking. Thus, a question asked may not only be a question, but a "cue" to counsel. As put by Justice Ruther Bader Ginsburg:

> [I]t seems to me, a waste of a lawyer's precious opportunity to use oral argument or attempt to use it just to recapitulate the briefing instead of trying to uncover what is in the decisionmaker's mind. Questions from the bench can give counsel a chance to satisfy the court on matters the questioner at least thinks significant and might resolve less satisfactorily without counsel's aid. Sometimes it is true, a question will be asked with persuasion of a colleague in mind, and the lawyer may sense at those times that she is being talked through, not to. Other times, the questioner may be trying to cue counsel, that an argument, pursued with gusto, is a loser and that counsel would be well advised to move on. A counsel too intent on a prepared script may miss that kind of cue.[9]

---

9. Hon. Ruth Bader Ginsberg, *Remarks for American Law Institute Annual Dinner (May 19, 1994)*, 38. St. Louis L.J. 881, 885 (1994).

You should hope for, plan for, and expect to have multiple questions during your argument. These questions can come at any time (opening, body, or closing) and can be about anything (the issue you are currently discussing, a totally different issue you planned to discuss later, or an issue you did not plan to discuss at all). Answering questions from the bench is both a skill and an art.

1. How to respond to questions

When asked a question from a judge, it is important to know not only the answer, but generally how to respond. Questions can come at any point during the oral argument. You might not so much as state your name before a judge interrupts you with a question. Below are some guidelines to follow when answering questions during oral argument.

Step one: Stop talking and immediately listen.

As soon as the judge starts asking a question, you should immediately stop talking, even if you are mid-sentence, or even if you are mid-syllable. As soon as the judge starts to speak, you stop speaking. No matter what. Stop. Talking over a judge is a mistake and a sign of disrespect to the court. As the judge is asking his or her question, you should be intently listening. This means you should be making eye contact with the judge. You should not be looking down at your notes or looking away.

Step two: Pause.

After the judge asks the question, you should pause for a moment. The purpose of the pause is three-fold. First, a pause allows you to make sure the judge is finished asking the question. You do not want to accidentally interrupt the judge by beginning to answer a question before the judge has finished speaking. Second, a pause gives you time to make sure you understand the question. Importantly, if you do not understand the question, you should ask the judge to clarify, rephrase, or repeat the question. You might say, "Your Honor, I apologize, but would you mind repeating your question." Or, you may ask, "Your Honor, if I understand your question, you are asking whether but-for causation in the context of an undue influence claim is similar to but-for causation in the context of a negligence claim?" This will allow the judge to clarify or rephrase the question if you do not understand it. Note that asking for clarification on a question is one of the only times you (the lawyer arguing) ever get to ask the court a question. Simply put, your job is to answer questions, not to ask them. Finally, a pause allows you to take a moment to formulate your answer.

Step three: Answer the question directly and then explain.

After you have paused, you should answer the question directly and then explain your answer. This is similar to what you learned in Part Two, Section II.D, regarding writing your brief answer in an objective memo. You begin with your direct answer (yes or no), and then you explain.

If the judge asks a yes/no question, you should begin with a direct and short answer: "Yes, Your Honor" or "No, Your Honor." Some variation of "yes" or "no" is also okay as long as you begin by directly answering the question. For example, "Absolutely, Your Honor" or "Definitely not, Your Honor." After you respond "yes" or "no," then, and only then, do you explain why. For example:

Judge: Counsel, is it true that you are arguing a disposition of a will is always natural when made to any charity, regardless of what that charity is?

Counsel for Defendant Happiness of Life: No, Your Honor. It is not de facto natural every time anyone makes a disposition to any charity. Rather, the law says that dispositions to charities should generally be upheld as a matter of public policy and that when the person was involved in the charity during her life, as here, where Ms. Bell was involved with Happiness of Life before she died, the disposition to the charity is not unnatural because there is a reasonable explanation for the disposition.

Even if the judge does not ask a yes/no question, you should still begin with your direct and short answer before explaining your reasoning. For example:

Judge: Counsel, how can you say that there is not at least a fact issue as to the second element of undue influence when, at the time Ms. Bell executed her new will, she was drinking that mushroom tea that altered her state of being?

Counsel for Happiness of Life: Because, Your Honor, there is no evidence Ms. Bell's free agency was destroyed by the tea. To prove the second element of his claim, Plaintiff must show evidence that Happiness of Life actually overwhelmed Ms. Bell's free agency or ability to decide for herself. Here, the evidence shows the opposite. The tea, which she did not just drink the morning of the will's execution but had been drinking for months prior, did not affect her ability to perform at her job, take care of her home, or otherwise complete her daily tasks.

By beginning with a short and direct answer to the judge's question and then explaining your answer, you do not leave the judge guessing or waiting for an answer. We all find it annoying when we ask a direct question, and, in response, we get a rambling, long-winded answer that is not responsive to our question or leaves us in suspense for a while before getting an answer to the question that we asked.

Imagine this exchange with your friend:

You: Are you going to travel home for Thanksgiving?

(Annoying) Friend: I have so many finals to study for and feel like I am really falling behind. Also, I am short on money. Law school is expensive. I told my mom that I could not come home for Thanksgiving break, and she was sad about it. The next day, my dad called me and said that he would pay for my flights. He also said that, if I come home, he would set up a quiet room with a desk for me at the house so that I could study in peace and not be disturbed by family. So, I am now traveling home for Thanksgiving.

That's super irritating, right? You would rather your friend start with, "Yes, I am traveling home for Thanksgiving." Then, she can explain the details behind why. At this point, you will have your answer and be free to listen (or maybe not listen) to the explanation. Judges are the same way. Judges want the direct answer to their question to come first and then the explanation for that answer.

Step four: After answering the question, transition back to your planned argument.

After you have answered the question asked, you must transition back to your planned argument. Arguably the hardest part about answering questions is not the actual answer, but, rather, it is the transition from answering a question back to your planned argument.

Think of telling a story. Your friend "interrupts" your story with a question or series of questions. If your friend only asks one question and the question relates to the part of the story you were just telling, it is easier to answer the question and get back to the rest of your story. However, if your friend asks you numerous questions in a row and the questions are not at all related to the part of the story you were previously telling, getting back to your story will be harder. After answering all your friend's questions and detouring from your story, you might have forgotten where you left off. You may think or say aloud, "Now, what was I saying before?"

A similar scenario can happen when answering a judge's question or questions, especially if the question is not related to the argument you are making at that time. However, you cannot ask a judge, "Now, what was I saying before?" Instead, you must know how to answer any question (or series of questions) and get back to your argument. This is difficult and takes practice.

Being able to transition goes hand in hand with being flexible. You may not transition back to exactly where you left off. For example, if you were just starting your discussion of your first issue and were asked back-to-back questions on that issue, it may be that, after answering those questions, you feel like issue one has been sufficiently addressed. In that case, you would not return to your planned argument on issue one, but, instead, you would make the choice to transition to issue two. As you can imagine, this requires quite a bit of quick thinking on your feet.

2. Additional guidelines for responding to questions

Below are a few additional guidelines to follow when answering questions.

- Do not call a judge "sir," "ma'am," "you," "Mrs.," "Mr.," etc. Call the judge "Your Honor."
- Do not patronize the judge by saying "Great question," "I am so glad you asked that," "I thought you'd never ask," or the like. This can be interpreted as disrespectful.
- Do not put off a question until later. When asked a question, you must answer it. You cannot say, "Your Honor, I will get to that question in a moment when I discuss the third element." Rather, you must answer whatever question is asked at that moment, even if the question is wholly unrelated to what you are currently discussing.
- Do not answer a hypothetical question by saying, "That's not our case." Duh! It is a hypothetical, which necessarily means it is a different set of facts than the facts of your case. You may get hypothetical questions designed to test your position, and you should answer them.
- Do not ask the judges questions. Besides asking for clarification of a question that a judge asked or asking to speak after your time has expired, you should never ask the judge a question.
- Do not argue with a judge or take a combative tone. Some judges will seem difficult. It is important that you maintain respect. For example, let's say that a judge misstates your position. The judge could do this repeatedly. A good way to handle this would be to say, "Respectfully, Your Honor, that is not a correct characterization of my client's position. Our position is that . . ." A bad way to handle this would be to say, "That's not what I said" or "You're wrong."
- Do not fight softball questions. Sometimes, a judge will ask you a question that seems too simple or too good to be true because it is so favorable to your position. For example, if you represented Happiness of Life, the court could give you the following softball question: "Counsel, is it correct that Ms. Bell actually did provide for Plaintiff in the new will?" You should recognize this question as a softball, be internally grateful for it, answer it, and use it to move your argument forward: "That is precisely correct, Your Honor. Ms. Bell did not disinherit the Plaintiff; rather, she devised him . . . ." Some lawyers make the (cringeworthy) mistake of fighting easy questions.
- Do not make up an answer. If you do not know the answer to a judge's question, the worst thing you can do is to invent an answer. You do not want to end up

saying something that is incorrect and hurt your credibility. Instead, if you do not know the answer, you should state, "Your Honor, I apologize, but I do not know the answer to that question" and move on. Alternatively, if the question seems important to the court, offer to get the court the answer to the question by filing a post-hearing or post-oral argument letter brief. For example, you might say: "Your Honor, I do not know the answer to that question at this time, but I will provide an answer to the court by letter brief tomorrow."

E. *Conclusion*

Your argument will end either when (1) you have nothing left to say or (2) your time is up, whichever comes first.

1. Concluding with some time left

If time is remaining, but you have nothing left to say, you should conclude. You need not "run out the clock." After all, courts appreciate brevity. As noted by one Fifth Circuit judge, "There never has been a panel that resented an advocate's using less than all of his or her allotted time."[10]

How you conclude will depend on how much time is left on the clock. If you have plenty of time left after finishing the body of your argument, you may (1) give a brief summary of your main points; (2) restate the overall relief you want (e.g., deny summary judgment); and (3) end by saying something like, "Unless the Court has further questions [pause in case the court does], that concludes my remarks. Thank you." You would then sit down.

If you only have, say, 30 seconds remaining, you do not have time to give a brief summary. Instead, you may conclude by (1) restating the overall relief you want and (2) end by saying, "Unless the Court has further questions [pause in case the court does], that concludes my remarks. Thank you." You would then sit down.

If you have less than 30 seconds remaining, you may conclude by simply saying, "Unless the Court has further questions [pause in case court does], that concludes my remarks. Thank you." You would then sit down.

2. Concluding when your time has expired

If time runs out and you are in the middle of speaking, you should stop speaking when you are out of time, say thank you, and sit down. The only exception to this rule is if you are in the midst of answering a judge's question. If you are in the middle of answering a judge's question and your time expires, you may ask, "Your Honor, I see my time has concluded. May I briefly finish answering your question?" If the court agrees and grants you permission to finish answering the question, do not do anything

---

10. Honorable Jacques L. Wiener, Jr., *Ruminations from the Bench: Brief Writing and Oral Argument in the Fifth Circuit*, 70 Tul. L. Rev. 187, 204 (1995).

else. You should answer the question or finish answering the question, say "thank you," and sit down. You should not "conclude" or make another point.

F. *Rebuttal (Movant/Appellant)*

If you are the movant or appellant (the party that argues first), you may have the opportunity for rebuttal. Recall that in the opening of your argument, you will need to reserve time for rebuttal if you wish to present a rebuttal. If you do not reserve the time, you waive rebuttal. For example, if your argument is 20 minutes long, you may choose to reserve two or three minutes for rebuttal.

Rebuttal can be a powerful tool because it is the last word of oral argument the court hears before making its decision. During rebuttal, you should not raise new points or re-argue points that you argued during your previous time. Rather, you should rebut the strongest points that the other side just argued to the court. While the non-movant or appellee is arguing, you should be taking notes of the points you want to rebut. If by the court's questioning, you sense that the court is having doubts about your position on an issue after hearing oral argument from the other side, you should make sure to address these doubts head-on in your rebuttal. Rebuttal is usually very short. Most lawyers do not recommend reserving more than two or three minutes for rebuttal. Given the brevity of rebuttal, you must use your time judiciously and address only the most significant point or points you need to win.

III. Preparing for your argument

Now that you understand the structure of an oral argument and how challenging making an oral argument can be, how do you prepare for it? Preparing is two-fold: (1) you must be prepared substantively to argue the issues before the court by knowing the law, the record, and how to present your argument; and (2) you must be prepared to present as a public speaker before the audience of the court.

A. *Preparing substantively for your oral argument*

1. Review the motions or briefs, the law cited therein, and the record or any exhibits

The good news about preparing substantively for oral argument is that you have done most of the heavy preparation during the writing process. To be prepared for an oral argument, you must be intimately familiar with what you have written, as well as what the other side has written, the law cited therein, and the facts of the case as set forth in the exhibits or the record. For example, if you represented Happiness of Life, you would prepare by reviewing your client's motion, the Plaintiff's opposition, the caselaw relied upon by your client and by the Plaintiff, and the facts of the case as found in the exhibits.

In reviewing the written papers at issue (the motion and opposition, or the briefs), you need to understand your argument and what the other side is arguing. You should assess your best points, as well as the best points the other side makes that you may need to address in oral argument. You also need to pull the law relied on by your side and the other side from the written papers. You need not memorize all of the legal authority, but you should read through it all. For the most important cases you rely on and the other side relies on, you should know some key details. It is helpful to create a case chart "cheat sheet" to help you jog your memory during oral argument. For the important cases relied upon by the other side, you may include on your cheat sheet ways to distinguish the cases.

Before oral argument, you should also do some quick research to make sure nothing changed between the time you submitted your papers and the date of the oral argument. You should make sure that none of the cases have been overturned or questioned by Shepardizing™ (LexisNexis®) or KeyCiting® (Westlaw®) the cases. You should also run a search to see if any new, relevant cases on the issue have been decided since you filed your motion or brief. A quick way to do this is to run the relevant search and then organize the search results by date so the newest cases are on the top of the search results.

In reviewing the record and/or exhibits, you need to become the expert on the facts of your case. Not knowing the facts of your own case or confusing the facts of your own case is especially damaging to your credibility.

2. Next, prepare your oral argument content

After you have reviewed the motions or briefs, the law, and the record and exhibits, you need to prepare the substance of your oral argument. Remember, you do not have time to cover the entire content of your motion or brief; you should not simply read from it. Instead, you need to list (in order of priority) your side's main points that you need to argue combined with the other side's strongest points that you need to address.

For example, if you represent Happiness of Life, in your Motion for Summary Judgment, you will have three issues (element one, element two, and element three of the undue influence claim). To win, you only need to show no genuine issue of material fact as to one of the elements. In your oral argument, you may decide to omit element one and spend your time arguing only elements two and three because they are stronger. You also may decide to start with element three, if you think that will be your best chance of winning.

Once you have your main points, you will need to prepare your opening, your argument body, and your closing. Preparing the opening and closing is simple. To prepare your opening, you should write out a script and memorize it (*see* Part Five, Section II.A, above). To prepare your closing, you should write out and memorize different versions of it, so you are prepared to conclude with ample time, limited time, or no time (*see* Part Five, Section II.E, above).

To prepare your body, you should list the main points you need to make for your Conclusion and, underneath those points, list the "R/A"—the law and facts that support that main point (*see* Part Five, Section II.C, above). Unlike your opening and closing, it is not necessary to write out the body of your argument word for word because, unless you have a silent court, you cannot script an oral argument. Rather, as set forth above, you will be interrupted with questions, and, based on those questions, you may need to move parts of your argument around or change your argument. Additionally, if you are the non-movant or appellee, you may need to change your argument based on what the other side argued or the questions asked to the other side. Because you must be flexible and because oral argument is a conversation, not a speech, an outline will be more helpful than a script.

a) Predict the questions you will be asked and prepare answers

The scariest part of preparing for anything is the unknown. The unknown in oral argument is the questions the court will ask you. To prepare for this "unknown," you need to do your best to anticipate and predict what questions you may be asked. For example, it is likely that a court will question you about weaknesses of your case and strengths of the other side. You should write out those possible questions and prepare answers to them.

b) Create an outline to bring with you to oral argument

After you have figured out the substance of your oral argument, you should create a short outline to bring with you to oral argument. You cannot bring to oral argument a stack of cases or a thick binder to flip through. The reason is because you will not have time to search through documents during oral argument, and, regardless, fumbling and flipping through papers is distracting to the court.

To prepare your outline, the best advice is to use the manila folder method. Yes, it is that simple. Use a regular manila folder. When you open the folder, it will lay flat like a book and have two sides. On each side, you will staple to each corner of (or otherwise affix) an 8.5x11 piece of paper that sets forth your outline material. The manila folder method allows you to see a two-page outline without having to flip anything or move papers around.

There is no one "right" way to create your two-page outline. However, we recommend putting your planned argument outline with your main points on the left side of the manila folder. For your main points, make them bold, and, under your main points, include a bullet-point list of law and facts that support each of your main points. On the right side of the manila folder, we recommend putting information you may need to answer anticipated questions and group the information by anticipated subjects. If you need a personal reminder (e.g., eye contact, speak louder, stay still), we recommend writing those on your outline in your own handwriting and in a color that stands out. For example, if you are a fast-talker, you could write "slow down!!!" somewhere on your outline to remind yourself to speak slowly. On the back of the folder (i.e., the back of the folder when it is closed), we will sometimes staple a one-page case chart. The hope is that you do not need to "flip" or "turn" to this, but it will be there just in case you get a question about a case and need to jog your memory.

Note that you should not include your scripted opening and closing in your outline. The reason for this omission is that, if they are written out, you may be tempted to look down and read them, instead of maintaining eye contact and delivering your opening and closing from memory. We have seen students in oral argument look down at their outline when saying "My name is . . . ." Obviously, these students know their names, but because they have brought with them a script of their opening, they are looking down and reading it instead of confidently stating it from memory.

c) Practice, practice, practice

The best way to prepare the content of your oral argument is to practice. It is meaningless if you have everything you need to say in your brain or written in your outline, but you are unable to communicate it orally. Therefore, you must practice communicating your argument orally numerous times.[11] You should also practice your oral argument under different conditions. For example, practice your argument without being interrupted with questions so you are prepared for the (unfortunate) situation where the bench is quiet or "cold." Practice making your points in different orders in case you are asked by a judge to address an issue in an order other than what you had planned. Ideally, during some of your practices, you should have someone (a friend, a colleague, or a family member) play judge and interrupt you with questions. The practice questions could be the questions that you have predicted and written out.

The benefits of practicing aloud are numerous. First, when you practice your argument orally, you will find that things, which sounded one way in your head or on paper, sound differently when spoken aloud and will need to be adjusted. Second, you will also figure out the timing and pace of your argument and whether you are spending too much or too little time on any point. Third, you will hear how your argument flows and how you are moving from point to point. It may be that your argument, while organized and logical on paper, becomes confusing when spoken such that you need to add more signposts or transitions. Fourth, practicing answering questions orally will allow you not only to refine the substance of your answer, but also to commit the art of answering questions to "muscle memory." Recall that when asked a question by the court, you should immediately stop talking, keep eye contact during the question, pause, give a direct answer, explain, and then—the hardest part—transition back to your argument. Finally, practicing orally will allow you to understand any weaknesses you have as a speaker, as discussed in the next section.

B. Refining your oral argument presentation skills

Mastering the content of your oral argument is half the battle. You must be able to deliver that content to the court in a persuasive, strong, non-distracting, credible way.

---

11. Consider videotaping yourself practicing your oral argument. By watching yourself on video (as painful as it may be) you will be able to isolate substantive and presentation-based weaknesses in advance of your "real" argument.

For example, it does not matter how brilliant the point you are making is if the court cannot hear it because you speak too softly. Therefore, part of being a strong oral advocate is having strong oral presentation skills. Below are some general tips for presenting a strong oral argument.

PRESENTATION TIPS	
Keep eye contact	You should strive to make eye contact with the judge or judges of the court. While it is okay to briefly look down at your outline, for the majority of your time you should be maintaining eye contact with your audience—the court.
Speak to be heard	In order to best deliver your message, you should speak loudly, you should speak slowly, and you should enunciate your words. In order to ensure that you are speaking to he heard, either record your oral argument to review it yourself or have someone watch you to provide feedback.
Make your tone conversational, but respectful	You should not sound like you are reading off your notes or performing off a memorized script. Instead, your tone should be conversational. Conversational does not mean that you are informal; you should always address the court with respect. However, you should treat an oral argument like a conversation between you and the judge (or among you and the judges), rather than as a performance where you are on stage and the judges are idle audience members watching.
Stand straight and still	When giving your oral argument, you should stand. Normally, you will stand behind a podium or lectern. While standing to deliver your oral argument, you should maintain good posture by keeping your shoulders back and head up. You should stand still. Unlike arguing before a jury, when arguing before a court, you should not move around or make gestures with your arms. You should also take care to not be unintentionally distracting by, for example, nervously tapping the podium, shuffling your papers, or otherwise fiddling with something.

Avoid filler words	Avoiding filler words, such as "um," "like," "uh," "er," and "ah," is easier said than done. Recording yourself arguing is the best way to know if you use a filler word. If you use a particular filler word, stopping its use is not something that necessarily happens overnight or on command. This is because your use of a filler word is not a cognizant decision made by you, but it is a habit and something that you are doing without thinking. However, filler words can be distracting and can make you sound less confident in what you are saying. Filler words are used more when you are unprepared or under-prepared, which causes you to trip over your words or be unsure in what you are saying. The more prepared you are, the fewer words you will use. Additionally, to eliminate filler words or, at least to reduce them, you should slow down your speaking pace and practice replacing filler words with pauses.
Avoid first person pronouns	When presenting the substance of your argument, you should avoid the use of first-person pronouns such as "I think," "I feel," "I believe," "I anticipate," etc. Put bluntly, the court does not care what you personally think, feel, or believe. The court cares about what the law says and what the facts of the case are. Keep yourself out of it.
Dress professionally	It should go without saying that on the day of your oral argument, you should dress in formal, courtroom attire. You do not want the court to be distracted from what you are saying by what you are wearing.
Keep the nerves at bay	Some of you are terrified of public speaking and an oral argument, by definition, is public speaking. To help keep your anxiety to a minimum, in addition to being very prepared, you should arrive early to the court, and, if possible, you should watch other people argue before the same court before you go so you know exactly what to expect. If when you get to the podium or lectern you are shaking or otherwise nervous, try discreetly squeezing the edges of the podium or lectern to release that nervous energy. Then, take a deep breath.

6 | Bar Preparation: MEE and Bar-Style Essays and MPTs

The type of writing you are doing affects the structure, the substance, and the format of your writing. In other words, formal legal writing, such as motions, objective memos, or briefs, looks different and contains different content than the writing you will do for law school exams and the bar exam, which takes the form of essays and, for the latter, Multistate Performance Tests (MPTs). While the foundational legal writing skills you learn in your legal writing courses will help you with other forms of legal writing, bar essays and MPTs are different than traditional legal writing in several ways. The biggest difference is that bar essays and MPTs are required to be written under strict time pressure. The chart below highlights some additional differences (and similarities) between the legal writing you will do in law school, on the bar, and in practice.

	OBJECTIVE MEMOS	LAW SCHOOL EXAM ESSAYS	BAR EXAM ESSAYS	MPTS
Citation and use of cases	Correct form and placement of citations from appropriate jurisdiction	Limited use of citations. Correct form not required.	No citations.	Limited use of citations. Correct form not required.
Organization	CRAC for each issue (i.e., each element of multi-element cause of action or defense).	Same.	Same.	Same, but can use abbreviated. Most important part of MPT organization is to explain law then apply the law (RA).
Facts	Separate statement of facts (SOF) and trigger facts weaved into Analysis ("A").	No separate SOF. Trigger facts weaved into Analysis ("A").	Same.	Same (unless instructions of task provide otherwise).
Headings, Conclusion sentences, and topic sentences	Use conclusion-based headings. After heading, the CRAC will begin with a Conclusion that is similar to the conclusion-based heading. Each paragraph under the heading should have a well-developed topic sentence.	Use conclusion-based headings. After heading, no need to start with a formal Conclusion. While paragraphs are divided topically, no topic sentence is required.	Same.	Same.
Rules	Lengthy description of rule and subrules for the issue, defense, or element being discussed. Rules include key language, terms, and often quotations from case law and/or statutes. Rule also includes full case illustrations.	Accurate rule statement and inclusion of key subrules related to the particular issue, defense, or element being discussed. No quotations are needed. Case illustrations are not usually necessary.	Same.	Same, but a modified version of a case illustration may be needed depending on the legal authority you are given and the task you are asked to complete.

	OBJECTIVE MEMOS	LAW SCHOOL EXAM ESSAYS	BAR EXAM ESSAYS	MPTS
Analysis and Counter-analysis	Includes rule-based reasoning plus extensive analogical reasoning that focuses on comparing/contrasting precedent cases to fact pattern at issue (or arguing case is like/unlike precedent case in persuasive writing).	Limited analogical reasoning, instead engaging mostly in rule of reason analysis (applying the rule to the facts to predict outcome). Both sides are discussed.	No analogical reasoning. Instead, a more limited analysis focused on applying the facts to the rule to yield a conclusion. Counter-analysis/counter-arguments are raised to provide a fully explained answer.	Includes mix of rule-based reasoning and analogical reasoning (if cases are illustrated). Counter-analysis not required unless instructed otherwise in assignment.

This part of the book will go into more detail on the process, format, and content for drafting law school and bar essay-exam answers and MPTs.

I. Bar (and bar-style law school) essays

The Multistate Essay Exam ("MEE") is drafted by the National Conference of Bar Examiners and administered as part of most states' bar exams. The MEE exam is designed to "test an examinee's ability to (1) identify legal issues raised by a hypothetical factual situation; (2) separate material which is relevant from that which is not; (3) present a reasoned analysis of the relevant issues in a clear, concise, and well-organized composition; and (4) demonstrate an understanding of the fundamental legal principles relevant to the probable solution of the issues raised by the factual situation."[1] Unlike the multiple-choice portion of the bar exam, the MEE portion requires students to communicate their knowledge of the law in an organized, written form under time pressure. In other words, the MEE is testing your knowledge of the law **and** your ability to communicate that knowledge like a lawyer. This chapter will introduce you to MEE and bar-style law school essay exams. In addition, it will provide you with a basic construct for using your critical legal writing skills to excel in essay writing.

A. Format of an MEE or bar-style essay question

During the time of the Paper Chase[2] and still in many law schools across the country, law school professors pride themselves in drafting lengthy and challenging end-of-the-semester essay exams. Some of these seemingly impossible exams cover hundreds of potential issues (i.e., causes of action and defenses) between numerous litigants such that no student can realistically identify or fully analyze all of them within the time allotted. MEE essays and bar-style law school essays, however, are different. Do not misunderstand: they are time pressured just like traditional issue-spotter exams. But, MEE and bar-style essay exams have a distinct question or set of questions and do not contain any extraneous facts. In other words, they are asking a specific question or set of questions and each fact in the hypothetical presented is legally relevant and likely has an impact on one of the questions asked. Below is a sample bar-style essay exam question annotated to help you understand the different parts of this type of essay question.

Hypothetical scenario with legally relevant facts

Jack and Annie were married in January of 1998 and filed for divorce in October of 2018. They lived in Texas throughout their marriage. Annie is a real estate investor, earning a good salary. Near the end of their marriage, Annie's business had grown enough that she received $500,000 bonuses each year in 2016 and 2017. Jack was a lawyer. He has worked and continues

1. National Conference of Bar Examiners, Multistate Essay Examination Purpose, http://www.ncbex.org/exams/mee/ (last visited June 21, 2019).

2. THE PAPER CHASE (Twentieth Century Fox 1973).

to work for Happy Lawyer, LLP and earns a good salary. Jack and Annie put all of their work-related income into a joint bank account.

Both Jack and Annie had received property from their families. In 1997, Jack's father had given him a mineral estate in Oilygas Ranch. Oilygas yielded $10,000 in royalties each year. Annie's father died in 2010. As part of his will, he bequeathed Annie a 50% interest in Birchwood, their Wisconsin summer home. In 2011, Annie's brother (to whom her father had bequeathed the other 50% of Birchwood) hit hard financial times. Annie and Jack borrowed $1.5M from Saveabuck Bank to purchase her brother's 50% interest in Birchwood, and then titled the entire property in Jack's name so he could manage the property in his spare time.

When their marriage hit rocky times, Jack attempted to woo Annie back to him by giving her a bronze statue of Donald Trump, her favorite President, for their back yard. Jack purchased the statue with funds from his retirement account, which he opened through Happy Lawyer after he and Annie married. The statue was valued at $120,000 because it was signed by President Trump himself—"the best signature ever." During 2017, their last year of marriage, the couple charged $50 per guest to visit the statue and earned $10,000 in cash related thereto.

On the other hand, when faced with their marital strife, in early 2019, during the pendency of their divorce, Annie gifted Birchwood to their (she and Jack's) two children, Pip and Sancho.

Three specific questions

1. To whom will the court award the following property: the joint bank account, Oilygas Ranch, the royalties from Oilygas Ranch, the bronze Trump statue, the income from the Trump statue, and Annie's 2017 bonus? Explain.
2. If Jack and Annie fail to pay the mortgage for Birchwood, from whom can Saveabuck collect? Explain.
3. Will the trial court void Annie's gift of Birchwood to Pip and Sancho? Explain.

B. How to format an answer to an MEE or bar-style essay question

Bar takers and law students alike struggle to understand what constitutes a bad, a better, and the best essay-exam answer. This age-old problem has resulted in speculations that professors grade by throwing papers down a staircase (the As traveled the farthest down the staircase, the Fs barely landed at the nearby top), that law school and even bar exam grading is arbitrary, and that all professors or bar-graders are looking for something different. It certainly is true that different graders or different professors have and value different styles in terms of writing, but all graders and all professors want and reward essay answers that are organized to mirror the way a lawyer reasons (CRAC) and that set forth precise and accurate rules.

Given these universal truths, below are two examples that illustrate acceptable formats for organization and a third example of what not to do—the "rule-dumping" organization that law professors warn against. There is no failsafe formula for how to identify issues and subdivide your answers properly, because, unfortunately, that is a question-specific struggle. Similarly, this short section of this book does not purport to instruct you on how to draft a thoughtful analysis that avoids the dreaded "fact dump" or "conclusory descriptions." Those lessons are for another day. Instead, the goal here is to provide you with a macro formula for drafting bar and bar-style essay answers and to provide you with our top five tips for maximizing the points you receive on a bar or bar-style essay exam.

1. The basic formula

An excellent essay response will subdivide the answer into bite-sized pieces—that is, into causes of actions and then further into elements or sub-issues. Each piece will then have its own CRAC.

GENERIC FORMULA

I. Conclusory Heading on Question I

a. Conclusory Heading Sub-Issue I	= C
GR.[3] SR[4] 1. SR2. SR3.	= R
A SR[5] 1. A SR2. A SR3.	= A
C	= C
b. Conclusory Heading Sub-Issue II	= C
GR. SR 1. SR2. SR3.	= R
A SR 1. A SR2. A SR3.	= A
C	= C

II. Conclusory Heading on Question II

a. Conclusory Heading Sub-Issue I	= C
GR. SR 1. SR2. SR3.	= R
A SR 1. A SR2. A SR3.	= A
C	= C
b. Conclusory Heading Sub-Issue II	= C
GR. SR 1. SR2. SR3.	= R
A SR 1. SR2. A SR3.	= A
C	= C

3. GR = general rule
4. SR = subrule
5. A SR = analysis of subrule

If you look at the sample bar-style essay question on pages 224–25, how many question headings will you have? There are three questions, so you will have three conclusory question headings. But, if you read each question more carefully, you will discover that you need additional subheadings (and additional CRACs) under each large question heading. For example, look at the first question:

> 1. To whom will the court award the following property: the joint bank account, Oilygas Ranch, the royalties from Oilygas Ranch, the bronze Trump statue, the income from the Trump statue, and Annie's 2017 bonus? Explain.

By carefully reading this question, you will notice that there are multiple questions within this single question. So, you will need a separate conclusory subheading and a separate CRAC for each piece of property included and asked about in the question. See below for the skeletal structure for a response to the first question presented by this bar-style essay.

I. The court will award [INSERT PROPERTY] to Annie and [INSERT PROPERTY] to Jack.

a. The court will award the joint back account to [INSERT].
b. The court will award Oilygas Ranch to [INSERT].
c. The court will award the royalties from Oilygas Ranch to [INSERT].
d. The court will award the bronze Trump statue to [INSERT].
e. The court will award the income from the bronze Trump statue to [INSERT].
f. The court will award Annie's 2017 bonus to [INSERT].

2. Top five tips for maximizing points on your MEE and bar-style essay exam responses

Tip # 1: Read the call of the question first, and then *read the hypothetical.*

Tip #2: Instead of highlighting and taking notes on the facts in the hypothetical, write out the rules on the side of the hypothetical that are triggered by each of the facts presented. The facts are written down in the problem, and they will not disappear. But you need to pull the rules from your head that are triggered by the questions presented and then the particular facts included. Given the time pressure, it is most efficient if you note the rules that are triggered by the main facts as you navigate your way through the hypothetical.

Tip #3: Do not forget CRAC. Each question should have at least one CRAC. Most will have sub-issues or elements, in which case each sub-issue or element will also have its own CRAC.

Tip #4: Answer the question or questions asked—not the question or questions you wish the essay had asked you.

Tip #5: Practice makes perfect. When studying for law school essay exams and/or the MEE, you must practice writing essays and then you must evaluate and rewrite your essays after reviewing a sample answer. What did you miss in terms of the legal rules? How did your organization compare to the organization of the sample answer? Did you include extraneous information or rules?

C. How MEE or bar-style essay questions are graded

Typically, professors and bar essay graders use detailed point sheets or rubrics to grade MEE or bar-style essays. But the intricacies of those grading sheets are not as important as understanding this: your professors and graders are grading quickly and always appreciate well-organized essays because, in many ways, organized essays grade themselves. The success of an essay response will turn on the following:

1. Is the essay well organized by issue?
2. Does the essay response address all the issues presented by the question?
3. Does the essay response follow CRAC?
4. Does the essay response correctly state the rules of law (and all the relevant elements)?
5. Does the essay response demonstrate that the student can engage in real analysis (that is, tie the relevant facts from the hypothetical to the identified rules of law to show how she reaches her conclusion)?
6. Does the essay response address all the legally relevant facts in the hypothetical?
7. Does the essay response reach the correct conclusion on each question presented?

These tell-tale measurements of essay excellence may seem "squishy" or unclear to you as a new law student. But, truthfully, they are easy for professors to identify and objectively measure. Given this reality, you need to focus on mastering the law and organizing your essay responses to answer the question(s) asked in the CRAC format.

II. MPT

The Multistate Performance Test or MPT is drafted by the National Conference of Bar Examiners and administered as part of the bar exam in most states. Some states' bar exams consist of one MPT, while other states use two MPTs. Unlike the multiple-choice and essay questions on the bar exam, which test substantive knowledge of the law, the MPT is unique in that it does not test substantive knowledge of the law. Rather, the MPT "is designed to test an examinee's ability to use fundamental lawyering skills in a realistic situation and complete a task that a beginning lawyer should be able to accomplish."[6] That is, the MPT is not testing your knowledge of the law, but whether you know how to do what lawyers do—solve a problem by applying the law to a set of facts. In fact, the MPT problem is not even set in a "real" jurisdiction but is set in the fictitious state of "Franklin." Thus, knowledge of the substantive law does not help you with the MPT because the law used in the MPT is fake Franklin law.

The MPT tests six fundamental lawyering skills: (1) problem solving; (2) legal analysis and reasoning; (3) factual analysis; (4) communication; (5) organization and management of a legal task; and (6) recognizing and resolving ethical dilemmas.[7]

A. *Format of an MPT exam*

In an MPT, the examinee is given (1) a "file," which consists of an "assigning memorandum" or "task memo" with a task you must complete from a supervising lawyer and the facts of the case (which can come from interviews, client documents, court documents, depositions, reports, articles, etc.); and (2) a "library," which consists of the legal authority (cases, statutes, rules, etc.) relevant to the task you are being asked to complete.

If this sounds familiar to something you have already done in first-year legal writing, it is because it is! An MPT is similar to your closed-packet objective memo. In the first semester of legal writing, you are given a problem from a supervising lawyer (the "assigning memorandum"), the facts of the case (the "file"), and packet of law (the "library"). Moreover, for your first-semester legal writing assignment, you are not allowed to do any outside research, but, rather, everything that you will use to write your answer is given to you. An MPT is similar—everything you will use to complete the task is provided to you. Just like when you did your closed-packet problem in legal writing, when doing an MPT, even though you are provided a packet with the legal authority (the "library"), not all of the legal authority provided will necessarily be

6. National Conference of Bar Examiners, *Multistate Performance Test Purpose*, http://www.ncbex.org/exams/mpt/ (last visited June 15, 2019).

7. National Conference of Bar Examiners, *MPT Skills Tested (2014)*, http://www.ncbex.org/pdfviewer/?-file=%2Fdmsdocument%2F54 (last visited June 15, 2019).

relevant or need to be used; and, with respect to the facts (the "file"), some will be relevant, some will not be, and some that would be helpful are missing.[8]

Importantly, in an MPT you have everything you need to complete the task at hand and you are working in a closed universe where you are not to bring in your outside knowledge of the substantive law, although you will bring with you generally the analysis and legal writing and reading skills you learned in law school.[9]

What makes the MPT difficult is not that the task you will be asked to complete is hard, but rather that you must read the materials and write your response in 90 minutes. It is up to you how to allocate your 90 minutes between reviewing the materials and writing. The 90 minutes goes by quickly and this time pressure is what makes the MPT especially challenging.

B. *How the MPT is graded*

While the actual rubrics and score sheets for how the MPT is graded vary state by state, MPT graders are looking for the following:

- **Answers that follow instructions.** For example, if you are told to be objective, your tone should be objective. If you are told to omit the statement of facts, you should omit it. If you are told to write a memorandum, your response should look like a memorandum.

- **Answers that are organized per the instructions and look organized.** Remember that people who grade the MPT are grading dozens or maybe hundreds of exams. They need to be able to grade answers quickly and visually see that your answer is complete and organized. Therefore, the use of noticeable (bold, underlined, etc.) headings is especially important on the MPT.

- **Answers that reach all issues such that it is evident the examinee allocated his/her time efficiently.** On the MPT, if there are three issues, you must allocate your time such that you address all three issues.

- **Answers that include citation to legal authority.** On the MPT, your citations need not be in correct form, but you should reference the relevant legal authority by name and make the references noticeable (italic, underlined) so they look like a citation to the grader.

- **Answers that conduct strong legal analysis (showing both a good grasp of the facts and law).** The MPT is testing your ability to do what lawyers do. The most important skill that lawyers must have is the ability to analyze the facts, analyze the law, and apply the law to the facts. This is where "CRAC" comes in. For the MPT exam, you will use a simplified version of CRAC.

---

8. National Conference of Bar Examiners, *Multistate Performance Test Directions*, http://www.ncbex.org/pdfviewer/?file=%2Fdmsdocument%2F191 (last visited June 15, 2019).

9. *Id.*

C. How to tackle an MPT

You have 90 minutes to understand the problem, read the facts and the law, and organize and write your answer. How do you tackle all of this in 90 minutes?

Step one: Read the assigning memo ("task memo") to understand what you are being asked to write.

When you open your MPT exam, the very first thing you should do is go to the first document of the file, which is the assigning memorandum from the supervising lawyer that gives you the assignment or task you must complete. The assigning memorandum will give you some background on the problem, tell you what task you will complete (i.e., what you will write), and give you special instructions. Note that the task you will be given is meant to mimic something a lawyer would do in the real world. For example, the assigning memorandum may ask you to write a memorandum to a supervising lawyer, a portion of a persuasive brief, a statement of facts, or a letter.[10] The assigning memorandum may ask you to do something that is less familiar to you, like draft a contract or a will, write discovery, write a settlement proposal or agreement, outline a witness examination plan, or write a closing argument.[11] Regardless of what you are asked to do, whether it seems familiar or not, take peace in knowing that you will be given instructions on how to complete the assigned task. If you are asked to, for example, draft a letter to a client, you will be given detailed instructions as to what should be included in the letter.

After reading the task memo, ask yourself the following questions:

- What am I being asked to write?
- How will it be organized?
- Who is the audience?
- What will the tone be (objective vs. persuasive)?
- Are there any special instructions?

Step two: Create a shell document that follows the task memo's instructions.

After you understand what you are being asked to write, you should create a shell document that follows the instructions provided. A shell document is what you will type your response into, and it should include, based on the special instructions given to you, placeholders for the different parts of your response.

For example, let's say that you were asked to draft a letter to your client Sam Smith for the signature of your assigning lawyer Molly May, briefly discussing the facts and then

10. National Conference of Bar Examiners, Multistate Performance Test http://www.ncbex.org/exams/mpt/ (last visited June 15, 2019).

11. *Id.*

analyzing three issues. What should your response look like? A letter! If your response is anything other than something that looks like a letter, you did not complete the task you were asked to complete. Your shell document might look like the example below.

> Dear Mr. Smith,
>
> [discuss facts]
>
> [issue 1]
>
> [issue 2]
>
> [issue 3]
>
> Sincerely,
>
> Molly May

If, given the time pressure, you do not create a shell document right away, you risk having an incomplete or unorganized response. Some students simply begin to type a response rather than drafting a shell and, in so doing, totally forget the response is supposed to be a letter to the client. This omission means they will lose points. Therefore, we recommend that before moving on from the task memo you create a shell document such that you ensure, at minimum, your response is organized correctly and follows instructions.

Please do not underestimate the importance of following instructions. On the one hand, following instructions is the easiest thing to do. On the other hand, experience in grading MPTs demonstrates that following instructions is actually difficult. In fact, failure to follow instructions is, in our experience, the number one reason students fail the MPT.

Step three: Read the file (facts) and the library (law), taking notes and pre-outlining as you go.

After reading the task memo and creating your shell response, you need to read the rest of the file and the library. Which one should you read first? It depends. Some people prefer reading the file first. They need to first grasp the facts of their client's case in order to appreciate the law that will apply. Other people prefer to read the library first. They need to understand the law, so that when they read the facts of the client's case they can understand which facts are important. We suggest that, as you take practice MPTs, you switch off reading the file first and library first. After you complete several MPTs, you will figure out which approach is most helpful to you.

Regardless of what you read first, as you read through the file and library, you should be taking notes. You really only have time to read through the packet one time. Therefore, you should annotate the documents with notes. For example, if a case in the library goes to the first issue, you may write "issue 1" on the top of the case in the library. You should also take notes in your shell document. For example, as you read the case that goes to issue one, you might type rules from that case in your shell document under the placeholder heading for that issue. If in the file you read from a deposition with testimony that goes to issue one, you might annotate that on the deposition testimony and add notes from that deposition in your shell under the placeholder heading for issue one. In this way, you are beginning a pre-outline of your response.

Step four: Organize your response.

After you have finished reading through the packet, you should have in your shell the beginnings of an outline, although it might be a bit messy. Spend some time cleaning it up and getting organized before you begin to write. Make sure that, before you write, you know which facts and which law go to each issue.

Step five: Write your response.

While the MPT does not explicitly separate out reading time and writing time, generally speaking, you should spend about half of your 90 minutes of time doing each. Therefore, when the clock says you only have about 45 minutes left, you should begin writing.

Writing an MPT response differs a bit from the writing you complete in legal writing courses in a few ways. First, you do not need to include properly formed citations to the law. Rather, in an MPT, citing to the law can be done by simply referring to a case by name. Note that, as MPT exam graders are sometimes grading thousands of exams and are looking for you to use citations, it is worth spending time making sure your references to legal authority stand out by using boldface, italics, and/or underlining.

> In Franklin, courts use the substantial factor causation test. ***Jones.*** The substantial fact test requires that . . .

Also, in an MPT exam, unless instructed otherwise, you should not need to cite to the factual record (the "file").

Second, in an MPT exam, organization is king. This means that you should spend time, as we have mentioned, getting your response organized according to the assignment instructions. You should also spend time doing things like bolding and underlining headings, so they are easily spotted and differentiated from the text.

Third, when doing legal analysis for an MPT exam, it is not necessary to do a full-blown CRAC. Rather, time is limited, and it is okay to take short cuts. For example, if your heading for the issue is a conclusion, you need not waste time restating your conclusion under the heading as the first "C" of CRAC. In such a situation, you would draft a conclusory heading for the issue and then follow it with your rule and analysis for the issue. Additionally, in legal writing courses, the "R" or Rule of CRAC has three parts—the general rule, the subrules, and the case illustrations. In contrast, your Rules on an MPT may be abbreviated. Oftentimes on an MPT you will not have time to do complete case illustrations. That is okay. What is most important is that you explain the law (and cite/reference to it) and apply the law to the facts.

Therefore, when we counsel students on doing legal analysis for an MPT, we say legal analysis is a two-step process: (1) explain the law; (2) apply the law. Do not worry too much about the breakdown of CRAC—simply make sure you explain the law then apply the law. Additionally, unless specifically instructed to do so, on an MPT you do not need to do counter-analysis.

Finally, in writing your response, it is very important that you reach all of the issues. If, for example, there are three issues, it is much better to have completed "okay" analyses of all three issues than to have "perfect" analyses of only one issue. The MPT graders are evaluating you based on your ability to efficiently manage your time. Failing to reach all of the issues presented shows a failure of time management.

D. *Types of MPTs*

The tasks that each MPT asks you to complete vary from MPT to MPT. It is important as you begin to practice MPTs and, even more, as you begin to prepare for the MPT section of the bar exam that you become familiar with the various tasks that the MPT exam can ask you to complete. You might not have time to practice each type of MPT (or, your year, the creators of the MPT could present an entirely new MPT task), but by familiarizing yourself with past tasks, you will begin to understand how the core skills discussed in this chapter are applicable to all tasks you may face. Below is a list of some of the more recent tasks students were asked to complete on the MPT exam.

TASK
Objective Memo+
Persuasive Brief+
Response to a Demand Letter
Draft Arbitration Clause
Demand Letter
Draft Legislation
Draft Complaint
Dispute Resolution Statement
Bench Memo
Opinion Letter

+ = most commonly tested tasks

7 | Appendix

OBJECTIVE WRITING DOCUMENTS

PERSUASIVE WRITING DOCUMENTS

OTHER

APPENDIX A:
SAMPLE E-MAIL MEMORANDUM

From: Adams, Savi
Sent: Monday, June 24, 2018 8:15:32 AM
To: Partner, Alex B.
Subject: John Bell, Client 0001.555456: Elements Required for Undue Influence

Dear Mr. Partner:

The purpose of this email is to identify the legal requirements for Mr. Bell to set aside Ms. Bell's Revised Will based on Ms. Welsh's undue influence.

In Texas, a contestant is required to prove three elements to set aside a will based on undue influence:

1. The "existence and exertion of an influence";
2. The "effective operation" of such influence to "subvert or overpower" the mind of the testator at the time of the execution of the testament; and
3. The execution of a will that the testator would not have executed "but for" such influence.

Rothermel v. Duncan, 369 S.W.2d 917, 922 (Tex. 1963). For your convenience, I have attached the *Rothermel* case to this email and have highlighted the relevant language.

Please let me know if I can provide you with any additional help on this case or any future cases.

Best Regards,

Savi

Savi P. Adams
Partner & Partner LLC
1212 Moon Court, Suite 1400
Dallas, Texas 75219
(214) 555–1234 (telephone)
(214) 555–6709 (facsimile)

PRIVILEGED AND CONFIDENTIAL: Communication Subject to the Attorney-Client Privilege and the Attorney-Work-Product Doctrine

<table>
<tr><th>ITEM</th><th>DESCRIPTION</th></tr>
<tr><td>Case Name</td><td>Rothermel v. Duncan, 369 S.W.2d 917 (Tex. 1963)</td></tr>
<tr><td>Court and Date</td><td>The Supreme Court of Texas, 1963</td></tr>
<tr><td>Disposition and Procedural History</td><td>Disposition: Reversed the judgment of the trial court and rendered that respondents (those contesting the will) "receive nothing." (924).
Procedural History: Contestant Rothermel (among others) filed a suit against executor Rothermel contesting the validity of the will of Sallie Rothermel based on undue influence and incapacity. After a jury trial, the county court denied the contest. The contestants appealed to the district court, where the jury only took up the undue influence claim. The district court found undue influence. The court of civil appeals confirmed the district court's holding.</td></tr>
<tr><td>Question Presented
(i.e., the issue)</td><td>Whether there was sufficient evidence in the record to find that Louis Rothermel exercised undue influence over Sallie Rothermel in the execution of her will when Sallie was ailing and feeble, Rothermel managed her finances and took care of her, and Sallie changed her will near the end of her life to favor L. Rothermel over her other relatives?</td></tr>
<tr><td>Trigger (Legally Relevant) Facts</td><td><u>Background</u>: Sallie had an original will, but signed a new will in 1958, 8 months before she died. Sallie had a number of children and grandchildren with whom she reportedly had good relationships.
<u>Element 1</u>: L. Rothermel oversaw Sallie's business affairs, correspondence, and signed her checks. L. Rothermel drafted the new will, and was in the house but not the room when Sallie signed.
<u>Element 2</u>: For several years Sallie's feeble condition required care. L. Rothermel moved Sallie to his farm. Sallie was "very sparsely" visited by her other relatives
<u>Element 3</u>: When the husband of Sallie died, L. Rothermel, the oldest son, quit school and assumed the responsibility of providing support for the family. Sallie leaned more towards L. Rothermel than son Bill for help and assistance. Witnesses heard Sallie state multiple times within 5 years of her death she that intended to leave her estate equally to her grandchildren.</td></tr>
<tr><td>Plaintiffs/ Appellees Argument</td><td>Contestants claim that L. Rothermel unduly influenced Sallie Rothermel because: (1) her fragile condition due to age and sickness made her susceptible to influence; (2) L. Rothermel generally looked after and supervised most of the business affairs and business interests of Sallie Rothermel, so there was the opportunity for influence; (3) the circumstances surrounding the signing of this will evidence exertion of influence; and (4) the disposition in her revised will, which treated her grandchildren unevenly, was unnatural.</td></tr>
<tr><td>Defendants/ Appellants Argument</td><td>L. Rothermel argues that, although Sallie suffered from the common maladies of age, none of her disabilities (i.e. poor hearing and eye sight, shaky hands, arthritis, and diabetes) affected her ability to make decisions regarding the execution of her will. He also argues that he handled her business affairs and interests because she trusted him, and Sallie had relied on him for years to help manage her affairs. Last, L. Rothermel argues that he did not influence her during the actual signing the will because he was not even present in the room when she executed it.</td></tr>
<tr><td>Rule
(i.e., the law)</td><td><u>General rule</u>: The contestants must establish all three elements of undue influence: 1) the existence and exertion of an influence (and that the influence was exerted with respect to the creation of a new will); 2) the influence overpowering the mind of the testator (which can be based upon the testator's mental and physical health); and 3) the execution of the will only occurring because of the influence. (922). UI can be established by direct or circumstantial evidence. (922). The party contesting the will based on UI has the burden to establish the three elements. (922).
<u>Element 1</u>: Mere opportunity to exert an influence is not sufficient evidence to establish influence. Further, to show the relevant influence existed, there must be some evidence that the defendant exerted the influence with respect to the creation of a new will. Influence that is undue includes "force, intimidation, excessive importunity, ...deception" to overcome the mind of the will maker. (922). Whether influence was exercised/exerted turns on the following factors: "the opportunities existing for for the exertion of the type of influence or deception possessed or employed, the circumstances surrounding the drafting and execution of the testament, the existence of a fraudulent motive, and whether there has been habitual subjection of the testator to the control of another." (923).
<u>Element 2</u>: The existence of mental and physical frailty is evidence for opportunity to overpower the mind, but not evidence that the defendant actually exerted an influence that overpowered the testator's mind. (923). The words and conduct of the testator "bear upon" the testator's mental state. (923). Influence is not undue "unless the free agency of the testator was destroyed" and a testament was produced that expresses the will of the person exerting the influence. (922).
<u>Element 3</u>: The but-for causation element for UI turns on whether the disposition in the will is unnatural. (923). The mere existence of a will that gives more to one beneficiary than another is not unnatural.</td></tr>
<tr><td>Reasoning
(on each issue)</td><td><u>Element 1</u>: Because Sallie relied on L. Rothermel and trusted him completely to handle her affairs, L. Rothermel had "ample" opportunity to exert influence over Sallie. However, opportunity to exert influence alone is insufficient to establish the first element because there must be actual evidence that such influence was exerted. Because there is no such evidence, the first element is not satisfied.
<u>Element 2</u>: Although given her feeble state and dependency on L. Rothermel, she may have been a candidate being subject to for undue influence, opportunity to influence is not alone sufficient to establish the second element. Instead, there must be an exercise of that influence and, here, there is no evidence that L. Rothermel used his position over her finances or her frail/feeble state to unduly influence the disposition in her will. Accordingly, the second element is not satisfied.
<u>Element 3</u>: A jury may only determine that the influence caused the execution of the will based on unnaturalness if all explanation in affection for the devise is lacking. Accordingly, because there was a reasonable explanation or explanations for the devise, element three is not satisfied.</td></tr>
<tr><td>Holding
(on each issue)</td><td>There was not sufficient evidence for a jury to find that there was undue influence for any of the three elements; accordingly the revised will can go to probate because there was no undue influence.</td></tr>
<tr><td>Main Take-Away</td><td>This case sets forth the three elements of UI and a number of over-arching general rules for establishing UI.</td></tr>
</table>

From: Alex B. Partner
Sent: September 23, 2018
To: Adams, Savi
Subject: Bell: Undue Influence Claim

Dear New Associate:

Thanks for joining me in the meeting with Mr. Bell this morning. Our next step will be to determine whether Mr. Bell will be successful in contesting Ms. Bell's 2018 will based on a claim that Ms. Welsh exerted undue influence over Ms. Bell. The core facts, as we know them today, are set forth in the attached memo to file.

Please draft a formal memorandum that I can share with Mr. Bell, analyzing whether he is likely to succeed in establishing the three elements required to show undue influence: "(1) the existence and exertion of an influence; (2) the effective operation of such influence so as to subvert or overpower the mind of the testator at the time of the execution of the testament; and (3) the execution of a testament which the maker thereof would not have executed but for such influence." *Rothermel v. Duncan*, 369 S.W.2d 917, 922 (Tex. 1963). Your colleague, Ms. Davis, has done preliminary research on this issue already, and I have attached the cases she found to this email. As a cost-conscious law firm that places our client's interests first, I would like you to rely on the cases Ms. Davis found in her research (she is, after all, a thorough and excellent legal researcher) to draft your initial memo. If Mr. Bell decides to pursue an undue influence claim, we will update the legal research at that time.

Remember you will need to include all the requisite parts of a formal memo, employ legal citations, and use excellent grammar and style. I look forward to receiving your work product.

Respectfully,

Alex

PRIVILEGED AND CONFIDENTIAL COMMUNICATION:
Communication Protected by the Attorney-Client Privilege and
Attorney-Work-Product Doctrine

Memorandum

To: File
From: Alex B. Partner
Subject: 9/22/2018 Client Meeting with Mr. Bell Regarding Potential Undue Influence Claim

---

Mr. Bell shared the following facts with me today (9/22/2018) during our initial client meeting. He is interested in figuring out his chances of success if he were to contest:

- In February 2016, Ms. Bell executed her first will, which left $10k to her parents, $5k to her brother, Franklin Jessup, and the residuary of her estate to her husband, our client, Mr. Bell.
- In August 2017, Ms. Bell suffered a severe head injury and was given drugs for pain and anxiety. She was given Zoloft for depression, which was increased after she suffered another loss the following month.
- After two weeks of medical care, Ms. Bell's doctors reported that she was essentially fully recovered, with only an occasional memory slip. Ms. Bell returned to her job at Slate Furniture where she was described as smart.
- In January 2018, Ms. Bell met Ms. Welsh. Ms. Welsh introduced Ms. Bell to the non-profit organization called Happiness of Life, which has the purpose of helping people achieve a high level of personal happiness in their own lives. Ms. Welsh invited Ms. Bell to a meeting. Ms. Bell reported to Mr. Bell that the organization helped her rediscover happiness.
- To join the organization, Ms. Bell did not have to make a donation; rather, she only had to pledge to "pursue and support happiness" and agree to be assigned a "Happiness Mentor." Ms. Bell pledged to Ms. Welsh's organization, and Ms. Welsh became Ms. Bell's Happiness Mentor. As Ms. Bell's Happiness Mentor, Ms. Welsh checked in with Ms. Bell often ten times per day. After Ms. Bell joined the organization, Mr. Bell noticed that Ms. Bell changed her behavior: she stopped watching TV; she

started wearing all hemp clothing rather than her business-professional attire; she stopped wearing makeup; and she lost contact with her friends. In addition, Ms. Bell decided to stop taking her prescription medicine for depression—Zoloft—and, instead, opted to drink mushroom tea provided by Ms. Welsh. The mushroom tea was made of mushrooms "from the forest" and was said to bring its drinker into a state of intense calm and spiritualism.

- In April 2018, Ms. Welsh's organization started a capital campaign that promised, if a member donated $20K, that member would be promoted in the organization. Ms. Bell was told that quickest way to get the promotion and, thus, get closer to happiness, was via a change to her will to leave her estate to the organization.
- That same month, Ms. Bell told Ms. Welsh she wanted to change her will.
- The same day that Ms. Bell told this to Ms. Welsh, Ms. Welsh called her neighbor, an attorney named Dan Duke, to set up an appointment to change Ms. Bell's will, explaining that "time is of the essence."
- Thereafter, Ms. Welsh drove Ms. Bell to Mr. Duke's office (the attorney) to change her will.
- Ms. Bell's changed her will to leave $10K to her parents, $5K to Mr. Bell, and residuary of her estate to Ms. Welsh's organization. In addition, Ms. Bell appointed Ms. Welsh as the executor in her new will. The will was executed in May 2018.
- On the day of the will-change, Ms. Bell drank her morning mushroom tea and then drove to Mr. Duke's office. Mr. Duke described Ms. Welsh as quiet and nervous.
- A month later Ms. Bell died.

PRIVILEGED AND CONFIDENTIAL COMMUNICATION:
Communication Protected by the Attorney-Client Privilege and
Attorney-Work-Product Doctrine

MEMORANDUM

TO:	Alex B. Partner
FROM:	Savi Adams
DATE:	October 1, 2018
SUBJECT:	John Bell, Client 0001.555456: Undue Influence

QUESTION PRESENTED

Under Texas law, a contestant can get a will set aside based on the ultimate beneficiary's undue influence, if the prior beneficiary can establish the "existence and exertion of an influence"; the "effective operation" of such influence to "subvert or overpower" the mind of the testator at the time of the execution of the testament; and the execution of a will that the testator[1] would not have executed "but for" such influence. *Rothermel v. Duncan*, 369 S.W.2d 917, 922 (Tex. 1963). Ava Bell executed a will that left the majority of her estate to her husband, John Bell ("Original Will"). After suffering a head injury that left her with mild memory lapses and depression (for which her doctor prescribed her an antidepressant), Ms. Bell met Anna Welsh and became inspired by and involved in Ms. Welsh's non-profit, Happiness of Life ("HOL"). During the next five months, Ms. Welsh and Ms. Bell were in regular contact. Ms. Welsh suggested changes to Ms. Bell's medical and lifestyle practices, and Ms. Welsh advised Ms. Bell that the quickest way for her to achieve her desired happiness and to gain an honorary title through HOL was to financially provide for HOL in her will. After consuming a cup of mushroom tea, Ms. Bell met with Ms. Welsh's attorney-friend and changed her previously executed will to leave the majority of her estate to HOL, rather than to her husband ("Revised Will"). Under Texas law, can Mr. Bell prove that Ms. Bell's Revised Will was a product of the undue influence of Ms. Welsh?

BRIEF ANSWER

Likely, no. Although Mr. Bell can probably establish the first two elements required to set aside a will based on undue influence, he is unlikely to succeed in establishing the third element because of the charitable nature of the bequest. Accordingly, it is unlikely that a court would set aside Ms. Bell's Revised Will based on Ms. Welsh's undue influence.

1. I have used the term testator throughout for simplicity's sake. That said, the term testator is typically used to refer to a male testator and the term testatrix is typically used to refer to a female testator.

Adams, 2

STATEMENT OF FACTS

A. Ms. Bell's Original Will left the majority of her estate to her husband, Mr. Bell.

In February 2016, Ava Bell executed her Original Will that left $10,000 to her each of her parents, $5,000 to her brother, and the residual of her estate to her husband, Mr. Bell. Mem. from A. Partner to File (Sept. 22, 2018).

B. After executing her Original Will, Ms. Bell suffered head trauma and was treated for depression.

In August 2017, Ms. Bell suffered severe head trauma as a result of a car accident. *Id.* Following the accident, Ms. Bell's doctors reported that she fully recovered, but she continued to suffer from lapses in memory. *Id.* She returned to her job at a furniture store, but was prescribed medication to treat her lingering depression. *Id.* After Ms. Bell's brother died that same month, the doctor increased her antidepressant dosage. *Id.*

C. Ms. Bell met Ms. Welsh and joined HOL.

In January 2018, Ms. Bell met Ms. Welsh, who was the head of the non-profit organization HOL. *Id.* HOL's purpose was to help its members pursue and spread happiness. *Id.* Ms. Welsh recruited Ms. Bell to join the group, and Ms. Welsh was assigned as Ms. Bell's "Happiness Mentor" ("HM"). *Id.* As her HM, Ms. Welsh kept in close contact with Ms. Bell, including texting her ten times a day. *Id.*

D. After suffering head trauma and joining HOL, Ms. Bell's behavior changed.

After joining HOL, Ms. Bell began dressing in hemp clothing rather than her business-professional attire, stopped watching television, stopped wearing makeup, and grew distant from her friends. *Id.* She stopped taking her prescribed antidepressant and, instead, substituted mushroom tea to try to attain happiness. *Id.* The tea contained mushrooms "from the forest" and brought the drinker to a state of intense calm and spiritualism. *Id.*

E. Ms. Bell desired to achieve happiness and promotion within HOL.

In April 2018, HOL started a fundraiser, and Ms. Welsh informed Ms. Bell that, if she contributed more than $20,000 to HOL, she would come closer to achieving happiness and would be granted a promotion within the HOL organization. *Id.* Ms. Welsh told Ms. Bell that the quickest way to get the promotion and, thus, get closer to happiness, was to change her will to leave her estate to HOL. *Id.*

F. Ms. Bell revised her Original Will.

At the end of April 2018, Ms. Bell told Ms. Welsh she wanted to change her will because doing so was the quickest way to achieve happiness and promotion. *Id.* That same day, Ms. Welsh called her neighbor, Dan Duke, who was an attorney. *Id.* Ms. Welsh told Mr. Duke that Ms. Bell wanted an appointment to change her will and that time was of the essence. *Id.* A week later, Ms. Welsh drove Ms. Bell to Mr. Duke's office to change her will, after Ms. Bell drank a cup of mushroom tea. *Id.* Mr. Duke described Ms. Bell as quiet and nervous during the meeting. *Id.* Ms. Bell changed her will to leave $10,000.00 to her parents, $5,000.00 to Mr. Bell, and the residual of her estate to HOL. *Id.* In addition, Ms. Bell appointed Ms. Welsh as the executor in her Revised Will. *Id.* In June 2018, Ms. Bell died. Mr. Bell is now seeking to set aside Ms. Bell's Revised Will based on undue influence.

DISCUSSION

Mr. Bell is unlikely to establish that Ms. Welsh unduly influenced Ms. Bell in the execution of her Revised Will. In Texas, a court will set aside a will for undue influence when the plaintiff proves three elements: "(1) the existence and exertion of an influence; (2) the effective operation of such influence so as to subvert or overpower the mind of the testator at the time of the execution of the testament; and (3) the execution of a testament which the maker thereof would not have executed but for such influence." *Rothermel,* 369 S.W.2d at 922. Undue influence may be shown by direct or circumstantial evidence. *Id.* Mr. Bell will likely be able to show evidence sufficient to establish the first two elements required to set aside a will based on undue influence; however, he will likely not be able to establish the third element and, thus, will not be able to set aside Ms. Bell's Revised Will.

I. MR. BELL WILL LIKELY ESTABLISH THE EXISTENCE AND EXERTION OF AN UNDUE INFLUENCE OVER MS. BELL.

Mr. Bell will likely be able to prove the first element required to set aside a will based on undue influence. The first element of undue influence requires that a plaintiff prove the existence and exertion of an influence. *Id.* In determining whether there was the existence and exertion of an influence, courts weigh five factors: (1) "the nature and type of relationship existing between the testator, the contestants, and the party accused of exerting such influence"; (2) "the opportunities existing for the exertion of the type of influence or deception possessed or employed"; (3) "the circumstances surrounding the drafting and execution"; (4) "the existence of a fraudulent motive"; and (5) "whether there has been a habitual subjection of the testator to the control of another." *Id.* at 923. To establish this element, all of the factors need not be present. *See id.* at 922. Moreover, in examining the factors, a court is not limited to events taking place *during* the will's execution; instead, a court can "consider all evidence of relevant matters that occurred within a reasonable time before or after the will's execution." *Estate of Luthen*, No. 13-12-00576-CV, 2014 WL 6632952, at *4 (Tex. App.—Corpus Christi-Edinburg Nov. 24, 2014, no pet.) (mem. op.). The existence and exertion of an influence may be shown by direct or circumstantial evidence; however, when circumstantial evidence is used, the "circumstances must be so strong and convincing and of such probative force as to lead a well-guarded mind to a reasonable conclusion not only that undue influence was exercised, but that it controlled the will power of the testator at the precise time the will was executed." *Green v. Earnest*, 840 S.W.2d 119, 121 (Tex. App.—El Paso 1992, writ denied). Evidence showing "[m]ere requests or efforts to execute a favorable instrument are not sufficient to establish undue influence unless the requests or efforts are so excessive so as to subvert the will of the maker." *Estate of Clifton*, No. 13-11-00462-CV, 2012 WL 3139864, at *2 (Tex. App.—Corpus Christi-Edinburg Aug. 2, 2012, no pet.) (mem. op.) (citing *Curry v. Curry*, 270 S.W.2d 208, 212 (Tex. 1954)).

Evidence that the alleged influencer had the opportunity to exercise undue influence is insufficient standing alone to satisfy the first element of undue influence; instead, the opportunity to influence must be coupled with evidence of actual exertion of an undue influence. In *Estate of Steed*, the court determined that there was insufficient evidence to establish the first element of undue influence based on the absence of evidence related to each of the element's five factors. 152 S.W.3d 797, 811 (Tex. App.—Texarkana 2004, pet. denied). In that case, the testator's sons (the contestants) argued that a will leaving the residual of the testator's estate to his wife (the alleged influencer) was a product of undue influence. *Id.* at 807, 813. The court first looked at the nature of the relationship between the wife and the testator. *Id.* at 809. The court determined that this relationship was a "close" and "loving" relationship. *Id.* In contrast, the court found that the relationship between the testator and his contestant-sons was "for some time estranged." *Id.* The court reasoned that, given the strong relationship between the wife and the testator and the estranged relationship between the contestants and the testator, the first factor weighed against finding "exertion of influence." *Id.* The court then looked at the opportunity for exertion of influence and reasoned that, because the testator and his wife did not live together daily, the second factor also weighed against a showing of exertion of influence by the wife. *Id.* With respect to the third factor—the circumstances surrounding the will's execution—the court reasoned that it also weighed against finding the exertion of influence because the wife did not participate in the will's preparation. *Id.* With regard to the fourth factor, the court held there was no evidence of fraudulent motive; instead, the court found that the evidence showed the husband and wife worked together on a shared business. *Id.* Finally, with respect to the fifth factor, the court held that there was no evidence that the wife controlled the testator's actions because he was an "independent, opinionated, take-charge type of person." *Id.*

On the other hand, the opportunity to exert influence can be combined with other factors—such as an alleged influencer's habitual control of a testator and use of relationship manipulation—to show the existence and exertion of an undue influence. In *Estate of Johnson*, the court held that evidence of the opportunity to influence, coupled with evidence of actual exertion, was sufficient to show that a will had been secured by undue influence. 340 S.W.3d 769, 783 (Tex. App.—San Antonio 2011, pet denied). In that case, the testator was "habitual[ly] subject[ed]" to the alleged influencer's control. *Id.* at 780. For example, the alleged influencer was interested in the testator's estate, attended estate planning meetings, and persuaded the testator to quit his favorite hobby of hunting. *Id.* at 780, 782. In addition, the alleged influencer used "relationship poisoning" to influence the testator to change his will by making negative remarks about his children. *Id.* at 782–83. The court reasoned that evidence of the opportunity to influence, coupled with evidence of exertion of influence and the combination of relationship poisoning and habitual control over the testator's finances and hobbies, demonstrated both the opportunity for and actual exertion of undue influence. *Id.*

A. On balance, the five factors used to analyze the first element of undue influence weigh in favor of finding that Ms. Welsh both wielded and exerted undue influence over Ms. Bell.

Unlike in *Estate of Steed*, where the evidence established only an opportunity to influence, the evidence in Mr. Bell's case is more like that in *Estate of Johnson*, where there was evidence of a number of the factors employed to assess the first element of undue influence. *Estate of Steed*, 152 S.W.3d at 811; *Estate of Johnson*, 340 S.W.3d at 783. Accordingly, like the contestant in *Estate of Johnson*, Mr. Bell will likely be able to demonstrate circumstantial evidence of enough factors to establish the first element of undue influence.

1. The first factor—the nature and type of relationship between the parties—likely weighs against finding that Ms. Welsh both wielded and exerted undue influence over Ms. Bell.

With respect to the first factor related to element one—the nature and type of relationship between the parties—the evidence shows that the relationships between Mr. Bell, Ms. Bell, and Ms. Welsh, are similar to the relationships in *Estate of Steed* and distinct from those in *Estate of Johnson*; accordingly, a court is likely to follow *Estate of Steed* and find that the first factor for element one weighs against a finding of the existence and exertion of influence. In *Estate of Steed*, the court found that the relationship between the testator, contestants, and beneficiary did not support a finding of undue influence because the relationship between the alleged influencer and the testator was a loving and caring one, and the relationship between the contestants and the testator was estranged. 152 S.W.3d at 811. Here, over the three months preceding her death, Ms. Bell arguably developed a "close" relationship with Ms. Welsh (the alleged influencer) through her pursuit of happiness and involvement with HOL. Mem. from A. Partner to File (Sept. 22, 2018). Although at this time there is no evidence—direct or circumstantial—that Ms. Bell during that time period had become estranged from Mr. Bell like the contestants in *Estate of Steed*, the evidence of Ms. Bell's proximity to Ms. Welsh is probably sufficient to find this factor weighs against the first element. *Id.*; *Estate of Steed*, 152 S.W.3d at 811.

2. The second factor—the opportunity to exert influence—weighs in favor of finding that Ms. Welsh both wielded and exerted undue influence over Ms. Bell.

With respect to the second factor related to element one—the opportunity to exert influence—the evidence related to Ms. Welsh's opportunity to influence Ms. Bell is more akin to the evidence in *Estate of Johnson* than *Estate of Steed*; accordingly, a court is likely to follow *Estate of Johnson* and find this factor weighs in favor of finding the existence and exertion of undue influence. At first blush, the opportunity Ms. Welsh had to influence Ms. Bell may seem similar to *Estate of Steed* because, like the alleged influencer in *Estate of Steed*, Ms. Welsh did not live with Ms. Bell. *Estate of Steed*, 152 S.W.3d at 809; Mem. from A. Partner to File (Sept. 22, 2018). However, the fact that the couple in *Estate of Steed* did not live together was only important because it meant that they were not in daily contact. 152 S.W.3d at 809. Here, unlike in

Estate of Steed, Ms. Welsh was in regular contact with Ms. Bell, even though they did not live in the same home. Mem. from A. Partner to File (Sept. 22, 2018). As Ms. Bell's HM, Ms. Welsh texted her ten times a day. *Id.* This regular contact between Ms. Welsh and Ms. Bell echoes the regular contact between the testator and alleged influencer in the *Estate of Johnson* case. *Id.*; *see Estate of Johnson*, 340 S.W.3d at 779–83. In *Estate of Johnson*, the alleged influencer imbedded herself in the testator's life such that her regular presence affected the testator's decisions. *See* 340 S.W.3d at 779–83. Similarly, once Ms. Welsh came into Ms. Bell's life, not only was she in constant contact with Ms. Bell, but Ms. Bell's behavior and preferences began to shift after this constant contact started—for example, she changed her clothing, her medications, and her interactions with friends. Mem. from A. Partner to File (Sept. 22, 2018). This consistent and daily contact, dissimilar from the not-daily contact between the testator and alleged beneficiary in *Estate of Steed*, created an opportunity to exert influence, weighing in favor of finding undue influence. *Id.*; *Estate of Steed*, 152 S.W.3d at 811.

3. <u>The third factor—the circumstances surrounding the drafting of the will—weighs in favor of finding that Ms. Welsh both wielded and exerted undue influence over Ms. Bell.</u>

With respect to the third factor related to element one—the circumstances surrounding the drafting of the will—Mr. Bell's case is similar to *Estate of Johnson* because both Ms. Welsh and the alleged influencer in *Estate of Johnson* were involved in the execution of the testator's new will. 340 S.W.3d at 780; Mem. from A. Partner to File (Sept. 22, 2018). Although at this point there is no evidence that Ms. Welsh had a hand in redrafting the will, it was Ms. Welsh who suggested that Ms. Bell change her will to name HOL as her main beneficiary, and it was Ms. Welsh who introduced Ms. Bell to Mr. Duke, an attorney who was Ms. Welsh's neighbor. Mem. from A. Partner to File (Sept. 22, 2018). Moreover, Ms. Welsh's involvement in the handling of Ms. Bell's will appears more significant when contrasted with the alleged influencer's involvement in crafting the will in *Estate of Steed*. *Id.*; *Estate of Steed*, 152 S.W.3d at 809. In that case, the testator was a lawyer who prepared his own will, and the court indicated that the lack of evidence that the alleged influencer "was with [the testator] when he drafted the will or that she participated in the preparation of the will" was "very important" to its holding. *Estate of Steed*, 152 S.W.3d at 809. Here, unlike *Estate of Steed*, Ms. Bell was not a lawyer, but, instead, she relied upon Ms. Welsh to facilitate the execution of her Revised

Will. Mem. from A. Partner to File (Sept. 22, 2018). In that capacity, Ms. Welsh advised Ms. Bell to change her will, introduced her to an attorney to help with the redrafting process, and ultimately drove her to the attorney's office to execute her Revised Will. *Id.* Accordingly, a court is likely to see Ms. Bell's case as aligned with *Estate of Johnson* and distinct from *Estate of Steed*, and, thus, find this factor weighs in favor of element one.

4. <u>The fourth factor—fraudulent motive—weighs against finding that Ms. Welsh both wielded and exerted undue influence over Ms. Bell.</u>

With respect to the fourth factor, fraudulent motive, although one can speculate that Ms. Welsh may have had a fraudulent motive, as of now there is limited—if any—circumstantial evidence that Ms. Welsh befriended Ms. Bell simply to ascertain her inheritance. Here, Ms. Welsh merely made Ms. Bell aware of the HOL fundraiser. Mem. from A. Partner to File (Sept. 22, 2018). She suggested that the easiest way to donate the requisite funds might be to adjust her will and "leave [her] estate to the organization." *Id.* Moreover, like in *Estate of Steed*, where the court did not find fraudulent motive when the alleged influencer and the testator shared a business, here, Ms. Bell and Ms. Welsh shared in an organization—HOL—about which they were both passionate. *Estate of Steed*, 152 S.W.3d at 809; Mem. from A. Partner to File (Sept. 22, 2018). This shared interest in HOL gave them a mutual interest in the organization's success, including its financial success. Accordingly, at most, Ms. Welsh made a "[m]ere request[]" which is "not sufficient to establish undue influence." *Estate of Clifton*, 2012 WL 3139864, at *2 (citing *Curry*, 270 S.W.2d at 212).

5. <u>The fifth factor—habitual subjection—weighs in favor of finding that Ms. Welsh both wielded and exerted undue influence over Ms. Bell.</u>

With respect to the fifth factor of habitual subjection, Ms. Welsh's behavior toward Ms. Bell is similar to the behavior of the alleged influencer toward the testator in *Estate of Johnson*. 340 S.W.3d at 782. Both Ms. Welsh and the alleged influencer in *Estate of Johnson* demonstrated interest in the testator's property and exercised mental control over the testator. *Id.* at 780, 782; Mem. from A. Partner to File (Sept. 22, 2018). Like the alleged influencer in *Estate of Johnson*, who showed explicit interest in the testator's estate, here, Ms. Welsh sought Ms. Bell's money with the financial motive of benefiting her organization, HOL. *Estate of Johnson*, 340 S.W.3d at 780; Mem. from A. Partner to File (Sept. 22, 2018). Similarly, like *Estate of Johnson*, where the alleged influencer exercised control over the testator's life choices and decisions such that the testator changed course on his preferred hobbies to appease the alleged beneficiary, here, there is circumstantial evidence that Ms. Welsh exerted influence over Ms. Bell's life decisions. *Estate of Johnson*, 340 S.W.3d at 782; Mem. from A. Partner to File (Sept. 22, 2018). After Ms. Bell met Ms. Welsh and joined HOL, she began dressing in hemp clothing rather than her business-professional attire, stopped watching television, stopped wearing makeup, and grew distant from her friends. Mem. from A. Partner to File (Sept. 22, 2018). Moreover, unlike in *Estate of Steed* where the testator was fully able and "independent," there is no evidence here that, after meeting Ms. Welsh, Ms. Bell maintained a sense of strength and independence. *Estate of Steed*, 152 S.W.3d at 809; Mem. from A. Partner to File (Sept. 22, 2018). Accordingly, a court reviewing Mr. Bell's case will likely follow *Estate of Johnson* and find that Mr. Bell can establish that the fifth factor weighs in favor of finding the first element of undue influence.

Accordingly, the second, third, and fifth factors related to element one weigh in favor of finding the exercise and exertion of an influence, while the first and fourth factors weigh against. Given that the factor analysis requires weighing rather than that "all factors be present," on balance, a court is likely to find that Mr. Bell can establish the first element of his undue influence claim. *See Rothermel*, 369 S.W.2d at 923.

II. MR. BELL PROBABLY CAN ESTABLISH THAT THE UNDUE INFLUENCE OF MS. WELSH OVERPOWERED MS. BELL'S MIND AT THE TIME SHE EXECUTED HER REVISED WILL.

Mr. Bell will likely be able to prove the second element required to set aside a will based on undue influence. The second element of undue influence requires that a plaintiff prove that the improper influence overpowered the testator's mind at the time of the will's execution. *Rothermel*, 369 S.W.2d at 922. To establish the second element, courts look at four factors: (1) "the state of the testator's mind at the time of the execution"; (2) "the testator's mental or physical incapacity to resist or the susceptibility of the testator's mind to the type and extent of the influence exerted"; (3) "the words and acts of the testator"; and (4) the "weakness of the mind and body" of the testator. *Id.* at 923. Susceptibility to influence alone is insufficient to establish this element; instead, evidence must demonstrate that "efforts actually overwhelmed [the testator's] free agency" or, put another way, "overpowered [the testator's] ability to decide for [her] self." *Matter of Kam*, 484 S.W.3d 642, 653 (Tex. App.—El Paso 2016, pet. denied);

Adams, 10

Mackie v. McKenzie, 900 S.W.2d 445, 449 (Tex. App.—Texarkana 1995, writ denied) (quoting *Rothermel*, 369 S.W.2d at 922) ("Not every influence exerted on a person is undue. It is not undue unless the free agency of the testator was destroyed and the will produced expresses the wishes of the one exerting the influence."). To demonstrate that the testator's mind was, in fact, overpowered or subverted, courts look at the "testator's mental or physical incapacity to resist or the susceptibility of the testator's mind to the type and extent of the influence exerted." *Rothermel*, 369 S.W.2d at 923.

Evidence that a testator suffers from depression is insufficient to satisfy the second element of undue influence as long as the testator is able to conduct her affairs and is physically capable. In *Estate of Steed*, the court overturned the jury's finding that the testator's mind was overpowered and, accordingly, the jury's finding of undue influence. 152 S.W.3d at 811. In that case, although the testator suffered from depression and anxiety and was taking Prozac, he was able to conduct his business affairs (for example, he worked as an attorney) and was a physically able person. *Id.* The court reasoned that it was "clearly wrong and unjust" for the jury to find that the wife overpowered the testator's mind because the testator was "a meticulous, detail[ed] person" who "worked regularly to the date of his death" and was "not physically or mentally impaired from performing his daily tasks." *Id.*

Evidence that a testator was using drugs or alcohol around the time of the will's execution is sufficient to prove that the testator was susceptible to an undue influence overpowering her mind. In *Estate of Johnson*, the court held the testator's alcohol abuse coupled with his memory dysfunction made him increasingly susceptible to undue influence such that the second element of the *Rothermel* test was satisfied. 340 S.W.3d at 778. In that case, the testator was an alcoholic and had an ongoing drinking problem. *Id.* In addition to the alcohol use, there was also evidence that the testator suffered memory dysfunction. *Id.* The court reasoned that drinking had an adverse effect on his reasoning and left him less capable of resisting the undue influence brought on by the beneficiary to change his will. *Id.* Furthermore, the court reasoned that due to the testator's alcohol abuse and the effect it had on his mental capacity to resist, the testator was susceptible to undue influence and that ample opportunity existed for the beneficiary to unduly influence the testator while he was drinking. *Id.*

Mr. Bell will likely be able to establish that Ms. Welsh overpowered Ms. Bell's mind because (1) like the testator in *Estate of Johnson*, who abused alcohol, she was under the influence of mushroom tea provided to her by Ms. Welsh during the execution of her Revised Will; and (2) although Ms. Bell was generally capable like the testator in *Estate of Steed*, she suffered from depression coupled with other cognitive limitations that distinguished her situation from that presented in *Estate of Steed*. In *Estate of Johnson*, the testator suffered from alcohol abuse that, the court found, rendered him less able to resist the influence of others. 340 S.W.3d at 778. Like the testator in *Estate of Johnson*, Ms. Bell was under the influence of an unknown allegedly psychotropic drug (the mushroom tea) during the months before and at the time of her will's execution. Mem. from A. Partner to File (Sept. 22, 2018). After Ms. Bell met Ms. Welsh, Ms. Welsh substituted Ms. Bell's antidepressant prescription for HOL's mushroom tea. *Id.* This tea was designed specifically to bring the drinker into a state of intense calm and spiritualism. *Id.* Given the psychotropic effects of the mushroom tea, a court is likely to draw a parallel to the alcohol use in *Estate of Johnson* and find that Ms. Bell, like the testator in *Estate of Johnson*, was especially susceptible to influence given her use of the tea.

Moreover, although depression alone is insufficient to establish the second element required for undue influence, Ms. Bell did not suffer only from depression like the testator in *Estate of Steed.* 152 S.W.3d at 811. In contrast, Ms. Bell battled depression coupled with lingering effects of head trauma. Mem. from A. Partner to File (Sept. 22, 2018). Additionally, the testator in *Estate of Steed* was depressed but otherwise capable of handling his own affairs; in fact, he was a "detailed person" who "worked daily" and was not "mentally impaired from performing his daily tasks." 152 S.W.3d at 811. In contrast, although there is some evidence that Ms. Bell, like the testator in *Estate of Steed*, was independent and capable (i.e., after her head trauma the doctors reported that she "fully recovered," and she "returned to work") Ms. Bell's story is not as simple as that of the practicing attorney in *Estate of Steed.* Mem. from A. Partner to File (Sept. 22, 2018). Ms. Bell suffered a brain trauma shortly before meeting Ms. Welsh, and, after her trauma, she suffered from depression and memory lapses. *Id.* Given this distinction, the reasoning of *Estate of Steed* does not squarely apply to Ms. Bell's situation, and, instead, a court in Mr. Bell's case is likely to find that the "pivotal" second element of undue influence is satisfied. *See Matter of Kam*, 484 S.W.3d at 653.

III. MR. BELL CAN PROBABLY NOT ESTABLISH THAT MS. BELL WOULD NOT HAVE EXECUTED HER REVISED WILL BUT FOR MS. WELSH'S INFLUENCE.

Mr. Bell will not likely be able to prove the third element required to set aside a will based on undue influence. The third—and final—element of undue influence requires that a plaintiff show that the testator would not have executed her will but for the alleged influence. *Rothermel*, 369 S.W.2d at 922. This element turns on whether the will provided for an unnatural disposition of property. *Estate of Davis*, 920 S.W.2d 463, 467 (Tex. App.—Amarillo 1996, writ denied). In deciding whether a disposition is unnatural, courts look to evidence that a "testator unexpectedly disinherited close family members previously provided for." *Estate of Luthen*, 2014 WL 6632952, at *7.

Although an alleged influencer's reasonable explanation for an unnatural disposition is not dispositive, *Estate of Johnson*, 340 S.W.3d at 784, a reasonable explanation as to the otherwise unnatural disposition can result in a court finding no but-for causation, *Estate of Luthen*, 2014 WL 6632952, at *8. Complicating the legal analysis involved in this element, well-settled Texas public policy favors leaving one's estate to charity because such bequests are less susceptible to undue influence given the "selfish reasons" for exerting undue influence are presumed absent for charitable institutions. *Caruthers' Estate*, 151 S.W.2d 946, 948 (Tex. App.—Beaumont 1941, writ dism'd judgm't cor.) ("Our courts have ever been diligent to guard the right of a testator to dispose of his property as he pleases and to uphold bequests made for charitable and religious purposes. Obviously, such bequests are less apt to be the result of undue influence than those made to private individuals who might for selfish reasons be inclined to exert influence upon the testator.").

Absent a reasonable explanation, a disposition that disinherits close relatives and charities previously provided for is evidence of an unnatural disposition and, thus, undue influence. In *Estate of Reno*, the court held that the testator would not have made the dispositions in his revised will, which disinherited family members and charities previously provided for, but for the influence of the alleged influencer. 443 S.W.3d 143, 154 (Tex. App.—Texarkana 2009, no pet.). In that case, the testator executed an original will bequeathing the estate to the children, grandchildren, and multiple non-profits, such as hospitals and churches. *Id.* After execution, one daughter severed all ties with the testator and the alleged influencer assisted the testator in preparing a revised version of the will. *Id.* The revised will was "completely different" from the testator's original will because it disinherited certain family members and charities for which the original will had provided. *Id.* The court reasoned that, because there was no reasonable explanation for the revisions to the will and the revisions made were "self-serving" to the alleged influencer, the revised will was unnatural and without a reasonable explanation. *Id.* Accordingly, the court determined that the testator would not have executed the revised will but for the influence of the alleged influencer. *Id.*

On the other hand, in instances where a charitable beneficiary assists the testator with the execution of the challenged will, courts find that a disposition to a charity at the expense of a close family member is not unnatural if there is a reasonable explanation for such a disposition, such as direct connection with the charity. *Estate of Davis v. Cook*, 9 S.W.3d 288, 294–95 (Tex. App.—San Antonio 1999, no pet.). In *Cook*, the court held that a disposition to a charity, at the expense of inheritance by family members, was not an unnatural disposition because there was a reasonable explanation for the devise. *Id.* In that case, with the assistance of a charitable organization, the testator disinherited family members in favor of a number of charitable organizations with which the testator has "direct connection[s]." *Id.* Despite the fact that the charitable beneficiary assisted the testator in the creation of his will, the court held there was no evidence that the testator would not have made the challenged will but for the influence of the charitable organization due to the direct connection between the testator and the charities at issue. *Id.* Moreover, the court reasoned that the state has a public policy interest in favoring wills that leave property to charity. *Id.*

Mr. Bell's case is distinct from *Estate of Reno* and akin to *Cook*; accordingly, a court is likely to follow *Cook* and find that Mr. Bell cannot satisfy the third element. At first blush, Mr. Bell's case seems aligned with *Estate of Reno*, where the alleged influencer, acting in self-interest, helped recraft the testator's will in a way that completely changed the original will and served to the alleged influencer's advantage. 443 S.W.3d at 154. *Estate of Reno*, however, is positioned differently than Mr. Bell's case. In *Estate of Reno*, the alleged influencer was a relative and the resulting revised will disinherited charities and other relatives previously provided for without explanation. *Id.* In contrast, in Mr. Bell's case, Ms. Bell's Original Will provided only for her relatives. Mem. from A. Partner to File (Sept. 22, 2018). Her Revised Will then lessened her allotted inheritances to her family members and identified a charity—HOL—as the primary beneficiary of her estate. *Id.* Taking this difference in posture into account, *Estate of Davis* explains that omitting prior beneficiaries from one's will in exchange for a charitable organization is not unnatural unless there is no reasonable explanation for the switch. 9 S.W.3d at 294. *Cook* further explains that in the case of a charity a reasonable explanation is a connection or link between the testator and the charity to which she bequeathed her estate. *Id.* The reason for the public policy enforcing wills with charitable gifts is because charitable bequests are usually less susceptible to undue influence because a private individual beneficiary's "selfish reasons" for exerting influence are absent when the beneficiary is a large, established charitable institution. *See, e.g., Caruther's Estate*, 151 S.W.2d at 948 (upholding a will where testator, who was not married, left the bulk of his estate to charities supported by the Catholic church of which he was a devoted member). Because there is no evidence at this point in Mr. Bell's case undercutting this rationale, given Ms. Bell's connection to HOL, it is likely a court would follow *Cook* and find that Mr. Bell cannot establish the requisite but for causation. *Id.*

CONCLUSION

Mr. Bell can probably establish the first two elements required to set aside a will based on undue influence—the existence and exertion of an influence on Ms. Bell and the overpowering of Ms. Bell's mind at the time of the execution of her will. However, because Ms. Bell's Revised Will effectively disinherits Mr. Bell for the benefit of a charitable institution to which Ms. Bell had strong ties, Mr. Bell is unlikely to succeed in establishing but for causation as required by the third element. Accordingly, Mr. Bell is unlikely to be able to set aside Ms. Bell's Revised Will on the ground of undue influence.

EXHIBIT I

LAST WILL AND TESTAMENT OF AVA BELL

I, AVA BELL, of Dallas County, Texas, make this my Last Will and Testament, and I revoke all Wills and Codicils previously made by me.

ARTICLE I. Identification

A. Husband. My husband's name is JOHN BELL. All references in this Will to "my husband" are to him.

B. Children. I have no children or descendants.

ARTICLE II. Specific Gifts

A. Personal Property. All of my interest in any motor vehicles, boats and personal watercraft, household goods, appliances, furniture and furnishings, pictures, silverware, china, glass, books, clothing, jewelry or other articles of personal use or ornament, and other personal property of a nature, use or classification similar to the foregoing shall be distributed to my husband; provided, however, if my husband fails to survive me, such property shall be distributed in the same manner as the residue of my estate, with such property to be divided and allocated as such beneficiaries may agree, or if they cannot agree, as my Executor shall decide. If any beneficiary hereunder is a minor, my Executor may distribute such minor's share to such minor or for such minor's use to any person with whom such minor is residing or who has the care or control of such minor without further responsibility, and the receipt of the person to whom such minor's share is distributed shall be a complete discharge of my Executor. The cost of packing and shipping such property to any such beneficiary shall be charged against my estate as an expense of administration.

B. First Additional Specific Bequest. I give the sum of Ten Thousand Dollars ($10,000.00) in cash (or other property of equivalent fair market value) to each of my parents who survives me to be split equally between them; provided if any one of my parents fails to survive me, the gift to such individual shall lapse. These gifts shall not bear interest from the date of my death until paid.

C. Second Additional Specific Bequest. I give the sum of Five Thousand Dollars ($5,000.00) in cash (or other property of equivalent fair market value) to my brother, Franklin Jessup; provided, however, if my brother fails to survive me, this gift shall lapse. This gift shall not bear interest from the date of my death until paid.

ARTICLE III.
Residue

I give all of the residue of my estate to my husband if he survives me. If my husband fails to survive me, I give all of the residue of my estate to my parents. If all of the beneficiaries listed above fail to survive me, then I give all of the residue of my estate to my heirs.

ARTICLE IV.
Executor Appointments

A. Executor. I appoint my husband, JOHN BELL, to be Independent Executor of my Will and estate.

B. Bond; Independent Administration. No bond or other security shall be required of my Executor in any jurisdiction. No action shall be required in any court in relation to the settlement of my estate other than the probating and recording of my Will and, if required by law, the return of an inventory, appraisement, and list of claims of my estate. An affidavit in lieu of inventory may be substituted for an inventory, appraisement, and list of claims if permitted by law.

C. Expenses and Compensation. Every Executor shall be reimbursed for the reasonable costs and expenses incurred in connection with such Executor's duties. No Executor shall receive any compensation for serving under this Will.

ARTICLE V.
Executor Powers

Each Executor shall, to the extent permitted by law, act independently and free from the control of any court as to my estate (and as to all of the property of my estate). Each Executor shall have and possess all powers and authorities conferred by statute or common law in any jurisdiction in which such Executor may act, except for any instance in which such powers and authorities may conflict with the express provisions of this Will, in which case the express provisions of this Will shall control.

ARTICLE VI.
Miscellaneous

A. Spendthrift Provisions. Prior to the actual receipt of property by any beneficiary, no property (income or principal) distributable under this Will shall, voluntarily or involuntarily, be subject to anticipation or assignment by any beneficiary, or to attachment by or to the interference or control of any creditor or assignee of any beneficiary, or taken or reached by any legal or equitable process in satisfaction of any debt or liability of any beneficiary, and any attempted transfer or encumbrance of any interest in such property by any beneficiary hereunder prior to distribution shall be void.

B. **Survivorship Provisions.** No person shall be deemed to have survived me if such person shall die within 60 days after my death; however, my Executor may make distributions from my estate within that period for the support of my husband. Any person who is prohibited by law from inheriting property from me shall be treated as having failed to survive me.

C. **Payment of Debts.** I direct that all of my legal debts, funeral and testamentary expenses, costs and expenses of administration of my estate, and all estate, inheritance, transfer and succession taxes (Federal, State and others) upon or with respect to any property required to be included in my gross estate under the provisions of any law, and whether or not passing hereunder, shall be paid as soon after my death as in the opinion of my Executor is practical and advisable. If at the time of my death any of my property is subject to a mortgage, lien, or other debt, I direct that the devisee taking such property shall take it subject to such mortgage, lien, or other debt, and that such person shall not be entitled to have the obligation secured thereby paid out of my general estate. My Executor is specifically given the right to renew, refinance and extend, in any form that my Executor deems best, any secured or unsecured debt or charge existing at the time of my death. Under no circumstances shall my Executor be required to prepay any debt of mine.

IN TESTIMONY WHEREOF, I have placed my initials on each of the foregoing pages of this, my Last Will and Testament, and in the presence of two witnesses, who are acting as witnesses at my request, in my presence and in the presence of each other, I hereunto sign my name, on the 14th of February, 2016.

Ava Bell

AVA BELL, Testatrix

The foregoing instrument was signed by the testatrix in our presence and declared by her to be her Last Will and Testament, and we, the undersigned witnesses, sign our names hereunto as witnesses at the request and in the presence of the testatrix, and in the presence of each other, on the 14th of February, 2016.

Debbie May
DEBBIE MAY

1234 Main Street
Street Address

Plano, Texas 75023
City, State and Zip Code

2016 LAST WILL AND TESTAMENT OF AVA BELL

Jack June
JACK JUNE, Witness Signature

1234 Front Street
Street Address

Plano, Texas 75023
City, State and Zip Code

SELF-PROVING AFFIDAVIT

STATE OF TEXAS §
§
COUNTY OF DALLAS §

Before me, the undersigned authority, on this day personally appeared AVA BELL, DEBBIE MAY and JACK JUNE, known to me to be the testatrix and the witnesses, respectively, whose names are subscribed to the annexed or foregoing instrument in their respective capacities, and, all of such persons being by me duly sworn, the said AVA BELL, testatrix, declared to me and to the witnesses in my presence that such instrument is her last will and testament, and that she had willingly made and executed it as her free act and deed; and the witnesses, each on his or her oath stated to me, in the presence and hearing of the testatrix, that the testatrix had declared to them that such instrument is her last will and testament, and that she executed same as such and wanted each of them to sign it as a witness; and upon their oaths each witness stated further that they did sign the same as witnesses in the presence of the testatrix and at her request; that she was at that time eighteen years of age or over (or being under such age, was or had been lawfully married, or was then a member of the armed forces of the United States or of an auxiliary thereof or of the Maritime Service) and was of sound mind; and that each of the witnesses was then at least fourteen years of age.

Ava Bell

AVA BELL, Testatrix

Debbie May
DEBBIE MAY, Witness Signature

Jack June
JACK JUNE, Witness Signature

Subscribed and sworn to before me by AVA BELL, testatrix, and by DEBBIE MAY and JACK JUNE, witnesses, on February 14, 2016.

Matt Knot
Notary Public, State of Texas

EXHIBIT 2

CAUSE NO. 2019-55555

	§	
ESTATE OF AVA BELL,	§	IN THE PROBATE COURT
Deceased	§	
	§	
	§	
	§	OF DALLAS COUNTY, TEXAS
	§	
	§	
	§	
	§	
	§	
	§	PROBATE COURT NO. 2

DEPOSITION OF JOHN BELL

The deposition of John Bell, plaintiff in the above-listed cause, taken before Teresa Defarge, Notary Public in and for Dallas County, Texas, at 1818 Georgia Street, Dallas, Texas, on the 9th of January, 2019, commencing at 3:00 p.m.

In attendance: Adele Smith, Smith & Jones LLP
Alex B. Partner, Partner & Partner LLC
Teresa Defarge, Notary Public
John Bell, Plaintiff

Q: Good afternoon, Mr. Bell.
A: Hello.
Q: My name is Adele Smith. I'm an attorney, and I'm here representing Happiness of Life. You have filed a lawsuit against them regarding your late wife's will. I am going to ask you some questions about your allegations. Do you understand that?
A: Yes, I do.
Q: Okay, good. I'll be asking you a few questions about why you believe Happiness of Life unduly influenced your wife. You understand that you're under oath today, and that you have to tell the truth just like you would if you were in court?
A: Yes.
Q: If I ask any questions that you don't understand, or if you can't hear me, let me know, and I'll ask the question again or ask it in a different way.
A: Okay.
Q: And I need you to answer everything out loud so that the reporter can take down your answers. Okay?
A: Okay.
Q: And since the reporter will be taking down everything we say, we need to make sure we don't talk over each other.
A: Okay.
Q: Can you give me your full name, please?
A: John Lowell Bell.
Q: And where do you live, Mr. Bell?
A: I live at 223 East 33rd Street, in Dallas.
Q: How long have you lived there?
A: Ava and I moved there in 2016 when she began law school.
Q: And where did you live before that?

A: After we got married in 2014, we lived in Plano. That was before she began law school.
Q: I know that this may be difficult for you, but I need to ask you some questions regarding your wife's death and your allegations about her will.
A: I understand.
Q: Did you and your wife have wills?
A: Yes, after a couple years being married, we did in February 2016. We were so happy then.
Q: Did an attorney prepare your wills?
A: Yes, we used a friend of ours, Ray Jeffrey.
Q: Do you remember who the beneficiaries of your wife's 2016 will were?
A: I remember because our wills were pretty much the same. We did them together. She left $10,000.00 to each of her parents, $5,000.00 to her brother, Franklin, and the rest of her estate to me. My will left $10,000.00 to my mother and $5,000.00 each to my brother and my sister. My father died when I was young. I, then, left the rest of my estate to Ava.
Q: After your wife died, when did you find out that she had changed her will?
A: After her death, I went to our safe in our master closet to get out the will. I found a new one that I had not seen before. I was shocked.
Q: Why were you shocked?
A: Her new will still left $10,000.00 to her parents, but the new will left me only $5,000.00 and left the bulk of her estate to Happiness of Life. Before Ava's accident, we were very close, and we told each other everything. I had no idea that she had changed her will. I also could not believe that she changed it to give the bulk of her estate to Happiness of Life. It is all Welsh's fault; she is a bloodsucker disguised in a meditation-loving, tree-hugger costume.
Q. We will talk about Ms. Welsh in a few minutes. First, I want to talk about Ava Bell's accident and her recovery thereafter. What happened in August 2017?
A. On August 15, Ava was in a really bad car accident due to a woman's drunk driving after being over-served. She almost died.

Q. I understand that lawsuit regarding the car accident settled?
A. Yes.
Q. What do you mean when you say Ms. Bell almost died?
A. Ava lost consciousness for 72 hours. After she woke up in the hospital, she was severely confused and agitated. She did not remember what had happened or who she was. She was in an extreme amount of pain. It was unbearable.
Q. How long was Ms. Bell in the hospital following her accident?
A. Two weeks. She was on high doses of pain and anti-anxiety medication the whole time we were there. She slowly got better physically, and her memory started coming back.
Q. After she was discharged from the hospital, was her memory back?
A. I would say her memory was at about 80 percent. She remembered most big things, but she had frequent lapses.
Q. What do you mean by that?
A. She used to have a steel trap of a memory and after the accident she started forgetting things. Like she didn't remember her Starbucks order or the song we danced to at our wedding. Little stuff, I guess.
Q. How was she physically after she left the hospital?
A. Miraculous. The doctors said her recovery was incredible. They told her to take it easy for a few months, but she was physically really good. Ava was a strong woman.
Q. Did she return to law school after she was discharged from the hospital?
A. No, she took a leave of absence from law school. It was just too much to make up all of the missed work. I think she would have liked to go back the following year.
Q. Did she work?
A. Yes, worked in sales at Slate Furniture. Went back after the accident on October 15, 2017.
Q. How did that go?

A. I think she did okay, but her heart wasn't really in it. She would say things like "life is too short" to spend time at work. I always told her we could live off of my income alone, that I wasn't forcing her to work, but she went in every day. She was like an emotionless zombie. I know that sounds mean, but I don't mean it that way. She just wasn't herself. It is all Ms. Welsh's fault.

Q: What do you mean that this is all Ms. Welsh's fault?

A: After Ava's accident, she struggled. She was not herself. She was depressed, and she began drinking.

Q. How much did she drink?

A. A lot. She would drink alone in her room. She became a recluse. She would go to work, but her heart was not in it. She is really smart so Ava got good performance reviews, but she got there late, left early, did the bare minimum. Before, she was really involved in work, ran the social committee. After the accident, she never did anything. I got really worried.

Q. You were worried because she seemed a little more reclusive?

A. A little? My Ava was gone. I didn't know this person. She stopped eating. Lost a ton of weight. All she did was drink and stay in her room. I thought she was depressed maybe.

Q. Did you call a doctor about this?

A. I did. In early November, I made an appointment for Ava at her primary care doctor. The doctor tested her and concluded she suffered from depression, which is common after accidents like Ava went through.

Q. You were at the appointment with Ava?

A. Yes, I was in the room. The doctor said this was normal after head trauma, which made me feel good. I thought there was hope. The doctor prescribed her Zoloft for depression, and she took it every day.

Q. So after she took the Zoloft, Ms. Bell was back to normal?

A. Yeah, we had a really good Thanksgiving, and she seemed happy. But then, her brother Franklin Jessup died in a skiing accident. Ava and Frank were really close, and the accident sent Ava back over the edge. She became deeply depressed and the doctor actually increased her Zoloft.

Q. Did the increased Zoloft work?

A. No. Ava was numb again. She didn't leave her room again, besides going to work. She drank heavily. I remember between Thanksgiving and Christmas Eve, she was constantly drunk at home, throwing things, and stumbling. It was awful.

Q. What happened on Christmas Eve?

A. She snapped back. She promised me she was done drinking. She said she wasn't herself and was just mourning Frank in her own way. She apologized for how difficult it had been since the accident. She promised for a better 2018. I felt hopeful. We actually booked the cruise that night. It was on both of our bucket lists.

Q. The June 16, 2018 cruise to the Caribbean?

A. Yeah. If I had only known. We were really excited to start a new year, and everything looked good. And, then she met Ms. Welsh.

Q: Can you explain what you mean by that?

A: Ava met Ms. Welsh as Ava was jogging. At first, I was happy for Ava to have a new friend. She seemed more at peace than she had been since the accident, and she enjoyed spending time with Ms. Welsh. But, it just got to be too much.

Q: What do you mean by that?

A: Ms. Welsh would not leave Ava alone once she joined Happiness of Life. Ms. Welsh appointed herself as Ava's "Happiness Mentor." Happiness of Life appoints Happiness Mentors for all new members. Ava was supposed to check in with Ms. Welsh once a day; but instead, Ms. Welsh texted Ava ten times a day and sometimes more. Ava consulted Ms. Welsh on everything from buying new shoes to whether to return to law school.

Q: Did you view Ms. Welsh's relationship with Ava as problematic?

A: Absolutely.

Q: How do you think the relationship was harmful to your wife?
A: It was one thing for Ms. Welsh to give Ava advice on shoes, but Ms. Welsh began to give Ava advice on things she had no business giving advice on.
Q: Can you give me an example of what you are talking about?
A: Ava suffered from depression. Her doctor prescribed Zoloft for Ava's depression. Ms. Welsh, who does not have a medical degree as far as I know, convinced my wife to stop taking Zoloft because it wasn't from nature. Instead of taking medicine that a doctor prescribed for her, Ava drank some kind of mushroom tea with Ms. Welsh.
Q. How often did she drink this mushroom tea?
A. Almost every morning.
Q. Do you know what was in the mushroom tea?
A. I don't know exactly, but I know it wasn't something you could buy at Whole Foods. It had magic mushrooms in it. The kinds from the 60s.
Q. Would Ms. Bell, for lack of a better term, be "tripping" every morning after drinking the tea?
A. No, not like that. Maybe it was a milder dose or something? I don't know. She said it made her feel instantly calm and spiritual.
Q. Did this concern you?
A. Everything Ava did after she met Ms. Welsh concerned me to some degree. But I couldn't stop her. She is, I mean, she was an adult.
Q: I understand that you believe that Ms. Welsh and the Happiness of Life exerted undue influence on your wife. Is that right?
A: Yes, that is absolutely true. It consumed her life. From sunup to sundown. For crying out loud, she woke up every morning and meditated on the grass in the front lawn after she met Ms. Welsh. Ava became someone I didn't know. They brainwashed her
Q: Why do you say that?

A: She stopped thinking for herself. She started dressing like them, only in hemp. She had asked for a fur coat for her birthday two years ago. It was ridiculous. She wouldn't watch TV anymore or wear makeup. She stopped calling her law school or work friends. It was 24/7 Happiness of Life stuff. And then, Ms. Welsh began to pressure Ava for money.

Q: How did Ms. Welsh pressure your wife for money?

A: Happiness of Life was raising money to buy a place to hold their meetings. Ms. Welsh tried to get Ava to donate to the building fund. Even though Ms. Welsh told Ava that members should donate what they could, she also told Ava that anyone who contributed to their means would receive the honorary title of Happiness Expert. To someone in Ava's unsettled state, who had gone through all that she had been through in the prior year, this was a not very well disguised extortion plot.

Q: Did your wife donate to the building fund?

A: I assume that was what her will was for. She didn't give anything while she was alive. I watch the finances pretty closely, but she certainly changed her will after learning of the building fund. I assume that qualified her as a Happiness Expert. Total nonsense.

Q: Given these changes you've described in your wife, how would you describe your marriage at the time of her death?

A: Rocky at times, but we were committed to one another. We loved each other. I took care of her during her darkest times. For better or worse, right? She said that she wanted to get back to us again. During her last Christmas, she actually talked about trying to have a baby in 2018. We both always wanted to start a family, but life got in the way. I had actually suggested we go to marriage counseling and she seemed really receptive to it. Ava said she would find us a counselor to get us back to a good place before we tried for a baby.

Q. Did she find a counselor?

A. Yes, some wacko from Happiness of Life. We never discussed marriage counseling again.

Q. Do you think Happiness of Life came between your marriage?

A. Absolutely. Not only was Ava doing Happiness of Life stuff 24/7, Ms. Welsh was poisoning me to Ava all the time.
Q. What do you mean by that?
A. Ms. Welsh told Ava that I was holding her back from achieving peak happiness, that I wasn't supportive.
Q. How do you know that?
A. I saw the texts! And, Ava would say things like how Ms. Welsh said that I should do this or that. Like how I should mediate with Ava or how I should give her daily affirmations.
Q. You said your marriage was "rocky." Can you describe that more for me?
A. I mean, yes, we had our difficulties. But we loved each other, as I said. We thought about cancelling the cruise we went on in June, but we had already paid for the trip, and we couldn't get our money back. When we left for the cruise on June 16, Ava actually seemed happy. We had a really fun first day on the cruise. We sunbathed, read, and even took a dancing class. The best thing about the day was that it was just the two of us; Ms. Welsh wasn't there. For the last six months it has been as if Ava and Ms. Welsh were the ones in a relationship, and I was on the sidelines watching my wife become someone she was not.
Q: Ava died on June 17, 2018, correct?
A: Yes, we were doing a yoga class on the boat. Ava, who recently had deemed herself a master at yoga due to all of her classes with Ms. Welsh, fell overboard attempting some yoga move. She died instantly. I blame Ms. Welsh for that.
Q: I don't have any further questions for you Mr. Bell. Thank you for your time. I am sorry for your loss.

CERTIFICATION

I hereby certify that the foregoing answers of John Bell, the witness forenamed, were signed and sworn to before me on the 9th of January, 2019, by said witness.

NOTARY PUBLIC STATE OF TEXAS

Notary Public's Signature

EXHIBIT 3

CAUSE NO. 2019-55555

	§	
ESTATE OF AVA BELL,	§	IN THE PROBATE COURT
Deceased	§	
	§	
	§	
	§	OF DALLAS COUNTY, TEXAS
	§	
	§	
	§	
	§	
	§	PROBATE COURT NO. 2

DEPOSITION OF ANNA WELSH

The deposition of Anna Welsh, a defendant in the above-listed cause, taken before Teresa Defarge, Notary Public in and for Dallas County, Texas, at 1818 Georgia Street, Dallas, Texas, on the 18th of January, 2019, commencing at 11:00 a.m.

In attendance: Adele Smith, Smith & Jones LLP
Alex B. Partner, Partner & Partner LLC
Teresa Defarge, Notary Public
Anna Welsh

Q: Good afternoon, Ms. Welsh.

A: Hello.
Q: My name is Alex Partner. I'm an attorney, and I'm here representing John Bell, who has filed a lawsuit contesting his wife's May 6, 2018 will that left the residuary of her estate to Happiness of Life. Do you understand that?
A: Yes. I am at a loss to understand why. All we did was allow Ava to get in touch with a happiness that she had lost for a long time.
Q. You have been designated by Happiness of Life as the person most knowledgeable, do you understand that?
A. Yes.
Q. And you are the owner of Happiness of Life?
A. No one owns Happiness of Life. It is a 501(c)(3), non-profit. All of our members, currently 12, have equality in the organization.
Q. But you are in charge, correct?
A. No, no one is in charge. Happiness is in charge. I am, however, a Happiness Expert Level 5. We call it H.E.5 for short.
Q. What does that mean, what does H.E.5 mean?
A. It means I have achieved the highest level of happiness on this earth. I am entrusted with helping others achieve similar happiness in their own lives.
Q: Okay, well, I am going to ask you a few questions today about your relationship with Ms. Bell and what you knew about her May 2016 Will. You understand that you're under oath today, and that you have to tell the truth just like you would if you were in court?
A: Yes.
Q: If I ask any questions that you don't understand, or if you can't hear me, let me know that and I'll ask the question again or ask it in a different way.
A: Okay.

Q: And I need you to answer everything out loud, so that the reporter can take down your answers. Okay?
A: Okay.
Q: And since the reporter will be taking down everything we say, we need to make sure we don't talk over each other.
A: Okay.
Q: Can you give me your full name, please?
A: Anna Nicole Welsh.
Q: And where do you live, Ms. Welsh?
A: I live with a number of Happiness of Life members in a community house on Sunshine Lane in Dallas.
Q: How long have you lived there?
A: I moved into this community house in the spring of 2016.
Q: And where did you live before that?
A: I lived with my parents in Plano, Texas.
Q: Did you go to college?
A: I attended the University of Texas for one year, but then I saw the light. I realized that ultimate knowledge comes from the earth and from yourself, and so I left college and moved back to Dallas to live in the Happiness of Life community home.
Q: Did you consider moving back to live with your parents?
A: No. My parents do not live in community with their truths; they are consumed by the material world. I could not live with people who don't understand and follow the basic tenets of Happiness of Life.
Q: When was Happiness of Life started?
A: It was started on January 3, 2016. We just celebrated our three-year anniversary.
Q: Were you a founding member?

A. Yes.
Q. Who else founded Happiness of Life?
A. We have one other H.E.5 member. His name is Meadow River. He is my boyfriend.
Q. What do you do on behalf of Happiness of Life?
A. Everything. I am the person who plans, publicizes, and organizes our weekly meetings. I assign new members to their Happiness Mentors, and I check in weekly with our Happiness Mentors to see how their relationship is progressing with their mentees.
Q: Do you have any responsibility for the finances of your chapter?
A: We don't really focus on the material, but I am the signatory on the chapter's bank account.
Q: Does anyone other than you have access to the chapter's bank account or financial records?
A: No, for simplicity, I keep all of our chapter's financial records.
Q: Can you tell me when you met Ms. Bell?
A: I met her in early January of 2018.
Q: How did you meet her?
A: I was meditating in the Happiness of Life meditation teepee at White Rock Lake. We set the teepee up at the lake every Saturday and Sunday. Ava was jogging at the lake and stopped by to ask me about the teepee.
Q: What else did you talk about during that conversation?
A: It really wasn't a long conversation. I told Ava briefly about Happiness of Life. I explained that Happiness of Life members believe that happiness comes from within and from becoming one with nature. Ava asked if she could attend our next meeting.
Q: When did you next see Ms. Bell?
A: A few days later when she came to one of our meetings.
Q: What did you do at the meeting?
A: Ava's first meeting was typical of most of our meetings. We meditated, sang, and danced. We find that song and movement allow us to connect with our authentic selves. Ava felt

comfortable with the other members, and she told me that she had not felt such peace in a very long time. I asked Ava if she wanted to join Happiness of Life.

Q: How did she respond?

A: Ava immediately said that she wanted to join the group. She said the meeting made her the most happy she had been in years. And, that was after only one meeting.

Q: How does that work? What did Ms. Bell have to do in order to become a Happiness of Life member?

A: All we ask a new member to do is to pledge in front of the group that he or she promises to pursue and support happiness from within and from around at all costs and to be assigned to a Happiness Mentor.

Q: Did Ms. Bell make this pledge?

A: Yes, she did following her first meeting.

Q: Was Ms. Bell assigned a Happiness Mentor?

A: Yes.

Q: Who was Ms. Bell's Happiness Mentor?

A: I was.

Q: Can you explain the duties of a Happiness Mentor?

A: Sure. As you can imagine, the Happiness of Life approach to our world is a change from how most people deal with the stress of everyday life. It is difficult to arrive at the centering place where you can truly pursue and support happiness from within you and from around you without resorting to artificial and unnatural tools such as prescription drugs and alcohol. Most new members need help on this road to self-fulfilling happiness. A Happiness Mentor is that guide on the road to self-discovery and contentment. If a new member is having a difficult time forsaking the unnatural stimulants that rob you of the essence of yourself, a Happiness Mentor can encourage the mentee and guide the mentee on the quest for happiness.

Q: How often do new members and Happiness Mentors meet?
A: We don't have any particular rules about that. Our expectation is that a new member will check in with his or her Happiness Mentor at least once a day.
Q: Isn't it true Ms. Welsh that you were in contact with Ms. Bell much more than once a day?
A: I don't know. It varied, I guess.
Q: Didn't you often text Ms. Bell ten times a day?
A: That could be true. The minimum contact is once a day, but, as I explained, especially in the beginning, this transition is difficult. Often, new members need a lot of support.
Q: Would you say that your relationship with Ms. Bell was more than a mentor/mentee relationship?
A: Well, it started as a mentor/mentee relationship, but we just clicked. We became really good friends. We were attached at the hip.
Q: In fact, didn't Ms. Bell rely on you for all kinds of advice from what kind of shoes to buy to whether to return to law school or not?
A: No more so than good friends rely on each other. We went shopping together; we did yoga together; and we attended Happiness of Life meetings together. I think you come to rely on anyone you spend a lot of time with. I gave Ava a lot of advice on a lot of things. I didn't hold a gun to her head and tell her to do anything. We all have free will. Ava had free will.
Q. Did Ms. Bell ever go against your advice?
A. I don't think so. Ava wanted to have what I had, she wanted Level 5 happiness. It is a long road to get there. I was there to help her. She listened to me, but she was always her own person.
Q: As a result of the time you spent with Ms. Bell, you learned about the car accident she was involved in in August of 2017 didn't you?
A: Yes.

Q: You knew that Ms. Bell suffered serious mental and emotional injuries as a result of that accident didn't you?
A: I wouldn't say that. I do know that Ava was not happy when I met her. She felt lonely after her brother's death and was looking for community. She was looking to change the direction and focus of her life, and she felt that Happiness of Life could help her with her search.
Q: In what ways was Ms. Bell unhappy with her life?
A: Her accident and the recovery process following her accident gave her a lot of time to think about her priorities. For example, Ava told me that before her accident she was very materialistic. She spent a lot of money on clothes and make-up. She was caught up in non-spiritual things. She liked gossip magazines and was too tied in to the ways of the physical world. After becoming enlightened with the Happiness of Life approach to life, she realized that true happiness comes from within and from the earth, not from Nordstrom and reading about the Kardashians. Also, Ava was miserable with her husband.
Q. Why do you say she was miserable with her husband?
A. Just an honest observation. John was holding her back. He thought Happiness of Life was nonsense. I told her she couldn't achieve true happiness with that negativity in her life. He was too invested in the material world; he liked his things. He also didn't seem to be happy with some of Ava's choices such as her decision not to wear make-up and to dress in natural hemp clothing instead of expensive restrictive clothing. John tried to get Ava to take prescription drugs and he liked it when she drank wine with him after work. Things had become difficult at home for Ava.
Q. So you told Ava to leave her husband?
A. No, I told her to invite him into her new life. And, if he wouldn't, that a marriage between two people with different values is devastating to a pursuit of true happiness.
Q. Did Mr. Bell ever express interest in Happiness of Life?
A. No, he was toxic to Ava's journey to happiness. He was making her depressed.

Q: You don't have a medical degree do you?
A: No.
Q: You are not a licensed psychiatrist or therapist are you?
A: No.
Q: Isn't it true that you advised Ms. Bell in March 2018 that she should stop taking the anti-depressants that her doctor had prescribed for her?
A: Well, I did suggest that because happiness comes from within, it was better not to rely on drugs to create your happiness for you. Too often people rely on artificial remedies in order to achieve internal peace. After joining HOL, Ava was happy. She didn't need medication.
Q: But didn't you and Ms. Bell drink some sort of medicated-type mushroom tea in order to commune with nature?
A: We did, but an organic mushroom tea is much different from a manufactured pharmaceutical or from alcohol for that matter.
Q. Did Ms. Bell drink this tea with you often?
A. Yes. We drank it together quite a bit. It is very relaxing. It helps your mind achieve a state of peace so that happiness can enter.
Q. How often is "quite a bit"?
A. I would say most days. I start each morning with a cup. Ava really enjoyed it. I believe she drank it in the mornings.
Q. What was in this tea?
A. Mushrooms. We find them in the forest. There is a secret place where they grow. If you ask me where, I will plead the fifth. It is a Happiness of Life trade secret.
Q. Okay. I am more interested in what type of mushrooms they are?
A. Let's just say they are magic.
Q. Does that mean this is a hallucinogenic tea that produces a, how do you say it, psychedelic trip?

A. It brings you to a natural state of intense calm and spiritualism.
Q. How long does this "natural state" last after you drink the tea?
A. Most of the day. But, let me be clear, it does not make you "trip out" or make you lose control of your own sense of being. It's not that kind of a tea. To be truly happy you must always have a sense of self. Does that make sense?
Q. Let's talk about finances. Happiness of Life raises money and needs money to run correct?
A. I wish we lived in a world without the realities of money, but, yes, we needed money.
Q: Isn't it also true that Happiness of Life is raising funds to purchase a permanent meeting space?
A: Yes. We started a fundraiser on the first of April 2018.
Q: Did you ask Ms. Bell to contribute to this capital campaign?
A: Well, yes, in the same way that I talked about the campaign to all of our members.
Q: How much did you expect Ms. Bell to contribute to the capital campaign?
A: The same as all of our members—what she could. We asked each of our members to contribute, but we only asked them to contribute what they could.
Q: Didn't you tell your members, however, that if they contributed more than $20,000 they would get the title of Happiness Expert?
A: Yes.
Q. Do a lot of your members just have $20,000 lying around that they could give?
A. Some do. Most don't.
Q. *So how can they achieve* Happiness Expert?
A. Another option is to vow to leave money to Happiness of Life after your departure from the physical world.
Q. Did you tell Ava to do that?
A. I told her that it was an option. During the membership process, each member submits their finances. Ava did not have enough money to make a one-time $20,000 gift.

Q. So you told Ava that she could achieve Happiness Expert if she left money in her will to Happiness of Life?

A. I told her it was one way to do it, yes. But, Ava was young and a lot of our members reach their $20,000 mark by donating as little as $5 a day over the course of 5 years. Or some members donate services with a monetary equivalent. There are lots of roads to achieving expert happiness.

Q. But all of them involve money?

A. They all involve capital, but that capital could be human contribution. For instance, if Ava became an attorney, she could donate legal services to Happiness of Life that would work toward her minimum $20,000 contribution.

Q: How much did Ms. Bell say she wanted to contribute to the capital campaign?

A: She didn't really say. I do think she wanted to be a Happiness Expert, of course.

Q. Did you suggest she change her will?

A. No, she told me that she wanted to change her will after I told her it was the quickest way to becoming an immediate Happiness Exert.

Q. When did she tell you this?

A. April 28, 2018. I remember because it was at my boyfriend's birthday brunch.

Q. And, you called attorney Dan Duke to change Ms. Bell's will that same day, correct?

A. Yes, Ava said she wanted to do it quickly, and Dan is my neighbor so I figured I would call him right away.

Q. Is Dan affiliated with Happiness of Life?

A. No, he is my neighbor.

Q. So you and Ms. Bell visited Mr. Duke together?

A. Yes and no. I made an appointment with Mr. Duke for Ava. He is very busy so she needed me to call to get her on his schedule. We had yoga later that day together so I drove her there.

Q. This was on May 6, 2018, correct?

A. Yes.

Q: Were you present when Ms. Bell changed her will?

A: I tried to go in the room with her. Not to influence her or anything. I just wanted to be supportive if she needed anything. However, Mr. Duke said that I should wait in the reception area, so I did.

Q: What was Ms. Bell's mood like that day?

A: She was a little more quiet than usual. We had done some meditating exercises in the car on the way there. So, that could have been why.

Q. Had Ms. Bell consumed any of the mushroom tea with you that day?

A. I believe so. Whenever we were together, one of us usually whipped up a couple of cups.

Q. To the best of your recollection you had both drunk the mushroom tea the day you went to see Mr. Duke?

A. That's correct.

Q. Just to be clear, Ms. Bell was no longer taking her prescribed Zoloft at this point?

A. Not to my knowledge. After she joined Happiness of Life, she did not need Zoloft. She wasn't depressed.

Q: Just to confirm, you knew when you were at Mr. Duke's office that Ava was there to change her will so that she could leave the bulk of her estate to Happiness of Life?

A: Yes.

Q: You were pleased about this?

A: Of course. Happiness of Life brings real goodness into the world. Ava's decision showed her loyalty to the organization and also showed a real commitment on her part to change her priorities and her life.

Q. Those are all of the questions I have for now. Thank you for your time.

A. Sure thing.

CERTIFICATION

I hereby certify that the foregoing answers of Anna Welsh, the witness forenamed, were signed and sworn to before me on the 18th of January, 2019, by said witness.

Notary Public's Signature

EXHIBIT 4

CAUSE NO. 2019-55555

	§	
ESTATE OF AVA BELL,	§	IN THE PROBATE COURT
Deceased	§	
	§	
	§	
	§	OF DALLAS COUNTY, TEXAS
	§	
	§	
	§	
	§	
	§	
	§	PROBATE COURT NO. 2

DEPOSITION OF DAN DUKE

The deposition of DAN DUKE, a witness in the above-listed cause, taken before Teresa Defarge, Notary Public in and for Dallas County, Texas, at 1818 Georgia Street, Dallas, Texas, on the 23rd of January, 2019, commencing at 3:00 p.m.

In attendance: Adele Smith, Smith & Jones LLP
Alex B. Partner, Partner & Partner LLC
Teresa Defarge, Notary Public
Dan Duke

Q: Good afternoon, Mr. Duke.
A: Hello.
Q: My name is Alex Partner. I'm an attorney, and I'm here representing Mr. Bell. Mr. Bell has filed a lawsuit contesting his wife's will, specifically the disposition to Happiness of Life. I assume you are very familiar with depositions being an attorney yourself?
A: Yes, I am
Q: Okay, good. Let's get started. Please state your full name for the record.
A: Dan Marvin Duke.
Q: What is your address?
A. 3102 Sunshine Lane, Dallas, Texas.
Q. How do you know Anna Welsh?
A. She is my neighbor. She lives in an apartment complex down my street. We met outside one day.
Q. Would you consider Anna Welsh a friend?
A. I would consider her my neighbor. We do not interact socially other than for neighborhood gatherings and such.
Q. Are you familiar with Happiness of Life?
A. I am familiar with it because of Ms. Welsh. She has told me about it several times.
Q. What has she told you?
A. Just basically what it is and how to join.
Q. Have you ever thought of joining Happiness of Life?
A. No, I have not.
Q. How did you come in contact with Ava Bell?
A. Ms. Bell was referred to me by Ms. Welsh on April 28, 2018.
Q. Is that pretty normal? To be referred a client?
A. Extremely normal.

Q. So how did the referral happen?

A. Ms. Welsh called to tell me that her friend wanted to change her will and that time was of the essence. She asked if I had any openings. Usually my schedule is very tight, but I was able to squeeze Ms. Bell in the following week after Ms. Welsh called.

Q. On May 6, 2018?

A. That's right.

Q. Did she say anything else on the phone call?

A. She told me that it would be an easy will to change because Ms. Bell had an old will and only a few provisions needed to have names changed. She walked me through it on the phone. She said the main thing was that Ms. Bell now wanted to leave the residuary of her estate to Happiness of Life instead of her husband.

Q. Did you speak with Ms. Welsh again after that phone call?

A. No, I saw her again when she arrived with Ms. Bell. I told her to wait in the waiting room and from there on out I only engaged with my client, Ms. Bell.

Q. Did Ms. Welsh ask to go into your office with Ms. Bell?

A. She did, but once I explained that it would be better for her to stay outside, she complied without question.

Q. When Ms. Bell was in your office, what did she say?

A. Just that she wanted to change her will because a lot of things had changed. She didn't elaborate much.

Q. How did her mood seem?

A. Quiet, a little nervous. I actually asked her if anything was bothering her, and she just said that changing her will made her think of death, which was scary. I hear that from a lot of clients.

Q. How did the process of changing Ms. Bell's will go?

A. Very normal. She told me that she wanted to change a few provisions, which were the ones Ms. Welsh told me about. You see the provisions she changed when you compare the two wills.

I typed up a new will, she signed it with witnesses, and we were done. I told her to put the will someplace safe, and I kept a copy as well.

Q. Was Ms. Welsh waiting for Ms. Bell when she was done in your office?

A. Yes, I assume they drove together.

Q. What was their interaction?

A. I think Ms. Welsh said something like "are you okay?" and Ms. Bell said "yes, glad that is over with. Let's go to yoga."

Q. What time did Ms. Bell arrive at your office?

A. I believe it was an 11 a.m. appointment.

Q. What time did she leave?

A. These things usually take about an hour and half. So let's say 12:30.

Q: Thank you for your time, Mr. Duke. I have no further questions.

A: Thank you.

CERTIFICATION

I hereby certify that the foregoing answers of Dan Duke, the witness forenamed, were signed and sworn to before me on the 23rd of January, 2018, by said witness.

Notary Public's Signature

EXHIBIT 5

LAST WILL AND TESTAMENT
OF
AVA BELL

I, AVA BELL, of Dallas County, Texas, make this my Last Will and Testament, and I revoke all Wills and Codicils previously made by me.

ARTICLE I.
Identification

A. **Husband.** My husband's name is JOHN BELL. All references in this Will to "my husband" are to him.

B. **Children.** I have no children or descendants.

ARTICLE II.
Specific Gifts

A. **Personal Property.** All of my interest in any motor vehicles, boats and personal watercraft, household goods, appliances, furniture and furnishings, pictures, silverware, china, glass, books, clothing, jewelry or other articles of personal use or ornament, and other personal property of a nature, use or classification similar to the foregoing shall be sold and the proceeds distributed in the same manner as the residue of my estate.

B. **First Additional Specific Bequest.** I give the sum of Ten Thousand Dollars ($10,000.00) in cash (or other property of equivalent fair market value) to my parents who survive me to be split equally between them; provided if any one of my parents fails to survive me, the gift to such individual shall lapse. These gifts shall not bear interest from the date of my death until paid.

C. **Second Additional Specific Bequest.** I give the sum of Five Thousand Dollars ($5,000.00) in cash (or other property of equivalent fair market value) to my husband, John Bell; provided, however, if my husband fails to survive me, this gift shall lapse. This gift shall not bear interest from the date of my death until paid.

ARTICLE III.
Residue

I give all of the residue of my estate to Happiness of Life.

ARTICLE IV.
Executor Appointments

A. Executor. I appoint ANNA WELSH to be Independent Executor of my Will and estate.

B. Bond; Independent Administration. No bond or other security shall be required of my Executor in any jurisdiction. No action shall be required in any court in relation to the settlement of my estate other than the probating and recording of my Will and, if required by law, the return of an inventory, appraisement, and list of claims of my estate. An affidavit in lieu of inventory may be substituted for an inventory, appraisement, and list of claims if permitted by law.

C. Expenses and Compensation. Every Executor shall be reimbursed for the reasonable costs and expenses incurred in connection with such Executor's duties. No Executor shall receive any compensation for serving under this Will.

ARTICLE V.
Executor Powers

Each Executor shall, to the extent permitted by law, act independently and free from the control of any court as to my estate (and as to all of the property of my estate). Each Executor shall have and possess all powers and authorities conferred by statute or common law in any jurisdiction in which such Executor may act, except for any instance in which such powers and authorities may conflict with the express provisions of this Will, in which case the express provisions of this Will shall control.

ARTICLE VI.
Miscellaneous

A. Spendthrift Provisions. Prior to the actual receipt of property by any beneficiary, no property (income or principal) distributable under this Will shall, voluntarily or involuntarily, be subject to anticipation or assignment by any beneficiary, or to attachment by or to the interference or control of any creditor or assignee of any beneficiary, or taken or reached by any legal or equitable process in satisfaction of any debt or liability of any beneficiary, and any attempted transfer or encumbrance of any interest in such property by any beneficiary hereunder prior to distribution shall be void.

B. Survivorship Provisions. No person shall be deemed to have survived me if such person shall die within 60 days after my death. Any person who is prohibited by law from inheriting property from me shall be treated as having failed to survive me.

C. Payment of Debts. I direct that all of my legal debts, funeral and testamentary expenses, costs and expenses of administration of my estate, and all estate, inheritance, transfer and succession taxes (Federal, State and others) upon or with respect to any property required to be included in my gross estate under the provisions of any law, and whether or not passing hereunder, shall be paid as soon after my death as in the opinion of my Executor is practical and advisable. If at the time of my death any of my property is subject to a mortgage, lien, or other debt, I direct that the devisee taking such property shall take it subject to such mortgage, lien, or other debt, and that such person shall not be entitled to have the obligation secured thereby paid out of my general estate. My Executor is specifically given the right to renew, refinance and extend, in any form that my Executor deems best, any secured or unsecured debt or charge existing at the time of my death. Under no circumstances shall my Executor be required to prepay any debt of mine.

IN TESTIMONY WHEREOF, I have placed my initials on each of the foregoing pages of this, my Last Will and Testament, and in the presence of two witnesses, who are acting as witnesses at my request, in my presence and in the presence of each other, I hereunto sign my name, on the 6th day of May 2018.

Ava Bell

AVA BELL, Testatrix

The foregoing instrument was signed by the testatrix in our presence and declared by her to be her Last Will and Testament, and we, the undersigned witnesses, sign our names hereunto as witnesses at the request and in the presence of the testatrix, and in the presence of each other, on the 6th day of May 2018.

Jamie July

JAMIE JULY, Witness Signature

1234 Ocean Ave.

Street Address

Dallas, Texas 75219

City, State and Zip Code

Marcus August

MARCUS AUGUST, Witness Signature

1234 Beach Street.

Street Address

Dallas, Texas 75219

City, State and Zip Code

2018 LAST WILL AND TESTAMENT OF AVA BELL

SELF-PROVING AFFIDAVIT

STATE OF TEXAS §
§
COUNTY OF DALLAS §

Before me, the undersigned authority, on this day personally appeared AVA BELL, JAMIE JULY and MARCUS AUGUST, known to me to be the testatrix and the witnesses, respectively, whose names are subscribed to the annexed or foregoing instrument in their respective capacities, and, all of such persons being by me duly sworn, the said AVA BELL, testatrix, declared to me and to the witnesses in my presence that such instrument is her last will and testament, and that she had willingly made and executed it as her free act and deed; and the witnesses, each on his or her oath stated to me, in the presence and hearing of the testatrix, that the testatrix had declared to them that such instrument is her last will and testament, and that she executed same as such and wanted each of them to sign it as a witness; and upon their oaths each witness stated further that they did sign the same as witnesses in the presence of the testatrix and at her request; that she was at that time eighteen years of age or over (or being under such age, was or had been lawfully married, or was then a member of the armed forces of the United States or of an auxiliary thereof or of the Maritime Service) and was of sound mind; and that each of the witnesses was then at least fourteen years of age.

Ava Bell

AVA BELL, Testatrix

Jamie July
JAMIE JULY, Witness Signature

Marcus August
MARCUS AUGUST, Witness Signature

Subscribed and sworn to before me by AVA BELL, testatrix, and by JAMIE JULY and MARCUS AUGUST, witnesses, on May 6, 2018.

Tim Kay
Notary Public, State of Texas

EXHIBIT 6

CAUSE NO. 2019-55555

	§	
ESTATE OF AVA BELL,	§	IN THE PROBATE COURT
Deceased	§	
	§	
	§	
	§	OF DALLAS COUNTY, TEXAS
	§	
	§	
	§	
	§	
	§	
	§	PROBATE COURT NO. 2

DEPOSITION OF SHIREE SMITH

The deposition of Shiree Smith, a witness in the above-listed cause, taken before Teresa Defarge, Notary Public in and for Dallas County, Texas at 1818 Georgia Street, Dallas, Texas, on the 20th of January, 2019, commencing at 3:00 p.m.

In attendance: Adele Smith, Smith & Jones LLP
Alex B. Partner, Partner & Partner LLC

Teresa Defarge, Notary Public

Shiree Smith

Q: Good afternoon, Ms. Smith.
A: Hello.
Q: My name is Alex Partner. I'm an attorney, and I'm here representing John Bell. Mr. Bell has filed a lawsuit against Happiness of Life regarding his wife's will. Do you understand that?
A: Yes, I do.
Q: Okay, good. I'll be asking you questions about your relationship with Ms. Bell both before and after her car accident in August 2017. You understand that you're under oath today, and that you have to tell the truth just like you would if you were in court?
A: Yes.
Q: If I ask any questions that you don't understand, or if you can't hear me, let me know that and I'll ask the question again or ask it in a different way.
A: Okay.
Q: And I need you to answer everything out loud, so that the reporter can take down your answers. Okay?
A: Okay.
Q: And since the reporter will be taking down everything we say, we need to make sure we don't talk over each other.
A: Okay.
Q: Can you give me your full name, please?
A: Shiree Elizabeth Smith.
Q: And where do you live, Ms. Smith?
A: I live at 103 Lakeview Drive, apartment number 458 in Dallas.
Q: How long have you lived there?

A: About 5 years.
Q: How did you meet Ms. Bell?
A: We met the first day of our 1L year in law school. We sat next to each other during the orientation presentation for the evening law students.
Q: How would you describe your relationship with Ms. Bell?
A: We were very close during our first year. We were in the same study group, and we also socialized outside of school. We were both married, and our husbands also became friends.
Q: How would you describe Ms. Bell's relationship with her husband?
A: I always thought of Ava and John as the perfect couple. They spent a lot of time together, and he was very supportive of her going to law school. I remember that he would often hide encouraging notes in her backpack that she would find as we were studying in the library.
Q: What kinds of things did you and Ms. Bell do together before her accident?
A: In the little bit of free time that we had, we would go shopping or get our nails done. One of our favorite things to do was to escape by reading gossip magazines and discuss the lives of the rich and famous. I know that it sounds silly, but we found ways to simply hang out together. Ava had so many friends. I felt proud to be one of them.
Q: How would you describe your relationship with Ms. Bell after her accident?
A: She became very withdrawn—a different person. She never returned my phone calls and was totally disinterested in the things she used to be into. She didn't want to hear about the latest law school gossip or celebrity gossip. She didn't want to chat on the phone. She didn't return text messages. She seemed like she didn't want to be my friend.
Q: Have you seen Ms. Bell since the accident?
A: In late October, after she hadn't returned my calls for weeks, I stopped by her house. It was awkward.
Q: Can you explain what you mean by awkward?

A: Well, for one thing I barely recognized Ava when she opened the door. She looked very frail, and she either did not recognize me or she pretended that she did not recognize me.

Q: What do you mean when you say she looked frail?

A. I don't know, I guess she seemed really out of it and weak. She looked like a shell of a person I once knew.

Q: You said she did not recognize you, is that right?

A: She acted like she didn't know who I was.

Q: Was October the last time you her before she died?

A: Yes. Unfortunately, yes.

Q: Thank you for your time, Ms. Smith. I have no further questions.

CERTIFICATION

I hereby certify that the foregoing answers of Shiree Smith, the witness forenamed, were signed and sworn to before me on the 20th of January, 2019, by said witness.

Notary Public's Signature

NO. 2019-55555

		IN THE PROBATE COURT
ESTATE OF AVA BELL, Deceased.		OF DALLAS COUNTY, TEXAS
		PROBATE COURT NO. 2

HAPPINESS OF LIFE's MOTION FOR SUMMARY JUDGMENT ON PLAINTIFF JOHN BELL'S CLAIM OF UNDUE INFLUENCE

I. INTRODUCTION

This Court should grant summary judgment on Contestant John Bell's ("Plaintiff's") undue influence claim brought to contest the will of Ava Bell, dated May 6, 2018 ("Revised Will"). To set aside a will on the ground of undue influence, Plaintiff has the burden to prove: "(1) the existence and exertion of an influence; (2) the effective operation of such influence so as to subvert or overpower the mind of the testator at the time of the execution of the testament; and (3) the execution of a testament which the maker thereof would not have executed but for such influence." *Rothermel v. Duncan*, 369 S.W.2d 917, 922 (Tex. 1963). First, Plaintiff cannot prove the existence and exertion of an influence by Anna Welsh—a member of Happiness of Life ("HOL")—when the evidence shows that Ms. Bell had a tumultuous relationship with Plaintiff; Ms. Welsh and Ms. Bell were close friends through HOL; Ms. Welsh did not participate in the drafting of the Revised Will; and Ms. Bell was a strong, smart business woman. At most, Plaintiff will show that Ms. Welsh had the "opportunity" to influence Ms. Bell, but there is no evidence that Ms. Welsh actually exerted an influence over Ms. Bell. Second, Plaintiff cannot prove that Ms. Welsh overpowered the mind of Ms. Bell at the time the Revised Will was executed. To the contrary, the evidence shows that Ms. Bell was both mentally and physically capable, and there is no evidence that Ms. Welsh overpowered Ms. Bell's mind. Third, Plaintiff cannot prove the third element of undue influence, which requires showing that the disposition of property to HOL was "unnatural," given that HOL is a charitable organization about which Ms. Bell was passionate during her life. *Rothermel*, 369 S.W.2d at 922–23. Because there is no genuine issue of material fact as to any of the three elements of Plaintiff's undue influence claim, this Court should grant summary judgment.

II. STATEMENT OF FACTS

A. After executing her first will, Ms. Bell suffered an accident, lost her brother, and became depressed.

On February 14, 2016, Ms. Bell executed a will ("Original Will") that left $10,000 to each of her parents, $5,000 to her brother Franklin Jessup, and the remainder of her estate to her husband, Plaintiff John Bell. Last Will and Testament of Ava Bell, dated Feb. 14, 2016, attached as Ex. 1. Ms. Bell had a closed-head injury as a result of a car accident on August 15, 2017. John Bell Dep. (Jan. 9, 2019) 4:3–6, attached as Ex. 2. After a mere two weeks, Ms. Bell was almost fully recovered, and her only vestige of the accident was an occasional memory slip regarding "little stuff" like a coffee order. *Id.* at 4:10–19. On October 15, 2017, Ms. Bell returned to her job and, even though she was less committed to her job than before the accident and not fully "herself," Ms. Bell received strong performance reviews. *Id.* at 4:23–5:7. Plaintiff described Ms. Bell as "really smart," "a strong woman," and "physically really good." *Id.* at 4:17–19; 5:10.
In November 2017, a primary care doctor prescribed Zoloft to Ms. Bell for her depression. *Id.* at 5:16–6:2. The Zoloft worked well until Ms. Bell's brother died—causing Ms. Bell to become depressed and start drinking. *Id.* at 5:24–6:6.

B. Ms. Bell met Ms. Welsh, joined HOL, and became "the most happy she had been in years."

On January 1, 2018, while on a jog, Ms. Bell met Anna Welsh. Anna Welsh Dep. (Jan. 18, 2019) 4:12–17, attached as Ex. 3. After conversing, Ms. Welsh introduced Ms. Bell to the 501(c)(3) non-profit organization called HOL, which has the purpose of helping people achieve a high level of personal happiness in their own lives, and invited Ms. Bell to a meeting. *Id.* at 2:11–13; 4:18–23. After attending the HOL meeting, Ms. Bell said "the meeting made her the most happy she had been in years," and Ms. Bell subsequently joined the organization. *Id.* at 4:18–5:5. To join the organization, Ms. Bell did not have to make a donation; rather, she only had to pledge to "pursue and support happiness" and to agree to be assigned a "Happiness Mentor." *Id.* at 5:6–14. Ms. Welsh became Ms. Bell's Happiness Mentor, and, in this role, Ms. Welsh checked in on Ms. Bell and encouraged Ms. Bell in her goal to become happy. *Id.* at 5:17–26. The mentee/mentor relationship between Ms. Welsh and Ms. Bell soon turned into a close friendship. *Id.* at 5:17–6:12.

By March 2018, Ms. Bell no longer suffered from depression nor needed her depression medication. *Id.* at 8:5–9. Ms. Bell was happy in all areas of her life except for her marriage. *Id.* at 7:6–21.

C. Plaintiff did not support Ms. Bell's newfound happiness through HOL, and their marriage became "miserable."

Ms. Bell told Ms. Welsh that her marriage to Plaintiff was "miserable" and her home life was "difficult." *Id.* at 7:6–21. Mr. Bell did not support Ms. Bell's membership in HOL or her choices to stop taking prescription drugs, stop drinking, and stop being materialistic. *Id.* Indeed, Plaintiff admitted that his marriage to Ms. Bell was "rocky." Ex. 2, John Bell Dep. 8:16–23.

D. Ms. Bell executed a new will, decreasing Plaintiff's share and leaving the residuary of her estate to the non-profit HOL, of which she was an avid member.

On April 1, 2018, HOL started a fundraiser for a new permanent meeting space. Ex. 3, Welsh Dep. 9:8–10. HOL asked each member to contribute or to pledge only to his or her means. *Id.* at 9:11–15. HOL assigned to large contributors of $20,000 (either through a monetary donation or the donation of services of equivalent value) an honorary title of Happiness Expert. *Id.* at 9:16–9:18.

Ms. Welsh never suggested that Ms. Bell change her will. *Id.* at 10:13–15. Rather, on April 28, 2018, Ms. Bell—on her own accord—decided to change her will. *Id.* at 10:13–17. Ms. Welsh referred Ms. Bell to attorney Dan Duke on April 28, 2018. Dan Duke Dep. (Jan. 23, 2019) 2:1–2, attached as Ex. 4. Mr. Duke is Ms. Welsh's neighbor, but he is in no way affiliated with HOL. *Id.* at 1:15–25.

On May 6, 2018, Ms. Bell drove with Ms. Welsh to Mr. Duke's office. Ex. 3, Welsh Dep. 10:23–11:1. While Ms. Welsh sat in the waiting room, Ms. Bell executed a new will. Ex. 4, Duke Dep. 2:19–24; Last Will and Testament of Ava Bell, dated May 6, 2018, attached as Ex. 5. Mr. Duke described Ms. Bell as "a little nervous" because changing her will made her think of death, but Mr. Duke said this was very common when changing a will. Ex. 4, Duke Dep. 2:22–3:7. Ms. Bell explained that she wanted to change her will because a lot of things had changed. *Id.* at 2:22–24. Overall, Mr. Duke said the execution of the Revised Will was "very normal." *Id.* at 3:3–7. The Revised Will left $10,000 to Ms. Bell's parents, $5,000 to Plaintiff, and the remainder of her estate to HOL. Ex. 5, Revised Will. On June 17, 2018, Ms. Bell died. Ex. 2, John Bell Dep. 9:17–20. Ms. Bell's husband, Plaintiff, is contesting the Revised Will on the ground of undue influence.

III. SUMMARY JUDGMENT EVIDENCE

Pursuant to Texas Rule of Civil Procedure 166a, and in addition to the pleadings and other papers on file with the Court, the following summary judgment evidence is being filed concurrently with this Motion and is incorporated in full by HOL as if set out at length:

1. Last Will and Testament of Ava Bell, dated February 14, 2016, attached as **Exhibit 1.**
2. Deposition of John Bell, dated January 9, 2019, attached as **Exhibit 2.**
3. Deposition of Anna Welsh, dated January 18, 2019, attached as **Exhibit 3.**

4. Deposition of Dan Duke, dated January 23, 2019, attached as **Exhibit 4.**
5. Last Will and Testament of Ava Bell, dated May 6, 2018, attached as **Exhibit 5.**

IV. SUMMARY JUDGMENT STANDARD

Texas Rule of Civil Procedure 166a(c) provides that summary judgment must be granted if "there is no genuine issue as to any material fact," and "the moving party is entitled to judgment as a matter of law." Tex. R. Civ. P. 166a(c). Summary judgment provides a means to eliminate "patently unmeritorious claims," and it should be granted if the record establishes the right of the defendant to judgment as a matter of law. *Swilley v. Hughes*, 488 S.W.2d 64, 68 (Tex. 1972). When a defendant moves for summary judgment on a plaintiff's cause of action, it does not need to disprove all elements; instead, it must only disprove one. *Henkel v. Norman*, 441 S.W.3d 249, 251 (Tex. 2014). In the instant case, the evidence establishes that there is no genuine issue of material fact as to the existence of each of the elements of undue influence. Accordingly, this Court should grant summary judgment.

V. ARGUMENT AND AUTHORITIES

There is no genuine issue of material fact as to Plaintiff's claim of undue influence. To set aside a will on the ground of undue influence, the Plaintiff has the burden to prove: "(1) the existence and exertion of an influence; (2) the effective operation of such influence so as to subvert or overpower the mind of the testator at the time of the execution of the testament; and (3) the execution of a testament which the maker thereof would not have executed but for such influence." *Rothermel*, 369 S.W.2d at 922. Because there is no genuine issue of material fact as to any of these elements, this Court should grant summary judgment.

A. Plaintiff cannot prove the existence and exertion of an undue influence.

This Court should grant summary judgment because Plaintiff cannot prove the existence and exertion of an undue influence by HOL on Ms. Bell. The first element of undue influence requires Plaintiff to prove the existence and exertion of an undue influence. *Rothermel*, 369 S.W.2d at 922. If a plaintiff uses circumstantial evidence to prove the first element, the "circumstances must be so strong and convincing and of such probative force as to lead a well-guarded mind to a reasonable conclusion not only that undue influence was exercised but that it controlled the will power of the testator at the precise time the will was executed." *Green v. Earnest*, 840 S.W.2d 119, 121 (Tex. App.—El Paso 1992, writ denied). Evidence showing a mere opportunity to exert an improper influence, and nothing more, is insufficient to establish the first element. *Rothermel*, 369 S.W.2d at 923. Furthermore, "[m]ere requests or efforts to execute a favorable instrument are not sufficient to establish undue influence unless the requests or efforts are so excessive so as to subvert the will of the maker." *In re Estate of Clifton*, No. 13-11-00462-CV, 2012 WL 3139864, at *2 (Tex. App.—Corpus Christi–Edinburg Aug. 2, 2012, no pet.) (mem. op.) (citing *Curry v. Curry*, 270 S.W.2d 208, 212 (Tex. 1954)).

To determine whether there was an existence and exertion of an undue influence, courts examine the *Rothermel* factors, which include: (1) "the nature and type of relationship existing between the testator, the contestants, and the party accused of exerting such influence"; (2) "the opportunities existing for the exertion of the type of influence or deception possessed or employed"; (3) "the circumstances surrounding the drafting and execution of the testament"; (4) "the existence of a fraudulent motive"; and (5) "whether there has been an habitual subjection of the testator to the control of another." *Rothermel*, 369 S.W.2d at 923. Courts regularly hold that leaving one's estate to charity is "less apt to be the result of undue influence than those made to private individuals who might for selfish reasons be inclined to exert influence upon the testator." *In re Caruthers' Estate*, 151 S.W.2d 946, 948 (Tex. App.—Beaumont 1941, writ dism'd judgm't cor.).

An opportunity to exercise undue influence alone is insufficient to meet the first element—there must also be the actual exertion of an undue influence. In *In re Estate of Steed*, the court overturned the jury's affirmative finding on the first element of undue influence. 152 S.W.3d 797, 810 (Tex. App.—Texarkana 2004, pet. denied). In that case, the testator's sons, the contestants, argued that a will leaving the residuary of the testator's estate to the testator's wife was a product of undue influence. *Id.* at 807, 813. The court first compared the nature of the relationship between the wife (the party accused of undue influence) and the testator, which was "close" and "loving," to the nature of the relationship between the testator and his sons, which was "for some time estranged," and reasoned the first factor "shows no exertion of influence." *Id.* at 809. Second, the court looked at the opportunity for exertion of influence and reasoned that, because the testator and wife did not live together daily, that factor weighed against a showing of exertion of influence by the wife. *Id.* With respect to the third factor—the circumstances surrounding the execution of the will—the court reasoned that it also weighed against finding the exertion of influence because the wife did not participate in the preparation of the will. *Id.* With respect to the fourth factor, the court held there was no evidence of fraudulent motive, and, instead, the evidence showed that the husband and wife worked together on a shared business. *Id.* Finally, with respect to the fifth factor, the court held that there was no evidence that the wife controlled the testator's actions because he was an "independent, opinionated, take-charge type of person." *Id.*

Similarly, in *Smallwood v. Jones*, the court overturned a jury verdict in favor of the contestant, the testatrix's son, on the ground of undue influence, holding that there was no evidence of the existence and exertion of an undue influence. 794 S.W.2d 114, 119

(Tex. App.—San Antonio 1990, no writ). In that case, the testatrix's son contested a will that left 80 percent of the testatrix's estate to the testatrix's sister, the party accused of undue influence, and 20 percent to him. *Id.* at 116–17. The contestant (testatrix's son) argued that he had a "close relationship" with his mother. *Id.* at 117. He argued that the existence and exertion of an influence existed at the time the will was executed because the testatrix lived with the sister three weeks before executing the will, and the sister helped to arrange for a lawyer to draft the testatrix's will. *Id.* at 117–18. The sister made the appointment with the lawyer, drove the testatrix to the lawyer's office, and waited in the reception area while the testatrix executed the will. *Id.* at 118. Additionally, evidence indicated that the sister pressured the testatrix as to how the testatrix should dress and keep her home, and the sister made the testatrix aware of the sister's financial problems. *Id.* The court held that the evidence was insufficient to support a finding of undue influence because, at most, the evidence demonstrated that the sister "may have had the opportunity to exert influence upon the [testatrix] as to the execution of her will," but that there was no evidence the influence was actually exerted with respect to making the will. *Id.* at 118–19.

Here, this Court should hold there is no genuine issue of material fact as to the first element of undue influence because, while HOL may have had the *opportunity* to unduly influence Ms. Bell, there is no evidence that it actually *exerted* an undue influence that destroyed Ms. Bell's free agency. All five *Rothermel* factors weigh against finding the first element is satisfied. With respect to the first factor, like *Estate of Steed*, where the testator had a "close" relationship with the party accused of exerting influence but was somewhat "estranged" from the contestants, here Ms. Bell had a close friendship with Ms. Welsh and was estranged from her "rocky," "miserable" marriage to Plaintiff. *Estate of Steed*, 152 S.W.3d at 809; Ex. 2, John Bell Dep. 8:16–23; Ex. 3, Welsh Dep. 5:17–6:12; 7:6–21. Thus, the first factor—the nature of the relationship between Ms. Bell and Plaintiff versus that of Ms. Bell and Ms. Welsh—shows no exertion of influence.

With respect to the second factor—the opportunity for exertion of influence—like *Estate of Steed*, where the party accused of exerting influence and the testator did not live together, here, Ms. Welsh did not live with Ms. Bell such that the factor likewise weighs against a finding of undue influence. *Estate of Steed*, 152 S.W.3d at 809; Ex. 2, Welsh Dep. 3:9–15. With respect to the third factor—circumstances surrounding the drafting of the will—this case is similar to *Smallwood* and *Estate of Steed*. Like *Smallwood*, where the court held the there was no evidence of exertion of undue influence when the party accused of undue influence made the appointment with the lawyer, drove the testatrix to the lawyer's office, and waited in the reception area while the testatrix executed the will, here, even though Ms. Welsh did the same, these acts are insufficient to show the exertion of an undue influence. *Smallwood*, 794 S.W.2d at 117–19; Ex. 3, Welsh Dep. 10:13–11:5. Rather, at most, it shows that Ms. Welsh "may have had the opportunity to exert influence upon the [testatrix] as to the execution of her will," but opportunity alone is insufficient. *Smallwood*, 794 S.W.2d at 117–19. Also, like *Estate of Steed*, where there was no evidence that the party accused of undue influence participated in the preparation of the will, here, there is likewise no evidence Ms. Welsh participated in the preparation of the will. *Estate of Steed*, 152 S.W.3d at 809; Ex. 3, Welsh Dep. 10:13–11:5. Rather, the evidence shows that it was solely Ms. Bell's decision to change her will, and Ms. Welsh only helped facilitate a meeting between Ms. Bell and an independent lawyer. Ex. 3, Welsh Dep. 10:13–11:5. Thus, the third factor weighs against finding the existence and exertion of an undue influence.

With respect to the fourth factor of fraudulent motive, similar to *Estate of Steed* and *Smallwood*, there is no evidence that Ms. Welsh had a fraudulent motive. Like *Smallwood*, where the party accused of undue influence made the testatrix aware of her financial problems, here, Ms. Welsh merely made Ms. Bell aware of the HOL fundraiser. *Smallwood*, 794 S.W.2d at 117–19; Ex. 3, Welsh Dep. 9:8–18. At most, Ms. Welsh made a "[m]ere request[]" and that is "not sufficient to establish undue influence." *Estate of Clifton*, 2012 WL 3139864, at *2 (citing *Curry*, 270 S.W.2d at 212). Like *Estate of Steed*, where fraudulent motive was not found when the party accused of undue influence and the testator shared a business, here, Ms. Bell and Ms. Welsh shared in an organization—HOL—about which they were jointly passionate. *Estate of Steed*, 152 S.W.3d at 809; Ex. 3, Welsh Dep. 4:18–5:14. And, because HOL is a charitable organization, this Court should be "less apt" to find Ms. Bell's disposition to HOL to be a product of undue influence because, unlike dispositions to private individuals, there are no "selfish reasons" for one to request a disposition to a charitable organization. *Caruthers' Estate*, 151 S.W.2d at 948.

Finally, with respect to the fifth factor—whether there has been habitual subjection of the testatrix to the control of another—like *Smallwood*, where evidence that the party accused of undue influence told the testatrix how to dress and keep her home was insufficient to show control, here, evidence that Ms. Welsh encouraged Ms. Bell to make healthy choices (like quitting prescription drugs, drinking, and materialism) is insufficient. *Smallwood*, 794 S.W.2d at 117–19; Ex. 3, Welsh Dep. 7:6–21. Moreover, like the testator in *Estate of Steed*, who was described as "independent," Ms. Bell was described as "a strong woman." *Estate of Steed*, 152 S.W.3d at 809; Ex. 2, John Bell Dep. 4:17–19; 5:10.

Each of the five *Rothermel* factors weighs against a finding of the existence and exertion of an influence by Ms. Welsh over Ms. Bell. Accordingly, Plaintiff will be unable to meet his burden to prove the first element, and this Court should grant summary judgment.

B. Plaintiff cannot prove HOL overpowered Ms. Bell's mind.

This Court should grant summary judgment because Plaintiff cannot prove HOL overpowered Ms. Bell's mind. The second element of undue influence requires Plaintiff to prove that the improper influence overpowered the testatrix's mind at the time of the will's execution. *Rothermel*, 369 S.W.2d at 922. To establish the second element, courts look at the following factors: (1) "the state of the testator's mind at the time of the execution"; (2) "the testator's mental or physical incapacity to resist or the susceptibility of the testator's mind to the type and extent of the influence exerted;" (3) "the words and acts of the testator"; and (4) "the weakness of the mind and body of the testator." *Id.* at 923. However, "[a] testatrix's weakened physical and mental condition is only indicative of her susceptibility to influence; it is no evidence that such influence exists in fact." *Guthrie v. Suiter*, 934 S.W.2d 820, 832 (Tex. App.—Houston [1st Dist.] 1996, no writ). Rather, the "pivotal" second element of undue influence requires a plaintiff to show that the person's "efforts actually overwhelmed [the testatrix's] free agency" or, put another way, "overpowered [the testatrix's] ability to decide for [her]self." *Matter of Kam*, 484 S.W.3d 642, 653 (Tex. App.—El Paso 2016, pet. denied); *Mackie v. McKenzie*, 900 S.W.2d 445, 449 (Tex. App.—Texarkana 1995, writ denied) ("Not every influence exerted on a person is undue. It is not undue unless the free agency of the testator was destroyed and the will produced expresses the wishes of the one exerting the influence.").

The fact that a testatrix suffers from depression is insufficient to meet the second element of undue influence when the testatrix is still able to conduct her business affairs and is physically capable. In *Estate of Steed*, the court overturned the jury's finding that the testator's mind was overpowered and, as such, the jury's finding of undue influence. 152 S.W.3d at 811. In that case, although the testator suffered from depression and anxiety and was taking Prozac, he was able to conduct his business affairs and was a physically able person. *Id.* The court reasoned that it was "clearly wrong and unjust" for the jury to find that the wife overpowered the testator's mind because the testator was "a meticulous, detailed person" who "worked regularly to the date of his death" and was "not physically or mentally impaired from performing his daily tasks." *Id.*

Even where there is evidence of what is arguably extreme mental incapacity, the second element of undue influence is not satisfied absent actual coercion of the testatrix's mind. In *Guthrie*, the court held that there was no evidence that the beneficiary of the will overpowered the testatrix's mind. 934 S.W.2d at 832. In that case, the testatrix, who had a lobotomy, was unable to care for herself at the time she executed the will. *Id.* at 827–28. The contestant of the will presented evidence that, around the time of the will's execution, the testatrix "appeared to be like a person who had Alzheimer's disease," "stared blankly without normal emotion or attention," had a home "strewn with garbage," and was in "a continuous and chronic state of confusion." *Id.* The court reasoned that, even though the testatrix's lobotomy "may have rendered her susceptible to undue influence," there was no evidence that her mind was overpowered. *Id.* at 832.

Here, there is no genuine issue of material fact as to whether HOL overpowered Ms. Bell's mind because the evidence demonstrates that Ms. Bell was physically and mentally capable, such that she was not susceptible to influence. Like the testator in *Estate of Steed*, who suffered from depression but was able to conduct business affairs and was physically able, here, although Ms. Bell may have suffered from depression, there is no evidence that the depression hindered her business affairs or physical capability. *Estate of Steed*, 152 S.W.3d at 811; Ex. 2, John Bell Dep. 4:17–19, 4:23–5:10. To the contrary, Ms. Bell received strong performance reviews at her job, and her husband described her as "really smart," "a strong woman," and "physically really good." Ex. 2, John Bell Dep. 4:17–19, 4:23–5:10. Additionally, unlike the testator in *Estate of Steed*, who was still on depression medication at the time he executed his will, here, at the time of the will's execution, Ms. Bell was no longer in need of depression medication because she was no longer depressed. *Estate of Steed*, 152 S.W.3d at 811; Ex. 3, Welsh Dep. 8:5–9. Moreover, there can be no dispute that Ms. Bell's mental condition—even at her worst after her brother died—fell grossly short of that of the testatrix in *Guthrie*, whose condition the court held did not meet the second element of undue influence, even though she was unable to care for herself, was constantly confused, and suffered a lobotomy. *Guthrie*, 934 S.W.2d at 827–28; Ex. 2, John Bell Dep. 5:24–6:6. Ms. Bell did not have a weakened physical or mental state, and, even if she did, such "is only indicative of her susceptibility to influence; it is no evidence that such influence exists in fact." *Guthrie*, 934 S.W.2d at 832. Nothing in the record proves that Ms. Welsh's "efforts actually overwhelmed [Ms. Bell's] free agency" or that Ms. Bell lost the "ability to decide for [her] self"—to the contrary, it was Ms. Bell who initiated a new will, and the day Ms. Bell executed her Revised Will was "very normal." Ex. 3, Welsh Dep. 10:13–15; Ex. 4, Duke Dep. 3:3–7.

Therefore, like the courts in *Estate of Steed* and *Guthrie*, Plaintiff cannot establish the second, "pivotal" element of undue influence. *See Matter of Kam*, 484 S.W.3d at 653.

C. Plaintiff cannot prove Ms. Bell would not have executed her Revised Will "but for" the alleged influence of HOL.

This Court should grant summary judgment because Plaintiff cannot prove Ms. Bell would not have executed her Revised Will but for the alleged influence of HOL. Under the third element, a plaintiff will not meet his burden to prove undue influence unless he proves the execution of a testament that the testatrix would not have made but for the influence. *Rothermel*, 369 S.W.2d at 922. The third element is not satisfied unless the testament is "unnatural." *Id.* A testament is unnatural only when "all reasonable explanation in affection for the devise is lacking." *In re Estate of Luthen*, 13-12-00576-CV, 2014 WL 6632952, at *7 (Tex. App.—Corpus Christi–Edinburg Nov. 24, 2014, no pet.) (internal citations and quotations omitted). Circumstantial evidence that is "equally as consistent with the proper execution of the testator's intent as with undue influence is considered no evidence" of an unnatural disposition such that a court will not find undue influence. *Smallwood*, 794 S.W.2d at 118 (citing *Rothermel*, 369 S.W.2d at 922). In upholding Texas's policy favoring charitable giving, when determining whether a disposition is unnatural, "courts have ever been diligent to guard the right of a testator to dispose of his property as he pleases and to uphold bequests made for charitable and religious purposes." *Caruthers' Estate*, 151 S.W.2d at 948.

Leaving the majority of one's estate to a charity instead of to a family member is not considered an unnatural disposition. In *Mackie*, the court upheld the trial court's grant of summary judgment with regard to the plaintiffs' claims of undue influence, holding that the testator leaving the residuary of his estate to charity was not unnatural. 900 S.W.2d at 450. In that case, the testator changed his will to leave the residuary of his estate to two charities instead of to his family. *Id.* at 447. The testator's first will left $50,000 and personal effects to his niece, and $600,000 to her children. *Id.* In the final will at issue, the testator left $265,000 to his niece, $10,000 and personal effects to her children, and the rest of his estate to two charities, the Baylor University Medical Foundation and Presbyterian Hospital of Dallas, both with which the testator was involved during his life. *Id.* at 447, 450. The Baylor University Medical Foundation paid for an attorney to change the testator's will. *Id.* The court held that the disposition in the testator's final will—favoring charities over his relatives—was not unnatural, reasoning that the testator was "proud" of his associations with the charities and had made past statements that he wanted to leave money to charities. *Id.* at 450. In *Guthrie*, the court held that the testatrix's exclusion of her only living son from her will was not an unnatural disposition. 934 S.W.2d at 832. In that case, the evidence showed that the testatrix and her only living son were not on good terms and that the testatrix expressed dissatisfaction with her son's "neglect" of her. *Id.* The court reasoned that disposition was not "unreasonable" "[g]iven the evidence of the strained relationship" between the testatrix and her son. *Id.*

Here, Plaintiff will be unable to prove that Ms. Bell's disposition to the charitable organization HOL was unnatural. Like the testator in *Mackie*, who left the bulk of his estate to charities that he was proud of and closely associated with, it is undisputed that Ms. Bell was proud of and closely associated with the charitable organization HOL such that Ms. Bell's leaving money to HOL was not unnatural. *Mackie*, 900 S.W.2d at 450; Ex. 3, Welsh Dep. 8:5–9. Following Texas policy, this Court should "diligent[ly]" protect the right of Ms. Bell "to dispose of h[er] property as [s]he pleases" and leave money to charity. *See Caruthers' Estate*, 151 S.W.2d at 948. Any argument that it was "unnatural" for Ms. Bell to reduce her husband's share should be rejected because, like *Guthrie*, where the testatrix had a "strained relationship" with her son, here, Plaintiff admitted his relationship with Ms. Bell was "rocky," and Ms. Bell confided that she was "miserable" in her "difficult" marriage. *Guthrie*, 934 S.W.2d at 832; Ex. 3, Welsh Dep. 7:6–21; Ex. 2, John Bell Dep. 8:16–23. Given that Mr. Bell was not supportive of Ms. Bell's newfound happiness or her membership in HOL, like the testatrix in *Guthrie*, it was not unreasonable for Ms. Bell to reduce her husband's inheritance. *Guthrie*, 934 S.W.2d at 832; Ex. 3, Welsh Dep. 7:6–21; Ex. 2, John Bell Dep. 8:16–23. Moreover, unlike *Guthrie*, where the testatrix excluded her son from the will, it is undisputed that Ms. Bell did not exclude her husband—rather she left him $5,000, which is not an insignificant amount of money. *Guthrie*, 934 S.W.2d at 832; Ex. 5, Revised Will at 1. Accordingly, this Court should hold there is no genuine issue of material fact as to the third element of undue influence.

VI. CONCLUSION

HOL respectfully requests that this Court grant its Motion for Summary Judgment on Plaintiff's Claim of Undue Influence.

Respectfully submitted,

SMITH & JONES LLP
4102 Crescent Court, Suite 1100
Dallas, Texas 75219
(214) 867-5309 (telephone)
(214) 555-5555 (facsimile)

By:

Adele Smith

ADELE SMITH
Texas State Bar No. 1234567

CERTIFICATE OF SERVICE

The undersigned certifies that a true and correct copy of the foregoing document has been served on all counsel for Plaintiff, via LexisNexis, on the 22nd day of March, 2019.

Adele Smith

Adele Smith

NO. 2019-55555

	'	IN THE PROBATE COURT
ESTATE OF AVA BELL, Deceased.	'	OF DALLAS COUNTY, TEXAS
	'	PROBATE COURT NO. 2

PLAINTIFF JOHN BELL'S OPPOSITION TO HAPPINESS OF LIFE'S MOTION FOR SUMMARY JUDGMENT ON PLAINTIFF'S CLAIM OF UNDUE INFLUENCE

I. INTRODUCTION

This Court should deny summary judgment on Plaintiff/Contestant John Bell's claim of undue influence. Happiness of Life ("HOL" or "Defendant") fails to meet its burden to prove that there is no genuine issue of material fact as to any of the three elements of undue influence: "(1) the existence and exertion of an influence; (2) the effective operation of such influence so as to subvert or overpower the mind of the testat[rix] at the time of the execution of the testament; and (3) the execution of a testament which the maker thereof would not have executed but for such influence." *Rothermel v. Duncan*, 369 S.W.2d 917, 922 (Tex. 1963). First, Defendant fails to prove the absence of a genuine issue of material fact with respect to whether HOL exerted an undue influence on Mrs. Bell when it poisoned Mrs. Bell against her husband; alienated Mrs. Bell from her friends and hobbies; controlled Mrs. Bell's daily decisions, had access to Mrs. Bell's finances; solicited Mrs. Bell to change her will in exchange for an honorary title; and assisted Mrs. Bell with the drafting and execution of her new will. Second, Defendant fails to prove the absence of a genuine issue of material fact with respect to whether HOL overpowered Mrs. Bell's mind at the time of the new will's execution when the evidence shows that Mrs. Bell was under the influence of mind-altering magical mushroom tea, given to her by HOL's founding member Anna Welsh, at the time of the will's execution. Third, Defendant fails to prove the absence of a genuine issue of material fact as to the third element when the evidence supports that Mrs. Bell made an unnatural disposition when she left the bulk of her estate to a

12-member, cult-like organization joined only four months prior instead of her husband.

Because the Defendant fails to meet its burden of negating Mr. Bell's undue influence claim, and because there exists, at a minimum, a fact issue as to each element of undue influence, this Court should deny summary judgment.

II. STATEMENT OF FACTS

A. Mrs. Bell's 2016 Will left the bulk of her estate to her husband, Mr. Bell.

In 2014, John and Ava Bell were married. John Bell Dep. (Jan. 9, 2019) 2:26–3:1, attached as Ex. 2. They shared a "happy" life and were "very close." *Id.* at 3:5–6, 17–20. Friends thought of them as the "perfect couple." *See* Shiree Smith Dep. (Jan. 20, 2019) 3:8–11, attached as Ex. 6. In February 2016, the couple executed wills together. Ex. 2, John Bell Dep. 3:17–20. Mrs. Bell executed a will that left $10,000 to each of her parents, $5,000 to her brother, and the remainder of her estate to Mr. Bell. Last Will and Testament of Ava Bell, dated Feb. 14, 2016 ("Original Will"), attached as Ex. 1. Mr. Bell was also named as executor. *Id.* Mrs. Bell worked as a salesperson at a furniture company, where she was "very involved" and even ran the company's social committee. Ex. 2, John Bell Dep. 4:23–5:12. In fall 2016, while still working during the day, Mrs. Bell began attending law school at night—something Mr. Bell was "very supportive" of her doing, often hiding encouraging notes to Mrs. Bell in her backpack. Ex. 6, Smith Dep. 3:8–11. Mrs. Bell made several friends at law school and, in her free time, enjoyed shopping, reading celebrity gossip, and discussing the lives of the rich and famous. *Id.* at 3:12–21.

B. Mrs. Bell suffered severe head trauma and was treated for depression.

On August 15, 2017, a drunk driver hit Mrs. Bell, and Mrs. Bell suffered severe head trauma as a result of the car accident. Ex. 2, John Bell Dep. 3:23–4:6. Following the accident, Mrs. Bell became a "different person." Ex. 6, Smith Dep. 3:17–21. Mrs. Bell's memory was at only 80 percent, and she had frequent lapses in remembering things like her coffee order and the song she danced to with her husband to at their wedding. Ex. 2, John Bell Dep. 4:8–16. Mrs. Bell was forced to take a leave of absence from law school. *Id.* at 4:20–22. In October 2017, Mrs. Bell returned to her job, but "her heart was not in it," and she only performed the bare minimum. Ex. 2, John Bell Dep. 4:23–5:12. Mrs. Bell stopped eating and began drinking, at times alone in her bedroom. *Id.* at 5:6–15. In November 2017, Mrs. Bell's doctor diagnosed her with depression and prescribed her Zoloft, an antidepressant. *Id.* at 5:16–6:2. The Zoloft worked well until Mrs. Bell's brother died that same month; and, thereafter, Mrs. Bell became more depressed and began drinking heavily. *Id.* at 5:16–6:2; Ex. 3, Welsh Dep. 7:3–5. Mrs. Bell's doctor then increased her Zoloft dosage. Ex. 2, John Bell Dep. 6:3–6.

After her increase of Zoloft, Mrs. Bell eventually "snapped back" and was back to her normal self by Christmas Eve. *Id.* at 6:7–14. Mrs. Bell promised a better new year to her husband, talked about having a baby, and booked a cruise for June 2018 with her husband. *Id.*

C. Mrs. Bell met Anna Welsh, joined HOL, and became brainwashed.

In January 2018, Mrs. Bell met Anna Welsh, head of the organization HOL. Anna Welsh Dep. (Jan. 18, 2019) 2:11–4:13, attached as Ex. 3. Formed in January 2016 by Ms. Welsh and her boyfriend, the 12-member group's purpose is to "help its members pursue and spread happiness." *Id.* at 2:10–18. Ms. Welsh is the sole person with access to HOL's financials and lives in the HOL "community home." *Id.* at 3:9–11, 4:4–11. Ms. Welsh recruited Mrs. Bell to join the group at the first meeting in January, and, after Mrs. Bell joined, Ms. Welsh assigned herself as Mrs. Bell's "Happiness Mentor." *Id.* at 4:18–5:26. Thereafter, the women became "attached at the hip." *Id.* at 6:9–18. Ms. Welsh obsessively texted Mrs. Bell, often more than ten times a day. Ex. 2, John Bell Dep. 6:20–26. Mrs. Bell consulted Ms. Welsh on everything from minor decisions to major life decisions in personal and financial matters. *Id.* at 6:20–7:3. Mrs. Bell never went against Ms. Welsh's advice. Ex. 3, Welsh Dep. 6:19–22. Also, after joining HOL, Mrs. Bell—like all members—was required to submit her finances to the group. *Id.* at 9:24–25.

Ms. Welsh, who is not a licensed physician, convinced Mrs. Bell to stop taking her prescribed Zoloft in January 2018. Ex. 2, John Bell Dep. 7:1–16. Ms. Welsh also convinced Mrs. Bell to stop drinking and, instead, encouraged Mrs. Bell to regularly drink "special tea." *Id.* at 7:4–16; Ex. 3, Welsh Dep. 8:10–9:5. The tea had "'magic mushrooms' [like] from the 60s." Ex. 2, John Bell Dep. at 7:13. The mushrooms were from "the forest" and brought the drinker to a state of "intense calm and spiritualism [for] most of the day." Ex. 3, Welsh Dep. at 8:21–9:3.

Mrs. Bell's life became consumed by HOL, and it completely changed her. For example, Mrs. Bell began dressing in hemp clothing like the HOL members, stopped watching TV and wearing makeup, and even stopped calling her law school and work friends. Ex. 2, John Bell Dep. 7:22–8:4. HOL "brainwashed" Mrs. Bell to the extent she "stopped thinking for herself." *Id.* Ms. Welsh told Mrs. Bell that Mr. Bell "was holding her back from achieving peak happiness," and that "she couldn't achieve true happiness with that negativity in her life." Ex. 2, John Bell Dep. 9:1–8; Ex. 3, Welsh Dep. 7:13–26. This brainwashing caused the relationship between Mrs. Bell and her husband to deteriorate, and Mr. Bell testified that Ms. Welsh "was poisoning [him] to Ava all the time" through text messages about how he was unsupportive. Ex. 2, John Bell Dep. 9:1–8.

D. After brainwashing Mrs. Bell, Ms. Welsh told Mrs. Bell the "quickest way" to gain an honorary title in HOL was to change her will to leave HOL a substantial sum of money.

In April 2018, HOL started a fundraiser to purchase a permanent meeting space and began to "pressure [Mrs. Bell] for money." Ex. 3, Welsh Dep. 9:10–18; Ex. 2, John Bell Dep. 8:14–15. Ms. Welsh asked Mrs. Bell to contribute and told her that, if she contributed more than $20,000 to HOL, she would be given the title of "Happiness Expert." Ex. 3, Welsh Dep. 9:10–18. Mrs. Bell did not have $20,000, but Ms. Welsh informed Mrs. Bell that "the quickest way to becoming an immediate Happiness Expert" was by changing her will. Ex. 2, John Bell Dep. 8:4–11; Ex. 3, Welsh Dep. 10:1–15. On April 28, 2018, Mrs. Bell told Ms. Welsh she wanted to "quickly" change her will. Ex. 2, Welsh Dep. 10:14–20. Ms. Welsh "right away" called her neighbor, Dan Duke, who was an attorney. *Id.* at 10:18. Ms. Welsh told Mr. Duke that "time was of the essence." Dan Duke Dep. (Jan. 23, 2019) 2:6–7, attached as Ex. 4. Ms. Welsh set up the appointment with Mr. Duke and, over the phone, walked him through the changes to Mrs. Bell's will, which would now leave the residuary of her estate to HOL. Ex. 3, Welsh Dep. 10:23–11:1; Ex. 4, Duke Dep. 2:6–15.

E. Accompanied by Ms. Welsh and under the influence of "mushroom" tea, Mrs. Bell changed her will to leave the bulk of her estate to HOL.

On May 6, 2018, Ms. Welsh and Mrs. Bell drank the mushroom tea—which has effects that last "most of the day"—and then Ms. Welsh drove Mrs. Bell to Mr. Duke's office. Ex. 3, Welsh Dep. 9:1–3, 11:9–13. Ms. Welsh tried to go in the office with Mrs. Bell, but she was denied and, instead, stayed in the waiting room throughout the appointment. *Id.* at 10:23–11:1; Duke Dep. 2:19–24. Mr. Duke described Mrs. Bell as "quiet" and "nervous" during the meeting. Ex. 4, Duke Dep. 2:22–3:2. Mrs. Bell changed her will to leave $10,000 to her parents, $5,000 to Mr. Bell, and the remainder to HOL. Last Will and Testament of Ava Bell, dated May 6, 2018 ("Revised Will), attached as Ex. 5. The Revised Will also appointed Ms. Welsh as the independent executor. *Id.*

On June 16, 2018, Mr. and Mrs. Bell left for a cruise, and, the next day, Mrs. Bell died unexpectedly when she fell overboard. Ex. 2, John Bell Dep. 9:18–20. Mr. Bell is now seeking to set aside his late wife's Revised Will on the ground of undue influence.

VIII. SUMMARY JUDGMENT EVIDENCE

Pursuant to Texas Rule of Civil Procedure 166a and in addition to pleadings and other papers on file with the Court, the following summary judgment evidence is being filed concurrently with this Opposition and is incorporated in full by Plaintiff as if set out in length:

1. Last Will and Testament of Ava Bell, dated Feb. 14, 2016, attached as **Exhibit 1.**
2. Deposition of John Bell, dated January 9, 2019, attached as **Exhibit 2.**
3. Deposition of Anna Welsh, dated January 18, 2019, attached as **Exhibit 3.**
4. Deposition of Dan Duke, dated January 23, 2019, attached as **Exhibit 4.**
5. Last Will and Testament of Ava Bell, dated May 6, 2018, attached as **Exhibit 5.**

6. Deposition of Shiree Smith, dated January 20, 2019, attached as **Exhibit 6.**

VI. SUMMARY JUDGMENT STANDARD

Under Texas Rule of Civil Procedure 166a(c), a court must deny summary judgment unless the movant establishes that there is no genuine issue of material fact, and, therefore, the movant is entitled to judgment as a matter of law. Tex. R. Civ. P. 166a(c). In deciding whether there is a genuine issue of material fact precluding summary judgment, evidence favorable to the non-movant will be taken as true. *Nixon v. Mr. Prop. Mgmt. Co., Inc.*, 690 S.W.2d 546, 548–49 (Tex. 1985). Every reasonable inference must be indulged in favor of the non-movant, and any doubts must be resolved in the non-movant's favor. *Id.* at 549. Here, the evidence establishes that there is a genuine issue of material fact as to all three elements of undue influence. Accordingly, this Court should deny summary judgment.

V. ARGUMENT AND AUTHORITIES

There are genuine issues of material fact as to Mr. Bell's claim of undue influence. A will must be set aside when the plaintiff proves: "(1) the existence and exertion of an influence; (2) the effective operation of such influence so as to subvert or overpower the mind of the testat[rix] at the time of the execution of the testament; and (3) the execution of a testament which the maker thereof would not have executed but for such influence." *Rothermel*, 369 S.W.2d at 922. No two cases of undue influence are exactly alike. *Id.* at 921. When examining an undue influence claim, this Court should consider "all of the circumstances shown or established by the evidence . . . even though none of the circumstances standing alone would be sufficient to show the elements of undue influence," and, "if when considered together they produce a reasonable belief that an influence was exerted that subverted or overpowered the mind of the testat[rix] and resulted in the execution of the testament in controversy, the evidence is sufficient" to establish an undue influence claim. *Id.* at 922. While undue influence may be shown by direct or circumstantial evidence, it is usually established by circumstantial evidence. *See id.* The facts in this case raise genuine issues of material fact as to each element of Mr. Bell's undue influence claim, and this Court should, therefore, deny Defendant's Motion for Summary Judgment in its entirety.

A. There is substantial evidence that HOL exerted undue influence on Mrs. Bell.

This Court should deny summary judgment because there is, at a minimum, a fact issue as to whether there was an existence and exertion of undue influence by HOL. The first element of the undue influence is established whenever the evidence shows the existence and exertion of an undue influence. *Rothermel*, 369 S.W.2d at 922. In determining whether there was the existence and exertion of an influence, courts look at five *Rothermel* factors: (1) "the nature and type of relationship existing between the testat[rix], the contestants, and the party accused of exerting such influence"; (2) "the opportunities existing for the exertion of the type of influence or deception possessed or employed"; (3) "the circumstances surrounding the drafting and execution"; (4) "the existence of a fraudulent motive"; and (5) "whether there has been a habitual subjection of the testat[rix] to the control of another." *Id.* at 923. All of the factors need not be present; rather, all of the matters shown by the evidence should be considered together even if standing alone the matters would not be sufficient. *Id.* at 922. Moreover, in examining the *Rothermel* factors, a court is not limited to matters at the time of the will's execution, but, instead, "it is proper to consider all evidence of relevant matters that occurred within a reasonable time before or after the will's execution." *Estate of Luthen*, No. 13-12-00576-CV, 2014 WL 6632952, at *4 (Tex. App.—Corpus Christi-Edinburg Nov. 24, 2014, no pet.) (mem. op.). Necessarily, "undue influence is usually a subtle thing," and it "usually involves an extended course of dealings and circumstances." *In re Estate of Johnson*, 340 S.W.3d 769, 777 (Tex. App.—San Antonio 2011, pet denied).

When the effect of an influence continues until the time of the will's execution, it is immaterial if the beneficiary was not physically present in the room when the will was signed. In *In re Olsson's Estate*, the court upheld a jury finding of undue influence. 344 S.W.2d 171, 178-79 (Tex. App.—El Paso 1961, writ ref'd n.r.e.). In that case, the testatrix disinherited her daughter and son in favor of her new husband, the beneficiary. *Id.* Shortly after marrying the beneficiary, the testatrix became ill and became wholly dependent on her husband. *Id.* at 175-76. The beneficiary had a "yen" for the testatrix's property and spent a considerable amount of her money. *Id.* at 177. The beneficiary encouraged the testatrix to believe that her family did not care for her and alienated her from her friends and family. *Id.* The beneficiary "dominated" the testatrix's every decision and activity, including who she visited and when she exercised. *Id.* at 179. Although he waited in the reception room, the beneficiary accompanied the testatrix to the lawyer's office to discuss her will on the day she signed it. *Id.* at 178. The court reasoned that the effect of the beneficiary's influence before the testatrix signed the will continued until the time of the execution such that it was immaterial that he was not physically present when the testatrix signed the will. *Id.* at 179. The court reasoned that, because the "influence and dominance" was "frequently" asserted prior to the execution of the will, there was an existence and exertion of an undue influence. *Id.*

A beneficiary's habitual control of the testatrix and use of relationship poisoning demonstrates the existence and exertion of an undue influence. In *Estate of Johnson*, the court held the beneficiary exerted undue influence on the testator. 340 S.W.3d at 783. In that case, there was evidence that the testator was "habitual[ly] subject[ed]" to the beneficiary's control. *Id.* at 780. The beneficiary was very interested in the testator's estate and attended estate planning meetings; and, the testator quit his favorite hobby of hunting in order to appease the beneficiary. *Id.* at 780, 782. Additionally, the beneficiary used "relationship poisoning" to influence the testator to change his will by making negative remarks about his children. *Id.* at 782-83. The court reasoned that the combination of relationship positioning and habitual control over the testator's finances and hobby demonstrated that undue influence existed and was actually exerted. *Id.*

Here, following *Olsson's Estate* and *Estate of Johnson*, this Court should find there are genuine issues of material fact as to the existence and exertion of an influence on Mrs. Bell by HOL. First, examining the first and second *Rothermel* factors—the nature of the relationship between the parties and the opportunities existing for exertion of influence—the evidence shows, at a minimum, a fact issue proving that HOL (via Ms. Welsh) engaged in "relationship poisoning" with respect to the marriage of Mr. and Mrs. Bell. *Estate of Johnson*, 340 S.W.3d at 782. Like *Estate of Johnson*, where the beneficiary used "relationship poisoning" to influence the testator to change his will by making negative remarks about his children, here HOL/Ms. Welsh turned Mrs. Bell against her husband. *Estate of Johnson*, 340 S.W.3d at 782–83; Ex. 2, John Bell Dep. 9:1–8; Ex. 3, Welsh Dep. 7:13–26. Before meeting Ms. Welsh and joining HOL, Mrs. Bell had a "happy" marriage to Mr. Bell—so much so that they were talking about having a baby. Ex. 2, John Bell Dep. 6:7–14, 8:16–23. After Mrs. Bell joined HOL, Ms. Welsh "was poisoning" her against Mr. Bell "all the time." Ex. 2, John Bell Dep. 9:1–8; Ex. 3, Welsh Dep. 7:13–26. Ms. Welsh told Mrs. Bell that Mr. Bell was holding her back from achieving peak happiness" and that "she couldn't achieve true happiness with that negativity in her life." Ex. 3, Welsh Dep. 7:13–26.

Similarly, like *Olsson's Estate*, where the beneficiary encouraged the testatrix to believe that her family did not care for her and alienated her from her friends and family, here, HOL/Ms. Welsh caused Mrs. Bell to become alienated from not only her husband, but also her friends, whom she stopped calling. *Olsson's Estate*, 344 S.W.2d at 177; Ex. 2, John Bell Dep. 7:22–8:4. Instead, Mrs. Bell became "attached to the hip" to Ms. Welsh, who obsessively texted Mrs. Bell, often more than ten times a day. Ex. 3, Welsh Dep. 6:9–18; Ex. 2, John Bell Dep. 6:20–26.

Next, examining the third, fourth, and fifth *Rothermel* factors—the circumstances surrounding the will's drafting and execution; the existence of a fraudulent motive; and habitual subjection of control—the evidence shows, at a minimum, a fact issue proving that HOL/Ms. Welsh exerted an undue influence on Mrs. Bell. *Rothermel*, 369 S.W.2d at 922. With respect to the will's drafting and execution, like *Olsson's Estate*, where the beneficiary was not physically present at the will's signing but was in the next room and drove her to the appointment, here, Ms. Welsh made the appointment with the lawyer, drove with her to the office, and waited in the next room. Ex. 3, Welsh Dep. 10:23–11:13; Ex. 4, Duke Dep. 2:19–24. Moreover, like *Estate of Johnson*, where the beneficiary attended estate planning meetings, here, over the phone, Ms. Welsh walked Mr. Duke through the changes to Mrs. Bell's will, which would leave the residuary of her estate to HOL. *Estate of Johnson*, 340 S.W.3d at 782; Ex. 3, Welsh Dep. 10:23–11:1; Ex. 4, Duke Dep. 2:6–15.

Like both *Olsson's Estate* and *Estate of Johnson*, where the beneficiaries were very interested in the testators' property, here, HOL required Mrs. Bell to submit her finances to the organization before she became a member. Ex. 3, Welsh Dep. 9:24–25; *Olsson's Estate*, 344 S.W.2d at 177–79; *Estate of Johnson*, 340 S.W.3d at 782–83. Even more than those cases, the evidence of Ms. Welsh/HOL's fraudulent motive is overwhelming given that HOL pressured Mrs. Bell for money and told her that changing her will was "the quickest way to becoming an immediate Happiness Exert." Ex. 2, John Bell Dep. 8:4–11; Ex. 3, Welsh Dep. 10:1–15.

Moreover, like *Olsson's Estate*, Ms. Welsh/HOL "frequently" asserted "influence and dominance" before the execution of the will by "dominat[ing] Mrs. Bell's daily decisions such that she was subject to Ms. Welsh/HOL's habitual control to the point where she was "brainwashed" and "stopped thinking for herself." *Olsson's Estate*, 344 S.W.2d at 177–79; Ex. 2, John Bell Dep. 7:22–8:4. Like *Estate of Johnson*, where the testator quit his favorite hobby of hunting in order to appease the beneficiary, here, Mrs. Bell changed everything about herself, including her appearance and her hobbies, to fit in with HOL. *Estate of Johnson*, 340 S.W.3d at 782; Ex. 2, John Bell Dep. 7:22–8:4. HOL had such power over Mrs. Bell that she quit taking her prescribed depression medication at the advice of Ms. Welsh/HOL. Ex. 3, Welsh Dep. 7:1–16. Because there is, at a minimum, a fact issue with regard to whether there was the existence and exertion of an influence by HOL, this Court should deny summary judgment.

HOL's reliance on *Smallwood v. Jones*, 794 S.W.2d 114 (Tex. App.—San Antonio 1990, no writ) and *Estate of Steed*, 152 S.W.3d 797 (Tex. App.—Texarkana 2004, pet. denied) is misplaced. Def.'s M. for Summ. J. 7–10. The key fact upon which the *Smallwood* court relied in holding that there was not exertion of undue influence was that the beneficiary was a caretaker of the testatrix and "like a daughter" to the testatrix. *Smallwood*, 794 S.W.2d at 118–19. Unlike the beneficiary in *Smallwood*, Ms. Welsh/HOL and Mrs. Bell were not in a caretaker-type relationship. *Smallwood*, 794 S.W.2d at 118–19; Ex. 2, John Bell Dep. 7:22–8:4. Also, unlike *Smallwood*, where there was little evidence of a fraudulent motive, here, the evidence of fraudulent motive is overwhelming because HOL was motivated to get Mrs. Bell to change her will in order to build a new, permanent meeting space. *Smallwood*, 794 S.W.2d at 118–19; Ex. 2, John Bell Dep. 8:4–15; Ex. 3, Welsh Dep. 9:10–18.

There are also key distinctions from *Estate of Steed*. First, unlike *Estate of Steed*, where the court found "very important" that the testator was an "independent" lawyer who prepared his own will, and there was no evidence that the beneficiary "was with [the testator] when he drafted the will or that she participated in the preparation of the will," here, Mrs. Bell was not a lawyer and Ms. Welsh/HOL were involved in every aspect of the will's drafting and execution. *Estate of Steed*, 152 S.W.3d at 809; Ex. 3, Welsh Dep. 10:23–11:1; Ex. 4, Duke Dep. 2:6–15. Ms. Welsh discussed the will's terms over the phone with the lawyer, drove Mrs. Bell to the lawyer's office, and tried to join Mrs. Bell for the will's execution. Ex. 3, Welsh Dep. 10:23–11:1; Ex. 4, Duke Dep. 2:6–15. Second, unlike *Estate of Steed*, where it was important to the court's holding that there was "no evidence of any other occasions when [the beneficiary] controlled [the testator's] actions," here, there is ample evidence that HOL controlled Mrs. Bell's relationships, hobbies, and decisions and pushed Mrs. Bell to change her will in order to achieve a made-up title in the HOL organization. *Estate of Steed*, 152 S.W.3d at 809; Ex. 3, Welsh Dep. 9:10–18, 6:19–22; Ex. 2, John Bell Dep. 7:22–8:4. This Court should not find either *Smallwood* or *Estate of Steed* persuasive.

Ms. Welsh/HOL's influence—like most undue influence—involved an "extended course of dealings and circumstances" that dramatically influenced every area of Mrs. Bell's life and this Court—considering "all evidence of relevant matters that occurred within a reasonable time before or after the will's execution"—should hold there exists, at a minimum, genuine issues of material fact as to the existence and exertion of undue influence such that summary judgment should be denied. *Estate of Luthen*, 2014 WL 6632952, at *3–4; *Estate of Johnson*, 340 S.W.3d at 777.

B. There is substantial evidence that HOL overpowered Mrs. Bell's mind.

This Court should deny summary judgment because there is, at a minimum, a fact issue as to whether HOL overpowered Mrs. Bell's mind. The second element of undue influence is established whenever the influence overpowered or subverted the testatrix's mind at the time the will was executed. *Rothermel*, 369 S.W.2d at 922. To demonstrate that the testatrix's mind was overpowered or subverted, courts look at the "testat[rix's] mental or physical incapacity to resist or the susceptibility of the testat[rix's] mind to the type and extent of the influence exerted." *Rothermel*, 369 S.W.2d at 923. Evidence of a testatrix's "weakness of mind or body," whether produced by infirmities of age or by disease or otherwise" is a "material circumstance" establishing the second element. *See id.* A court may also look at a testatrix's words or acts in order to establish her mental state. *Id.*

Evidence that a testatrix was using drugs or alcohol around the time of the will's execution is sufficient evidence to prove that a testatrix was susceptible to an undue influence overpowering her mind. In *Estate of Johnson*, the court held the testator's alcohol abuse, coupled with his memory dysfunction, made him increasingly susceptible to undue influence such that the second element was satisfied. 340 S.W.3d at 778. In that case, the testator was an alcoholic. *Id.* There was evidence that the testator suffered memory dysfunction as well. *Id.* The court noted that drinking had an adverse effect on his mind and cognitive reasoning, leaving him "vulnerable to undue influence." *Id.* The court reasoned that due to the testator's alcohol abuse and the effect it had on his mental capacity to resist, the testator was "susceptible to undue influence" and that "ample opportunity" existed for the beneficiary to unduly influence the testator while he was drinking. *Id.*

Here, the Court should also find that there is sufficient evidence to create a fact issue as to whether Mrs. Bell had her mind subverted or overpowered by HOL. Like in *Estate of Johnson*, where the testator was under the influence of alcohol around the time of the will's execution such that there was "ample opportunity" for undue influence, here, because Mrs. Bell drank the magic mushroom tea every day, which had the effect of altering her mental state, there was "ample opportunity" for Ms. Welsh/HOL to unduly influence her. *Estate of Johnson*, 340 S.W.3d at 778; Ex. 2, John Bell Dep. 7:4–16; Ex. 3, Welsh Dep. 8:10–9:5. More than *Estate of Johnson*, where there was no direct evidence of the testator drinking on the day of the will's execution, here, there is direct evidence that, immediately before executing the Revised Will, Mrs. Bell drank mushroom tea with Ms. Welsh. *Estate of Johnson*, 340 S.W.3d at 778; Ex. 3, Welsh Dep. 11:9–13. Additionally, like the testator in *Estate of Johnson*, who had memory deficiencies around the time of the will's execution, here, there is evidence that Mrs. Bell lost 20 percent of her memory capacity few months before executing the Revised Will. *Estate of Johnson*, 340 S.W.3d at 778; John Bell Dep. 4:8–16. Moreover, given her recent traumatic car accident and the abrupt stop to her prescribed depression medication, like *Estate of Johnson*, there is, at a minimum, a fact issue that Mrs. Bell was uniquely "susceptible" to undue influence given her weakened mental capacity to resist. *Estate of Johnson*, 340 S.W.3d at 778; Ex. 2, John Bell Dep. 7:4–16; Ex. 3, Welsh Dep. 8:10–9:5. Accordingly, like in *Estate of Johnson*, this Court should hold that Mrs. Bell was susceptible to undue influence and that ample opportunity existed for HOL to unduly influence Mrs. Bell such that such that summary judgment should be denied.

HOL's reliance on *In re Estate of Steed*, 152 S.W.3d 797 (Tex. App.—Texarkana 2004, pet. denied), to support that HOL did not overpower Mrs. Bell's mind is incorrect. Def.'s M. for Summ. J. 11–13. Unlike in *Estate of Steed*, where the testator suffered from depression but was actively taking his prescribed medication, Mrs. Bell was not taking her prescribed medication and was, instead, drinking "magic" tea. *Estate of Steed*, 152 S.W.3d at 811; Ex. 2, John Bell Dep. 7:4–16; Ex. 3, Welsh Dep. 8:10–9:5. Moreover, unlike *Estate of Steed*, where there was no evidence that the testator was "emotionally dependent" on the beneficiary, and, instead, there was ample evidence that he was independent; here, there is evidence that Mrs. Bell was extremely dependent on Ms. Welsh and HOL for all life decisions, whether big or small, making her more susceptible to undue influence. *Estate of Steed*, 152 S.W.3d at 811; Ex. 2, John Bell Dep. 6:18–7:16; Ex. 3, Welsh Dep. 8:10–9:5. Accordingly, this Court should not follow *Estate of Steed*.

Likewise, HOL's reliance on *Guthrie v. Suiter*, 934 S.W.2d 820 (Tex. App.—Houston [1st Dist.] 1996, no writ) is unpersuasive because HOL misleads the Court as to the

Guthrie court's holding. Def.'s M. for Summ. J. 12–13. In *Guthrie*, the will contestant relied on evidence that the testator had a lobotomy and the appearance of an Alzheimer's patient in order to demonstrate the existence and exertion of an undue influence—the first element of *Rothermel*. 934 S.W.2d at 832. The *Guthrie* court held that, while such evidence of a weakened mental condition rendered the testator susceptible to undue influence (the second element of *Rothermel*), it was insufficient to prove the first element. *Id.* Thus, *Guthrie's* holding lends no support to HOL and, instead, at most, supports that Mrs. Bell's weakened mental condition "rendered her susceptible to undue influence." *See id.*

Because there is, at a minimum, a fact issue as to whether HOL overpowered Mrs. Bell's mind, this Court should deny summary judgment.

C. There is substantial evidence that Mrs. Bell would not have executed the Revised Will but for HOL's undue influence.

This Court should deny summary judgment because there is, at a minimum, a fact issue as to whether Mrs. Bell would have executed the Revised Will but for the undue influence exerted by HOL. The third element of undue influence is satisfied whenever the evidence shows that the testatrix would not have executed the will but for the influence. *Rothermel*, 369 S.W.2d at 922. If the will provides for an unnatural disposition of property, the third element of the *Rothermel* test is satisfied. *Id.* at 923. In deciding whether a disposition is unnatural, courts look to evidence that a "testat[rix] unexpectedly disinherited close family members previously provided for." *Estate of Luthen*, 2014 WL 6632952, at *7. A disposition can still be considered "unnatural" even if there is a reasonable explanation. *Estate of Johnson*, 340 S.W. at 784 ("[E]vidence of a reasonable explanation for an unnatural disposition does not prevent a jury from finding undue influence."). As such, when "competing explanations" for a disposition exist, whether the testament is unnatural is a question for the jury and granting summary judgment is improper. *Id.*; *see also Estate of Luthen*, 2014 WL 6632952, at *8.

Leaving one's estate to someone a testatrix met only a few months before executing the will is evidence of an unnatural disposition. In *In re Estate of Fiedler*, the court held there was sufficient evidence of an unnatural disposition. No. 13-09-00386-CV, 2011 LEXIS 2856, at *11 (Tex. App.—Corpus Christi–Edinburg April 14, 2011, no pet.) (mem. op.). In that case, the testator left his estate to a beneficiary whom he met only 15 months prior to executing his will. *Id.* The court reasoned that excluding family in favor of a woman the testator met only 15 months prior to executing his will was unnatural and that the jury reasonably held that the beneficiary unduly influenced the testator "to devise his will to her advantage." *Id.* at *11–12.

Here, this Court should reach the same result as *Estate of Fiedler* and hold that Mrs. Bell's Revised Will, leaving the residuary of her estate to HOL and "unexpectedly disinherit[ing]" her husband, was an unnatural disposition. *See Estate of Luthen*, 2014 WL 6632952, at *7. Even more than *Estate of Fiedler*, where the testator left his estate to a woman he met only 15 months prior, here Mrs. Bell left the bulk of her estate to HOL, which she had joined ***only four months*** prior to executing her Revised Will. *Estate of Fiedler*, 2011 Tex. App. LEXIS 2856, at *11; Ex. 5, Revised Will; Ex. 3, Welsh Dep. 2:11–13, 4:12–13, 4:18–5:26. Accordingly, this Court should follow *Estate of Fiedler* and hold there is, at a minimum, a fact issue as to whether the Revised Will's disposition to HOL was unnatural.

Defendant's reliance on *Mackie v. McKenzie*, 900 S.W.2d 445 (Tex. App.—Texarkana 1995, writ denied) is misplaced. Def.'s M. for Summ. J. 14–15. First, unlike *Mackie*, where the testator left the bulk of his estate to charities that he was involved in throughout his life, here, Mrs. Bell had joined HOL ***only four months prior*** to executing her Revised Will. *Mackie*, 900 S.W.2d at 450; Ex. 5, Revised Will; Ex. 3, Welsh Dep. 2:11–13, 4:12–13, 4:18–5:26. Second, unlike the *Mackie* charity beneficiaries—Baylor University Medical Foundation and Presbyterian Hospital of Dallas—that are large, well-established, and reputable, HOL is a 12-member, newly-founded, cult-like group. *Mackie*, 900 S.W.2d at 450; Ex. 5, Revised Will; Ex. 3, Welsh Dep. 2:10–18. Third, the present case is distinguishable from *Mackie* because, unlike Mrs. Bell, the *Mackie* testator did not have a spouse. *Mackie*, 900 S.W.2d at 447; Ex. 2, John Bell Dep. 2:26–3:1. Accordingly, this Court should not follow *Mackie*.

Finally, this Court should reject Defendant's public policy argument. Def.'s M. for Summ. J. 15. While it is true that Texas protects bequests to charities, such bequests are usually less susceptible to undue influence because a private individual beneficiary's "selfish reasons" for exerting influence are absent when the beneficiary is a large, established charitable institution. *See, e.g., In re Caruther's Estate*, 151 S.W.2d 946, 947–48 (Tex. App.—Beaumont 1941, writ dism'd judgm't cor.) (upholding will where testator, who was not married, left the bulk of his estate to charities supported by the Catholic church of which he was a devoted member). Here, the same policy does not apply because Ms. Welsh had clear self-interest in inducing Mrs. Bell to leave the bulk of her estate to HOL given that Ms. Welsh is the founding member of the small group of 12, lives in its community home, and is the sole signatory on the HOL bank account. Ex. 3, Welsh Dep. 2:11–4:13.

In summary, HOL's explanation for the unnatural disposition—that Mrs. Bell's relationship with Mr. Bell has deteriorated—is not dispositive, and "competing explanations" are an issue for the jury and require summary judgment to be denied. *See Estate of Luthen*, 2014 WL 6632952, at *8. Accordingly, this Court should deny summary judgment because there is, at a minimum, a fact issue as to whether Mrs. Bell would have executed the Revised Will but for the undue influence exerted by HOL.

VI. CONCLUSION

For the foregoing reasons, this Court should deny Defendant's Motion for Summary Judgment.

Respectfully submitted,

Partner & Partner LLC
1212 Moon Court, Suite 1400
Dallas, Texas 75219
(214) 555–1234 (telephone)
(214) 555–6709 (facsimile)

By: *Alex B. Partner*

ALEX B. PARTNER
Texas State Bar No. 91011121

CERTIFICATE OF SERVICE

The undersigned certifies that a true and correct copy of the foregoing document has been served on all counsel for Defendant, via LexisNexis, on the 19th day of May, 2019.

Alex B. Partner

Alex B. Partner

Appeal and Error ⚷790(3)

Federal court orders requiring desegregation of schools operated by defendants precluded them from spending public funds for purpose contrary thereto and rendered moot questions presented on defendants' appeal from decision of Court of Civil Appeals that defendants be enjoined from expenditure of money for erection and maintenance of school buildings for segregated use, and Supreme Court would grant writ of error, vacate judgment of Court of Appeals and order case dismissed.

William S. Lott, Georgetown, Bracewell, Reynolds & Patterson, Houston, for petitioners.

Ashton, Allen & Smith, L. Hamilton Lowe, Austin, for respondents.

PER CURIAM.

Petitioners, the Board of Trustees of Georgetown Independent School District, have filed their motion to declare this case moot and order its dismissal. Attached to the motion is a copy of the order of the United States District Judge for the Western District of Texas, Austin Division, in Civil Action No. 1311, dated June 12, 1963, holding unlawful and unconstitutional the racial segregation policy and practice of petitioners, and directing the desegregation of the public schools of the Georgetown Independent School District pursuant to the plan and schedule set forth in the order. Petitioners are subject to this order and to such further orders as may be entered by the United States District Court or by any Federal courts of appellate jurisdiction in event an appeal of the case is prosecuted.

Also attached to the motion of petitioners is a copy of the resolution of petitioners adopted June 25, 1963, reading, in part, that "in connection with the building program heretofore adopted, that all school buildings and facilities in the Georgetown Independent School District, including the Westside School, will not be segregated schools but will be desegregated in accordance with the order of the aforesaid United States District Court, and that all such schools will be occupied and used in accordance with such rulings."

Respondents oppose the motion of petitioners but do not challenge the correctness of the order and resolution attached to the motion of petitioners and referred to above.

Since petitioners are now subject to orders of the Federal courts requiring desegregation of the schools operated by the Georgetown Independent School District, and may not expend the funds of the District for a purpose contrary to such orders, we declare this case moot. Cf. State v. Society for Friendless Children, 130 Tex. 533, 111 S.W.2d 1075; United States and Interstate Commerce Commission v. Alaska Steamship Company et al., 253 U.S. 113, 40 S.Ct. 448, 64 L.Ed. 808.

The application for writ of error is granted, the judgment of the Court of Civil Appeals, 368 S.W.2d 873, is vacated and, without further proceedings, the case is ordered dismissed. No motion for rehearing will be entertained.

Louis F. ROTHERMEL, Individually and as Independent Executor, Petitioner,

v.

Sarah R. Rothermel DUNCAN et al., Respondents.

No. A-9542.

Supreme Court of Texas.

July 10, 1963.

Rehearing Denied July 31, 1963.

Will contest on theory of mental incapacity and the exertion of undue influence by testatrix' son wherein county court denied the contest and, on trial of the case, the District Court, Waller County, Ernest Coker, J., entered judgment in favor of contestants and son appealed. The Beaumont Court of Civil Appeals, Ninth Supreme Judicial District, 365 S.W.2d 398, affirmed and son appealed. The Supreme Court, Smith, J., held that evidence did not establish that son, who had managed affairs of testatrix during her lifetime and with whom testatrix had lived for most part until her death, had exercised undue influence over testatrix so as to subvert or overpower her will and cause execution of a testament preferring son over widow and children of deceased son.

Judgment of Court of Civil Appeals and trial court reversed and judgment rendered that contestants take nothing.

1. Wills ⟹155(1)

"Undue influence" in procurement of testament is ground for its avoidance separate and distinct from ground of testamentary incapacity; while testamentary incapacity implies want of intelligent mental power, undue influence implies existence of testamentary capacity subjected to and controlled by dominant influence or power.

See publication Words and Phrases for other judicial constructions and definitions.

2. Wills ⟹163(1)

Before testament may be set aside on grounds of undue influence contestant must prove existence and exertion of influence; effective operation of such influence so as to subvert or overpower mind of testator at time of execution of testament; and execution of testament which maker would not have executed but for such influence.

3. Wills ⟹155(1)

Every influence exerted by one person on will of another is not undue, for influence is not undue unless free agency of testator was destroyed and a testament produced that expresses will of one exerting influence; however, "undue influence" may take nature of force, intimidation, duress, excessive importunity or deception and exertion of such influence is species of fraud.

4. Wills ⟹155(3)

One may request or even importune and entreat another to execute favorable dispositive instrument; but unless importunities and entreaties are shown to be so excessive as to subvert will of maker, they will not taint validity of instrument with undue influence.

5. Wills ⟹166(12)

In absence of direct evidence of undue influence in executing testament all of circumstances shown or established should be considered; and even though none of circumstances standing alone would be sufficient to show elements of undue influence, if when considered together they produce reasonable belief that such influence was exerted, evidence is sufficient to sustain such conclusion but testament should not be set aside on bare suspicion of wrongdoing.

6. Wills ⟹158

Establishment of existence of undue influence is based upon inquiry as to nature and type of relationship existing between testator, contestants and party accused of exerting such influence and is predicated upon inquiry as to opportunities for exertion of type of influence or deception possessed or employed, circumstances surrounding drafting and execution of testament, existence of fraudulent motive and whether there has been habitual subjection of testator to control of another.

7. Wills ⟹156

Where there is competent evidence of existence and exercise of undue influence, issue as to whether it was effectively exercised turns the inquiry and directs it to state of testator's mind at time of execution of testament.

8. Wills ⟹164(7)

Establishment of subversion of overpowering of will of testator by undue influence is generally based upon inquiry as to testator's mental or physical incapacity to resist or susceptibility of testator's mind to type and extent of influence exerted; words and acts of testator may bear upon his mental state and weakness of mind and body, whether produced by infirmities of age or by disease, may be considered.

9. Wills ⟹164(3)

Establishment of fact that testament executed would not have been executed but for undue influence is generally predicated upon consideration of whether testament executed is unnatural in its terms of disposition of property.

10. Wills ⟹166(7)

Will cannot be set aside on proof of facts which at most do no more than show opportunity to exercise undue influence.

11. Wills ⟹166(2)

Establishment of circumstances of having opportunity to exert undue influence due to being in position of caring for person upon whom influence is supposed to be exerted is equally consistent with theory of innocence as it is with theory of wrongdoing.

12. Wills ⟹163(8), 166(1, 12)

Exertion of influence that was undue cannot be inferred alone from opportunity, but there must be some testimony, direct or circumstantial, to show that influence was not only present but that it was in fact exerted with respect to making of testament itself.

13. Wills ⟹164(7), 166(8)

Fact that testatrix was old and suffered from common maladies of age may be considered as establishing testatrix' physical incapacity to resist or susceptibility of her mind to influence exerted; however, such evidence does not establish that her mind was in fact subverted or overpowered at time of execution of testament.

14. Wills ⟹1

Person of sound mind has perfect right to dispose of his property as he wishes.

15. Wills ⟹166(5)

Mere fact that testament makes unnatural disposition of property in that one child is preferred over widow and children of another child is not enough to show undue influence; it is only where all reasonable explanation in affection for devise is lacking that this circumstance may be taken as badge of disorder or lapsed mentality or of its subjugation.

16. Wills ⟹166(2)

Evidence did not establish that son who had managed affairs of testatrix during her lifetime and with whom testatrix lived for most part until her death had exercised undue influence over testatrix so as to subvert or overpower her will and cause execution of a testament preferring son over widow and children of deceased son.

W. H. Betts, Hempstead, for petitioner.

Roland B. Voight, Williams, Lee & Lee, Houston, McLain & Harrell, Conroe, J. C. McEvoy, Hempstead, for respondents.

SMITH, Justice.

This is a suit filed by Sarah R. Rothermel Duncan et al. in the County Court against Louis F. Rothermel, individually and as independent executor of the estate of Sallie A. Rothermel, contesting the validity of the will of Sallie Rothermel, deceased. On March 7, 1960, trial was held in the County Court, and the contest was denied. Upon the trial of the case in the District Court the plaintiffs pleaded both mental incapacity and undue influence, but the latter ground was the only issue submitted to the jury. The jury found that the contested will was the result of undue influence exercised upon the deceased by her son, Louis Rothermel. Based on the jury verdict the trial court entered judgment in favor of the contestants. The Court of Civil Appeals affirmed. 365 S.W.2d 398.

The issue before this court is whether the record contains any evidence of probative force to support the finding of the jury that undue influence was exercised by Louis F. Rothermel in the execution of the will of Mrs. Sallie A. Rothermel. We have concluded that such evidence does not exist in this record. Therefore, the judgments of both the trial court and the Court of Civil Appeals are reversed.

We shall confine our statement of the evidence to that relied upon by the contestants to sustain the jury finding. The record reveals that Sallie Rothermel was the mother of three children; Louis, a daughter and Bill. In 1906 Sallie Rothermel's husband died. At the time of their father's death Louis was sixteen years of age and Bill was one. Upon the death of his father, Louis left school and assumed the responsibility of providing support for his mother, sister and Bill. Louis' sister died in 1916.

In 1918 Louis was married, and in 1920 Louis and his wife, Mrs. Rothermel and Bill moved from Pennsylvania to Houston, Texas. Since Bill was sixteen years younger than Louis, Mrs. Rothermel leaned more towards Louis than Bill for help and assistance, especially in the earlier years of her widowhood. Mrs. Rothermel did not remarry. The record reflects that at all times the Rothermel family was a close one, and that Louis continued to support his mother until investments made by him for and in Mrs. Rothermel's name became sufficient to provide for her. Mrs. Rothermel was equally devoted to her two sons, and in 1939 she executed her first will whereby her estate was devised equally to her two sons.

Subsequently, Bill and Louis associated in the very successful business of the Maritime Oil Company, and in 1952 Bill became a partner of Louis in this business. The partnership lasted until Bill's death in 1955. Mrs. Rothermel was greatly grieved over the loss of her younger son.

After Bill's death Mrs. Rothermel resided with Bill's family from October, 1955, to March, 1956. From March, 1956, to October, 1956, she resided with Louis. From October, 1956, to October, 1957, Mrs. Rothermel was in residence at an old ladies' home in Houston. On or about October 1, 1957, Louis took his mother to his farm in Waller County, some 50 miles from Houston. Thus, began the chain of events leading to the filing of this suit.

Louis maintained and operated a poultry and egg business on his farm and had employed a single woman named Mary Blumberg who cared for the business. From the time of her arrival at the farm, Mrs. Rothermel lived with Mary in her 4-room house on the farm. Mrs. Rothermel was then 93 years of age, and suffered from the common maladies of age: she was hard of hearing, her eyesight was bad, her hands shook, and she suffered from arthritis and diabetes. For several years Mrs. Rothermel's feeble condition required care and companionship—this became the responsibility of Mary Blumberg.

Soon after she was taken to the farm, Mrs. Rothermel fell and suffered a broken rib. On this occasion she was taken to a hospital in Hempstead, Texas, where she remained for two or three days. At the farm Mrs. Rothermel was "very sparsely" visited by her other relatives.

Mrs. Rothermel was devoted to Louis; she trusted him completely and relied entirely upon him to handle her affairs, which he did. Louis took care of all of her business correspondence and affairs and signed her checks. All of Mrs. Rothermel's papers, including the 1939 will, were kept in Louis' safe-deposit box in Houston.

Louis' testimony reveals that in the latter part of 1957 or in the early part of January of 1958 his mother requested that he bring to her the 1939 will, which he did. The 1939 will remained in her possession for several days, and she conferred with Louis and informed him that she wanted to make another will and leave everything to him. Although he was aware of the possible double federal tax consequences of being the sole beneficiary of his mother, Louis did not try to explain this to his mother. Louis testified that he drew the new will in Houston, and either used the 1939 will or one of his own as a pattern, and that he suggested to his mother that her will provide that if he predeceased her, his daughter would be her executrix and that her property be divided equally among her grandchildren and great grandchildren. No attorney was consulted; and after the new will was drawn, Louis took it to his mother who kept it several days.

On January 30, 1958, the new will was signed by Mrs. Rothermel before two witnesses, Mary Blumberg and her brother, August Blumberg, who was another farm employee of Louis. The witnesses were gathered by Louis. The will was signed by Mrs. Rothermel without comments, questions or suggestions, and at a time when Louis was in the house but not in the room where the signing of the will took place. No one read or explained the will to her or saw her read the will.

After the will was signed, it was delivered to Louis by his mother. He took possession of the will and placed it in his safe-deposit box, and no one knew of its execution except the witnesses thereto and Louis until sometime after his mother's death. Mrs. Rothermel discussed the execution of this will with no one except Mary Blumberg. Mrs. Rothermel continued to live with Mary Blumberg until her death in October of 1958 at 94 years of age. The new will appointing Louis independent executor of his mother's estate was probated by the County Court on October 7, 1958.

After this suit was filed Louis went to the home of two witnesses at the trial to inquire if either of them had knowledge of any prior will of Mrs. Rothermel. It further appears that, shortly after the probate of the will, and before this suit was filed, Louis made out checks for $1000 each: one was sent to Mary Blumberg, and a check in a like amount was mailed to each of his two nieces, two nephews (respondents herein), a daughter and two grandchildren, totaling $8000.

Other evidence in the record reveals that Mrs. Rothermel loved the children of her two sons equally. Disinterested witnesses had heard Mrs. Rothermel declare numerous times, within five years of her death, that she intended to leave her estate equally to her grandchildren.

It would unnecessarily lengthen this opinion to attempt to analyze each item of evidence which the contestants claim is some evidence of undue influence. Mental incapacity and undue influence was alleged, and the record reflects that evidence was introduced in an effort to support both grounds.

The contestants select from the summarized evidence above three sets of circumstances which they deem sufficient to bring this case within the holding of this court in the case of Long v. Long,[1] 133 Tex. 96, 125 S.W.2d 1034, that the evidence introduced would support a finding of the exercise of undue influence. The particular facts of this case which the contestants claim should support a similar conclusion are: (1) the fragile condition of Mrs. Rothermel due to age and sickness; (2) Louis, the beneficiary, "generally looked after and supervised most of the business affairs and business interests of his mother"; and (3) the circumstances surrounding the signing of this will.

No two cases involving undue influence are alike, and each case must stand or fall depending upon the legal sufficiency of the facts proved. Because of this it does not

1. See: Long v. Long, Tex.Civ.App., 98 S.W.2d 236; Long v. Long, Tex.Civ.App., 129 S.W.2d 1206; Long v. Long, 133 Tex. 623, 138 S.W.2d 798.

necessarily follow that it should be held in this case, as it was in the Long case, that the finding of undue influence has support in the record.

[1, 2] Undue influence in the procurement of a testament is a ground for its avoidance separate and distinct from the ground of testamentary incapacity; for while testamentary incapacity implies the want of intelligent mental power, undue influence implies the existence of a testamentary capacity subjected to and controlled by a dominant influence or power. Long v. Long, supra; Besteiro v. Besteiro, Tex. Com.App., 65 S.W.2d 759. Thus, before a testament may be set aside on the grounds of undue influence the contestant must prove: (1) the existence and exertion of an influence; (2) the effective operation of such influence so as to subvert or overpower the mind of the testator at the time of the execution of the testament; and (3) the execution of a testament which the maker thereof would not have executed but for such influence. See: Stewart v. Miller, Tex.Civ.App. (1925), 271 S.W. 311, wr. refused; Olds v. Traylor, Tex.Civ.App. (1944), 180 S.W.2d 511, wr. refused.

The burden of proving undue influence is upon the party contesting its execution. It is, therefore, necessary for the contestant to introduce some tangible and satisfactory proof of the existence of each of the above stated elements of undue influence. Scott v. Townsend, 106 Tex. 322, 166 S.W. 1138.

[3, 4] It cannot be said that every influence exerted by one person on the will of another is undue, for the influence is not undue unless the free agency of the testator was destroyed and a testament produced that expresses the will of the one exerting the influence. Long v. Long, supra. Indeed it has even been held that one may request or even importune and entreat another to execute a favorable dispositive instrument; but unless the importunities and entreaties are shown to be so excessive as to subvert the will of the maker, they will not taint the validity of the instrument with undue influence. See: Curry v. Curry, 153 Tex. 421, 270 S.W.2d 208, and cases cited therein.

Influence that was or became undue may take the nature of, but is not limited to force, intimidation, duress, excessive importunity or deception used in an effort to overcome or subvert the will of the maker of the testament and induce the execution thereof contrary to his will. The courts of Texas treat the exertion of such influence in the execution of a dispositive instrument as a species of legal fraud. See: Curry v. Curry, supra.

[5] The exertion of influence that was or became undue is usually a subtle thing and by its very nature usually involves an extended course of dealings and circumstances. Thus, it is settled that the elements establishing undue influence may be proved by what is known as circumstantial, as well as by direct, evidence. Long v. Long, supra. In the absence of direct evidence all of the circumstances shown or established by the evidence should be considered; and even though none of the circumstances standing alone would be sufficient to show the elements of undue influence, if when considered together they produce a reasonable belief that an influence was exerted that subverted or overpowered the mind of the testator and resulted in the execution of the testament in controversy, the evidence is sufficient to sustain such conclusion. Barksdale v. Dobbins, Tex. Civ.App (1940), 141 S.W.2d 1035, wr. refused. However, the circumstances relied on as establishing the elements of undue influence must be of a reasonably satisfactory and convincing character, and they must not be equally consistent with the absence of the exercise of such influence. Stewart v. Miller, supra. This is so because a solemn testament executed under the formalities required by law by one mentally capable of executing it should not be set

aside upon a bare suspicion of wrongdoing. Burgess v. Sylvester, 143 Tex. 25, 182 S.W.2d 358.

[6–9] Generally, the establishment of the existence of an influence that was undue is based upon an inquiry as to the nature and type of relationship existing between the testator, the contestants and the party accused of exerting such influence. The establishment of the exertion of such influence is generally predicated upon an inquiry as to the opportunities existing for the exertion of the type of influence or deception possessed or employed, the circumstances surrounding the drafting and execution of the testament, the existence of a fraudulent motive, and whether there has been an habitual subjection of the testator to the control of another. Where there is competent evidence of the existence and exercise of such influence, the issue as to whether it was effectually exercised necessarily turns the inquiry and directs it to the state of the testator's mind at the time of the execution of the testament, since the question as to whether free agency is overcome by its very nature comprehends such an investigation. Scott v. Townsend, supra. The establishment of the subversion or overpowering of the will of the testator is generally based upon an inquiry as to the testator's mental or physical incapacity to resist or the susceptibility of the testator's mind to the type and extent of the influence exerted. Words and acts of the testator may bear upon his mental state. Curry v. Curry, supra. Likewise, weakness of mind and body, whether produced by infirmities of age or by disease or otherwise, may be considered as a material circumstance in establishing this element of undue influence. Long v. Long, supra. Finally, the establishment of the fact that the testament executed would not have been executed but for such influence is generally predicated upon a consideration of whether the testament executed is unnatural in its terms of disposition of property. Long v. Long, supra.

[10–12] The evidence in the case at bar establishes that Mrs. Rothermel trusted Louis completely and relied entirely upon him to handle her affairs. The evidence likewise establishes that Louis had ample opportunity to exert influence upon his mother as to the execution of the testament in controversy, but evidence as to any deceit or fraud is lacking. It is the law in Texas that a will cannot be set aside on proof of facts which at the most do no more than show an opportunity to exercise influence. Burgess v. Sylvester, Tex.Civ. App. (1944), 177 S.W.2d 271; affirmed, 143 Tex. 25, 182 S.W.2d 358. The establishment of the circumstances of having an opportunity to exert such influence due to being in a position of caring for the person upon whom the influence is supposed to be exerted is equally consistent with the theory of innocence as it is with the theory of wrongdoing. Price v. Taliaferro, Tex.Civ. App. (1952), 254 S.W.2d 157, wr. ref. n. r. e. The exertion of influence that was undue cannot be inferred alone from opportunity, but there must be some testimony, direct or circumstantial, to show that influence was not only present but that it was in fact exerted with respect to the making of the testament itself. There is no such evidence here.

[13] The evidence likewise establishes that Mrs. Rothermel was old and suffered from the common maladies of age. This evidence may be considered as establishing Mrs. Rothermel's physical incapacity to resist or the susceptibility of her mind to an influence exerted. However, such evidence does not establish that her mind was in fact subverted or overpowered at the time of the execution of the instrument in question.

[14, 15] A person of sound mind has a perfect legal right to dispose of his property as he wishes, and the testament in the case at bar makes an unnatural disposition of the property only in the sense that one child was preferred over the widow and children of another child. This circum-

stance is frequently present in cases involving the issue of undue influence, and it is only where all reasonable explanation in affection for the devise is lacking that the trier of facts may take this circumstance as a badge of disorder or lapsed mentality or of its subjugation. See: Craycroft v. Crawford, Tex.Com.App. (1926), 285 S.W. 275; Curry v. Curry, supra. The evidence in the case at bar does not support the conclusion that Mrs. Rothermel's testamentary disposition of her estate was unnatural.

[16] The elements of the exertion and the effective operation of any influence possessed by Louis over his mother so as to subvert or overpower her will and cause the execution of this testament are not supported by any tangible evidence. Because of the disposition we make of this case we need not consider the other issues raised on this appeal.

The judgments of the Court of Civil Appeals and the trial court are reversed and judgment is here rendered that respondents take nothing.

Ex parte J. D. THETFORD and Wife, Mamie Thetford.

No. A-9649.

Supreme Court of Texas.

July 24, 1963.

Proceeding for habeas corpus relief from indefinite jail sentence. The Supreme Court, Calvert, C. J., held that judgment holding paternal grandparents in contempt for failing to comply with order to produce grandchildren over whom they were not shown to have had possession and control after allegedly wrongfully aiding their son in obtaining their possession in violation of court order was void, and grandparents were entitled to habeas corpus relief, where condition of purging themselves was production of the children, an act impossible of performance.

Relators ordered discharged.

1. Habeas Corpus ⟹22(2)

Habeas corpus proceeding is collateral attack on contempt judgment, and one may be relieved of its impositions only if judgment is void.

2. Contempt ⟹61(4)

Contempt judgment imposing coercive restraint is void if condition for purging contempt is impossible of performance.

3. Habeas Corpus ⟹22(2)

Judgment holding paternal grandparents in contempt for failing to comply with order to produce grandchildren over whom they were not shown to have had possession and control after allegedly wrongfully aiding their son in obtaining their possession in violation of court order was void, and grandparents were entitled to habeas corpus relief, where condition of purging themselves was production of the children, an act impossible of performance.

Doss Hardin, Fort Worth, Sid L. Hardin, Edinburg, for relators.

Toby Goldsmith, Fort Worth, for respondent.

CALVERT, Justice.

Petitioners seek relief from an indefinite sentence to jail imposed by a judgment of the District Court of the 17th Judicial District, Tarrant County.

Petitioners are the grandparents of three minor children, Cynthia Kay Thetford, VaLinda Gay Thetford and Timothy Jason Thetford. Carlton Allen Thetford, petitioners' son, is the father of the children. Carlton and his wife, Dorothy Ann, were divorced in February, 1961 and legal cus-

Works Cited

Teaching—both in terms of pedagogy and content—amasses from the work of those who have taught and studied in years prior. The content of this book would not have been possible without the scholarly and pedagogical contributions of the myriad of experts in the field of legal writing that have preceded this book's creation. We are deeply appreciative of the work of all of our legal writing colleagues around the country and, in particular, of the authors and of the works listed below. We want to acknowledge their contributions to the content of this book and the quality of the learning that happens in our legal writing classrooms.

Deborah L. Borman, A Short & Happy Guide to Legal Writing (2019).

Matthew Butterick, Typography for Lawyers: Essential Tools for Polished & Persuasive Documents (2d ed. 2015).

Catherine Martin Christopher, Tackling the Texas Essays: Efficient Preparation for the Texas Bar Exam (2018).

Christine Coughlin, et al., A Lawyer Writes: A Practical Guide to Legal Analysis (2d ed. 2013).

Linda H. Edwards, Legal Writing: Process, Analysis, and Organization (5th ed. 2010).

Elizabeth Fajans, et al., Writing for Law Practice: Advanced Legal Writing (3d ed. 2015).

David C. Frederick, The Art of Oral Advocacy (3d ed. 2019).

Bryan A. Garner, Legal Writing in Plain English (2001).

Bryan A. Garner, et al., The Redbook: A Manual on Legal Style (4th ed. 2018).

Bryan A. Garner, The Winning Brief: 100 Tips for Persuasive Briefing in Trial and Appellate Courts (3d ed. 2014).

Bryan A. Garner, The Winning Oral Argument: Enduring Principles with Supporting Comments from the Literature (2d ed. 2009).

Antonio Gidi & Henry Weihofen, Legal Writing Style (3d ed. 2018).

Adam Lamparello & Megan E. Boyd, Show, Don't Tell: Legal Writing for the Real World (2014).

Michael D. Murray & Christy H. DeSanctis, Advanced Legal Writing and Oral Advocacy: Trials, Appeals, and Moot Court (2d ed. 2014).

Richard K. Neumann, Jr., Legal Reasoning and Legal Writing: Structure, Strategy, and Style (6th ed. 2009).

Richard K. Neumann, Jr. & Sheila Simon, Legal Writing (2d ed. 2011).

Susan E. Provenzano, Sarah O. Schrup, Carter G. Phillips & Jeffrey T. Green, Advanced Appellate Advocacy (2016).

Teresa J. Reid Rambo & Leanne J. Pflaum, Legal Writing by Design: A Guide to Great Briefs and Memos (2d ed. 2013).

Mary Barnard Ray, The Basics of Legal Writing (Revised 1st ed. 2008).

Joan M. Rocklin, et al., An Advocate Persuades (2016).

Antonin Scalia & Bryan A. Garner, Making Your Case: The Art of Persuading Judges (2008).

Wayne Schiess, Writing for the Legal Audience (2nd ed. 2014).

Helene S. Shapo, et al., Writing and Analysis in the Law (6th ed. 2013).

Helene S. Shapo, et al., Writing and Analysis in the Law: Teacher's Manual (6th ed. 2013).

Richard C. Wydick, Plain English for Lawyers (5th ed. 2005).

Index